MEDIEVAL STUDIES

for

J. A. W. Bennett

MEDIEVAL STUDIES

for

J. A. W. Bennett

———— ◆ ————

AETATIS SUAE LXX

Edited by

P. L. HEYWORTH

CLARENDON PRESS · OXFORD

1981

Oxford University Press, Walton Street, Oxford, Oxford OX2 6DP

London Glasgow New York Toronto
Delhi Bombay Calcutta Madras Karachi
Kuala Lumpur Singapore Hong Kong Tokyo
Nairobi Dar es Salaam Cape Town
Melbourne Auckland

and associate companies in
Beirut Berlin Ibadan Mexico City

Published in the United States by
Oxford University Press, New York

British Library Cataloguing in Publication Data
Medieval studies for J. A. W. Bennett.
1. English literature—Middle English,
1100–1500—History and criticism—
Addresses, essays, lectures
I. Bennett, Jack Arthur Walter
820'.9'001   PR251   80–041783
ISBN 0–19–812628–X

Printed in Great Britain by
Butler & Tanner Ltd,
Frome and London

TO JACK BENNETT

We present this book to you as a declaration of our respect, admiration, and affection. You will understand our wish to set with your name that of Gwyneth, to whom many of us also owe gratitude and thanks, but who did not live to see our work completed.

Jack Bennett died on 29 January 1981 in Los Angeles while on his way to New Zealand. He is buried in Cambridge beside his wife Gwyneth.

Contents

List of Plates

ex. Written space 120 × 68mm. Very deep lower margin, 108mm or more.

Aristotle, De interpretatione, in the translation attributed to Boethius. The whole page contains from 23.b.29 'contradiccionis' to 24.a.5 'contraria': ed. L. Minio-Paluello (1965), pp. 36/8–37/7.

4b Part of fo.96ᵛ of Corpus Christi College, Oxford, MS 114. England. s.xiii. ex. See below p. 355. The manuscript was in Oxford in 1294 and was then deposited as a pledge in the Cista Reginae by John Beneger and his brother William, 'et ponunt predictus Iohannes et Willelmus Dominum Walterum de goldecote procuratorem eorum ad predictum librum aquietandum quandocumque uenerit', fo. 331ᵛ. The columns are numbered and the lines are numbered by fives between the columns.

Beginning of 11.9 (369.a) of Aristotle, Meteora, in the translation attributed to Gerard of Cremona. The initial is blue.

4c Part of Merton College, Oxford, MS 269, fo.248. See below p. 371.

Beginning of bk.12 of the commentary on the Metaphysics. Initial C and beside it a pencil sketch to help the illuminator.

Abbreviations

—————— ◆ ——————

BL   British Library
BN   Bibliothèque Nationale
EETS   Early English Text Society
ELH   *English Literary History*
ELN   *English Language Notes*
HLQ   *Huntington Library Quarterly*
JEGP   *Journal of English and Germanic Philology*
MÆ   *Medium Ævum*
ME   Middle English
MED   *Middle English Dictionary*
MLN   *Modern Language Notes*
MHG   Middle High German
MLR   *Modern Language Review*
MP   *Modern Philology*
OED   *Oxford English Dictionary*
PG   J. P. Migne, *Patrologiae cursus completus, Series Graeca*
PL   J. P. Migne, *Patrologiae cursus completus, Series Latina*
PMLA   *Publications of the Modern Language Association of America*
RES   *Review of English Studies*
SP   *Studies in Philology*
TES   *Times Educational Supplement*
TLS   *Times Literary Supplement*

J. A. W. Bennett

When Jack Bennett retired from the Chair of Medieval and Renaissance English at Cambridge University on 30 September 1978 and subsequently passed his seventieth birthday on 28 February 1981 two appropriate occasions for the publication of these essays in his honour slipped by. That they were allowed to do so will scarcely distress him, for, like the poet whose work he has done so much to illuminate, Jack Bennett has never set much store by 'stellification'. There is an unmistakable irony in any attempt such as the present to memorialize him; but those who are party to it hope that any embarrassment he may feel at being accounted meritorious will be allayed by the knowledge that, if he is the victim of a conspiracy, it is an amiable and affectionate one.

Jack Arthur Walter Bennett was born at Auckland, New Zealand in 1911, the elder son of Ernest and Alexandra Bennett. His parents were natives of Leicester and it was from Leicester that they emigrated to New Zealand, his father in 1907, followed two years later by his mother, and it was there that his parents married.

He got his early schooling at Mt. Albert Grammar School whence a Lizzie Rathbone Scholarship took him to Auckland University College, where he sat under a remarkable teacher, Philip Sidney Ardern. Ardern had returned from Oxford twenty years before to plough a lonely furrow, spending his leisure compiling massive editions of Old English and Middle English texts, editions which never reached print but which displayed acumen, accuracy, and a degree of intellectual rigour not surpassed in the published works of better-known scholars. Astringent and sceptical in temper, Ardern had a sympathy with and an intuitive understanding of the medieval mind not often found in the Antipodes, or anywhere else for that matter, and Jack Bennett, in Ben Jonson's words, owed to him 'all that I am in arts, all that I know'. It was Ardern who first turned his mind to Middle English.

But that interest in Middle English was slow to develop. At Auckland he was preoccupied with literature more broadly defined and especially with modern literature, as his earliest publications show. And while still an undergraduate he joined with a friend, James Bertram—it was to Bertram that he owed his introduction to modern poetry—and Charles Brasch, a young poet who had just returned from St. John's College, Oxford, to plan and publish a magazine, *Phœnix*, that might be said to mark the beginning of modern New Zealand literature.

At Oxford, where a postgraduate scholarship took him to Merton in 1933, he was persuaded to build on the foundations so solidly laid by 'Pip' Ardern, and apart from a term's tutorials from Edmund Blunden—from which grew a friendship that did not close till Blunden was buried in Long Melford churchyard forty years later—he devoted himself to philology, attending the lectures of C. L. Wrenn and J. R. R. Tolkien on Old English philology, of C. T. Onions on Middle English philology, and of Gabriel Turville-Petre on Old Norse. Under Turville-Petre, then preparing his thesis in a tall house in Beaumont Street, Bennett attended more to the sagas than to the *Ormulum*, taking four papers in Old Norse in the Final Honour School.

In that School Bennett was examined by (among others) C. T. Onions and E. V. Gordon, and he has always suspected he owed his First to their charitable view of some notably erratic papers. If that was the case, his debt to Gordon was compounded because it was Gordon's generous comments on his New Zealand scholarship papers which had opened the way for him to go to Oxford two years before. Meanwhile, from Walton Street and the offices of the Clarendon Press, a New Zealander of an earlier generation had been keeping a benevolent eye on him, and it was Kenneth Sisam who urged him not to spend the time bought for him by Merton's electing him to a Harmsworth

Senior Scholarship on *Piers Plowman*, which would have been his preference, but rather on channelling his enthusiasm for Old Norse into an exploration of the beginnings of Old English and Norse studies in England.

Under Sisam's guidance it proved a rewarding subject, embracing as it did the extraordinary flowering of medieval scholarship in English which took place in the late seventeenth and early eighteenth centuries, in the work of Francis Junius, George Hickes, Edmund Gibson, Humfrey Wanley, Thomas Hearne, and others, and which two centuries later was to give confidence and direction to the second flowering of the latter part of the nineteenth century. By a lucky chance it was also to keep him in Oxford. In 1938, his D.Phil. completed and his Harmsworth (which had been extended for a year) running out, he decided to go for a Junior Research Fellowship at Queen's, and much to his surprise (since Queen's had never before had a Fellow in English) he was successful. R. H. Hodgkin had just completed his *History of the Anglo-Saxons* and had returned to Queen's as Provost; he knew some Anglo-Saxon and something of the Queen's Saxonists and it seems likely that he persuaded the college to elect Bennett. Bennett celebrated by lecturing in the Schools on *Piers Plowman* and (under the influence of Helen Waddell) on the Medieval Lyric.

At the outbreak of the Second World War Bennett was on a visit to New Zealand, and he made his way from there via the Huntington Library to New York. As he waited for a ship to take him to England he was asked by the British Information Services to help out for a few weeks. The few weeks lengthened into five years, and he served first as Head of the Research Department, later as a Director. When not distracted by official business—which included reading (for the first time) John of Salisbury's *Policraticus*, at a sitting, in order to supply Lord Halifax the British Ambassador with a suitable speech to accompany the presentation of a first edition to Harvard Library, and tracking down the Great Seal of William IV by way of a junk shop in New Jersey to an elegant West Side apartment—he took the opportunity to read medieval manuscripts in the Pierpont Morgan Library, to study medieval painting at the Metropolitan Museum, and, remote in spirit as in place from the cheerful uproar of Manhattan, medieval sculpture at the Cloisters, on its lovely eyrie overlooking the Hudson River. And only New York could have provided (on the top floor of a fashionable department store) an exhibition of the sunless treasures of William Randolph Hearst, ranging from a complete Spanish Romanesque cloister to stacks of stained glass, some of which Sir William Burrell was to retrieve, and which will eventually be on view in Glasgow—all fresh from the crates in which they had been shipped from Europe, and all for sale.

Bennett probably learned more about the Middle Ages in those unexpected years than if he had never moved from the common rooms of Oxford. This was borne in on him on his return to England in September 1945; those who had stayed on to teach the diminished rump of the wartime English School were—with the notable exceptions of C. S. Lewis, J. R. R. Tolkien, and Nevill Coghill—exhausted or about to retire. Bennett soon found himself teaching every paper in the Final Honour School to men and women from eighteen colleges, often finishing a long week of tutorials at lunch-time on Sunday. In those overcrowded and energetic post-war days, while work was not difficult to find jobs were less easy to come by. When the call came (in 1947) it was from Magdalen. Why that college having just elected Neil Ker to a fellowship decided to elect Bennett also he never knew: all he remembers is meeting C. T. Onions in the High Street and Onions saying gruffly, 'We're thinking of making you a fellow. Any objections?'

Magdalen at that time was superabundant in talent: Gilbert Ryle, J. L. Austin, and T. D. Weldon; C. T. Onions and Godfrey Driver; R. W. Chapman, C. S. Lewis, Colin Hardie (zealous for Dante), and A. P. D'Entreves; A. J. P. Taylor and K. B. MacFarlane; and foremost among scientists J. Z. Young and Peter Medawar—though both were already poised for departure. C. C. J. Webb still made an occasional lunch-time appearance.

John Betjeman—at that time more of a local butt than a national figure—would bring in Osbert Lancaster. Chapman would bring in G. M. Young, Lewis, John Wain, Colin Hardie, Arnold Toynbee, and T. S. R. Boase, newly elected head of this learned *familia*, Sir Kenneth (as he then was) Clark.

It was only slowly that Bennett became a full-blown medievalist. In 1951–2 two sabbatical terms spent in New Zealand gave him the opportunity to draft—'by the long wash of Australasian seas'—his study of *The Parlement of Foules*, although it was not published until 1957. But seventeenth-century interests competed with his earlier ones for several years, invigorated by the seventeenth-century teaching for Schools which at the time of his election he had agreed to relieve Lewis of, and an edition of Bishop Corbett begun in 1938 was not completed until 1955. In the same year he published for the Scottish Text Society an edition of devotional pieces from two late Scots manuscripts; this grew from an early liking for Gavin Douglas stimulated by Gavin Bone, and he undertook it at the suggestion of Sir William Craigie. It was an interest which was to remain with him and resulted in his regular supervision over the years of theses on late Scottish themes.

Bennett had first met Craigie in the thirties and was a regular visitor to him in his retirement at Christmas Common, above Watlington, both before and after the war. Craigie was an affable host who used to delight in talking philology while walking around the orchard, where each tree was named after an American scholar, stopping to see how, for example, 'Edith Rickert' was bearing. Bennett did several stints for Craigie on slips for the *Dictionary of the Older Scottish Tongue*, and he accounts it a very great privilege to have known and learned from not one but two editors of the *Oxford English Dictionary*.

The second, of course, was C. T. Onions, who ruled over Magdalen Library and with benign vigour edited *Medium Ævum* out of an old shoe-box. His relationship with Onions was never close—it found, perhaps, its most relaxed expression in the affectionate biographical sketch which prefaced the bibliography Bennett compiled for the Clarendon Press in honour of Onions's sixty-fifth birthday—but Onions soon enlisted Bennett's help as a member of the editorial board of *Medium Ævum* and subsequently deputed editorial tasks for some time before relinquishing both the editorship and the shoe-box to him in 1956. That perhaps marked Bennett's perpetual profession to medievalism, and some would argue that it is in the editing of that journal that he has performed his most signal service to medieval studies. In the following year his *Parlement of Foules* was published, and in 1958 the first volume of the Clarendon Medieval and Tudor Series appeared under his General Editorship.

During these years too he was beginning to give thought to possible ways of improving the lot of graduate students, who were coming to Oxford in increasing numbers, very often from overseas, to find a university rich in resources but with no very clear notion of how to employ them to the best advantage of those hoping to prepare themselves for a career in university teaching. Bennett's long-held reservations about traditional 'research' in literary studies and its products are stated in a radio talk he gave in 1961, with a title eloquent of the views it expresses—'Research: the Tyrant'. The issue had been faced a decade earlier by the Oxford philosophers under the leadership of Gilbert Ryle and H. H. Price; their answer had been to institute the B.Phil. degree, with its emphasis on classes and seminars which exposed postgraduates to a wide range of philosophical expertise, within the framework of a carefully articulated curriculum, rounded off by three or four rigorous examination papers with a short dissertation as an option for one of them. That experiment had by the late fifties proved itself a decided success. Bennett saw that at Oxford a similar scheme in medieval studies might offer a programme scarcely capable of being matched elsewhere and one that would bring advanced students' experience more nearly in line with their expectations than had been the case in the past.

He gave a great deal of his time and energy to getting the

B.Phil. established, time and energy that with the onset of illness that was never very far away in those and subsequent years he could hardly afford, and it was surprising to some that he was prepared to expend so much of himself in such a cause. But it is worth pointing out—since the evidence is not available in very public places—that throughout his career Bennett has espoused reforming causes and written thoughtfully about them. As an undergraduate at Auckland in his first published essay, 'A Future for Our Language Departments', he made a plea for more imaginative teaching of literature in New Zealand universities, drawing attention, for example, to the possibilities offered by the study of comparative literature. A paper, 'English as you teach it in America', written during his American years, is a sympathetic but critical assessment of the state of English studies in the USA against the background of his own New Zealand and Oxford experience. And even as he worked to make the B.Phil. a reality he was already exploring a much bolder idea, a proposal to establish in New Zealand a small residential collegiate graduate institution with teaching staff and students drawn from the (then) four New Zealand universities to create 'some form of local but unparochial postgraduate institution which will both provide an environment in which students of proved ability can mature, and act as a source for the supply of some of those teachers whom the universities will otherwise be at a loss to find. ... a single institute or college, not crushed under the weight of metropolitan life, and more flexible and more experimental than a national university for graduates could be; distinct in function and in location from the present universities, and sufficiently flexible in its constitution for its programmes to be easily modified in the light of experience.'[1]

If this owes something to the example of Nuffield and St. Antony's at Oxford, the Institute of Advanced Studies at Princeton, the Pontifical Institute of Mediaeval Studies at Toronto, and France's Royaumont, it is also deeply rooted in Bennett's

[1] 'Sketch-Plan for a College', *Landfall*, vol. 14 no. 3 (September 1960), p. 278.

own experience of the Oxford college system 'and in the conviction which underpinned his support of the Oxford B.Phil.
proposal, that the only worthwhile format in graduate education—at least in the humanities—is one in which the teacher
can 'act with his whole mind on the pupil's whole mind', and
it perhaps owes most of all—and this explains his choice of
Landfall, the New Zealand quarterly edited by his old friend
Charles Brasch, as the forum for the proposal—to his powerful
sense of the needs of New Zealand and its universities, isolated
by accident of geography from the chief centres of higher
learning and scholarship in the West. The proposal met with no
favour in New Zealand, but a pupil of Bennett's at Magdalen,
Ian Donaldson, was to direct just such a centre when it was
founded some years later at the Australian National University
in Canberra, and Bennett greatly enjoyed a visiting fellowship
there in 1976.

In November 1963 C. S. Lewis died at the end of a long and
debilitating illness, having resigned from the Chair of Medieval
and Renaissance English at Cambridge some months earlier. He
had left Magdalen and Oxford for Cambridge in 1954 and his
departure had been a severe blow to Bennett; it had taken him
several years to feel comfortable riding in tutorial harness with
Lewis and longer than that to perceive the full bearings of
Lewis's scholarly writing. The possibility of succeeding him in
the Cambridge chair did not present itself readily, or in many
ways very attractively, to Bennett's mind. After thirty years in
Oxford his thoughts were of the wrench of departing from there
rather than of the possibilities Cambridge offered. But he was
ill and Oxford could promise no relief from the terrible drain
of tutorial work. He cobbled an application together and
submitted it reluctantly and late, encouraged by one thought:
having got the Oxford B.Phil. going he looked forward to the
opportunity of devising an improved version at Cambridge.

He did not find Cambridge a friendly place. At Magdalene,
where he had followed Lewis in his fellowship, there was
generous acceptance and much kindness; but the Faculty, very

much at odds with itself on a divisive political issue, did little to welcome him. He put this down to his being an 'offcomer', but Lionel Knights, who in his second term came as King Edward Professor, later confessed that, though a native, he suffered from much the same feeling of indifference and estrangement.

Whatever the explanation, not much in the early Cambridge years went right. His hopes for an improved B.Phil. in medieval studies foundered on the impossibility of reconciling sophisticated and rigorous postgraduate courses with the meagre offerings in medieval subjects made available to undergraduates by the Faculty or required by the Tripos. By way of a remedy to this he did manage to inaugurate classes in elementary Middle English for beginners, and at the other end of the scale he got much pleasure from supervising a number of first-class Ph.D. candidates.

But his satisfactions were in large part those which he carried over with him from Oxford. Although *Medium Ævum* proved difficult to run from Cambridge, he managed to begin a new series of monographs. The first of these, Meg Twycross's *The Medieval Anadyomene*—which he supervised (as an Oxford B.Litt. dissertation), published (also acting as a financial guarantor), and finally reviewed (anonymously)—has since been reprinted twice, and no. X in the series has just (1979) appeared. Volumes in the Clarendon Medieval and Tudor series were published regularly throughout the sixties—including, forty years on, Bennett's homage to P. S. Ardern, an edition of *Piers Plowman*, B I–VII—before the enterprise fell a victim to inflation and the inflated publishing costs of the early seventies. And he continued, as for thirty years past, to act as reader and adviser on medieval literature for the Clarendon Press—an account of which will be found elsewhere in this volume.

With the increased time and freedom that his Chair gave him—the real blessing conferred by Cambridge—his health, though still uncertain, greatly improved and he had energy to direct towards his own work. The fruits were soon apparent. A collection of essays on Malory contributed by others at his invitation had marked his departure from Oxford; it was followed in 1966 by the Early Middle English Reader which he and Geoffrey Smithers had laboured on for many years. It was essentially an Oxford book, conceived with the demands of the Oxford Final Honour School in mind (as complementary to Sisam's *Fourteenth Century Verse and Prose*), but with a usefulness that extended far beyond that, a usefulness greatly enhanced by Norman Davis's exhaustive and invaluable glossary. In 1968 followed Bennett's study of *The House of Fame*, a work which brilliantly illuminated that obscure and problematical poem, and one notable for its unapologetic emphasis on the richness of Chaucer's imagination and the poem it had fashioned, rather than on the ingenuity of his own exposition. In the same year he published in the Clarendon Medieval and Tudor Series a selection from Gower, followed in 1972 by his Langland in the same series. In 1970, *en route* to New Zealand to visit his mother, then over ninety, he delivered the Alexander Lectures at University College, Toronto, taking as his subject 'Chaucer at Oxford and at Cambridge'. This appeared as a book under the same title in 1974.

Inevitably, honours began to accrue. In 1971 Bennett was elected Fellow of the British Academy. In 1976 he held a Visiting Fellowship at the Australian National University, and was elected a Corresponding Fellow of the Mediaeval Academy of America and an Honorary Foreign Member of the American Academy of Arts and Sciences. In 1978 he was elected to an Emeritus Fellowship of the Leverhulme Trust. In 1980 he was awarded the Sir Israel Gollancz Prize of the British Academy. But characteristically that which he took most pleasure in was his appointment as Keeper of the Old Library at Magdalene in 1968. If the post became something of a refuge for him, that was very much to the library's and the college's benefit. He supervised the recataloguing of the collection and installed Lord Fitzwilliam's loan of manuscript and printed books. He examined most of the books in the library personally, and scarcely a week passed but something interesting, and often something exciting, was turned up. Among others may be mentioned Ben Jonson's copy of Horace, a presentation copy of Bishop Percy's *Reliques*, and manuscript drafts of T. S. Eliot's *The Dry Salvages* and *Little Gidding*, which, after two memorable afternoons spent going over them with Valerie Eliot, he subsequently wrote about in the *Ampleforth Journal*.

Another unexpected pleasure of the later Cambridge years was his friendship with I. A. Richards. Richards was elected a Fellow of Magdalene in 1926, but had been absent for most of the time since, from 1944 holding a chair at Harvard. During his Harvard years Richards had regularly spent the Long Vacation in Cambridge and towards the end of his life returned to live there in a house at the edge of the college gardens. Nothing would seem more unlikely than that Bennett and Richards should have tastes and views in common, but so it proved; they saw each other constantly and delighted in each other's company.

By the early seventies those who visited Bennett, guiltily distracting him from his proper business, seldom came away unless with pleasure mixed with regret, regret which inevitably followed from contemplating the gap, increasing year by year, between the richness of the materials accumulated over an immense range of subjects, and the opportunities which remained—on any reasonable expectation—to put them into finished form. Thus the launching of the official Oxford history of Oxford was welcomed by some for no other reason than that it displaced and rendered impracticable Bennett's own dream of a comparative intellectual history of Oxford and Cambridge, for which he had amassed materials for more than thirty years. No more mourned was the refusal of the Syndics of the Cambridge Press to support a proposal submitted to them by Bennett and Owen Chadwick for a history of Cambridge along the lines of the Oxford scheme.

Yet no one needs to be reminded less than Bennett that in scholarship as in love the commonplace is also the truth: 'The lyf so short, the craft so long to lerne', and his unannounced decision to release into print material unpolished and, on his own admission, at times deliberately conjectural shows a clear-sighted pragmatism. Hence between 1972 and 1976 he published in four parts 'Supplementary Notes on Sir Gawain and the Green Knight', a more-or-less verbatim transcript by a professional typist of material in the form of lecture notes, accumulated in the course of half a lifetime's reading and teaching, printed by offset at the press in the Cambridge University Library, followed in 1976 by notes in four parts supplementary to his 'school' edition of *The Knight's Tale* (2nd edition 1958), reproduced in the same way. And a similar pragmatism lies behind his decision to put into publishable form—but beginning at the end and working backwards, since it is in discussion of the later passus that he believes he has most that is original to offer—his long-awaited commentary on *Piers Plowman*, perhaps to be issued in similar format.

That lies in the future, as do at the time of writing other works: a collection of essays on Gibbon, the fruit of reading begun in Canberra in 1976; a study of the Passion in English poetry from the *Dream of the Rood* to David Jones's *Anathemata*, based on the last of his Cambridge lectures; and, above all, the volume in the Oxford History of English Literature on Middle English literature to 1400 (but unfortunately not including Chaucer), inherited by him from the late Dorothy Everett. And if the Oxford History is the work which those who care about Jack Bennett and who care about Middle English studies are most anxious for, it is an anxiety he will not misunderstand. It arises from an awareness of the importance of what needs to be done and the conviction that it can be done by none so well as by him.

The Learned Adviser

DAN DAVIN

The world of learning resembles that notorious iceberg: beneath the pinnacles of published books, the escorting floes of reviews and scholarly journals, there is a submerged eight-ninths of supporting substructure. Each of these worlds, under and over, visible and invisible and together making a whole, owes its debt to Jack Bennett's lifetime labour—a labour, let it be said at once, in which he has delighted and which must often have physicked pain. Almost any reader of this book is likely to be familiar—though the familiarity will not have dispelled residual awe—with his published books, cairns which stand as high landmarks in the vast landscape of modern scholarship, monuments constructed not for himself but for others but making nonetheless his own unwitting House of Fame.

My present concern, however, is with his work in that world unseen by the layman where, assiduous and scrupulous for truth, the real toilers of scholarship are busy, a world known but to the scholar's peers, his pupils, and his publishers. The domain of the publisher is only a small part of all that bustle of letters, memoranda, conversations, arguments, and discussion where Jack Bennett has been a busier bee than most and with a keener scent for honey. But it is to this narrower theme of his relations with publishers, and in particular with the Clarendon Press, that I must confine myself.

All academic publishing houses nowadays seek the advice of 'grete clerkes' and men of 'auctorite' before agreeing to publish a learned book. The practice is especially venerable with the older university presses, as the files of the Clarendon Press amply reveal. From the time the records begin, they show the determination of the Delegates and their officers to ensure, as far as precaution can, that works of scholarship are free of blemish or error and are worthy of a great imprint. The tradition goes back to the editing of the Greek and Latin classics, and when in the nineteenth century men began to feel that the nobler texts of English literature merited a similar pious attention, the tradition was duly adapted without impairment to its rigour. The fundamental object was the same: to produce a text as close as possible to the original, with the essential minimum of justifying apparatus and such glossing and concise explanation as might be necessary to its accurate interpretation. The principles remained as before, but the new problems and the techniques to solve them were concerned now with the printed texts that followed the manuscript and with ridding them of the injuries they had suffered from careless editors and compositors; whereas the concern of the classical scholars had been for the great Jesse tree of manuscript transmission and the sins and oversights of scribes.

When I first came to the Clarendon Press, in 1945, I was not entrusted with any serious responsibility by my mentor, Kenneth Sisam, at that time Secretary to the Delegates, until I had spent a long time immersed in the files and familiarizing myself with this tradition in both its forms. As it happened, the pioneers of the editing of English texts were for the most part men trained in the classics, pupils as it might be of men like Bywater and Joachim or of scholars of similar stature in other universities. Many of these pioneers were still alive and some of them were among us in Oxford—though I was sternly enjoined to take no account of provenance in the pursuit of quality and reminded that, however *sui generis* a Chapman, a Garrod, a C. S. Lewis, or a Tolkien might be, there was always somewhere a counterpart: every Nichol Smith was matched somewhere by a Sherburn or a Lefty Lewis; and successors to Percy Simpson or Harold Williams might well be found across the Atlantic in a Fredson Bowers or a Louis Landa. Yet the *genius loci* must have its pious due, and my knowledge of the past and preparation for the future owed much to the Oxford ambience, to the osmotic influences so agreeably experienced in the halls and senior common-rooms of colleges like Oriel and Christ Church, Magdalen and Balliol.

It was while I was still undergoing preliminary indoctrination that I first met Jack Bennett, though his name was already known to me from an article on D. H. Lawrence he had printed in the early 1930s in a swiftly suppressed issue of *Open Windows*, a New Zealand S.C.M. magazine edited by him. And I had already heard Sisam praise his Oxford thesis, as something that ought to be published as a book. I had not heard him speak in such terms of a thesis before. I doubt if any other thesis ever provoked such a flagrant contradiction of his firm belief that a thesis and a book were two quite different things.

This first meeting took place informally in Sisam's office, later to be my own. As I now see it, Sisam must have been consciously and deliberately bringing us together, with an eye to the future after his retirement two years later. He had already discerned in Jack a scholar of enormous promise, and one well fitted to sustain the best traditions of Oxford scholarship. And in me he hoped no doubt to mould some sort of successor to himself, a recruit who would continue the aims and standards that he himself had inherited and gone on to maintain and develop. If I were to be of any use, I would need to be trained to see the quality of men like Jack and learn how to win their help and loyalty in our learned publishing.

So, each after our own potentialities, we were being adjured, though the eloquence was one of example rather than explicit precept, to make our energies complementary and pursue a common purpose—'Hold the hye way, and lat thy gost thee lede / And trouthe shal delivere, hit is no drede.'

Nor was Sisam to be disappointed in his hopes, at least in so far as Jack made part of them. Of course, he was only one of many advisers to give their services to the Press, services which could never be requited in proportion to their value and often, in any case, given without any thought of payment. But over a period of some thirty years there were few books published by the Press in the field of English language and literature of the Middle Ages in the presentation of which Jack did not play some part, a role which could seldom be acknowledged in authors' prefaces because it was necessarily anonymous.

It would be fascinating, but too indiscreet and too laborious, to trace through the Press files since 1946 how much he has done to polish the sometimes rude and uncut gems which scholars have submitted for publication. No one in that period was so sedulous to prevent the springing of 'cokkel in our clene corn'. There were few to compare with him in that disinterested devotion which enables a man to put aside his own work for the sake of the common cause, and to put aside his own prejudices also. More than most, he had the ability to identify with the author whose work he was scrutinizing and to pierce through to what was being attempted, even though it might be obscured by irrelevancies, rash judgements, straining of evidence, particular points of view pressed too hard, or details seen too close or insufficiently considered against a wider background. He could temper enthusiasm without extinguishing it and assist a man in pursuing his own argument with greater lucidity, concision, and proportion, so that the eventual conclusion could emerge, purged of clumsiness and error or any other dross that might clog its movement. Nor would discreet suggestions for the improvement be disdained. No man was ever more considerate at helping a lame dog over his style; for Jack never lost sight of 'Grammere, that grounde is of gode'.

Ruefully at times, no doubt, he must have called to mind when correcting his own proofs or the proofs of volumes in the Clarendon Medieval and Tudor Series Chaucer's admonition to Adam, his scribe:

> Under thy long lokkes thou most have the scalle,
> But after my makyng thou wryte more trewe;
> So ofte a-daye I mot thy werk renewe,

It to correcte and eek to rubbe and scrape;
And al is thorugh thy negligence and rape.

Yet the pains he took were never accompanied by petulance and, from my point of view as publisher, his unfailing courtesy was a blessing. Very often, the publisher is pig-in-the-middle between patronizing or arrogant adviser and affronted or infatuated author, and dangerously placed between the fell, opposed points. To keep sensibilities unruffled, he will often have to rewrite an adviser's comments before passing them on, the point buttoned and less likely to wound. And, to preserve anonymity, he will have to remove the identifying traits—a scornful reference, say, to the author's failure to consult some work that the adviser himself has published, a characteristic hobby-horse, or a give-away phrase. For authors under criticism are often fretful and spiky and apt to think the adviser an enemy, one whom to identify is somehow to diminish and discomfit.

With Jack's reports only the most superficial laundering was necessary. The heat of his intentness on truth was so fierce that the accidents of vanity or superciliousness or patronage were burned away. If he had a fault as an adviser it would be the perfectionism that made him spend too much time on the task, and the accessible good nature that made him too busy doing too much for too many people. There were times when he might well have pleaded, '"My speed is a warines," falters the mouse.'

There was that execrable handwriting of his, too. His reports often had to wait until I had time to decipher them so that they could be accurately typed—alas, those difficulties of reading exactly the exotic proper names and titles fetched from every corner of his extensive reading and wide-ranging memory. And there were the postscripts that had to be restored to the main body of the report, postscripts that would crowd the margins of his letters or even follow in a flight of postcards, evidence that the string of his mind's bow kept on vibrating and that the quiver was never empty.

Something, of course, of his personality would still show through in the edited report: he was not without his 'drei bobbes' which it would have been wrong to eliminate; he had a fastidiousness of language pleasingly paradoxical in one who is such a 'glotoun of wordes'; the liveliness of allusion and its range intimated that the writer was a man for whom literature lived and for whom the good books of all times and countries were irresistible friends. On the whole, though, one took a chance and, rather than dehydrate the report, would send it on with all its juices, trusting that the recipient would feel no surprise but would take it for granted that an adviser of the Clarendon Press, reporting on a book about Malory, say, would find it natural to mention Langland, Virgil, Dante, the Provençal poets, the French chronicles, Henry James, T. S. Eliot, Edith Wharton, and Alfred Tennyson.

No one in my time, then, has done better journeyman service in the workshop of letters or been a better foreman of the jury in the courts of scholarship. But he himself has perhaps expressed it best, that delight in the labour that physicks pain, in a Skeltonic *jeu d'esprit*, the sort of marginal gloss that occurs in so many medieval manuscripts and would have delighted Robin Flower:

Dignissime Daniele,
I can at last tell'ee
I've o'erseen the goodman's script
Here and there chipped and nipped
—For twas not easy to find
The sentence of his mind
—These earnest eggheads
Know their x's, y's and zeds,
But not their ABC—
Take witness of me!
So hold me excused
If I have not well perused
This English half-abused,
His Text at least is true
—Of that no need to rue—

And his Notes have some pith.
Let us be content therewith.
In fine—*Imprimatur*
Et Deus misereatur
On editors-in-chief
And send them some relief
From painful anthologists
Who from Time's kindly mists
Would rescue not only Lydgate
But those of lower rate
Such as Hoccleve and Hawes.
Ho! Here we must pause
And so NO NO NO
To P.H.D. and Co.
Let them try R.W.B.
Who prints such E.E.T.
Whether readable or not.
Now March suns grow hot
Let us leave such sad learning,
To spring daffodils turning
And praty birdes smale
Warbeling in the vale
—ug, ug,
  jug, jug
Good day and good luck
—But *Chuck*, I say, *chuck.*

Langland *Nel Mezzo Del Cammin*

———————— ◆ ————————

JOHN BURROW

I

At the beginning of Passus XII of the B Text of Langland's *Piers Plowman*, Imaginatif introduces himself to the dreamer Will as follows:

'I am ymaginatif', quod he; 'ydel was I neuere
Though I sitte by myself in siknesse ne in helthe.
I haue folwed thee, in feith, thise fyue and fourty wynter,
And manye tymes haue meued thee to mynne on thyn ende,
And how fele fernyeres are faren and so fewe to come;   5
And of thi wilde wantownesse whiles thow yong were
To amende it in thi myddel age, lest myght the faille
In thyn olde elde, that yuele kan suffre
Pouerte or penaunce, or preyeres bidde:
Si non in prima vigilia nec in secunda & c.
Amende thee while thow myght; thow hast ben warned ofte   10
With poustees of pestilences, with pouerte and with angres.'[1]

The Latin words in this passage allude, as Skeat noted, to one of the parables of Christ, reported by St. Luke: 'Let your loins be girt and lamps burning in your hands. And you yourselves like to men who wait for their lord when he shall return from the wedding; that when he cometh and knocketh, they may open immediately. Blessed are those servants whom the Lord, when he cometh, shall find watching. Amen I say to you that he will gird himself and make them sit down to meat and

---

[1] All B-Text quotations are from the edition by G. Kane and E. T. Donaldson (London, 1975), substituting *gh* for ȝ and *th* for þ. C-Text quotations are from W. W. Skeat's edition (Oxford, 1886).

passing will minister unto them. And if he shall come in the
second watch or come in the third watch [Vulgate: *Et si venerit
in secunda vigilia, et si in tertia vigilia venerit*] and find them so,
blessed are those servants.'[2]

The three *vigiliae* of the parable have to be understood here
in an allegorical sense. Just as the night, according to Hebrew
custom, was divided into three watches, so human life is divided
into the three ages specified by Imaginatif: youth (*yong*, 6),
middle age (*myddel age*, 7), and old age (*olde elde*, 8). This
interpretation of the three *vigiliae*, as Robertson and Huppé
observed, has a counterpart in the *Glossa Ordinaria*: 'Prima
ergo vigilia custodia pueritiae est, secunda juventutis, tertia
senectutis. Si quis vero in pueritia vigilare neglexerit, non tamen
desperet, sed etiam in juventute vel saltem tandem in senectute
resipiscat, quia pius judex moras nostras patienter exspectat.'[3]
Both passages speak of failures of vigilance in the first age, from
which a man may recover in his second age or even (though
Imaginatif doubts this) in his third. The term *pueritia*, in the
Glossa, corresponds to Langland's *yong*, *juventus* to his *myddel
age*, and *senectus* to his *olde elde*.[4]

Robertson and Huppé say that Imaginatif's statement is
'almost a paraphrase of the *Glossa Ordinaria*'; but (as often) it
is hard to be certain of Langland's exact source. The allegorical
interpretation of the *vigiliae* was already ancient in the twelfth
century, when the *Glossa* was compiled. The prime Latin
authority was one of the homilies of Gregory the Great. Gregory
identified the first watch as *pueritia*, the second as *adolescentia
vel juventus*,[5] and the third as *senectus*. Like the *Glossa*, but

---

[2] Douai–Reims version, Luke 12:35–8. Related passages are Matthew 24:42,
24:46, 25:13, and Mark 13:33–7; but these counsel vigilance without mentioning
the *vigiliae*.

[3] Cited from *PL* 114.298 by D. W. Robertson and B. F. Huppé, *Piers Plowman
and Scriptural Tradition* (Princeton, 1951), p. 149.

[4] *Pueritia* (usually 'boyhood' only) extends its semantic range in three-age sets.
Juventus, as in classical Latin, represents what Shakespeare in his sonnet of the
three ages (no. 7) calls 'strong youth in his middle age'.

[5] Gregory justifies the unusual use of *adolescentia* as a synonym for *juventus*
by citing Ecclesiastes 11:9: 'Laetare ergo, juvenis, in adolescentia tua'.

rather more elaborately, he went on to explain how failures of vigilance might be redeemed: 'Qui ergo vigilare in prima vigilia noluit, custodiat vel secundam, ut qui converti a pravitatibus suis in pueritia neglexit ad vias vitae saltem in tempore juventutis evigilet. Et qui evigilare in secunda vigilia noluit, tertiae vigiliae remedia non amittat, ut qui in juventute ad vias vitae non evigilat saltem in senectute resipiscat.'[6] Gregory's homily was widely read.[7] Indeed, his interpretation of the three *vigiliae* as the three ages of man became standard. Bede adopted it in his Commentary on Luke, as did the ninth-century Haymo of Auxerre in his homily 'De Confessoribus'.[8] It first appears in English in one of the homilies of Aelfric: 'Seo forme waecce is witodlice on cildhade, and seo oðer waecce is on weaxendum cnihthade, and seo þridde waecce is on forweredre ylde.'[9] Later the interpretation appears, not only in the *Glossa Ordinaria*, but also in the *Catena Aurea* of St. Thomas Aquinas.[10] As late as the early seventeenth century, the numerologist Petrus Bungus cites the exegesis, attributing it to *theologi* and mentioning particularly Haymo of Auxerre.[11]

Whatever his exact source may have been, Langland's indebtedness to the Gregorian interpretation of Luke 12:35–8 cannot

[6] *XL Homiliarum in Evangelia*, Book I, Homily 13, cited from *PL* 76.1125. The Greek father Cyril of Alexandria has the interpretation before Gregory, in his Commentary on Luke: *PG* 72.746–7.

[7] It was included in the influential eighth-century Homiliary of Paul the Deacon: see C. L. Smetana, 'Aelfric and the early Medieval Homiliary', *Traditio*, xv (1959), 178, item 109.

[8] Bede, *In Lucae Evangelium Expositio*, ed. D. Hurst, Corpus Christianorum: Series Latina, 120 (1960), p. 257. Haymo of Auxerre, *PL* 118.789. Haymo's version shares with Langland's one feature not found in any other version known to me. A man who has failed in vigilance in his first age should make amends in his second 'et dum virtus corporis viget, in bono opere se exerceat'. Compare Imaginatif: 'amende it in thi myddel age, *lest myght the faille*'.

[9] *Angelsächsische Homilien und Heiligenleben*, ed. B. Assmann (reprinted Darmstadt, 1964), p. 52. *Cnihthad* is Aelfric's regular rendering of *adolescentia*, here reflecting the peculiar biblical use (n. 5 above).

[10] *Catena Aurea*, in *Opera*, v (Venice, 1746), pp. 224–6. Aquinas also cites Cyril (n. 6 above).

[11] Petrus Bungus, *Numerorum Mysteria* (Paris, 1618), pp. 155–6.

be doubted. This tradition explains not only Langland's interpretation of the three *vigiliae* as the three ages of man, but also
his association of those ages with the idea of death. This goes
back to Gregory's interpretation of St. Luke's words, 'that when
he cometh and knocketh, they may open immediately': 'Venit
quippe Dominus cum ad judicium properat, pulsat vero, cum
jam per aegritudinis molestias esse mortem vicinam designat.'[12]
In *Piers Plowman*, the *molestiae* which announce the approach
of death are 'poustees of pestilences, with pouerte and with
angres'. These serve to warn Will that his 'ende' is near. They
represent, as it were, the knocking on Will's door, to which he
has not yet responded.

So the words of Imaginatif in Langland's poem have a long
tradition behind them. But Langland does not simply follow
this tradition: he brings it to bear on the specific circumstances
of Will the dreamer. Will is portrayed here as a man in middle
age reflecting upon the course of his life. Imaginatif represents
Will's own 'imaginative power'—his capacity, that is, to envisage
events beyond the immediate present, surveying the past and
picturing the future. Unlike Gregory, Imaginatif does not speak
in general terms. His version of the *vigiliae* is aimed directly at
Will. 'You have failed to be vigilant in your first age,' he says,
'and you must look to it *now*, in your second. You may not be
able to when you are old.' The tone is urgent and minatory.
Will has passed beyond the 'wilde wantownesse' (*pravitates* in
Gregory) of youth, and is now in middle age. Indeed, if one can
take literally the beautiful line whose full, luxuriantly alliterated
beginning is so expressively betrayed by its bald end, he is now
well past the middle point of his life: 'And how fele fernyeres
are faren and so fewe to come'. Old age is approaching; but even
now Will fails to 'amend'. Instead, as Imaginatif goes on to

[12] *PL* 76.1124. Three-age schemes are particularly often associated with the
thought of death. One English example is *The Parlement of the Thre Ages*: see
T. Turville-Petre, 'The Ages of Man in *The Parlement of the Thre Ages*',
Medium Ævum, xlvi (1977), 66–76. A less obvious example is Chaucer's
Knight's Tale. The main reason for this association is probably Gregory's
interpretation of Luke's parable.

assert scornfully, he is wasting his precious time writing useless poetry: 'thow medlest thee with makynges' (XII. 16).[13]

But Imaginatif appears to be even more specific and personal than that: 'I haue folwed thee, in feith, thise fyue and fourty wynter'. On the most natural interpretation, these words refer to Will's age. It has been argued that 'imaginative power' cannot properly be said to follow a man from the moment of his birth; but any alternative reading requires a more difficult supposition: that there was some specific age (seven? fourteen?) at which that power was generally known to start functioning. In the absence of evidence for this, I prefer to take 'fyue and fourty wynter' as an indication of age. But what kind of indication is it? One scholar suggests that forty-five is no more than a 'typical' number, developed from the round number forty for purposes of extra alliteration, and intended to suggest merely that Will has indeed already passed 'fele fernyeres'.[14] Such an interpretation will account for the line as it stands in revised form in the C Text: 'Ich haue yfolwed the in faith more than fourty wynter' (C xv.3). But the B text is more specific, and it will bear a more specific interpretation.

Medieval teaching about the ages of man exhibits a bewildering variety, not only in the number of ages into which life is divided (three, four, five, six, seven, ten), but also in the years at which the various divisions are held to occur. I believe it is significant, however, that Will's age, forty-five, figures in three important schemes as the point at which middle age (*juventus*) gives way to old age. Of these, the scheme least likely to have been known to Langland is that of the Roman writer Varro.

[13] John Scattergood points out to me that such failure to amend is treated in pious writings as a kind of sloth: e.g. *Book of Vices and Virtues*, ed. W. N. Francis, EETS, OS 217 (1942), p. 28. This may explain why Imaginatif introduces himself as he does: '"I am ymaginatif", quod he; "*ydel was I neuere*"'. The opposition between sloth and 'vigilance' in Langland's mind appears again in the confession of Sloth in B V. Sloth admits to neglecting 'vigilies' (409) and is brought to his senses by '*Vigilate* the veille' (442). See J. A. W. Bennett's note to the latter passage in his edition of the *Visio* (Oxford, 1972).
[14] F. Krog, 'Autobiographische oder typische Zahlen in *Piers Plowman*?', *Anglia*, lviii (1934), 318–32.

Varro divided life into five stages of fifteen years each: *pueri* up to 15, *adulescentes* up to 30, *iuvenes* up to 45, *seniores* up to 60, and *senes* up to 75.[15] Much closer to Langland is the four-age scheme expounded at length by Dante in his *Convivio*. According to Dante, the threescore years and ten allowed by the Psalmist (leaving aside *senio*, or decrepitude, the fourth and last age) are divided into three ages, symmetrically centring on 35. The first age, here called *adolescenza*, lasts up to 25, the second, *gioventute*, from 25 to 45, and the third, *senettute*, from 45 to 70.[16] Dante claims to derive his figure 45 from *la ragione propria*. Since all authorities agree, he says (quite wrongly), that adolescence lasts until 25, and since 35 is the centre point, it stands to reason that *gioventute* must have ten years on either side of that point, if the arc of human life is to be symmetrical: 'Avemo dunque che la gioventute nel quarantacinquesimo anno si compie'.[17] This passage from the *Convivio*, besides showing that a great fourteenth-century poet could take an interest in these frigid schemes, provides an exact parallel to the scheme implied

[15] Varro's scheme is reported by Censorinus, *De Die Natali Liber*, Ch. xiv: ed. O. Jahn (Berlin, 1845), pp. 33–4. On this scheme, see E. Eyben, 'Die Einteilung des menschlichen Lebens im römischen Altertum', *Rheinisches Museum für Philologie*, 116 (1973), 150–90, pp. 172–6.

[16] *Convivio*, Treatise iv, Ch. xxiii.

[17] Treatise iv, Ch. xxiv: ed. G. Busnelli and G. Vandelli, ii (Florence, 1964), p. 306. Charles d'Orléans also divides life into three (*enfance, jeunesse, vieillesse*); and in one of his ballades, No. XC in P. Champion, ed., *Poésies*, 2 vols. (Paris, 1971), he treats the age of forty-five as the beginning of the last age. Charles imagines a game of tennis with Aage (not Old Age, whom he always calls *Vieillesse*, but the passage of time in life): 'J'ay tant joué avecques Aage / A la paulme que maintenant / J'ay quarante cinq' (1–3). Charles has scored forty-five points (the equivalent in *jeu de paume* of forty in modern tennis?). So far, he goes on to say, he has been keeping his end up against his skilful opponents, the doubles partnership of Soussy and Fortune; but Vieillesse is angry that the game has lasted so long, 'Et dit, en son felon langage, / Que les chasses dorenavant / Merchera, pour m'estre nuisant' (17–19). Old Age, that is, will henceforth act as line-judge or umpire, to make things difficult for Charles. *Dorenavant* ('henceforth') suggests that the age of forty-five—represented, as all scholars agree, by the score in the game—marked for Charles the beginning of *vieillesse*. (I am indebted to my colleague Myra Stokes, who pointed out this poem to me.)

in *Piers Plowman*: a division of the seventy years of normal life into three ages, the middle one of which ends at forty-five. But Langland and his audience are more likely to have known another authority: the thirteenth-century friar Bartholomaeus Anglicus. In his encyclopedia entitled *De Proprietatibus Rerum*, which was widely copied and read in late medieval England, Bartholomaeus presents a six-age scheme of the ages of man, based mainly on Isidore of Seville, as follows: *infantia* up to 7, *pueritia* up to 14, *adolescentia* up to 21 (or 28, 30, or 35, according to different authorities), *juventus* up to 45 or 50, *senecta* up to an unspecified age, and then *senectus*. I quote what he says about *juventus*: 'Huic adolescentie succedit iuventus, et hec inter omnes etates est media et ideo fortissima, et pretenditur secundum Isidorum usque ad annos xlv vel usque ad l, in quo finitur.'[18] In fact, Isidore in different places gives 49 or 50 as the terminal point for *juventus*; and Bartholomaeus' 45 very likely derives from a scribal error.[19] But the figure of forty-five none the less acquired, for the many readers of *De Proprietatibus*, the considerable authority of Isidore.

I suggest that the age of forty-five has for Langland the significance attributed to it by Varro, Dante, and Bartholomaeus: it marks the boundary between 'myddel age' and 'olde elde'. Reread with this idea in mind, Imaginatif's words to Will acquire new urgency and point. What Imaginatif says, we now notice, is that he *already has* many times warned Will in his middle age to make amends for his wild youth. His present call for amendment, indeed, may be the very last that Will has the physical strength to respond to: 'Amende thee while thow myght'. So Imaginatif's scrap of Latin (not exactly matched in

---

[18] *De Proprietatibus Rerum* (Nuremberg, 1483), Book vi, Ch. i. John Trevisa translates the passage as follows: 'Aftir this *adholescencia* "striplynges age" cometh the age that hatte *iuuentus*, and this age is in the middil amonges ages, and therfore it is strengest. Isidir seith that this age lastith and durith to the 45 yere or to the fifty yere, and endith in that yere', *On the Properties of Things*, ed. M. C. Seymour *et al.*, i (Oxford, 1975), p. 292.

[19] Isidore, *Differentiae*, Book ii, Ch. xix (*PL* 83.81); *Etymologiae*, Book xi, Ch. ii (*PL* 82.415). See Eyben, art. cit., pp. 177–9.

the Vulgate, or in any other authority known to me) takes on
a touch of menace. *Si non in prima vigilia nec in secunda ...*
It is not so much that God, the 'merciful judge' of the *Glossa
Ordinaria*, patiently allows us three sets of chances. Rather: 'If
not in the first watch nor yet in the second ... perhaps never'.

II

Imaginatif is the last of a series of allegorical figures, representing
various powers and attributes of the mind, whose encounters
with Will make up the action of the Third Dream of *Piers
Plowman*. It was earlier in this dream that Langland broke off
when he first attempted to compose the poem. The A Text
ends abruptly at the moment when, talking with Clergy and
Scripture, Will breaks into an angry tirade against the injustice
of Providence. In the B continuation, this tirade is followed,
first, by a bewildering dream-within-a-dream (B XI), and then
by Imaginatif, who resumes and concludes the Third Dream
(B XII).

In the first part of the dream-within-a-dream, at the very
beginning of the B continuation, there is a section, XI.7–64,
which seems *prima facie* to bear some relation to the later
passage I have just been discussing. It begins with Fortune
carrying Will into the 'land of longing and love'. Here he meets
Fortune's two damsels, oddly named '*Concupiscentia Carnis*'
and 'Coveitise of Eiyes', with their follower, 'Pride of Parfit
Lyvynge'. In a little scene which evidently represents the false
hopes of the beginnings of life, the two damsels make their
flattering promises to Will:

> *Concupiscencia carnis* colled me aboute the nekke
> And seide, 'thow art yong and yeep and hast yeres ynowe
> For to lyue longe and ladies to louye...'
> The secounde seide the same: 'I shal sewe thi wille;
> Til thow be a lord and haue lond leten thee I nelle...'
>   (XI.17–19, 22–23)

Old Age warns Will that Fortune and her damsels will forsake him; but Recklessness is reassuring: 'thow hast wel fer til Elde'. So, led on by Faunteltee (Childishness), Will dreams that he comes to terms with the first of the damsels: '*Concupiscencia carnis* acorded alle my werkes'. Later he keeps company with the second, younger damsel:

> Coueitise of eiyes conforted me anoon after
> And folwed me fourty wynter and a fifte moore,
> That of dowel ne dobet no deyntee me thoughte.
>
> (XI.46–8)

But at last, old age catches up with him:

> By wissynge of this wenche I dide, hir wordes were so swete,
> Til I foryede youthe and yarn into Elde.
> And thanne was Fortune my foo for al his faire biheste.
>
> (XI.59–61)

Shortly after, this 'autobiographical' section comes to an end, rather awkwardly in the B Text. The Friars, who had cultivated Will while Fortune was his friend, lose interest once he is laid low by old age and poverty. This betrayal prompts a display of righteous indignation from Will, in the course of which his own dubious moral history is, for the time being, quite lost sight of.

It is not difficult, looking back from the opening of Passus XII, to see the outlines of Imaginatif's three-age scheme already emerging in the shadowy and fantastic 'autobiography' of this dream-within-a-dream. The relevant scriptural passage in this case is 1 John 2:16: 'For all that is in the world is the concupiscence of the flesh [Vulgate: *concupiscentia carnis*] and the concupiscence of the eyes [*concupiscentia oculorum*] and the pride of life, which is not of the Father but is of the world.' The first member of this triad is associated very naturally with the first age, in which Faunteltee leads Will into the life of mirth and 'liking' promised by *Concupiscentia Carnis*: 'to lyue longe and ladies to louye'. This is the youthful wantonness of which

Imaginatif later speaks (XII.6). The second member of the triad, *concupiscentia oculorum*, requires rather more explanation. It is clear, I think, that Langland, following a traditional interpretation, understands 'concupiscence of the eyes' as avarice.[20] The evidence for this is that Coveitise of Eiyes promises Will land and lordship (XI.23), advises him to 'haue no conscience ... how thow come to goode' (XI.53), and speaks with relish of being *'pecuniosus'* (XI.58). At the same time, she is the younger of the two damsels (XI.13–14). This means that the preoccupations which she represents develop later in life than those represented by *Concupiscentia Carnis*. Thus we see Will, in his dream, yield first to the elder damsel, and only later to the younger: 'Coueitise of eiyes conforted me anoon *after'*. The carnal desires of youth, in other words, are succeeded (without necessarily being displaced) by the worldliness and avarice of middle age. In late medieval sources, avarice is most often associated with old age; but Langland is plainly following an alternative tradition, which associates it with the middle of life. The latter tradition is clearly represented in another fourteenth-century alliterative poem, *The Parlement of the Thre Ages*. Here Youth is a lover, but Middle Age thinks of nothing but his money and his lands: 'alle his witt in this werlde was one his wele one'.[21]

In *The Parlement of the Thre Ages*, it is the third age, Elde, who dominates the discussion. He warns the two younger figures of the vanity of their lives, and announces the approach of death: 'Dethe dynges one my dore, I dare no lengare byde'.[22] In Langland's version, Elde performs a very similar function. He is not associated with the third member of St. John's triad, Pride of Life, whom Langland represents as no more than a

[20] On the tradition, see D. R. Howard, *The Three Temptations* (Princeton, 1966), Ch. ii.
[21] *The Parlement of the Thre Ages*, ed. M. Y. Offord, EETS, os 246 (1959), l. 149. The association of avarice with old age is illustrated in Benvenuto da Imola, below, p. 32.
[22] *Parlement*, l. 654. The image of death knocking probably derives, directly or indirectly, from Gregory's interpretation of the knocking in the parable.

shadowy attendant on Fortune's damsels (XI.15, 33). Langland's
Elde associates with Holiness:

'Allas, eiye!' quod Elde and holynesse bothe,
'That wit shal torne to wrecchednesse for wil to haue his likyng!'
(XI.44–5)

It is Elde who finally displaces Coveitise of Eiyes, when Fortune
turns against Will and reduces him to poverty. This development
occurs, significantly, after the younger damsel has followed Will
for 'fourty wynter and a fifte moore'. I cannot account for the
exact form of this expression. Why 'forty years and a *fifth*
more'? But in the absence of a convincing alternative (Langland
can hardly mean forty-*eight*), we must surely identify this, as
most readers have done, with Imaginatif's 'fyue and fourty
wynter'. If this is right, then we can say that the number forty-
five is associated in both places with the point at which middle
age, the age of lordship, wealth, and 'might', passes into the
poverty and weakness of old age.[23]

Unlike his interpretation of Luke's *vigiliae*, Langland's interpretation of the two *concupiscentiae* of St. John's Epistle does
not belong to the mainstream of exegetical tradition. It has a
curious parallel, however, in the opening scene of Dante's *Divine
Comedy*, as interpreted by one of Dante's earliest commentators.
In this scene, it will be remembered, Dante imagines himself, at
the exact middle age of thirty-five, lost in a dark wooded valley.
His attempts to escape up the slopes of a sunlit hill are barred
by three beasts: first, a leopard; second, a lion; and finally a

[23] There is a difficulty here, stated by A. S. Jack, 'Autobiographical Elements
in *Piers the Plowman*', *JEGP* iii (1901), 402: 'It is altogether arbitrary to make
this the entire period of his life. Why suppose that William is thinking that
"Coueityse of Eyghes" has followed him from his birth and not since twenty
or even thirty years after his birth?' It is true that the narrative makes Coveitise
of Eiyes follow *Concupiscentia Carnis* as Will's chief 'comforter'; but the
younger damsel is already present in the opening scene (22–4), and Langland
apparently thinks of her here as a lifelong companion. Otherwise the coincidence
of the two references to forty-five is impossible to explain.

she-wolf, who drives him back into the darkness. Fourteenth-and fifteenth-century commentators on the *Divine Comedy* commonly interpret these three beasts as *luxuria, superbia,* and *avaritia,* respectively. Three of the early commentators further associate this triad of vices with the three ages of man.[24] Particularly interesting is Benvenuto da Imola, whose *Comentum super Dantis Aldigherij Comoediam* is dated 1375–80. He writes: 'Autor noster fingit tantum tres feras occurrisse sibi, quia tria sunt principalia generalia vicia communiter occupantia hominem in triplici aetate, scilicet luxuria in juventute, superbia in viril-itate, avaritia in senectute. Unde Joannes: *omne quod est in mundo,* etc.'[25] Benvenuto here refers to the same passage of St. John's Epistle used by Langland ('For all that is in the world ...'). Unlike Langland, he associates all three members of John's triad with an age, and hence cannot preserve the Johannine order, according to which *avaritia (concupiscentia oculorum),* not *superbia* (pride of life), occupies the middle position. However, his commentary does show that Langland was not alone in associating the three ages of man with this particular biblical passage.

The early commentators' identification of Dante's three beasts with the three ages and their characteristic vices suggests a more general comparison between Passus XI–XII of the B Text of *Piers Plowman* and Canto I of the *Inferno.* In both, the narrator finds himself *nel mezzo del cammin di nostra vita.* Dante, at thirty-five, is exactly at the middle; Will, at forty-five, is at the end of the middle. Morally and spiritually, both have lost their way. Dante, in the world of his vision, is literally lost in the dark wood, which symbolizes, according to Benvenuto da Imola, 'mundanus status viciosus'.[26] Langland's Will has so bewildered himself with thinking about Dowel that he has lost

---

[24] Benvenuto da Imola, *Comentum super Dantis Aldigherij Comoediam,* ed. J. P. Lacaita, i (Florence, 1887), pp. 35–7. Anonimo Fiorentino, in *La Divina Commedia nella figurazione artistica e nel secolare commento,* ed. G. Biagi et al. (Turin, 1924–39), i. 23–4. Giovanni da Serravalle, ed. Biagi, i. 18.

[25] Ed. cit. i. 36–7.

[26] Ed. cit. i. 24.

faith in the justice of Providence. His own life is governed by appetite and unchecked by any thought of the Last Things. Like Dante, he has lost the straight way, *la diritta via*. It is in this state of alienation from God that the narrators in both poems are confronted with an admonitory vision—a vision of what their life has been, what it is, and what (if they do not amend) it will be. Both, from the dubious vantage-point of middle age, see all three ages of human life pass before their eyes. Recapitulating and anticipating their own experience, this vision is, or should be, profoundly shocking and chastening. It is like the awful death-experience of King Hezekiah, whose words Dante certainly had in mind: 'In dimidio dierum meorum vadam ad portas inferi', that is, 'In the midst of my days I shall go to the gates of hell'.[27]

In portraying their narrators 'in dimidio dierum suorum', both Langland and Dante reflect some of the contradictions inherent in medieval thinking about this middle period of man's life. On the one hand, *juventus*, and especially the age of thirty-five, stands at the top of the arc of human life, as we have seen from Dante's *Convivio*. This is the age when all man's powers are at their height—no longer developing, not yet in decline. Contrary to the melancholy implications of the modern expression 'middle age', it is an age of might, as Bartholomaeus says: 'hec inter omnes etates est media et ideo fortissima'. Its appropriate emblem, in the *Inferno* and elsewhere, is the lion.[28] At this age a man should be no longer slave to the passions of youth and not yet victim of the infirmities of old age. Hence he may have the strength to face up to his moral condition and bear the consequences of trying to put it right. Such a view is implicit in Imaginatif's plea to Will to 'amende thee while thow myght'. We may also find traces of it in Dante's opening scene, as did the author of another early commentary, the *Ottimo*

---

[27] Isaiah 38:10.
[28] Titian's painting *Allegory of Prudence*, in the National Gallery, London, portrays the three ages of man above three animal heads. The face of middle age is above a lion.

Commento: 'In questa etade debbono li uomini essere quanto si puote umanamente perfetti, e lasciare le cose giovanesche, partirsi da' vizj, e seguire virtù e conoscenza. E con questa motiva esemplifica sè l'Autore agli altri: duolsi del tempo passato in vita viziosa, e volge li passi a' migliori gradi.'[29]

But there is another, quite different way of looking at middle age, which seems more immediately relevant to both narrators. From this point of view the arc of human life appears inverted, so that middle age lies at the bottom. Christianity always had a special sense of the nearness of *pueritia* to God; and it inherited from ancient civilization a reverence for the spiritual value of *senectus*. Thus the two 'extreme ages' are both favoured with special grace.[30] By contrast *juventus*, in the middle, will appear worldly and unspiritual—the age at which man is furthest away from God and most likely to be spiritually lost. Thus, in reading the opening scene of the *Divine Comedy*, we may observe that the middle-aged narrator finds his escape from the wooded valley blocked by beasts representing the vices of all three ages of man. All three kinds of vice overlap, as it were, in this part of life: a person can be still lustful, now proud, and already avaricious. Similarly in *Piers Plowman*, it is during middle age that Will—now dominated by Coveitise of Eiyes, and evidently still accompanied by *Concupiscentia Carnis*[31] —loses all interest in Dowel:

> Coueitise of eiyes conforted me anoon after
> And folwed me fourty wynter and a fifte moore,
> That of dowel ne dobet no deyntee me thoughte;
> I hadde no likyng, leue me, the leste of hem to knowe.
> Coueitise of eiyes com ofter in mynde
> Than dowel or dobet among my dedes alle.

> (XI.46–51)

---

[29] *L'Ottimo Commento della Divina Commedia* (Pisa, 1827–9), i. 3.
[30] On 'Extrem-Alter', see C. Gnilka, *Aetas Spiritalis* (Bonn, 1972), pp. 105 and 139.
[31] This seems to be implied by XI.30.

III

Passus XI of *Piers Plowman*, then, confronts Will with an admonitory vision of what his life has been and may well be in the future. In the following Passus, after Will has awoken from his dream-within-a-dream, we further discover, from the direct words of Imaginatif, that he has already completed two of the three ages of his life. Here, in the outer dream, Will is forty-five years old, standing on the brink of old age. Imaginatif has given him many warnings (one of them, presumably, the vision from which he has just woken); but still he does not amend. Soon it may be too late. Together, these two 'autobiographical' passages present a portrait of spiritual crisis in middle age. I have already suggested that this portrait may be compared in certain particulars with that given by Dante in the first canto of the *Divine Comedy*; and I would like now to consider what part these portraits play in their respective poems. This more general comparison will leave us finally with an unavoidable, though embarrassing, question: Is the 'autobiography' of Passus XI–XII fact or fiction?

The first canto of the *Inferno* acts as a prologue to the whole *Divine Comedy*. Any comedy, according to Dante's own definition, will begin in 'asperitas'; and it is this that the first canto represents: a bitter state of alienation from God.[32] The comic action begins when Dante comes to himself and realizes that the *cammin di nostra vita*, which he has already followed blindly for half its length, has led him away from the *diritta via*. He tries to climb directly out of the darkness up the slopes of the sunlit hill; but he is frustrated by the three beasts, which represent the sinful habits of a lifetime. He must therefore try another, more circuitous road back to God: *altro viaggio* (*Inferno*, I.91). This is the visionary road followed in the *Inferno*, *Purgatorio*, and *Paradiso*; and it leads, at the end of the poem's

---

[32] Cf. Dante's description of comedy in the letter to Can Grande: 'Comedia vero inchoat asperitatem alicuius rei, sed eius materia prospere terminatur'. The dark wood is *aspra* (*Inf.* I.5).

last *cantica*, to the happy ending proper for comedy. Thus the whole of the *Comedy* may be said to represent, so far as 'Dante' is concerned, an ultimately successful response to the spiritual crisis of the opening. Like Hezekiah, Dante goes to the gate of Hell 'in dimidio dierum suorum'; but he passes through Hell, into Purgatory and Paradise.

Things are much less clear in *Piers Plowman*. For one thing, Langland's poem entirely lacks the consistent time-scheme according to which the whole action of the *Comedy* takes place, on the literal level, in the course of about a week in the narrator's thirty-fifth year. In the B Text of *Piers*, it is not until he reaches the two passages we have been considering, almost exactly half-way through the poem, that Langland gives any indication of the age of his narrator; and his only other reference to the matter comes at the very end, in the last Passus. Here Will is attacked by old age (Elde) and takes refuge, as death approaches, in the Church (xx.183–213). This later episode, admittedly, may seem to follow very closely from the episodes in XI–XII. Passus XII leaves Will on the brink of old age; in Passus XX he falls over it. Accordingly, some critics have been led to look for a consistent increase in the age of Will throughout the poem. If he is old at the end and middle-aged in the middle, must he not be young at the beginning?[33] But this inference gains no support at all from the first ten Passus of the B Text; and in the absence of such a confirming general pattern, the link between Passus XI–XII and Passus XX itself loses strength. The two sets of references are, after all, separated by some 3,000 lines of text; and there is nothing in those intervening lines to bring Will's age to mind.

Comparing Dante and Langland in this way, one is struck by a certain pointlessness in the English poet's portrait of his narrator in middle age—pointlessness, that is, within the overall plan of the work. The portrait, one might say, seems to make

---

[33] See e.g. J. F. Adams, '*Piers Plowman* and the Three Ages of Man', *JEGP* lxi (1962), 23–41. Adams observes the ages scheme in XI (p. 28), but not in XII. His essay is generally rather fanciful.

very little difference to the rest of the poem. The dream of Fortune's damsels and the words of Imaginatif both speak with unprecedented directness to Will's condition as an individual man at a specific moment in his life—but to what effect? It is not merely that Will himself seems quite unaffected, in what follows, by these urgent warnings. That is perhaps no more than another illustration of Will's customary imperviousness. The puzzle is rather that the *poem* seems just as unaffected. The Third Dream concludes with Imaginatif's delayed responses to the theological questions raised by Will back in Passus X—responses which take no account of the intervening 'auto-biographical' passages. There follows, at the beginning of Passus XIII, a summary of the Third Dream in which those episodes are represented only in the following lines:

> And of this metyng many tyme muche thought I hadde,
> First how Fortune me failed at my mooste nede;
> And how that Elde manaced me, myghte we euere mete;
> And how that freres folwede folk that was riche.

> (XIII.4–7)

The wording of this rather amnesic summary is taken from Elde's warnings to Will at the beginning of the dream-within-a-dream.[34] Line 6 carries us back to a point where old age was not yet the urgent matter that it became for Imaginatif, and casually leaves us there: 'And how that Elde manaced me, *myghte we euere mete*'. So it is not surprising to find that the ensuing dream, which concerns the dinner at Conscience's house and the encounter with Hawkin, drops the matter entirely. The 'autobiographical' episodes of Passus XI–XII turn out, in fact, to be strangely lacking in consequence. The contrast with Dante is most striking here; for the first canto of the *Inferno* has as its consequence nothing less than the whole action of the *Divine Comedy*.

We are left, then, with a question: Why did Langland

---

[34] "'Man', quod he, "if I mete with the, by Marie of heuene!/Thow shalt fynde Fortune thee faille at thi mooste nede"' (XI.28–9).

introduce into the middle of his poem two passages so carefully
worked, so far-reaching in their implications, yet so inconse-
quential for the rest of the poem? The only satisfactory answer,
I think, is frankly to take these passages as referring not to a
fictional narrator, 'Will', but to William Langland himself. If
their point cannot be found in any relation to other parts of the
poem, then it must be looked for elsewhere—in their direct
bearing upon Langland's own situation at the time when he
started work on the B-continuation. Such was the opinion of
one of Langland's best interpreters, R. W. Chambers. Chambers
wrote: 'Now this vision, telling how the poet in his youth
abandoned the search for *Do-Well*, and how, as old age
approached, he was urged to avow his vision among men, and
to reprove deadly sin ... can only be an apology for the fifteen
years' interval between the abandonment of the A-text by the
poet, about the age of thirty, and his resumption of his task, in
the revised B-text, about the age of forty-five—his "middle age",
as it is called later ... Either the vision means that, or it means
nothing.'[35]

The hypothesis that Langland wrote the first part of the B-
continuation at the age of forty-five was first put forward by
W. W. Skeat.[36] It has since been rejected by many students of
the poem on the grounds that numbers, and especially 'round'
numbers, are not to be trusted in medieval texts.[37] Even E. T.
Donaldson, who accepts much of the 'autobiographical' material
in *Piers* at face value, rejects this particular interpretation as
'credulous'.[38] However, I have argued in this essay that Langland's two references to the age of forty-five are more closely
related to their context than previous critics have realized. They

[35] *Man's Unconquerable Mind* (London, 1939), pp. 135–6.
[36] See, for example, Skeat's notes to B XI.46 and C XV.3 in his edition of 1886.
In the Preface to this edition, ii. 32, he is a little less confident.
[37] See the articles of Krog and Jack, already cited. Since every fifth number is
'round', we can hardly dismiss them all as purely conventional. Dante, after
all, actually *was* thirty-five in the Jubilee year of 1300, the year in which his
poem is set.
[38] *Piers Plowman: The C-Text and Its Poet* (2nd edn., London, 1966), p. 220.

form part, in fact, of a quite specific portrait—a portrait of Will at the end of his second age. Hence they cannot be dismissed as merely 'typical' large numbers. A portrait such as this might itself, of course, be invented—as part of a fictional biography, or even for general didactic purposes. But no such purposes are served in this case, so far as I can see. On the contrary, the portrait seems superfluous—almost, as the poem proceeds, an embarrassment. So why should Langland have invented it?

I myself believe that only an approach such as that of Chambers enables us to appreciate these passages for what they are. Langland is talking about himself. To assert this, as Chambers himself explains, is not to assert the veracity of every detail in the portrait. In much modern historical criticism, we find a very sophisticated awareness of literary convention coexisting with a very naïve notion of literal truth. Such criticism assumes that if a medieval writer were concerned (*per impossibile*) to deliver the truth of, say, his own moral history, he would do so in terms readily distinguishable from those elsewhere identified as purely conventional. But this is not the case. Conventions, after all, represent nothing less than the forms in which reality presents itself to any age, medieval or modern. So to show, for example, as has recently been done, that Thomas Hoccleve's description of a mental breakdown conforms to medieval 'conventions of madness' leaves quite untouched the question of whether Hoccleve himself actually suffered such a breakdown.[39] Supposing he did, how should we expect him to describe it in terms other than those customary in his day? Or even to experience it in any other terms? Similarly, the fact that Langland portrays the three ages of Will's life in conventional fashion leaves untouched the question of whether Langland is talking about himself. I believe he was.

[39] For a well-documented statement of the opposite opinion, see P. B. R. Doob, *Nebuchadnezzar's Children: Conventions of Madness in Middle English Literature* (New Haven, 1974), Ch. 5.

IV

When Langland came to revise the first part of his B-continuation, for the C Text, he omitted the autobiographical passage
at the beginning of B XII.[40] Hence Imaginatif, in C, makes no
allusion to the parable of the three *vigiliae*. Langland also
removed both the references to the forty-five years of Will's life.
The specific and immediate expression 'thise fyue and fourty
wynter' (B XII.3) is softened to 'more than fourty wynter' (C
XV.3); and the line in B XI explaining how Coveitise of Eiyes
'folwed me fourty wynter and a fifte moore' (B XI.47) is simply
cut out. In B, I have argued, the *vigiliae* passage and the
references to forty-five years together serve to define Will as one
who has reached, precisely, the end of middle age. The omission
of both in C quite destroys this exact definition, leaving only a
vaguely elderly Will:

> Ich haue yfolwed the in faith more than fourty wynter,
> And wissede the ful ofte what Dowel was to mene.
>
> (C XV.3–4)

It is not impossible to imagine purely literary reasons for this
group of changes in the C Text. Langland, we might suppose,
decided for some reason at one point in the B Text to present
his 'narrator' or 'persona' as a forty-five-year-old man; but
later, finding no use for this fiction, he abandoned it. But the
simplest explanation is the biographical one. Will is no longer
forty-five in the C Text because Langland himself was no longer
forty-five when he composed that last version of his poem. This
explanation, of course, follows very naturally from the biographical reading of B XI–XII. Indeed, Chambers and his

---

[40] See Donaldson, *The C-Text and Its Poet*, pp. 224–6. Donaldson's Ch. VII
('The Poet: Biographical Material') is chiefly concerned with the new autobiographical passage in C (VI.1–104). Will's dialogues there with Conscience and
Reason have some things in common with his dialogue with Imaginatif in B
XII, and may be said to take its place. But the C passage contains only one
vague reference to advancing years: '"Whanne ich yong was," quath ich,
"meny yer hennes"' (VI.35).

followers might have faced some tricky questions if Langland had *not* made such changes in his later version. To that extent, the changes in C may be said positively to support the bio-graphical reading of B XI–XII, by fulfilling a prediction implicit in it. Langland, as I believe, devoted part of B XI–XII to a precise and somewhat painful rendering of his own thoughts and fears at an age which tradition taught him to regard as the threshold of old age. We would not expect this to be carried over intact into a later version. For, if we do call Langland an 'autobiographical' poet, it is not because he shows any interest in his own *past*.

Addendum

Hoccleve's *Lerne to Dye*, a part of his so-called *Series*, provides further parallels to Langland's use of the parable of the three *vigilae*. A dying man says: 'þat man, as in holy writ is witnessid, / Which whan god comth and knokkith at the yate, / Wakynge him fynt, he blessid is algate': *The Minor Poems*, ed. F. J. Furnivall (E.E.T.S. ES 61, ·1892), *Lerne to Dye* lines 614–16. The Latin sidenote reads: *Beatus quem cum venerit dominus & pulsauerit &c.* Earlier in *Lerne to Dye* (162–4) the coming of death is associated with the three ages: 'youthe', 'middil age' and 'olde' age. Also, lines 824–6 counsel repentance while a man still has 'strengthe & force'. Investigation of Hoccleve's source, Suso's *Horologium Sapientiae*, might throw further light on Langland.

Music 'Neither Unpleasant nor Monotonous'

GEORGE KANE

The study of Langland's versification begins with the question why he chose to write in the alliterative long line, to which the answer must lie in his insight into the unsuitability of the 'octosyllabic' measure, the *lyght and lewed* four-stress rising rhythm with couplet rhyme, for his subject as he conceived it. From the indications of education and intellectual sophistication in his poem the choice was almost certainly deliberate and critically based rather than a matter of regional sentiment or cultural pressure. He discerned that of the two non-stanzaic verse systems available in the 1360s this was the one better suited to extended treatment of a grave and complex topic. A corresponding perception distinguishes his attitude to the alliterative tradition itself. This also appears judicious and critical: he employs very few of its distinctive mannerisms. Half a dozen synonyms for 'man' and one verb-formula are all that can be confidently related to the historical tradition.[1] Certain terms of Scandinavian origin with a dialect flavour, for instance *cairen*, *gate*, *silynge*, and *tyne*, are not in that category and the presumption is that he used them for alliterative convenience, as he evidently did the dialect alternatives *ayein/ageyn*, *chirche/kirk*, *ȝyue/gyue* and the pronoun *heo*.[2] He took from the tradition, as from the resource of dialect variety,

---

[1] The expressions are *freke, gome, lede, renk, segge, wye,* and *warpen ... word* as in *Ech a word þat he warp* (v.86).

[2] Compare *For þow shalt yelde it ayein at one yeres ende* (VI.43), *Wiþ gile þow hem gete ageyn alle reson* (XVIII.334); *And as chaste as a child þat in chirche wepeþ* (I.180), *Whan I come to þe kirk and knele to þe Roode* (v.105); *For he þat yeueþ yeldeþ and yarkeþ hym to reste* (VII.80), *And er he gyue any grace gouerne first hymselue* (v.51); *But sooþnesse wolde noȝt so for she is a Bastard*

what was conveniently serviceable, in that eclecticism instancing the same independence and originality which characterize the style and content of his poem.

Langland used the alliterative long line with remarkable virtuosity. It is paradoxical, in view of the consensus about his stature as a poet, and the progressive demonstration of modern *Piers Plowman* scholarship how careful and studied is his art, that the technical excellence of his versification is not appreciated. The old notion that his metre is 'uncouth', that he 'was not very particular' about it and 'frequently neglects to observe the strict rules',[3] that he had 'small regard for grammar',[4] and the misconception that because a fourteenth-century Englishman was educated primarily in Latin and French he would not be concerned about the spelling of English or understand its grammatical structure[5] still appear to influence critical attitudes: Langland's versification is unpolished, careless, and perfunctory.[6]

(II.24), *Hendiliche heo þanne bihiȝte hem þe same* (III.29). Quotation is from G. Kane and E. T. Donaldson, *Piers Plowman: the B Version* (London, 1975).

[3] *The Vision of William concerning Piers the Plowman*, ed. W. W. Skeat (10th edn. rev., Oxford, repr. 1968), pp. xxiii, xxxix, and *The Vision of William concerning Piers the Plowman in Three Parallel Texts*, ed. W. W. Skeat (3rd impression, Oxford, 1969), ii. lxi.

[4] *The Vision of Piers the Plowman ... Text B*, EETS, os 39 (repr. 1930), p. xli.

[5] George Saintsbury, *A History of English Prosody*, i (London, 1906), pp. 167, 168. Saintsbury simply misread the interpolation about teaching in English in Trevisa's Higden. Trevisa's points are that boys learn their grammar faster nowadays, and that ignorance of French is increasing. Saintsbury may not have realized that the grammar which they studied, whether in French or English, was Latin grammar. Any literate Middle English text is a demonstration that vernacular grammar could in that period (as indeed today) be interpreted through the study of Latin. As to the surviving inflexions, their rôle in Chaucer's verse line, and their remarkably correct use in manuscripts like Ellesmere, Hengwrt, and the Trinity College, Cambridge, B.15.17 manuscript of *Piers Plowman* imply knowledge transmitted by teaching, not just preserved by ear.

[6] Dorothy Everett, *Essays on Middle English Literature* (Oxford, 1955), p. 48: 'The greatness of *Piers Plowman* does not obscure its comparative lack of art, ... it still remains evident that its writer (or writers) felt no compulsion to polish his work.'

Poets generally have been more interested in the craft of versifying than their readers, and there is an *a priori* unlikelihood of a great poet being a careless technician. Langland was alive to the difference between good and bad performance: *is noon of þise newe clerkes*, says his text, *That kan versifie faire* (xv.373, 374). He left no sign that he might be unsure of his own ability. His Dreamer-poet is never made to invoke the modesty-topos, or to express concern about the possible technical shortcomings of his verse.[7] To write in verse about a topic is *To reden it in Retorik* (xi.102), hardly a modest expression. The hazard in verse-making is not doing it badly, but taking sinful pride in it, indulging in it to the neglect of spiritually more rewarding activity. Under rebuke of this the Dreamer makes a perfunctory excuse, as if for all the charge being well founded he does not take it seriously and means to continue in his way (xii.16 ff.). These attitudes are sketched by a poet in command of his style[8] who will, as a writer in English at that literary moment, have been not merely conscious of the form of his art but self-conscious about it. In terms of that appreciation the chance of his having been casual about his versification appears slight. Either he was unaware of his limitations or we have misconceived his purpose. The latter is undoubtedly the case. Two further reasons for the misconception must be added to the legacy of misdirection.

One is failure to value correctly in Langland's case the relation of a successful poet to his verse system. To conceive of it in terms of the remembered misery of schoolboy exercises, of how he 'manages to fulfil the requirements of the metre', is obfuscating. It is to himself that the mature poet is answerable for his management of the verse medium he adopts or adapts and uses. Some of the gratification he derives from his poetic activity will come from awareness of having said to his satisfaction what he was

---

[7] As does Chaucer's, for instance in *House of Fame*, 1096, 1098.
[8] See J. A. Burrow, *Ricardian Poetry* (London, 1971), pp. 34, 35 for an important insight in respect of this.

impelled to say within the self-imposed prescriptions.[9] These are truisms which should not have to be affirmed. A result of the poet's success is that his versification exists as part of the meaning of his poetic statements, not merely because the verse is effective in making that meaning more emphatic, clearer, more evidently interrelated, but also because it will engage the reader's auditory interest and confer the combination of physical and intellectual pleasure experienced when pattern and meaning are simultaneously apprehended. A kind of 'fallacy of rules' which over-emphasizes the need for the poet's regularity is possible. Certainly by writing in verse he undertakes a formal responsibility. But in his success it becomes a pleasurable one, a means of achievement, and he will cultivate it, not behave in respect of it like someone who cheats at patience. There will be an immeasurable difference of quality between his performance and that of a barely competent versifier such as Lydgate; this puts another set of standards into effect.

The second reason is misappreciation of the fourteenth-century alliterative long line as a verse medium. From the number of its syllables not being regulated, and its rhythm being indeterminately rising or falling, it has been judged incapable of modulation.[10] The systematicians who have tried to establish its nature by 'scanning' quantities of lines have been handicapped by inade-

[9] 'The poet reaps his triumphant reward because he has set himself so many obstructions to overcome.' S. Chatman, *A Theory of Meter* (The Hague, 1965), p. 207. Compare Robert Frost's 'Writing free verse is like playing tennis with the net down'. (Address to Milton Academy, Milton, Massachusetts, 17 May 1935.) My two colleagues who severally told me of and located this quotation have my thanks.

[10] Compare J. Lawlor, *Piers Plowman: an Essay in Criticism* (London, 1962), p. 190: 'the chief characteristic is the entire absence of any tension between the demands of speech (and thus sense) on the one hand, and a theoretically unvarying metrical pattern on the other'; p. 191: 'There can be no question of discrepancy, whether delicate or strident, between a theoretically unvaried scansion and the actual demand of speech and sense—that discrepancy ... for which the older term 'modulation' may be preferred'; p. 223: 'There can be no juggling within the phrase, and thus no scope for those skills of inversion and transposition which can contribute markedly to our pleasure in the foot-counted line. ... The 'prosody' of Langland does not allow patterned diction.'

quate means of notation which either obscure or fail to register the auditory interest of the alliterative long line in good use.[11] Moreover because they have in general neglected to make enough allowance for scribal damage, especially in texts uniquely preserved, the norms they propose are necessarily to some extent false. The indifferent quality of most alliterative 'poetry', however notable the exceptions, can make the long line seem a crude instrument.

If this were true of the alliterative long line as Langland uses it there would be slight regard for his poem and little pleasure to be derived from reading it. The greatness of a poem implies technical excellence: its metre, as a component of style and meaning and feeling, must be commensurate with its other features. What distinguishes Langland's use of the line is his evident perception that alliteration can have a substantive phonetic existence independent of the metrical accents[12] of a line, that the recurrence in a certain proximity of the same initial phoneme or conventionally associated initial phoneme sets up a pattern of a different character from the rhythmic pattern of the line,[13] one established

[11] See, for example, R. W. Sapora, Jr., *A Theory of Middle English Alliterative Meter with Critical Applications*, Speculum Anniversary Monographs, i (1977), p. 20; 'Non-stressed, non-alliterating syllables are not metrically significant', and p. 45: 'Some stress alternations occur in lines where both stressed and non-stressed readings would result in metrical lines. The method I have adopted in such cases is to assign or not assign metrical emphasis so as to produce the least complex reading, the only exceptions being those cases where the more complex reading seems to reflect the sense of the line better than the less complex one.' Any formulae that might emerge where such opinions and procedures are in force will bear little relation to the lines of poetry.

[12] The figure *paromoeon* was held to exist by virtue of the alliteration falling on the first syllable regardless of stress. (C. B. Kendall, 'Bede's *Historia ecclesiastica*: The Rhetoric of Faith', in J. J. Murphy, *Medieval Eloquence* (Berkeley, 1978), p. 159.)

[13] That is the pattern created by, within the line, the interplay of lexical stress, the phrase rhythm which will modify this, semantic stress, and possibly awareness of a rhythmic norm, and externally, the tone, emotional colour, and pace of the context. See, for discussions, e.g. O. Jespersen, *A Modern English Grammar*, i (Heidelberg, 1909), pp. 150 ff., G. Leech, *A Linguistic Guide to English Poetry* (London, 1969), pp. 103 ff., Chatman, *A Theory of Meter*, pp. 52 ff.

in the first instance by auditory experience of the recurrence, without necessary relation to the variations of tone, pitch and volume by which the rhythmic pattern is sensed.[14] The two patterns might coincide; lines where this occurred in the first three of four metrical accents would be normative. To make the patterns coincide only partially was to modulate the line. In such cases the pattern of metrical accents would be established and maintained by semantic stress;[15] the more or less different disposition of the alliterative pattern (still fulfilling its initial or historical function of 'genre specification'[16]) would both create auditory interest by disappointment of conventional expectation and generate poetic energy by provoking consideration of possible reasons for the departure from the norm. How strikingly Langland operates this principle has been variously noticed.[17]

[14] There are conveniently gathered references to phoneticians' studies of these phenomena in Chatman, A Theory of Meter, pp. 34 ff.

[15] 'What determines the metrical structure is the phrasing imposed by sense and normal stress.' W. Nowottny, The Language Poets Use (London, 1962), p. 109; and cf. n. 13 above. In Piers Plowman no aids are needed to 'pick out the stressed syllables' (T. Turville-Petre, The Alliterative Revival (Cambridge, 1977), p. 17). The notion that this was one of the conventional functions of alliteration seems supported by (and may indeed derive from) the absence of modulation in a great many lines of Middle English alliterative verse. But whether one charitably assumes that the writers of such verse thought themselves conventionally bound to produce relentlessly 'regular', metronomically accented lines, or judges them insensitive versifiers, their limitations are apparent. In Langland's case the choice is between assuming his inability to meet the formal demands of the verse convention and allowing him technical virtuosity which transcended them.

[16] Chatman, A Theory of Meter, p. 224.

[17] See, for instance, E. Salter, Piers Plowman: an Introduction (Oxford, 1962), pp. 21, 22: 'his general practice is to refuse alliteration the dominance it so often has in other contemporary works'. She may, however, be referring to Langland's style, his sparing use of 'exotic, colourful terminology', rather than his technical performance. Lawlor, Piers Plowman: an Essay in Criticism, p. 223: 'Langland's is emphatically a poetry to be read aloud—and, at that, stated, not intoned' is perceptive. Most recently Turville-Petre (The Alliterative Revival, p. 60) writes of Langland's use of grammatical words to alliterate: 'The result of this practice is to distort the basic rhythm of the alliterative line much more radically, and much more daringly, than anything attempted by the author of Gawain. Langland ... brings his verse much closer to prose. ... Paradoxically, in his flouting of prosodic norms, Langland is more consciously moulding his verse form that

The norm upon which he modulates his verses is a line containing four semantically determined metrical accents, divisible two and two at a grammatically tolerable point of pause, of which the first three accents fall upon syllables which alliterate, that is, begin with identical or conventionally associated consonant phonemes or with vowel phonemes. The rhythm of this norm is indeterminately rising or falling; the number of its unstressed or more lightly stressed syllables is not fixed. The immediately obvious possibilities of modulation are in the number of metrical accents, the extent and exactness of coincidence between the two patterns, accentual and phonemic, the presence of hyper-normative alliteration or of a second alliteration differing from the normative, and the position of the pause. From a presumption set up by the character of the poem the dominant pattern in a line is the semantically determined one of metrical accents: the rhythm of the line will be a performance-rhythm. The alliteration, the generically distinctive formal feature of the line, will contribute to its intellectual and emotional meaning as a second pattern.

The brilliance of Langland's versification begins with those lines of *Piers Plowman* which exemplify that norm and are therefore by definition not modulated. They illustrate how well he understood and exploited the potential of the option of rising or falling rhythm and the freedom of syllabic number. A few typical illustrations will have to suffice. There are lines of 'average'[18] length with rising rhythm: *Ac loue and lowenesse and leautee togideres* (III.291), *For his luþer lif þat he lyued hadde* (v.380).

---

the author of *The Destruction of Troy*, who is always content with the most regular metrical patterns.' Notwithstanding the unfortunate terms 'distort' and 'flouting', there are signs of understanding the mode of function of Langland's alliterative line in that quotation. But the same writer seems to find difficulty in reading the poem, or possibly is differentiating reading from scanning it: 'there is at times doubt about the stress-pattern of the line, so that the reader has to hesitate and go back over the line to discover its structure' (ibid., p. 59).

[18] I use the term subjectively. The indeterminacy of Langland's historical and grammatical final *e* compels this. See *Piers Plowman: the B Version*, pp. 215, 216, n. 184.

There are lines of similar length with falling rhythm: *Lurkynge þoruʒ lanes, tolugged of manye* (II.219), *Drede at þe dore stood and þe doom herde* (II.208). There are markedly long lines with rising rhythm: *For no cause to cacche siluer þerby, ne to be called a maister* (XI.174), *And dide hym assaie his surgenrie on hem þat sike were* (XVI.106); and lines as long with a falling one: *Lentestow euere lordes for loue of hire mayntenaunce?* (V.250), *Coueitise comþ of þat wynd and crepeþ among þe leues* (XVI.28). There are lines which give an effect of being appreciably shorter: with rising rhythm, *I shal seken truþe er I se Rome* (V.460), *In dolful deþ deyeden for hir faith* (XV.522); and with falling rhythm, *Adam and Eue he egged to ille* (1.65), *Falsnesse I fynde in þi faire speche* (XVI.154). There are lines with adjacent metrical accents in the first half: *For þat is þe book blissed of blisse and of ioye* (XI.168); and in the second half: *And is as glad of a gowne of a gray russet* (XV.167); and across the caesura: *Er I wedde swich a wif wo me betide* (III.121). It is not easy to find two lines which one would confidently 'scan' the same: the variety is huge.[19] Its first effect is constant auditory interest.

The interest, tension, generated by modulation is at least as much intellectual as it is sensory. Expert modulation implies for the reader/hearer the question why the poet undertook it, which directs him to the meaning of the line.

That appears even from the simplest kind of modulation to be found in *Piers Plowman*. This is represented in lines differentiated from the norm by the presence of a fifth (in a few cases even a sixth) semantically established metrical accent on an unalliterating syllable. Such accents, which necessarily alter the whole rhythm of the line,[20] surprise by their presence outside the norm,

[19] By 'scan' I mean read expressively in accordance with the metrical accents of the line, and taking account of the existence of stresses intermediate between light and heavy.

[20] 'The phrase is a single intonational unit, and the accent forms its center.... Any stressed syllable bears a potential for accent; whether that potential is fulfilled will depend on broader conditions of meaning and emphasis.... Accent ... is the prominence which one syllable in an uttered phrase receives when it

disappoint by not alliterating, and represent the contextual necessity or importance of the words where they fall as vindication of the modulated rhythm. Lines so modulated are quite common: discounting those where strong disagreement between good readers about relative grades of stress is possible, the type is well established.[21]

The additional metrical accent occurs at the beginning of the first half-line: *For béttre is a litel los þan a long sorwe* (Prol. 191), *The kýng haþ mede of his men to make pees in londe* (III.221), *And lásse he dredeþ deeþ and in derke to ben yrobbed* (XI.268), *And for góddes loue leueþ al and lyueþ as a beggere* (XIV.264), *How énglisshe clerkes a coluere fede þat coueitise hiȝte* (XV.415). Less often it occurs between the two alliterated metrical accents in the first half-line: *And riden fáste for Reson sholde rede hem þe beste* (IV.30), *Amonges crístene men þis myldenesse sholde laste* (XV.258), *And assoille men of álle synnes saue of dette one* (XIX.190). In a few lines it comes after both alliterated metrical accents in the first half-line: *Why sholde we þat nów ben for þe werkes of Adam* (X.115). It occurs before the alliterating accent in the second half-line: *And haue power to punysshe hem*; *þánne put forþ þi reson* (II.49), *And what meschief and maleese críst for man þolede* (XIII.77), *Til it bifel on a friday, a lítel bifore Pasqe* (XVI.139), *Which is lif þat oure lord in álle lawes acurseþ* (XVIII.107), *Conscience criede, 'hélp, Clergie or I falle* (XX.228). Very occasionally a line will have two additional metrical accents on unalliterating syllables unmistakably imposed by the sense in the context: *Ioye þat néuere ioye hadde of riȝtful lugge he askeþ* (XIV.111).

A more intricate modulation occurs when semantic emphasis appears to compete for attention with the alliterative pointing: a syllable, most often a monosyllabic word, adjacent to one of the three normative alliterating syllables, has as much as or more

is the center of the pitch contour; it is not fixed to the word but to the phrase.' Chatman, *A Theory of Meter*, pp. 57, 58.

[21] It was identified by Marie Borroff, *Sir Gawain and the Green Knight: A Stylistic and Metrical Study* (New Haven, 1962), p. 171.

semantic importance than this. Here the rhythm is not supplemented or extended but complicated by ambiguity. Depending on the meaning of the line in the context, the adjacency of the two kinds of distinction, phonetic emphasis and alliteration, either results in level stress (itself a kind of modulation) or raises doubt about which is dominant. Disappointment of expectation of the coincidence of patterns becomes auditory experience of their distinct effects.

Such words occur before the first alliterating syllable: '*Yé, lord*', *quod þat lady, 'lord forbede ellis!*' (III.112), *And keép som til soper tyme and sitte noȝt to longe* (VI.263), *And whát man he myȝte be of many man I asked* (VIII.5), *If fáls latyn be in þat lettre þe lawe it impugneþ* (XI.304), *The chíef seed þat Piers sew, ysaued worstow neuere* (XIX.406). They also occur before the second: *I wolde þat éch wight were my knaue* (V.117), *And breþeren as of óo blood, as wel beggeres as Erles* (XI.200), *Boþe to riche and to nóȝt riche þat rewfulliche libbeþ* (XIV.152), *Dos ecclesie þis day haþ ydronke venym* (XV.560), *So nede at grét nede may nymen as for his owene* (XX.20). And they occur before the third: *And in fastynge dayes to frete ér ful tyme were* (II.96), *And blody breþeren we bicome þere of ó body ywonne* (XI.202), *Wilynge þat men wende hís wit were þe beste*(XIII.291), *It is lighter to leeue in þré louely persones* (XVII.46), '*Alarme! alarme!*' *quod þat lord, 'éch lif kepe his owene!*' (XX.92). They occur before two of the alliterating syllables: *Forþi lakke nó lif ooþer þouȝ he moóre latyn knowe* (XI.214), *Goód hope, þat helpe sholde, to wánhope torneþ* (XVII.315); and even before three: *Thré leodes in oón lyth, noón lenger þan ooþer* (XVI.181). In at least one instance two occur before the third alliterating syllable: *And seide to Sathan, 'ló! here mý soule to amendes* (XVIII.327). Occasionally they follow the alliterating syllable: *And lawefulle men to lifhóly men liflode brynge* (XV.308), *And suwed þat Samaritan þat was so fúl of pite* (XVII.87).

There are, further, lines which, combining these two modulations, have both an unmistakable independent additional metrical accent and one that appears to compete with a normatively alliterating syllable for prominence. Examples are: *Wit and frée wil, to eúery wiʒt a porcion* (VIII.53), *And be we nóʒt únkynde of oure catel, ne of oure konnyng neiþer* (XI.212), *Leneþ hé nó lif lasse ne moore* (XIII.17), *Confortour of creatures; of hým comeþ álle blisse* (XVI.190).

The sense of competition for prominence between the two patterns of metrical accent and alliteration in lines modulated like the last two kinds relates to the distinctive function of the alliterative long line in expert use. The dominant pattern will always be the pattern of metrical accents corresponding to the semantic content of the line. This is because the intonation it implies is indispensable to effective communication. And in works where most lines are unmodulated the alliteration can become so associated with metrical accentuation that it comes to seem merely the generic mark of the verse form, unreflectively identified with tonal emphasis, or an aid to reading, or the ear can (in self-protection against monotony) become insensitive to it as an auditory experience.[22] In the modulated lines of *Piers Plowman*, which are numerous, the distinctiveness of alliteration as an indicator of prominence is clearer. The alliteration in modulated lines which does not coincide with or become lost in vocal emphasis appears in a rôle not so much secondary as functionally independent, makes its point less insistently and with subtler suggestion than, by its nature, does the energetic distinction of pitch, length and volume.

The kind of modulation which exhibits most clearly Langland's understanding that the two patterns exist independently and are separable occurs in lines where at some point metrical accent and alliteration must be differently located because the alliterating syllable is (less commonly occurs in) a 'grammatical' as opposed to a 'lexical' word, one which would not normally bear stress in connected speech[23] and upon which the context does not confer relative importance.

In the following lines the word is a monosyllabic preposition:

[22] Compare Turville–Petre, *The Alliterative Revival*, p. 48.
[23] Leech, *A Linguistic Guide to English Poetry*, p. 107.

It is noȝt by þe bisshop þat þe boy precheþ (Prol. 80), *Ye shul abiggen boþe, by god þat me made!* (II.128), *I dar not for fere of hym fiȝte ne chide* (IV.52), *Boþe afyngred and afurst, and for chele quake* (X.60), *And from fendes þat in hem was and false bileue* (XIX.47), *And flapten on wiþ flailes* fro *morwe til euen* (VI.184), *Tel me to whom þat tresour appendeþ* (I.45), *Treuþe herde telle herof, and to Piers sente* (VII.1), *And wommen* wiþ *childe þat werche ne mowe* (VII.101), *That þeiȝ we wynne worship and* with *Mede haue victorie* (III.352). The alliterating preposition and its metrically stressed object are not always adjacent syllables: *And a title, a tale of noȝt,* to *his liflode at meschief* (XI.300), *The bisshop shal be blamed* bifore *god, as I leue* (XI.311). The alliterating word may be a form of the verb *to be* without evident special contextual stress: *And as a Brocour brouȝte hire to* be *wiþ fals enioyned* (II.66), *That is baptiȝed* beþ *saaf, be he riche or pouere* (X.351), *And beden hire be bliþe: 'for we* beþ *þyne owene* (III.27), *Ooþerwise þan he* was *warned of þe prophete* (III.275), *I waitede wisloker and þanne* was *it soilled* (XIII.342), *Raþer þan to baptiȝe barnes þat* ben *Catecumelynges* (XI.77), *Ac wisdom and wit* were *aboute faste* (IV.81). It may be a negative particle: *He þat neuere* ne *dyued ne noȝt kan of swymmyng* (XII.165), *Noght of þe nounpower of god, þat he* ne *is myghtful* (XVII.316). It may be a possessive adjective: *And þe myddel of* myn *hand wiþoute maleese* (XVII.195).

If Langland's understanding of the separability and distinct modes of function of alliteration and metrical accent and his capacity to apply this were not otherwise evident there might be warrant for judging lines like those just quoted to be 'irregular' or 'incorrectly versified' or else to instance a perfunctory fulfilment of the generic requirement. But the *a priori* likelihood that the lines are purposefully modulated directs to scrutiny of the relation between the alliterative and metrically accented words. This proves to be closely phrasal: of preposition and object, linking verb and complement, quasi-preclitic adverb of negation and verb, possessive adjective and noun. The modulation disappoints expectation of alliteration on the accented syllable of the phrase, the centre of its 'pitch contour', but in compensation by separating the patterns divides and sets off its components and implies the government or modification which unites them. In such an understanding, which if Langland did not achieve himself he could find in his Priscian,[24] the modulation appears a function of meaning, calling for sensitive reading to be sure, but no more wayward or careless a distinction of an unstressable syllable than is the use in generic alliteration of grammatical words with special contextual importance, as for instance *So bi hise werkes þei wisten þat he wás Iesus* (XI.238) or *And ek, haue god my soule, ánd þow wilt it craue* (XIII.164).[25]

One extreme of sophisticated modulation in *Piers Plowman* is found in the poet's use of alliteration beyond the requirement of the generic norm. Such alliteration has been misconceived as 'not functional, but decorative'.[26] It is of course impossible for any element of a poem which has power of engagement to be inert ornament, 'not functional'.[27] In fact the modes of function of hypernormative alliteration in *Piers Plowman* correspond approximately to those recognized in classical times, that is the imitative and the associative.[28] The difference is that Langland's practice transcends the one and refines the other.

[24] Specifically of prepositional phrases: 'annititur semper praepositio sequenti dictioni et quasi una pars cum ea effertur'. (*Institutiones Grammaticae*, in H. Keil, *Grammatici Latini*, iii (Leipzig, 1859), p. 27). It would not take much reflection to see the extensions of the principle to other kinds of phrase.

[25] Lines with this feature are not uncommon: see, for instance, V.33, 269, 381; IX.143; XIII.74, 336; XIV.296; XVII.350.

[26] Turville–Petre, *The Alliterative Revival*, p. 17. The error again is a legacy from Saintsbury: 'The alliteration is not unfrequently a real set-off, and no mean one.' (*History of English Prosody*, i. 186.) By 'set-off' he means 'adornment, decoration or ornament'. See *OED*, s.v. 1.

[27] 'All artistic conventions are devices for creating forms that express some idea of vitality or emotion. Any element in a work of art may contribute to the illusory dimension in which such forms are presented, or to their appearance, their harmonization, their organic unity and clarity; it may serve many such aims at once. Everything, therefore, that belongs to a work is expressive; and all artifice is functional'. S. Langer, *Feeling and Form* (New York, 1953), p. 280.

[28] H. Lausberg, *Handbuch der Literarischen Rhetorik* (2nd impression, Munich, 1973), ii. 885: 'Die Wortanfangs-Alliteration tritt auf: 1) vorwiegend

The transcendence consists in understanding the particular applicability to alliteration of a principle that modern criticism accepts but finds hard to express definitively, namely that the patterns of sound experienced in reading verse are determinants of the effect of poetic statement beyond simply giving pleasure.[29] Our emotional and intellectual response to a passage, particularized by denotation and connotation, is intensified by auditory experience of pattern in its language; in the simultaneous apprehension of the whole we impute to the semantically empty constituents of the pattern, here to the initial sounds organized as pattern by their recurrence, the meaningfulnesses of the expressions where they occur, so that their a-logicality is not merely subsumed into, but greatly enhances, the entire significance.[30]

So, when the Dreamer expresses the criticism that *pilgrymes konne wel lye*,

> I sei3 somme þat seiden þei hadde ysou3t Seintes;
> To ech a tale þat þei tolde hire tonge was tempred to lye
> Moore þan to seye sooþ, it semed bi hire speche.
>
> (Prol. 50–2)

the additional alliteration is not 'senseless and tasteless stuffings of the line with five or even six alliterated words'[31] but a factor

lautmalend im Satzkontext, so die Wiederholung des Wortanfangs s- zur Wiedergabe des Zischens der Schlangen ... 2) vorwiegend gruppierend (auch als Vokal-Alliteration) in der Abfolge koordinierter kommata.' He refers, naturally, to good practice; what is criticized in, for example, *Ad Herennium*, IV. xii is pointless and excessive alliteration. (*Ad C. Herennium de Ratione Dicendi*, ed. with an English translation by H. Caplan (Cambridge, Mass., 1954), pp. 271–3.) For a sketch of classical attitudes and practice see J. Marouzeau, *Traité de stylistique appliquée au latin* (Paris, 1935), pp. 42–7.

[29] See, for example, I. A. Richards, *Practical Criticism* (London, 1929), pp. 217, 218; Nowottny, *The Language Poets Use*, p. 112; Chatman, *A Theory of Meter*, p. 198 (he properly recalls Richards's precedence by quoting him); Langer, *Feeling and Form*, p. 28.

[30] The force of this principle in application to statements of moment and concern should appear from the consideration that pattern can confer an illusion of significance upon nonsense as in some nursery rhymes.

[31] Saintsbury, *History of Prosody*, p. 192.

in our reaction to the speaker's disillusionment at the abuse of a pious institution. Even a fourth alliterating syllable, of whatever grade of stress, draws the three generically formal ones into prominence: the alliterative pattern seems momentarily to dominate, and in the impression of effortless fluency of alliteration we hear the glib fabrications and are drawn to the Dreamer's attitude.[32] So at the trial of Wrong in IV we hear multiple alliteration as the smooth persuasiveness of his defenders which might pervert justice;[33] it figures also in the speeches of the temptresses by the Mirror of Middle Earth.[34] But its function is not specialized: it can equally well lend persuasiveness to the explanation of a mystery or force to a rebuke, seem to imply the extreme gravity of an offence, suggest a state of moral confusion, or simply give an impression of increase of pace.[35] It can be used to rhetorical effect. Which of two men thrown into the Thames is in more peril, goes the question, the one who cannot swim

> Or þe swymmere þat is saaf by so hymself like
> Ther his felawe fleteþ forþ as þe flood likeþ?
>
> (XII.166, 167)

The sensory contrast between the even distribution of alliteration in 166 and its imbalance in 167 is an auditory inducement to compare their content. The two hypernormative alliterations, *so* in 166b and *forþ* in 167a, thrown into contrast by their respective prominence as a grammatical word and as the third in the half-line, further set off the adjacent opposites of choice and helplessness. We sense the point of the exemplum as a physical, an auditory experience; in the daring near-rhyme alliterating with itself and differentiated only by modal inflexion, however, the boundaries of physical and intellectual or emotional experience are less clearly definable.

---

[32] There is hyperalliteration in the speech of another liar, Hawkyn: see, for example, XIII.304, 310, 311.
[33] See IV.88, 89, 92, 93, 95, 97.
[34] See XI.19, 20, 22, and compare 35.
[35] See XVII.141, I.141, XVII.287, XIX.350 and XVII.83–5 respectively.

In that respect lines with vocalic alliteration are a special case. This is because the actual constituents of their alliterative pattern, the initial vowel phonemes, whether or not preceded by *h*, can be uttered with variable frequency (heard as pitch) and variable length. That is, the alliterating sounds themselves are capable of bearing stress and metrical accent. So the alliterating vowels play a larger part in the dramatic fabric of the line than is possible for alliterating consonants. In normative vocalically alliterating lines there can be exceptional force in the direction of the coinciding patterns to semantic importance: for instance in *Coueiteþ hé noon erþely good, but heueneriche blisse* (xv.175) to the exceptional identity in the pronoun, or in *For Antecrist and hise al þe world shul greue* (xix.219) to the appalling implications in the possessive. In lines with hypernormative vocalic alliteration, because the differentiations between the extremes of heaviest and most lightly stressed alliterating syllables can be so fine, there are special effects. The vocalic beginnings of words not metrically accented are assumed into the pattern formed where alliteration coincides with the metrical accents: the gradations of stress developed by the contextual meaning and feeling set up a kind of tune. For instance, in *To hem þat hengen hym heiȝ and his herte þirled* (1.174) the pronouns and possessive adjective are coloured by the emotion arising from the relation of their referents; in *For if heuene be on þis erþe, and ese to any soule* (x.305) *if, on* and *any* by their function in the 'contrary-to-fact' speculation acquire metrical importance as subtle exponents of the meaning; in *For hem þat haten vs is oure merite to louye* (xi.183) from the paradox in the doctrine the grammatical words which express it have very subtle graduations of stress. Such instances could be multiplied.[36]

Langland's refinement of the associative or 'grouping' function of alliteration[37] appears in a variety of highly sophisticated

---

[36] For a small sample of the variety of effects Langland obtained with hypernormative vocalic alliteration see 1.9, 65; v.164; xi.27; xiii.353; xiv.165; xviii.372, 419.

[37] See Lausberg's classification, n. 28 above. The function is like that of *annominatio* (Lausberg, ii. 885), a kind of analogy, *argumentum a simili* (ibid. i. 254),

modulations. A simple but extreme illustration of its operation is afforded by a number of lines where the phrasing or syntax compels deferment of the medial pause,[38] as in *Pardon wiþ Piers Plowman truþe haþ ygraunted* (VII.8) or *Lere hem litlum and litlum et in Iesum Christum filium* (XV.610). The effect is refined when, in lines already so modulated, he introduces secondary, extrageneric alliteration. This functions primarily as an intellectual rather than a sensory and emotional device, a figure of thought. We hear words with similar beginnings as a group: words so grouped by an alliteration other than the generic one are also by that feature set apart, and this directs us to consider how their meanings might be related. Then even the perception that the secondary alliteration is explicable as an accident of the vocabulary of the topic can enhance understanding. The range of application is considerable. Sometimes the secondary grouping appears merely for emphasis: *And flour to fede folk wiþ as* best be *for þe soule* (XIV.30). But often it is more subtly directive: for instance in *And gan wexe wroþ with lawe for* Mede *almoost hadde shent it* (IV.174) by setting off *almoost* it indicates that the King's anger is specifically at how close Mede came to destroying the legal system. And in *And somme seruen as seruauntȝ* lordes *and* ladies (Prol. 95) the secondary grouping points to the menial nature of the activity, not merely improper for a theologian, as is looking after the royal revenue, but also degrading.[39]

Similar functions are observable where, as is not uncommon, secondary alliteration occurs in otherwise normative lines. It is seldom safe to explain this as accidental. For instance in *Ac for þe beste ben* som *riche and* some *beggeres and pouere* (XI.198)

---

and an 'intellektueller Aufmerksamskeitserreger' (i. 323). Compare W. Empson, *Seven Types of Ambiguity* (2nd edn., London, 1949), pp. 11, 12, and Nowottny, *The Language Poets Use*, p. 5.

[38] See *Piers Plowman: the B Version*, p. 138.

[39] For examples of even more elaborate patterning see XIII.87 and XX.306 with four alliterating syllables before the pause and then secondary alliteration, and XIV.137 with deferred pause and two secondary alliterations.

Langland could have written *opere* for *some*;[40] or in *And in-obedient to ben vndernome of any* lif lyuynge (XIII.281) used any number of combinations such as *man lyuynge, lyues creature* and so on. And it is not material whether he consciously chose the alliterative combination; by virtue of existing it is functional: the two conditions of life are formally separated, the category is the broadest conceivable. The secondary alliteration occurs in various positions.[41] A refinement is to make it cross the generic one, as in *Suffraunce is a souerayn* vertue, *and a swift* vengeaunce (XI.379). The device generates engagement by raising the possi-bility of a significant relation between the concepts linked and set apart by the secondary alliteration and their joint bearing on the rest of the statement: in *Forþi* ech *a wis wiȝt* I *warne, wite wel* his owene (Prol. 208), where there is already from the hyper-normative generic alliteration a portentous quality about the mouse's wisdom after the event, the vocalic secondary allitera-tion, gradually forced on our notice, sets off the selfish triviality of the actual advice.[42]

There are lines with two possible generic alliterative patterns. In some the effect is merely formal: distributive, for instance in *Somme in Eyr, somme in erþe, somme in helle depe* (I.125). But often the patterns correspond to relations of meaning, as in *For I wol go wiþ þis gome, if god wol yeue me grace* (XIII.181). Here one significance is Conscience's rejection of the friar's evalu-ation of Patience implicit in his decision to accompany the latter as a pilgrim, the other his acknowledgement that he needs divine help in the enterprise. Each alliteration sets off both mean-ings, but in different proportion. The implication is of the paramountcy of the second.[43] There are even a few lines with two possible generic alliterations and a secondary one to

---

[40] He uses it, for example, at II.112, 160; VII.103; X.401.

[41] See, for instance, Prol. 58; I.43; IV.176; VI.63; X.333; XII.16; XV.178, 541; XVI.237; XX.12.

[42] Compare, for instance, V.503; XIII.258; XV.420; XVII.100; XX.306.

[43] Compare, for instance, III.72; VI.99; X.419; XIII.368; XV.48; XVII.254; XVIII.341.

boot, like *Sire Se-wel, and Sey-well, and* here-*wel þe* hende
(IX.20).

Langland's concept of language as *a game of heuene* (IX.104),
'a celestial diversion', and the abundant wit in his style confirm
the suggestion of effective playfulness here and in other places.
For instance in *I haue an Aunte to Nonne and an Abbesse boþe*
(V.153) there is a choice between a vocalic alliteration and one
produced by colloquial misdivision. In

> *Presul* and *Pontifex* and *Metropolitanus,*
> And oþere names an heep, *Episcopus* and *Pastor*
> (XV.42, 43)

the contrast between grand Latin and homely English, the modu-
lation in the separateness of alliteration and metrical accent in
Episcopus, and the secondary alliteration of its tonic syllable with
Pastor are elements in our impression of the Dreamer's misguided
elation. In *Thyn euenecristene eueremoore eueneforþ with þiselue*
(XVII.137) the near-*annominatio* is not accidental.

The extensions of this dimension of Langland's verse technique
into style and meaning which signal the end of my demonstration
are a study in themselves, too large for consideration here, but
they must be noticed. They can be briefly illustrated from the
names of his personages which alliterate. There the pattern can
have several functions. It will always constitute qualitative progression: call True-Tongue Tom and the name is apt and right
for him (IV.18).[44] It can generate meaning: calling Abstinence an
aunt (V.383) implies strict and uncomfortable but ultimately
beneficial correction. It can create dramatic humour, as with the
names of the two lawyers in the trial of Wrong in Passus IV. First
they are Warren Wisdom and his companion Witty (27), next
Widsom and Sir Warren the Witty (67), then Wisdom and Wit
(76, 81), and finally there is Warren Wisdom again (154).[45] Their

---

[44] See Kenneth Burke, 'Lexicon Rhetoricae', in R. W. Stallman, *Critiques and Essays in Criticism: 1920–1948* (New York, 1949), p. 235.
[45] Langland's making each in turn bear the name Warren suggests that this word had unfavourable connotations, but it is hard to be confident about them. The

variable names suggest shiftiness, unreliability, the bewilderment of the layman in a court of law.

There has been some welcome awareness of the stylistic intricacy of *Piers Plowman*.[46] Analysis of its metre would demonstrate a corresponding quality there. The technical excellence of Langland's verse has been repeatedly sensed through the barrier of amateurish misconceptions: even Saintsbury's could not put down his sensibility: 'There *is* music in this *un*metre; and, what is more, the music is neither unpleasant nor monotonous.'[47] Understanding will come with correct evaluation of differences. One is between the alliterative long line and the Chaucerian: no good purpose is served by looking for the qualities of the one in the other, since they simply function in different ways. The second is between Langland's alliterative long line and those of its other versifiers. In that dispersed and undocumented tradition there would be no consensus about a norm, or rules: the individual poet's conception of the verse form would be the accidental product of his special experience of it rather than a least common denominator. Some wrote wooden and regular verses, easy to scan, whether because they were conforming to what they conceived of as rules or through lack of ear and understanding. As for Langland, his alliterative long line works, and its effective operation is explicable in terms of modern criticism. This is unlikely to be an accident. More probably it reflects the quality of his sensibility, artistic insight, and control.[48]

word means 'a piece of land enclosed and preserved for breeding game'. (*OED*, s.v.1. The first citation is from *Piers Plowman* B Prologue, 163.) Maybe it carried some of the odium of such institutions. The difference of scale discourages connecting it with the family name of the earls of Surrey, even though the career of John de Warenne (ob. 1347) was unprincipled enough.

[46] For instance by A. C. Spearing in 'Verbal Repetition in Piers Plowman', *JEGP* lxii (1963), 722–37.

[47] *A History of English Prosody*, i. 185, 186.

[48] This is in the best medieval tradition. Compare the following: 'il domine son talent, discipline son style, conserve le contrôle de ses moyens d'expression. Il en résulte un surprenant alliage d'intensité et d'artifice, une extraordinaire combinaison de la sincérité avec les procédés. Le tout est beau, délectable à l'intelligence du lecteur aussi bien qu'à l'oreille de l'auditeur; n'oublions d'ailleurs

pas que, de son temps, le lecteur est aussi, et d'abord, auditeur: la qualité des sons est nécessaire pour que l'idée pénètre en l'esprit, la musicalité ne se peut séparer de la vérité. Art subtil, dans lequel seuls les plus grands excellaient.' (Dom Jean Leclercq, 'Sur le caractère littéraire des sermons de S. Bernard', in *Recueil d'études sur Saint Bernard et ses écrits*, iii (Rome, 1969), p. 199.)

The Girl with Two Lovers:
Four Canterbury Tales

———————— ◆ ————————

HELEN COOPER

J. A. W. Bennett's tracing of Chaucer's sources both literary and domestic, from Dante to the back streets of Oxford, has been constantly illuminating and fascinating. In this paper I want to look at the way that Chaucer, in the *Canterbury Tales*, uses his own works as sources for each other, so that the tales themselves present contrasting interpretations of genres, themes, and motifs. Such a reading lessens the emphasis on the *Canterbury Tales* as a dramatic work, with the tales as explorations and extensions of the characters of the individual tellers, and suggests that poetic variety for its own sake is even more important: that what matters is less that all of life and society is there in the *Tales*, than that all of art is there. There are four tales that illustrate this artistic variation particularly well, although the same idea could be applied more widely: the tales of the Knight, Miller, Merchant, and Franklin. The obvious relations between these stories place them in two pairs, the Miller's Tale 'quiting' the Knight's, and the Franklin's continuing the marriage debate in which the Merchant's Tale has been so prominent. Such a division has, however, tended to obscure the over-all relationship between the four tales, for they all share the same plot: the story of the girl with two lovers. The literary or oral sources of these tales are widely diverse, but Chaucer brings them into striking relationships with each other, so that they become variations on a series of connecting themes. As well as the central plot motif, episodes, conventions, images, and ideas are mirrored or distorted among the four tales.

The cross-linking between these tales is clear in their balance

of genre. Each pair—Knight and Miller, Merchant and Franklin—consists of a romance and a fabliau, so that while the tales
are contrasted within each pair the similarities are more striking
across them: the Knight's and Franklin's Tales are both courtly
romances, the Miller's and Merchant's both fabliaux. If the
Miller's Tale works in contrast to the courtliness and metaphysical depth of the Knight's, the Franklin's restores the
idealism so drastically lacking in the Merchant's. The first pair
illustrate romance and fabliau almost in their purest form—not
that there is anything else quite like them, but it is hard to
imagine either genre being better handled, or the conventions
of either being put to fuller use. The second pair is not so
easy to define. The Merchant's Tale is a fabliau dressed up as
a romance. Its themes and motifs, its choice of well-born
characters (citizens, peasants, and clerks, not knights and squires,
are the commonest protagonists of the fabliau), and its level of
style—a style that can include the idealistic argument on marriage and January's paraphrase of the Song of Songs—all link
it with the romance; but the debasement of the courtly form
through the crudity of its subject gives the tale a disillusionment
of tone almost as unexpected in fabliau as in romance. The
Franklin describes his tale as a Breton *lai*, and while this may
imply something old-fashioned and provincial about him, the
distinction between *lai* and romance may well be thematically
significant too, for *lais* tend to be much less about adventures
and much more about emotions. Certainly the *lais* of Marie de
France, or even *Sir Orfeo*, are more concerned with the inner
life, adventures of the spirit, than are the more strongly narrative-
based romances. Chaucer's *lai* has a clear story line, but in the
end it is much more about reactions than actions, about feelings
rather than events.

The similarities and differences in Chaucer's handling of the
same motifs and images in the four tales tend to highlight these
generic distinctions—courtly idealism for the Knight, open
fabliau for the Miller, perverted romance for the Merchant, the
delicate courtliness of *lai* for the Franklin. The parallels between

the four are many and striking. The basic similarity of plot in the tales is immediately obvious: Palamon and Arcite are rivals for Emily's favours, Nicholas and Absolon for Alison's, January and Damian for May's, Arveragus and Aurelius for Dorigen's. The variations in that basic pattern accord with the implications of the tales' genres. In the Knight's Tale the lovers' aim is marriage: the romance of courtship, with the idealized lady as the ultimate reward, is the most clearly idealistic form of romance. In the Miller's Tale the lovers' aim is adultery: Alison is married already, though her elderly husband John, despite his occasional flash of affection for her, can hardly be described as a contestant in the sexual game; he does not constitute a third rival, though the proliferation of men in the tale certainly contributes to its effect. January, the other elderly husband of the group, most definitely is a contestant. In the Franklin's Tale the characters are all young, and therefore, like Palamon and Arcite, act appropriately for their age in loving, but Arveragus and Aurelius parallel January and Damian socially and in plot-function as husband and amorous squire. At the level of plot, the Knight's Tale tends to stand out from the others in having an unmarried heroine—the lady who is all the more unattainable for never having been attained. It is this that helps to make Emily more of a symbol than a character, and contributes to the high idealism of the romance.

The working out of the plots continues the web of connections and cross-linking. In both the Knight's Tale and the Merchant's, it is the gods who intervene to bring about the final resolution. The Knight's Tale introduces the planetary deities, Saturn, Venus, Mars, and Diana, but their effects as portrayed in the temples raise the accidents and disorders associated with each of them to the level of divine principle. No room is left for the interaction of human and divine; Arcite is killed capriciously, in what amounts to mere accident. Sensed behind these gods, however, is the 'firste moevere' Jupiter, with his providential rather than irrational ordering of the world. The Merchant replaces these traditionally pre-eminent deities with a doubly debased set—gods of the underworld rather than the heavens, further reduced to bickering fairies. To introduce divine machinery implies romance elevation of style, and the philosophical reach of the Knight's Tale more than matches this; the Merchant's gods are brought down to the level of fabliau, to take part in the sexual deception. January's healing is a divine miracle as Arcite's death is not, but given his insistent mental blindness it is a miracle not worth the performing.

There has been some debate as to the artistic relevance of the Merchant's episode of the gods,[1] but at least part of its justification may lie outside the Merchant's Tale itself, in the contrast with the Knight's Tale. What supernatural there is in the other two tales is magic rather than divine, and in both of them the magic is rather less supernatural than it appears. In the Miller's Tale Nicholas claims to know of the approaching flood by astrological means, while there is of course really no flood and no astrology: life remains commonplace, and the marvellous never actually materializes. In the Franklin's Tale Aurelius prays to Apollo for help, but without results; there is no way out through divine intervention. The rocks are finally removed by 'magyk natureel'—or are they? 'It semed that alle the rokkes were aweye',[2] but Chaucer does not commit himself, and certainly nobody in the tale so much as goes to look. Magic is emphatically not what matters: it is used to make a point about human potential, not the supernatural, and magic can no more effect the final removal of the rocks than it can make Dorigen cease to love her husband. The gods affect the story in the Knight's and Merchant's Tales in despite of the characters; in the Franklin's Tale, the resolution of the plot lies in the people themselves. Divine machinery and magic are introduced there only to be rejected as answers, and to throw

[1] See, for example, Robert M. Jordan, 'The Non-dramatic Unity of the Merchant's Tale', *PMLA* lxxviii (1963), 293–9, and Karl P. Wentersdorf, 'Theme and Structure in the Merchant's Tale', *PMLA* lxxx (1965), 522–7.
[2] *The Works of Geoffrey Chaucer*, ed. F. N. Robinson (2nd edn., London, 1957), *CT* IV.1296.

the emphasis back on to the characters, their emotions and their virtues.

The imagery of the four tales shows the same interrelations and variations. Three of them contain gardens, the love-garden having been a traditional motif of courtly romance long before Guillaume de Lorris institutionalized it. Its absence from the Miller's Tale is of a piece with the essentially fabliau nature of the story: the garden is *par excellence* the setting for the romance of love. In the Knight's Tale, the garden provides the idealized courtly background against which the cousins glimpse the idealized courtly lady. Its freshness and hers are intermingled: she is fairer than the lily, her complexion 'strove' with the rose, she gathers a garland of red and white roses. In threatening juxtaposition to the garden, both geographically and symbolically, is the 'thikke and stroong' tower where the lovers are imprisoned. They cannot get into the garden, and it becomes a part of Emily's unattainableness—a *hortus conclusus*. The love-garden in the Merchant's Tale is all too vulnerable, and the heroine all too accessible, in spite of January's care with walls and locks, and in spite of the Song of Songs imagery that associates it with spiritual love—'the gardyn is enclosed al aboute'.[3] But this is not the *hortus conclusus*, nor even the garden of courtly wooing of the *Roman de la Rose*. As has often been pointed out, it is a secularized Eden with Damian as the serpent and the traditional apple tree replaced by a pear tree—a species that was a low joke in itself in the Middle Ages; that is why the comparison of Alison with a 'pere-jonette tree' is so loaded. The events that happen in January's garden, for all their setting, are emphatically not courtly—again romance elements are being debased into fabliau and deprived of symbolic

[3] IV.2143, cf. Song of Songs 4:12. Imagery from the Song of Songs is also used in the Miller's Tale and could be another aspect of the interlinking of these tales: see R. E. Kaske, 'The *Canticum Canticorum* in the Miller's Tale', *SP* lix (1962), 479–500, though some of the parallels adduced there seem to me rather far-fetched. Kaske stresses the comic incongruity of the imagery in the Miller's Tale; it certainly works rather differently there from in the Merchant's Tale, where its effect is decidedly unsettling.

significance. The garden of the Franklin's Tale too is described hyperbolically; the closest analogue of the tale, in the *Filocolo*, makes the blooming of the garden in midwinter the crucial marvel. But in the Franklin's Tale, unlike the Merchant's, the adulterous tryst in the garden never materializes. The baseness that brings May and Damian together is realized in the brutality of the language—May throwing the note in the privy, the coarseness of the love-making. In the Franklin's Tale, human *gentilesse* and *trouthe*—compassion, nobility, integrity—prevent the love-garden from fulfilling its usual function. It may be compared to 'the verray paradys', but, in this tale, the Fall never happens.

The season is as important as the setting in the same three tales. In Chaucer as in Malory, love and Maytime are inseparable. The main events of the Knight's Tale—the vision of Emily, the meeting in the woods, and the tournament—all take place in May, as does Aurelius's declaration of love in the Franklin's Tale. It is possible that the pear-tree episode also happens in spring: 'The wynter is gone with alle his reynes weete' is more than just a quotation, though perhaps it is slightly later in the season as the sun is about to enter Cancer (IV.2222–4), indicating late May or early June, and perhaps with the implication of more heat and less freshness. In the Miller's Tale, as befits a fabliau, the season is of supreme unimportance: all the events of any significance take place indoors, and it is the mundane days of the week rather than the connotation-laden months that are stressed.[4]

The season is all but inseparable from the heroine in the Knight's, Miller's, and Merchant's tales. The Franklin's Tale is an exception here: there is no formal description of Dorigen, except for a passing reference to her beauty, and by way of variation it is Aurelius who, like the Squire in the General Prologue, is compared to May. In the Knight's Tale Emily and the month of May seem to be almost interchangeable. The two

[4] In 'Why Does the Miller's Tale Take Place on Monday?', *ELN* xiii (1975), 86–90, John Hirsh suggests a basis in popular superstition.

are named or referred to alternately throughout the first section of the description of her (I.1034–48): 'It fil ones, in a morwe of May / That Emelye ... Fressher than the May with floures newe ... She was arisen and al redy dight, / For Maye wol have no slugardie ... This maked Emelye have remembraunce / To doon honour to May ...' It is a comparison pressed even more strongly than her linking with the sun (her early rising here, or the later 'Up roos the sonne, and up roos Emelye'), and it is certainly strong enough to affect our reading of the later heroine who is identified even more closely with the month—'fresshe May' herself. The May image stands for youth, beauty, and love in both heroines, but for Emily the associations are of profound symbolic import, while for May the constant repetition of *'fresshe* May' becomes increasingly sarcastic as the tale progresses. As with the garden, the denotation of the traditional romance image is being undermined. Alison too is described through an abundance of spring imagery; though the season is never explicitly mentioned, the morning milk, the 'newe pere-jonette tree', the swallow, kid and calf and primrose all bring spring or summer to mind. The season, again, is part of her youth, her attractiveness, even though the selection of imagery is totally and ludicrously different from Emily's. For Alison, the images are of the farmyard or of the lower senses, taste and smell ('bragot or the meeth', the 'hoord of apples'), and (not least important, for Alison) touch: 'softer than the wolle is of a wether'. For Emily, there are images of the angel, the lily; images of the nobler senses, sight and hearing, alone, that keep the reader as far from any physical contact with her as are Palamon and Arcite. In effect many of the images are spiritual rather than visual: Emily does not *look* like 'the lilie upon his stalke grene'—the analogy works at the symbolic level of spiritual association, indicating beauty and purity rather than the specific attributes of the lily that Chaucer mentions. By contrast with this use of apparently visual imagery to stand for something else, January's choosing of a bride is likened to setting up a mirror in 'a commune market-place'. His idea of womanhood is reduced to the merely visual; and the inadequacy of such vision becomes the central theme of the Merchant's Tale.

Conceptual relationships between the four tales—the level of *sentence* rather than *matter*—are more complex. The theme of marriage is clearly one of the most important of these. The close relationship between the series of tales initiated by the Wife of Bath has tended to blur some of the implications of the theme elsewhere in the *Canterbury Tales*, and not the least significant of its other appearances is in the Knight's Tale. This tale, as the first of the whole work, often sets patterns, norms of ideal behaviour or ideal artistry, on which the rest of the tales play variations, and this holds true as much for marriage as for the nature of the heroine or the use of the courtly garden. The wedding of Palamon and Emily is not a mere device to produce with a flourish a happy ending out of potential tragedy like a conjuror and his rabbit; and I do not agree either with the recent tendency to see it as a piece of political opportunism. It is true that Theseus suggests the marriage when he is wanting a political alliance, and the whole of his 'firste moevere' speech can be read in that light; making virtue of necessity thus becomes a euphemism for diplomatic expediency. But the strongly Boethian elements of the tale suggest a different interpretation, for in both the *Consolation of Philosophy* and a paraphrase from it in *Troilus and Criseyde* the 'faire cheyne of love' that Theseus speaks of holds nations in friendship and peoples in alliance, just as it governs the stable ordering of the universe and draws hearts together.[5] The political treaty and the wedding thus become an affirmation of faith in the providential ordering of the world, the assertion of a stabler and more rational order than that implied by the haphazard violence of Mars or the degradation of love into lust of the temple of Venus. In Chaucer's other great Boethian poem, Troilus's idealism was unable to come to terms with earthly mutability; Theseus's doctrine makes

[5] See Boethius, *De Consolatione Philosphiae*, esp. II, m. viii. 22–5 (Loeb Classical Library, repr. 1968), and its paraphrase in *Troilus*, III. 1764–9, where alliances and marriages are juxtaposed.

possible the affirmation of ideals within an unstable world. The passage makes a powerful opening statement on the symbolic implications of marriage; the irrelevance of matrimony except as a sexual inconvenience in the Miller's Tale is a delightful contrast. There is no Boethian macrocosmic correspondence there.[6]

The Knight's Tale places the wedding at the end, a scheme that helps to throw the emphasis on to structural ordering rather than human relationships. It is interesting that the key tale on marriage, the Wife of Bath's, should also end with a wedding and the restoration of harmony; marriage is given a value that was lacking in the tale apparently originally designed for her, the Shipman's, but which is absolutely right for this five-times-married practitioner of the art of matrimony. By contrast, the Miller's, Merchant's, and Franklin's tales reverse the pattern and start with a wedding—recounted briefly as a necessary preliminary in the Miller's and Franklin's, elaborated at a length that threatens to make the rest of the story become a mere appendage in the Merchant's. The Miller's Tale, like the Merchant's, is about an old husband with a young wife, but this never develops into a morally coherent theme and it would be hard to say that the tale contained any view of marriage as such—it is a work that is gloriously innocent of any 'sentence' whatsoever. The marriage theme in the Merchant's and Franklin's tales, and the contrast of the two, is a well-annotated area. As its courtly nature would indicate, however, the Franklin's Tale has more in common with the Knight's: both use marriage as a positive affirmation of order. Marriage in the Merchant's Tale is explicitly impugned from the beginning, with the sarcastic praise of the state[7] and the corrupt example the

[6] Morton W. Bloomfield sees the over-all lack of Boethian ordering as constituting the meaning of the tale: see 'The Miller's Tale: An UnBoethian Interpretation', in *Medieval Literature and Folklore Studies: Essays in Honor of Francis Lee Utley*, ed. Jerome Mandel and Bruce A. Rosenberg (New Brunswick, 1970), esp. p. 210.

[7] The sarcasm in the mouth of the Merchant is clear, though I agree with A. C. Baugh ('The Original Teller of the Merchant's Tale', *MP* xxxv (1937),

story shows. January starts out hoping to find heaven on earth in marriage, and his speech on the subject expresses as high an ideal of the relationship between husband and wife as is ever put forward in the *Canterbury Tales*:

> The blisse which that is bitwixe hem tweye
> Ther may no tonge telle, or herte thynke.
> (IV.1340–1)

The echo of St. Paul's ineffable mystical experience is no accident. Where a statement of ideals of this kind in the courtly tales represents an absolute, however, the idealism of the Merchant's Tale proves to be delusory. Marriage is not Paradise but a fallen Eden, not a symbol of harmony but the context for lust, jealousy, and deceit. The initial courtly treatment of the theme, with its implications of romance idealism, is entirely subverted by the ensuing fabliau plot. The Franklin's Tale, like the Merchant's, opens with courtship and marriage, followed by the intervention of the lovesick squire; but it ends not with the separation of husband and wife, but with their relationship strengthened. Marriage could hardly be called a symbol of harmony in this tale—the threat to it is too powerful for that—but it is a practical expression of harmony, of a mutually enriching relationship between two people. The theme of marriage comes round from metaphysical correspondence to the people involved.

The striking conceptual relationships between the four tales include, besides marriage, the way in which the characters have to face the consequences of chance, of interruptions to the normal ordering of the world. The series of misapprehensions that ends the Miller's Tale is again splendidly devoid of significance: not even poetic justice is served, as Alison gets off scot-free. In the courtly tales Chaucer makes a strong reassertion of human values in the face of such disruption. The irrational violence of the universe represented by the gods in the Knight's

15–26) that the passage makes more sense as an orthodox disquisition on the state of matrimony, spoken by an ecclesiastical narrator.

Tale is countered by Theseus's declaration of faith in a providential ordering behind the 'wrecched' appearance of the world, in the supremacy of Jupiter over Saturn. It is only by making 'vertu of necessitee' that human dignity can be reaffirmed, by a positive acceptance of the conditions of the world just as the knight-errant accepts the adventure that shall fall to him. The Franklin's Tale presents even more clearly the triumph of human 'vertu' over circumstance: the plot is set for the lady's fall; the husband, lover, and clerk vie in magnanimity to produce a happy ending. The virtue, in the modern sense, is even named—as *trouthe*, ultimately related to the Truth who is God in *Piers Plowman*, to Chaucer's *balade* on Truth, and to the Boethian *stabilis fides*. Arveragus and Dorigen meet necessity with *trouthe* and triumph. Neither here nor in the Knight's Tale is the ending facile. The world is still such that Arcite can be killed in his moment of triumph, that the natural order embodied in the rocks of the coast of Brittany threatens a ship and a love; but human goodness is all the clearer by such a contrast.

The close of the Merchant's Tale is an odd mixture. It bears superficial resemblances to the courtly tales: there is the supernatural intervention, the totally unpredictable 'chance' (to human minds) of January's eyes being opened, and May manages to convert the impending disaster into a 'happy ending' through wit and quick thinking. Again, a character is triumphing over circumstance; but what a triumph, and what circumstance. The theme of human virtue as the fixed point in an unstable world is being thoroughly degraded: May may be making a virtue of necessity, meeting her 'adventure' head-on, but the situation is the result of her own corruption, and what wins is not *trouthe*, as in the Franklin's Tale, but a neat bit of lying. Dorigen too is responsible for the situation she finds herself in, through her promise to give Aurelius her love, but the contrast with May underlines the fact that this time the wife has entered into a bond out of love for her husband, not out of disgust with him.

In some of the parallels I have discussed, most notably the use of the gods and the identification of the heroine with May, the Knight's Tale and the Merchant's stand out as being strikingly closely contrasted, in spite of their present distance from each other in the *Tales*. Their similarity is so marked as to suggest that Chaucer may at some stage have intended there to be a closer link between them. The Merchant's Tale was apparently composed originally with a different teller in mind:[8] lines such as 'thise fooles that been seculeer' (IV.1251) and 'I speke of folk in seculer estaat' (IV.1322) suggest an ecclesiastic. Critical opinion has generally favoured the Friar as the original narrator,[9] but the Monk has perhaps a stronger claim: for in the General Prologue, the Knight and the Monk are continuously and closely contrasted just as are the themes and images of the Knight's Tale and the tale now ascribed to the Merchant. As R. E. Kaske has ably demonstrated,[10] the Knight and Monk become antitypes. It is the Knight who has devoted his life to the service of Christ, while the Monk has devoted his to the pursuits of a country gentleman; in their occupations, their bearing, even in their horses, they are complete opposites. The tale now ascribed to the Monk, the series of tragedies, continues this contrast: the Knight asserts the providential ordering of the universe and the dignity of man in the face of Fortune, the Monk's tragedies deny the possibility of any stability in earthly affairs or of any

[8] The prologue giving the ascription to the Merchant does not figure in a large number of manuscripts. This may be because it was a late addition, or it may simply be due to the influence of the Hengwrt MS: see Germaine Dempster, 'A Chapter of the Manuscript History of the Canterbury Tales', *PMLA* lxiii (1948), esp. 466, 473.

[9] See especially Baugh's discussion of the probability of an ecclesiastic as narrator and the manuscript evidence for the placing of the tale. Baugh declares against the Monk as teller largely on grounds of character (he is not the right 'kind of person' for such a tale, p. 21); as I argue below, this approach does not seem to me to carry sufficient weight—and in any case, at least some of our idea of the Monk's character is derived from the tale now ascribed to him. Earlier, J. M. Manly was prepared to accept the Monk as narrator (see his edition of the *Canterbury Tales* (New York, 1928), p. 624) and suggested intriguingly that the Monk might have been 'retaliating for the satire on monks in the Wife of Bath's Tale (now the Shipman's)'.

[10] 'The Knight's Interruption of the Monk's Tale', *ELH* xxiv (1957), 251–8. Kaske goes on to point out the contrast in viewpoint between the tales of the Knight and the Monk.

control by man over the irrationality of the world. But just as the Wife of Bath seems to have lost the Shipman's Tale in order to tell a different, even more suitable, story, so the Monk may have lost his tale of January to contrast with the Knight's in order to be given the tragedies that still fulfil a similar function. One small relic of what may have been an intention to connect the Knight's Tale with a tale told by the Monk occurs in the link following the Knight's Tale, when the Host calls on the Monk to follow on:

> 'Now telleth ye, sir Monk, if that ye konne
> Somwhat to quite with the Knyghtes tale.'
>
> (I. 3118–9)

In fact, of course, the Miller interrupts, and it is he who 'wol now quite the Knyghtes tale'. 'Quite' implies more than just 'follow': the Miller's Tale is a rebuttal as much as it is a successor. Both the present Monk's Tale and the Merchant's Tale would serve the same function of 'quiting', as the Host invites the Monk to do, but the tale of January and May would certainly give a closer and clearer fit. If Chaucer once thought of putting that story next, he must have abandoned the plan at an early stage, as the Knight–Miller–Reeve group is the most consistently coherent series in all the manuscripts. The tale of January and May tends to float; if it was displaced from proximity to the Knight's Tale, it may have found another home only late in Chaucer's arrangement.[11] To have followed the tale of Palamon and Arcite with the story of January and Damian would have sabotaged the issues and ideals of the Knight's Tale; as it is, the Miller's Tale offers a light-hearted parody that sends up the Knight's Tale without destroying it. But the reference to the Monk in the link remains, and, given the possibility that it may have been he who told the story of January and May, the

---

[11] In a great many manuscripts the Merchant's Tale follows the Squire's Tale and precedes the Wife of Bath's; on the Merchant's Prologue, which links it to the Clerk's Tale and therefore necessitates its placing after the Wife of Bath's, see n. 8 above.

lines may well be calling attention to a connection between the tales.

In conclusion I would like to make a brief plea—polemical except that many readers must already agree with it—on behalf of the reading of the *Canterbury Tales* that a study of this kind suggests. The main implications affect, firstly, the pilgrim-tellers; and secondly, the aesthetic basis of Chaucer's art.

Four characters have scarcely been mentioned in this study: the Knight, Miller, Merchant, and Franklin themselves. The kind of reading of their tales I have attempted leaves a minimum of room for the tellers, and gives much more space to Chaucer himself. His declaration of non-intervention is an author's fiction[12]—after all, it is fiction he is writing:

> For Goddes love, demeth nat that I seye
> Of yvel entente, but for I moot reherce
> Hir tales alle, be they bettre or werse,
> Or elles falsen som of my mateere.
>
>   (I.3172–5)

A 'psychological' reading of the *Tales* is inadequate to explain the multiplicity of reflections and interlinkings that Chaucer provides. The importance of generic variation in the four tales I have studied here—the difference of tone and treatment between the courtly tales, fabliau, fabliau tricked out as romance—suggests a different kind of relationship of tale to teller: that of decorum, the rhetorical rule of appropriateness. Decorum refers especially to the fitting of style to speaker and subject-matter rather than to the actual choice of subject, but the concept provides a much closer analogy to Chaucer's procedure in the *Tales* than does any medieval psychological or dramatic practice. It is decorous for the churls to tell 'cherles tales', just as it is decorous for the Knight to tell a romance. There is no need to posit a social inferiority complex for the Franklin in his choice of genre; romances were one of the most

[12] There has been a recent tendency to take it at face value: see, for example, Charles A. Owen, *Pilgrimage and Storytelling in the Canterbury Tales* (Norman, Oklahoma, 1977), pp. 85, 87, 99.

important medieval literary kinds, and Chaucer had few appropriate characters to tell them. The Franklin, fittingly, tells a domestic rather than a metaphysically idealistic one. On this basis, the story of January and May would be decorous, appropriate, for either the Merchant or the Monk: the Merchant, because he occupies a social level half-way between the gentry and the townsmen, just as the tale looks towards both romance and fabliau; the Monk, because his portrait in the General Prologue has provided a breaking of decorum in the contrast of the office and the man, the spiritual ideal versus the worldly actuality, that parallels the stylistic indecorum of the reduction of romance into fabliau, the hollowness of the tale's ideals, and its inability to sustain its initial level of high sermon.[13] The tales expand the portraits of the tellers—Chaucer does not give a story to a pilgrim for whom it would be out of character, and the tone and nature of the tales do reflect back on to their narrators—but the stories are also an artistic creation in their own right, with a unity that can work in parallel to their setting in the pilgrimage, and not just a series of disparate viewpoints brought together by chance. The contents of the tales, like the pilgrims themselves, are no one's responsibility but Chaucer's; for the tales go beyond their framework, and become an encyclopedic exploration of the whole poetic and generic spectrum of the age.

[13] Sermon as distinct from irony or sarcasm, which is the reading the Merchant's Prologue forces on it: see the discussion in Baugh, pp. 17–18.

Chaucer's *Anelida and Arcite*

―――――――― ◆ ――――――――

J. NORTON-SMITH

The course of criticism abounds in tiny watersheds. In 1963, Professor Clemen's revision and English translation of his pre-war study of Chaucer's early poetry[1] summed up the general opinion of *The Boke of feire Anelida and fals Arcite*.[2] Thereafter an agreed silence fell over the poem—now broken nearly a decade later by a brace of re-evaluations.[3] The two essays alluded to are by critics of different interpretative persuasions.

[1] *Chaucer's Early Poetry* (London, 1963), pp. 197–209.

[2] I have used the title as given in MS Bodley 638 (closely supported by that in Fairfax 16). These MSS alone preserve the original Italian spelling of the name Analida (though, as in the title, 'Anelida' spellings alternate), whilst the form of the title preserves the Italian use of paired alliterating epithets, as found in the Florentine poem *L'Intelligenza*, stanza 75, where Chaucer came across the name: 'La bella Analida e lo bono Ivano'. Her literary origin could hardly be more obscure. The Italian poet establishes her aura of renown by modelling the line in stanza 75 on a formulation used in stanza 72 to present the famous lovers Tristan and Isolde: 'E la bell' Isaotta e 'l buon Tristano'. Similarly, Chaucer's use of the proleptic alliterating epithets gives the title an almost ballad-historical texture—as if these personages had been made famous by ancient folk art-forms. Chaucer reinforces the alliteration by substituting 'Arcite', thereby establishing the essential link with Statius's *Thebaid*. Medieval Celtic has been shifted into classical antiquity. The title is directly echoed in line 147. I cannot remember a similar collocating of epithets 'fair' and 'false' elsewhere in Chaucer, nor can I remember Arcita anywhere in the *Teseida* being described as 'false'. Boccaccio's character differs radically from that presented by Chaucer in the *Knight's Tale*. Creon is once called 'perfido' (II.31) but Arcita is usually called 'buono'. Chaucer obviously knew *L'Intelligenza* as did the author of *The Court of Sapience*. Robinson's note is far too cautious and ultimately misleading.

[3] Cf. J. I. Wimsatt, '*Anelida and Arcite*: A Narrative of Complaint and Comfort', *Chaucer Review*, 5 (1970), 1–8; M. D. Cherniss, 'Chaucer's *Anelida and Arcite*: Some Conjectures', ibid. 9–21.

But whatever helping hands are extended to this neglected work—fantastical 'conjectures' apart—the silent deeps at the heart of Clemen's chapter seem hardly stirred. For both recent writers are agreed on four main issues: (1) the poem is unfinished; (2) the poem is an early production; (3) the poem's predominant artistic quality resides in the plangent beauties of the Complaint section; (4) the poem's affiliation in Chaucerian chronology lies with early verses on a Theban subject taken from the *Teseida*, early verse yearning to become the *Knight's Tale*.

None of these assumptions, all as old as Skeat, seems capable of being controverted. They have become part of the modern *donnée* of the poem's scholarly setting.[4] I see no reason for not regarding all four notions as still hypothetical and unproven. I shall try to show that these points should be rethought and that four quite different and infinitely more reasonable hypotheses can be generated, namely: (1) the integrity of the text should be asserted: this is a complete, finished poem; (2) the poem is not an early composition but was written between the completion of *Troilus* and the evolution of the *Legend of Good Women*; (3) although the complaining letter is important in considering the nature of the poem's achievement, Chaucer is concerned with a larger, though related, poetic topic—that is, the author evolves a positive attitude towards the function of poetry as an 'art' which operates along the lines which classical poets and Renaissance writers had imagined for it: that poetry, closely allied to the function of the faculty of memory both preserves what otherwise would be lost, and confers a memorable record in terms of causes and effects in the area of human history both public and private;[5] (4) the most convincing affiliation with

---

[4] These basic critical assumptions persist to this day. The most recent repetition I notice is in Piero Boitani's *Chaucer and Boccaccio*, Medium Ævum Monographs, viii (Oxford, 1977), pp. 72–3.

[5] The recording function of *poesis* is closely connected with immortalization and the creation of memorable, valuable history. Cf. Horace, *Epistles*, II.i; *Odes*, IV.viii, ix (and Fraenkel's discussion, *Horace* (Oxford, 1957), pp. 423–6); *Ars Poetica*, 391–407. Brink's account, *Horace on Poetry* (Cambridge, 1971),

Chaucer's writings for *Anelida and Arcite* lies with the poet's Italian concerns, with the Theban material of Book V of *Troilus* and with the *Legend of Good Women*'s new mood of quasi-religious 'penance', elegant Ovidian complaining epistle, and poetry designed to redress the 'wrongs' (real and imaginary) done to womankind, verses demonstrating the constancy and good sense of the sex.

For Professor Clemen, *Anelida and Arcite*'s status as a 'transitional' work is guaranteed by its 'experimental, tentative' texture, and is faithfully reflected in 'the unfinished nature' of the text. The *Knight's Tale* will be the final narrative form towards which *Anelida* is stumbling. Now this is all unresisted fantasy if it can be shown that the poem is finished—for the narrative goal ahead as the *Knight's Tale* really has nothing in common with *Anelida*, unless you conjecture that the poem is only an uncompleted narrative, prefaced by a section of epical invocation.

The argument for the unfinished nature of the poem turns on the existence of a single stanza of rhyme royal which follows the end of Anelida's complaint. The first question must be 'Is the stanza genuine'? It does not appear in all the manuscripts; it appears in only four. These four manuscripts turn out (for a variety of reasons) to have no pre-eminent qualities which would make them indispensable for the establishing of a base text. Only Brusendorff saw that the classification evolved by Skeat and Koch (and finalized by Butterworth and followed openly by Robinson) obscured the real distinction between the manuscript groups.[6] Robinson's habit of accepting the conclusions and evidence of others on textual classification has led the editor into stemma-impelled misconceptions. Initially the manuscripts may be divided into three main groups: (1) whole and genuine

pp. 384–94, gives a clear history of the origins of this tradition as reflected in the Augustan period.

[6] A. Brusendorff, *The Chaucer Tradition* (Oxford, 1925), pp. 259–60: 'This peculiar and badly constructed stanza (note especially the concluding lines) is certainly a spurious addition, due to a copyist of the *Anelida*-booklet found among the circle of texts which formed the basis of the Hammond group.'

poem (with internal omissions in manuscripts copied by Shirley, irregularities resulting from Shirley's habit of copying partially from memory); (2) fragment (complaint only), one manuscript containing the extra and spurious stanza; (3) pseudo-incomplete poem with extra stanza. All other *differentiae* must be subordinated to these larger, substantial divisions. For example, MS Tanner 346 cannot simply be classified with Robinson's so-called 'archetype a' since it has been contaminated in transmission by acquiring the extra stanza. The stemma-derived category 'archetype a' may describe nothing which ever existed in reality and from which little usefully can be argued. The manuscripts, as suggested above, divide into the following groups:

1.   Bodley 638
    Fairfax 16
    Harley 372
    Harley 7333 (copied from a Shirley MS)
    Add. 16165 (Shirley MS)

2.   Trin. Coll. Cambr. R.3.20 (Shirley MS)
    Magd. Coll. Cambr. Pepys 2006
    Phillipps 8299
    Cambr. Univ. Lib. Ff. 1.6 (with extra stanza)

3.   Tanner 346
    Digby 181
    Longleat 258

The conclusion I draw from looking at the manuscripts again is that only group 1 manuscripts can be considered as evidence for forming a base text; it is the only form of the poem which the poet could have overseen *ipse*. Group 3 (supported by Ff. 1.6) contains a non-Chaucerian last stanza.[7] The rhymes are con-

---

[7] Bodley MS Tanner 346 contains an unusual feature which may account for the stanza. On fo. 65a, written in a hand related to that of the text, appearing just within the written area of the leaf towards the outer margin between the end of the poem and the extra stanza is the Latin adjective 'Belliger'. This could be the Latin transliteration of the scribe's name (this practice is not

We instinctively understand why Chaucer should appeal to the god of war, Mars, as an inspirational aid. Like *Troilus and Criseyde*, the confused social life of wartime provides the setting for the meeting and courtship of Sir Arcite and Lady Anelida. Such is the straightforward drift of Boccaccio's address. But why invoke 'thy Bellona, Pallas'? Although one is permitted to doubt, Robinson reminds us that 'The confusion appears in Boccaccio's *De Genealogia* ... where Bellona is also called sister of Mars and his charioteer'. But Chaucer, doubtless aware of the closeness of function of the Italian and Greek deities, nowhere makes any confusion. His memory is perfectly accurate. They are not confused or identified, they are only equated—equated in order to emphasize certain shared attributes. The Pallas Athene Chaucer is here appealing to is the armed goddess in her personification of the exercise of vigilance and reason, the opposer of anarchy and rebellious confusion. Athene acquired the epithet 'Pallas' as the destroyer of the Titan Pallas, one of the giants who opposed the civilizing rule and order of Olympus. The archetypical battle between order and presumptuous chaos was made famous to the Middle Ages from Ovid's account in *Metamorphoses* I. But here Chaucer is remembering the passage in Dante's *Purgatorio* XII which had already yielded him one of the memorable phrases and key images for *Anelida*, 'la punctura della rimembranza', 'the poynt of remembrance' of lines 211 and 350. In *Purgatorio* XII Dante gazes at the examples of the Proud set in effigy in amazing likeness of what they once had been and which 'many a time causes men to weep for them because of the prick of remembrance, which only to the pitiful gives spur ... in order that there be a memory of them'. A few lines later he says,

> Vedea Timbreo, vedea Pallade e Marte,
> armati ancora intorno al padre loro,
> mirar le membra de' giganti sparte.
>
> (31–3)

vocat pariter studiique locique Mnemonidas'; 'And she calls the Mnemonian sisters happy as well on account of their way of life as their place of living.'

(I saw Thymbraeus Apollo, I saw Pallas Athene and Mars, yet in arms, around their father Jove, gazing on the scattered limbs of the giants.)

This is why Mars and Pallas are invoked together by Chaucer—as any good humanist would have known—these are the aspects of Mars and Pallas as protectors of order and permanence against change and chaos. These are the deities of civilization in their preserving and protecting functions.

Robinson's note on the Muse Polymia is cryptic to say the least. Chaucer's eloquent lines we are told 'seem to be due to Dante'. The note goes on: 'The adjective "memorial" may even be due to Dante's *memoria* (Paradiso, 1.9), though it is appropriate on general grounds to the character of Polyhymnia.' The connection of memory with this Muse is more than general, it is essential. I suspect that Chaucer's remembering of Dante in this stanza has been affected by Boccaccio—affected by Boccaccio's commentary on Dante, *Inferno* II, where all of Dante's invocations are collected and discussed, together with all his classical sources and parallels. The mythographers, too, are quoted and brought in as explanatory material. Boccaccio also touches on the relation of poetry to history. The etymologizing of the name Polymia as 'the Muse of many memories', not the Muse of many songs, was known to Boccaccio, who gives this explanation. The same explanation is provided in Latin in the *De Genealogia*. Boccaccio's commentary to the *Commedia* is one of the unrecognized sources of much of Chaucer's knowledge of Renaissance literary aims; he had not just read the *De Genealogia*.

The nervous strength and classical elegance of the line

> singest with vois memoriale in the shade

on the other hand owes its modelling entirely to Chaucer—there is no corresponding use of the adjectives *memoriale/memorialis/memorabilis* in Latin or Italian in this or any earlier period I can find. 'Con voce memoriale' never

of the efficacy of literary activity and the poet's commitment to permanence of memorable fabricating in a world of hostile change and continuous erosion is distinct in each poem.

Professor Quinones in his study *The Renaissance Discovery of Time*[10] places the origin of the writer's dramatic, heroic personal contest against the triumph of time exclusively in Dante and Renaissance Italy—with scant regard for the facts. As for Chaucer, only Egeus's conventional words of comfort: 'And we been pilgrims, passing to and fro' are quoted—and somehow attributed to Chaucer as typical of a medieval passivity in accepting the oblivious garland extended by historical time: 'The world is but a highway ...'[11] 'Wrong again' one is tempted to write in his margins. From the evidence of the first three stanzas of *Anelida and Arcite* Chaucer was well aware of the necessity for such a heroic struggle, though with characteristic Chaucerian modesty he makes no grand gestures towards himself as the organ of inspiration. He allows the majesty of the created invocations to do that.[12] Chaucer, like Dante and Boccaccio (whom he paid the compliment of quoting and imitating in this poem), was fully conscious of the poet's contention with time, change, and impermanence. In common with these writers, his attitude varies from work to work and with the course of his own artistic life. In the *House of Fame* (wherever we eventually place it in Chaucerian chronology) the struggle against the slide into oblivion is seen with sceptical humour and a certain underlying Boethian philosophical abrasiveness—an acerbity which avoids involving directly the proud, self-confident solutions

[10] R. J. Quinones, *The Renaissance Discovery of Time*, Harvard Studies in Comparative Literature, 31 (Cambridge, Mass., 1972).

[11] Ibid., p. 15.

[12] The vague and abstract ('riposta e nascosa') and loosely 'pompous' syntax and literary programme of Boccaccio (*Teseida*, 1.2) is given personal intensity of feeling, philosophic definitiveness (*Meta.* 15), and vitality of metaphoric emphasis by Chaucer. Boitani (op. cit., p. 73) notes the similarity in elevated cadences but he does not comment on Chaucer's radical alterations. Later, in lines 47–8, Chaucer refers, without benefit of an assumed innocence, to the skill and cunning of his style of writing for this poem: 'And founde I wol in shortly for to bringe / The slye wey of that I gan to write ...'.

of the antique poetic spirit. But in its overt evaluation of the
literary act and the poet's concern for memorability, *Anelida
and Arcite* is totally distinct, and totally committed to the
seriousness of purpose which the *renascentia* assigned to the
verbal arts:

> Thou ferse god of armes, Mars the rede,
> That in the frosty contre called Trace,
> Within thy grisly temple ful of drede
> Honoured art, as patroun of that place;
> With thy Bellona, Pallas, ful of grace,
> Be present, and my song contynue and guye:
> At my begynnyng thus to the I crye.
>
> For hit ful depe is sonken in my mynde,
> With pitous hert in Englyssh to endyte
> This olde storie, in Latyn which I fynde,
> Of quene Anelida and fals Arcite,
> That elde, which that al can frete and bite,
> As hit hath freten mony a noble storie,
> Hath nygh devoured out of oure memorie.
>
> Be favorable eke, thou Polymya,
> On Parnaso that with thy sustres glade,
> By Elicon, not fer from Cirrea,
> Singest with vois memorial in the shade,
> Under the laurer which that may not fade,
> And do that I my ship to haven wynne.
> First folowe I Stace, and after him Corynne.

These humanistic concerns make the reader fully aware of the
poet's positive attitude in opposing oblivion and the erosion of
knowledge due to the process of time. The modern poet's
'Beneath it all, desire of oblivion runs' is not Chaucer's text.
The poetic reworking of these lines from Boccaccio's *Teseida*
has long been recognized, but other elements not directly
traceable to this work have passed almost without notice.[13]

[13] A small but typical point is that there is no note in Robinson on the phrase
'sustres glade', apart from trying to attribute the expression to Dante's *Paradiso*,
I. Chaucer is here remembering Ovid, *Metamorphoses*, v.267–8: 'Felicesque

tal' about the poem at this level of invention. It has a well-tried
poetic structure which is the result of Chaucer's reworking of
the Gransonian narrative-complaint hybridization.

Chaucer's innovation lies in the grafting together of stylistic
elements not found together in Middle English verse or in the
French and Italian schools, as far as I can discern. Anelida's
complaint-letter (already a hybrid) is written in a rich variety
of lyric measures (including leonine rhymes) which shows
Chaucer's mastery of the *musique artificielle* as defined by
Deschamps in his *Art de Dictier*. This highly elaborate French
mode is deliberately joined to the equally artificial but smoothly
modulated and richly severe neo-classical syntax and diction of
the *invocatio* and *narratio*. But these deliberate combinations
of elements have not pleased the poem's critics. If I may quote
from Professor Clemen's chapter:

... these lyrical passages stand almost isolated in the poem, and they
are not convincingly brought within the framework of the 'story'.
The epic and lyric elements do not harmonize, although Chaucer's
addition of narrative elements to the complaint shows that he was
aiming at a harmony of this kind.... One wonders what lies behind
it? Is it a wish to mystify the reader, a change of plan with the poem,
delight in experimenting with epic forms and themes, or skilful
'postponement' of the real beginning of the story?

The problem created by the view of the poem as an amalgam
of incompatibles is made a little less acute when we are no
longer obliged to see the poem as an 'unfinished' narrative or
unfinished epical narrative yearning to become the *Knight's
Tale*. But it still does not remove the charge of incompatibility
or explain the artistic intention for the combining of different
styles or even 'genres'. Yet the history of the presupposition of
incompatibility is obscure. Why should critics have imagined that
invocations, lyrical measures, and narrative units were topoi
more naturally confined to other genres? Such a view ignores the
use of long invocations in at least three of Horace's most
famous odes and in the introductory poem to Ovid's *Amores*, not

to mention the contemporary use of invocations and apostrophes to the Muses in Italian poetry, where there is extensive elaboration of neo-classical diction and imagery in the shorter poems of Petrarch and Boccaccio, and in Boccaccio's concluding, dedicatory sonnet to the *Teseida*. We should not be invited to see these invocations as inappropriate to shorter poetic fictions where the main component is personal and lyrical.

This assimilation of the invocation and the personal poem had already taken place in Italy according to the practice of the ancients. The reason for this recourse to the invocation of the Muses in Italian poetry of Chaucer's day is instructive. Examine each moment in Petrarch and Boccaccio and one sees that the poet's invoking of the Muses becomes a poetic creation of a personal, humanistic interval, a Parnassian incantation which mediates between the projected subject-matter and the *ingenio* of the poet's searching, creative memory. It emphasizes the seriousness of the poet's intention, not only by calling on inspirational aid from higher intelligences by means of a higher science, but by associating the poet's self-consciousness of expression with the gravity of thought of the classical authorities. The invocation calls into being an ancient religious affiliation, a sophisticated yet ancient mental ritual. The invocational moods of Petrarch and Boccaccio in Italian and Latin demonstrate how deeply assimilated these textures, the lyrical, the invocational, and the functioning of neo-classical poetic memory, had become by the time of Chaucer's visits to Italy.

What now remains of the four original assumptions about *Anelida and Arcite*? Not very much, for the case for 'earliness' disappears as soon as the Italian and humanist concerns are permitted their natural force and seriousness. The richness of Italian and Latin resonances and the steady maturity of their application should warn us that the poem is no early production but the considered result of the poet's absorbing of Renaissance verse and literary ideals. The poem should not be paired automatically with the *House of Fame*. The aesthetic evaluation

ceivably Chaucerian but the stanza is syntactically odd. The narrative style evolved for this poem grows out of the three invocational stanzas which open the poem; they show suspensive enjambment of movement (neo-classical 'continuousness' in Professor Auerbach's terminology), where the medial caesura is avoided altogether or much moved about in the manner of Surrey or Milton. The extra rhyme-royal stanza is mechanically made up of pleonastic hemistichs with intrusive, regular, and often awkward medial caesura dividing in six out of seven lines after the second foot. It reads:

3   2

Whan that Anelida / this woful quene

2   3

Hath of hir hande / written in this wise

2   3

With face deed / betwixe pale and grene

2   3

She fell a-swowe / and sith she gan to ryse

2   3

And unto Mars / avoweth sacrifice

2   3

Within the temple / with a sorowful chere

2   3

That shapen was / as ye shal after here

The sub-Lydgatian use of phraseological additive elements in this stanza is not the Chaucerian stylistic norm for this poem. The final and indisputable evidence is the use of 'betwexe' to specify some shade between paleness and greenness (the conventional colour sign for pallidness/lividness, the bleached pallor of Greek χλωρός). But Chaucer always uses 'betwexe' in colour contexts as the mediator between distinct states of emotional or complexional composition. He could and did write 'Betwixen yelow and red' (*Knight's Tale*, 2132) but it is highly unlikely

unknown). It could represent the surnames Marshall, Strong, Savage, Wild, Bold. A scribe might very well be the author of the stanza; it would hardly be the work of a professional poet.

that he used 'between' to mediate two colours virtually identical. 'Pale and grene' is a common phraseological unit in Middle English; it signifies a slight variation in an almost identical physiological and emotional state. I can find no other example in ME of 'betwexe' used with this phrase. It amounts to a verse solecism. Chaucer could have written 'in hues pale and grene' but not this. This is nonentity yawning in 70 syllables. I submit these lines could not have been written by Lydgate, much less Chaucer.[8] Remove the charge of 'incompleteness' and the 'tentative' and 'experimental' also evaporate. It is strange that critics always assume that 'unfinishedness' automatically signals an 'experimental' state. Of course, experiments, like everything Complaint written by Chaucer. First, the *Complaint of Mars*,

Banish the spurious stanza and suddenly the form of *Anelida and Arcite* closely resembles two types of Framed Amatory. Complaint written by Chaucer. First, the *Complaint of Mars*, which is divided into three sections (preface, *narratio*, complaint) where the *praefatio* shows a three-part sectioning which foreshadows the larger structure of the poem.[9] The *Anelida* invocatory preface is also cast into three stanzas with the central stanza enunciating one of the personal motives for the writing of the poem: the poet's strong desire to take an active role in opposing the destructive effects of Time. The second Framed Complaint which *Anelida* resembles is the *Complaint unto Pity*, which has a similar three-part structure and also uses the concluding device of verbal echoes, deliberate repetitions of words and images in the final stanza of opening lines and phrases from the exordium of the poem. No doubt Professor Burrow would wish to call this 'circular form', but it is really 'epanaleptic'—if we dare to revive the term. *Anelida* skilfully uses echoic phrases and metaphors to achieve the same concluding effect. There is, then, nothing whatever 'experimen-

[8] There is another peculiar usage recorded in this stanza: the sense of the verb *avowe* in the phrase 'avoweth sacrifice'. The attested ME sense 'to promise solemnly' does not occur anywhere in Chaucer's genuine work.

[9] Cf. J. Norton-Smith, *Geoffrey Chaucer* (London, 1974), pp. 16–34.

and poetic authority is allowed a modern, less erudite, more sceptical vantage point. The memorializing activity on behalf of womanhood takes the form of modern, Christian, fourteenth-century penance—a submission, obliquely comic, which calls for atonement in the appropriate hagiographic form (though subverted from its original seriousness). The freely expandable narrative form of the *Legend* places Chaucer's act of poetic memory amongst the religious artistic commissions of Richard the Connoisseur. The *Legend* has found a new, highly personal way to detach itself from the sober gravity and literary serious-ness of 'olde clerkes speache in forme of poetrie'—to give us light sophistication and charming social allegory whilst still preserving classical centres of interest: feminine psychology, the mutual interaction of vice and virtue, and eloquent poetic utterance. Philosophical seriousness is also preserved. This new freedom looks forward, too, to the triumphant relativity of literary authority which takes us down an older Kent road and knits up what Professor Bennett once called 'that special kind of *Canterbury Tales* contentment'.[20]

[20] *The Parlement of Foules* (Oxford, 1957), p. 193.

masculine attitude is repetitiously characterized as 'false') but
Chaucer establishes another quality in the martyrdom of love
which derives directly from Ovid's *Heroides*—the interdepend-
ence of virtue and vice. In common with the hagiographical
fashions he gently parodies in the *Legend*, Chaucer shows us in
Anelida and Arcite that each impulse, joy and pain, each role,
the wronger and the wronged, is not a simple dualism but arises
out of a mutual attraction. There exists a psychological nexus
which fascinated Ovid. The same relation exerted an equal
fascination on Chaucer. We can see this reflected in the reversal
of roles for false Arcite when he has taken up with his new
'lady', the cause of his having abandoned Anelida. In turn, he
becomes a victim—wholly subjugated in the service of love to
the cruel temperament of his new passion. By a simple dramatic
irony Anelida's persistent and uncomplicated belief in Arcite's
unfeeling caddishness is no longer valid. His realization of guilt
and contrition is more perfect perhaps than she could wish. The
reader is left to imagine the effect of her terrible, final letter on
the despairing Arcite. This psychological and moral connection,
exploited most effectively by Chaucer in the legend of St.
Lucrece, is that area which Angelo refers to when he says 'Amen'
to Isabella's prayer 'Heaven keep your honour safe', and adds
in a dazzling aside,

> For I am that way going to temptation
> Where prayers cross.

This affinity with the moral and formal interests of the *Legend
of Good Women* I find more convincing as a possible chronological affiliation than the accepted yet wholly hypothetical
connection of *Anelida and Arcite* with some earlier, quite non-
existent story of Thebes which is imagined to lie behind the
Knight's Tale. There are other elements which connect *Anelida*
with the last book of *Troilus*: for example, the presence in the
poem of the insistent note of doom and decline, the dominant
sense of fatalism, 'the olde wrathe of Juno to fulfille', the roll-
call of the famous Theban dead in stanza nine—all these details

recall the use of the historical sense of Theban nemesis in Troy's
eventual destruction—and the rolls of honour of the Theban
slain in *Troilus*, v.1499–1505.[19] The related fates of Thebes and
Troy perhaps indicate some fundamental connection between
the common origins of these two poems.

Briefly stated, I believe that *Anelida and Arcite* represents a
genuine transitional model, mediating between the tragic, declin-
ing pagan world of the last book of *Troilus* and the legendary,
ironically Christian, epistolary complaint material of the *Legend
of Good Women*—poetic material already promised in a vague
form at the very end of the same last book of *Troilus*. The
Legend (however ironically) belongs to the poetic, hagiographical memorials of the Christian New World. *Anelida and Arcite*
belongs to the poetic memorials of the pagan Old World, at
least in one half of its stylistic fascination and certainly in terms
of the poet's struggle against the declinations of *spatiosa vetustas*,
'longe time'. The extraordinary metrical and rhyming skills
exhibited in Anelida's letter suggest to me that Chaucer is here
inscribing his own memorial and farewell to the elaborate,
highly intricate *musique artificielle* of the French school. Henceforth, in the *Legend* and the *Tales of Canterbury*, we find
Chaucer interested in rendering his own time in a style which
calls for a plainer, more domestic modernity, no matter how
modified by the author's or his characters' experience of the
past. However intricately and beautifully contrived, *Anelida*
renders pain and suffering in the well-wrought style of classical
monumentalism. Its celebrated verbal qualities, its special
memorializing, involve the poet in very recondite fictional
manœuvring. The *Legend of Good Women* allows the poet new
creative room for manœuvre—where the scope for satire, irony,
and personal observation becomes broader, more obvious, more
informal and relaxed. Chaucer's treatment of history, evidence,

---

[19] The elegiac mood, verbal structure, and some names derive from a common
source in Boccaccio, *Teseida*, ii.10–11. Chaucer is not simply versifying the
twelve-line Latin summary of Statius's *Thebaid*, though Root's note (pp. 554–5)
seems to encourage this view. Skeat did not miss the connection.

truth of the authorial situation. If 'Statius' may be said to represent the written authorial aspect of the civilizing world which the poet wishes to preserve through imitation (though the actual passages of the *Thebaid* may be small), then 'Corryne' may be understood to represent the complementary inventive side of the poetic faculty, that aspect which works with personal experience, which speaks with the authority of *experiaunce*. This would be the 'author' who provides Chaucer with the untraceable parts of the poem—especially the letter of Anelida. This Corrina is not Ovid's mistress, nor the pseudonym of a historical figure, nor is she the lamenting mistress of the *Amores*. Rather, quite naturally, she represents the inspirational side of the poet's activity which derives from personal reality. These two aspects of her (inspiration and personal reality) were well known to readers of Ovid, though not, it would seem, to Chaucer's critics. In *Amores* II.xvii Ovid testifies to Corinna's inventive role:

> ingenio causas tu dabis una meo.

(You alone shall be the spur to my poetic genius.)

(II.xvii.34)

In the poet's famous autobiography in the *Tristia* (IV.x.60 ff.), Ovid testifies to her real existence and her unknowableness as fictional personage:

> moverat ingenium totam cantata per urbem
> nomine non vero dicta Corinna mihi.

(My poetic genius had been stirred by her who was sung henceforth throughout the city, whom I called, not by a real name, Corinna.)

I propose that this is the symbolic figure whom Chaucer names and says he follows after Statius. She is a secular, unwritten authority who summarizes the plangent, private side of the formal invention and contrasts with the figure of Statius who justly represents the general, classical eloquence of the invocation and narrative authorial modes. In this role she anticipates Chaucer's apostrophe in the Prologue to the *Legend of Good Women* (F 84–96) addressed to a fused fugure of Alceste and Queen Anne as the only Muse of all Chaucer's poetic labours.[18] It is this aspect of the poetic faculty which connects the poem *Anelida and Arcite* with Ovid's *Heroides* and Chaucer's own *Legend of Good Women*—that side of Chaucer's imagination which enters into the workings of feminine psychology and seeks to impersonate the anguished eloquence of the Ovidian heroine. It is no accident that Anelida's complaint takes the form of a letter in the process of being written—and that it draws on Dido's Letter to Aeneas (*Heroides*, VII) for the origin of two of its crucial images: the concluding pathetic simile of the dying swan which sings against its death, and the radical image of the 'sword of remembrance' which in line 212 acts as a gloss on the Dantean 'point of remembrance'. Although as yet unremarked, Ovid's lines (*Heroides*, VII.189–90) provided the basis for Chaucer's metaphor:

> nec mea nunc primum feriuntur pectora telo;
> ille locus saevi vulnus amoris habet.

(Nor does my heart now for the first time feel a sword's thrust: that spot already bears the wound of a cruel love.)

This is an important image, for it generates in Chaucer's imagination of series of related, destructive martial-amatory phrases. These expressions sharpen Dante's original *punctura* into something more destructive—which is both the forming cause of memory and foreshadows the means to eventual oblivion. The 'wounded heart' recurs in line 231, the 'sword of sorrow' is reinvoked in line 270, 'the self-murder with privy-thought' of line 291 reminds the reader how deeply the echoes of violence from the Theban situation had entered into the private life of Anelida.

Another important parallel with the *Legend of Good Women* remains to be drawn. Not only does the reader find himself in the intimate presence of wronged womanhood (where the

[18] J. Norton-Smith, op. cit., pp. 66–9.

seems to occur. Boccaccio in one place[14] speaks of the Muses as singing 'con vostre canto sottile e sonore', but the employment of the wonderful adjective which combines at least three senses, 'partaking of the quality of remembrance', 'conferring memorableness on the song uttered', and 'memorable now in its own right of quality of expression' is unknown to the poetic usage of Dante, Petrarch, or Boccaccio. The quality of Chaucerian *imitatio elegantiae* owes nothing to Dante's noun *memoria*. It owes much to Dante's and Boccaccio's concept of the poet's role, the exercise of his *alto ingenio*, in conferring eternalization and true fame through eloquence and memorableness. The material from Fulgentius and others discussed at length by Boccaccio in this same passage in the commentary to *Inferno* II reminds the reader of the Muses' connection not only with singing but with the production of eloquent speech and the training of the voice—'la formatione perfetta della nostra voce'.

Of course, the central stanza in the invocational preface introduces us to the concern of the poet in respect of the course of history, history as the wearing, decaying power of time in its long accumulating decadence, characterized by the linked physical images of 'biting' and 'destroying'. Robinson notices Boethius, *De Consolatione*, II, pr. vii ('obscura vetustas' as the enemy of books and authors) but fails to notice that the strength and force of the imagery as well as the personal urgency of tone are derived from the famous apostrophe in Ovid's *Metamorphoses*, XV.234–6 beginning 'Tempus edax rerum ...', a passage which inspired Guillaume de Lorris's long digression in the *Roman de la Rose* (ll. 351 ff.). Chaucer translated the French early in his career, but it is only in his mature works that he uses the substantive *elde* in this special appreciation of the Latin substantive *vetustas*.[15] He would seem to be the only Middle English writer to have invented a separate usage for this

---

[14] *Teseida*, XII. Sonetto, 8.

[15] In rendering the French, Chaucer shapes his general syntactical pattern to Guillaume's, with the result that he relies on the verb *elden* and the adjective *elde*. Guillaume's *Vieillese* (Chaucer's *Elde*) is not *vetustas*.

concept of endlessly destructive antiquity, 'invidiosa vetustas' in Ovid's phrase.

Although it might be profitable to recall Professor Curtius's excursus on the Muses and the popularity of the concept of eternalization amongst medieval poets great and small, his surveys of the topic call attention almost exclusively to the features which poets had in common.[16] The differences never seem to emerge. Chaucer's treatment here of the notion of eternalization seems to me to vary a little from the idea which Dante testifies that he had first learnt from Bruno Latini.[17] Chaucer, unlike his Italian mentors, seems not to insist on the attainment of Fame for the poet as an individual. He does not avoid or deny this emphasis, but he seems assured enough in the possession of his own genius not to need to. The primary function of Chaucer's memory and presiding Muse is to preserve and record eloquently documents of the remote past which would be otherwise lost to civilized letters.

Actually, the literary reality behind this statement is more complicated and not unattended by the Muse of Irony. The poet's written sources extend beyond Statius. The reader who knows his poets and something of Theban history is aware that very little of the narrative and no part of the epistolary complaint of Anelida (the private side of the public events of recorded history) is to be found in any written account. Obligingly, Chaucer has given us his authority for this, Corryne. Chaucer scholarship has evolved at least four complicated explanations for this mysterious *auctor*, and not one of them is in the least convincing. I wonder if the truth is not much more simple, and that Chaucer may be conveying to the reader something like the

[16] E. R. Curtius, *European Literature and the Latin Middle Ages* (London, 1953), pp. 228–46, 476–7.
[17] The general drift, the proper worth of literature, is the same. Professor Bennett rightly observes of *The House of Fame*, 1091 ff. and Chaucer's echoing of *Paradiso*, 1.13–15: 'And behind Chaucer's appropriation of this prayer lies the fact that he is the first Englishman to share Dante's sense of the worth of poetry and of the act of poetic creation.' (*Chaucer's Book of Fame* (Oxford, 1968), p. 101.)

1305–6 where it includes only half E 1305. It includes few passages not in later manuscripts, the only one of importance being the couplet A 252ab. There is no room to discuss all these extra items; CYT and the extra passages in WBP may stand for the rest.

Of the additional tales two, Beryn and the Plowman's Tale, are found only in later fifteenth-century manuscripts. CYT and Gamelyn are found in early manuscripts: CYT in El and most other manuscripts including Ha⁴, Gamelyn in Ha⁴ and about half the extant manuscripts but not in El. The attitude of scholars to these two could hardly be more different: CYT is accepted universally as genuine, but Gamelyn is as universally rejected—at best some feel that Chaucer may have had a copy of it because he intended to rewrite it. Attitudes to these two tales are so ingrained that it is rare to find any discussion about their genuineness or otherwise. The reasons for the acceptance of CYT are partly manuscript (its occurrence in El) and partly literary (its style and structure, both of which are said to resemble those of other tales). But if Hg is the earliest manuscript and if El is dependent upon it, there is no support in the manuscript tradition for the genuineness of CYT, for the occurrence of CYT in El would be no more telling than that of Gamelyn in Ha⁴. It is true that it may be inferred from Hg that CYT was in preparation,[10] but this is of no help to those who edit by method (3). Indeed the knowledge that it was in preparation should probably count against its genuineness for such editors. The acceptability of CYT can be decided solely on literary grounds.

The literary arguments in favour of CYT are the way it is worked into the framework of the poem and its style. But that it is worked in so adroitly may exhibit the hand of a more accomplished imitator than the author of Gamelyn. Indeed the facility with which CYT fits in could argue against its genuineness, for a conscientious imitator would try to make his creation as convincing as possible. It has often been claimed that the

[10] Blake, op. cit.

inclusion of CYT was 'most happy and successful'.[11] It could with equal validity be claimed than an imitator who wanted to include a tale about alchemy would be forced to add to the number of the original pilgrims since none of those mentioned in Pro is an alchemist. And whoever wrote CYT was clearly fascinated by alchemy and apparently had a grudge against its practitioners. Chaucer for his part shows no interest in alchemy in his genuine work, and alchemical vocabulary is not found there. As for the position of CYT in the order of the tales, it is linked to SNT through a reference in its prologue to 'the lyf of Seinte Cecile' (G 554). No reference is made to the nun, for it seems probable that SNT was not allocated to a teller in the original copy-text and that allocation to the nun was the work of the editor of Hg. It may well be that the imitator started on CYT before he knew which pilgrim was to be allocated SNT in Hg. CYT also has a verbal link with McT in that both contain a reference to the Blean forest. This reference caused SNT to be moved from its place in Hg between Fkt and ClT to the place it occupies in El between B² and H. CYT is thus unique in having a link with another tale outside its own group; it is also unusual in having such clear indicators of its position in the order of tales. These references arouse suspicion, for in a tale not found in the earliest manuscript they indicate a careful attempt to place the tale in the poem and make it seem genuine. Once CYT is introduced it forms a constant group with SNT. If CYT is genuine, we may wonder why two members of the constant group G became separated, for there is nothing to suggest that the members of any other constant group ever did.

The problems of style and structure are more difficult because more subjective. There has been no shortage of critics who have pointed out the weaknesses of CYT and how it differs from the other tales. Skeat noted its hasty composition, faulty metre, and marks of carelessness.[12] More recently Muscatine has remarked

[11] Skeat, op. cit., p. 7.
[12] W. W. Skeat, *The Complete Works of Geoffrey Chaucer*, vol. iii (Oxford, 1894), pp. 492–3.

already shown that later manuscript groups are either descended from or based directly on Hg and El,[9] there is no room in the manuscript tradition for the theory of prior circulation. To dispose of this assumption in no way diminishes the possibility that certain manuscripts represent different stages in Chaucer's revision of his text. Even if this view were acceptable, one would not be able to return to the carefree editorial attitude of earlier Chaucerian scholarship whereby editors took various parts from these revised versions to make up their edition of the poem. If, for example, Hg and El are two versions of the poem issued by Chaucer, they have the status of 'complete' editions by the author, and it is not in order to supplement them by including extra material. If Hg is an edition by Chaucer then an editor might choose it as his base manuscript to show what Chaucer's earliest version was like. Or he might choose a later manuscript to present a more mature version of the poem by Chaucer. But each version by Chaucer is discrete and the mixing of manuscripts is not permissible. No editor would try to offer an edition of *Piers Plowman* by amalgamating the A, B, and C texts; and if authorial versions are accepted for the *Canterbury Tales*, the amalgamation of its versions is equally improper.

If we accept there is a manuscript tradition which goes back to one manuscript, Hg, then there are three possible ways to edit the poem. (1) To include only what is in Hg on the assumption that what is in the earliest manuscript will represent all that was available of the poem when the author died. (2) To assume that several early manuscripts represent different stages of revision in the poem by the author. In view of the recent work on the text of the poem, this is likely to mean only Hg and El, though other early ungrouped manuscripts like Ha[4] might be considered. (3) To assume that all Chaucer wrote as part of the poem was not for one reason or another included in the earliest manuscript, which was assembled after his death.

[9] G. Dempster, 'A Chapter in the Manuscript History of the *Canterbury Tales*', *PMLA* lxiii (1948), 456–84, and 'The Fifteenth-Century Editors of the *Canterbury Tales* and the Problem of Tale Order', *PMLA* lxiv (1949), 1123–42.

This would open up the theoretical possibility that anything found in any later manuscript was genuine. Let us consider these options.

The third possibility is the least compelling now that the theory of prior circulation appears untenable. If there is a linear manuscript tradition, then editors choosing this possibility would need to show not only why they include pieces from later manuscripts but also why those pieces are not found in the earliest manuscripts. As some sections in neither El nor Hg are included, it is not a question of simple omission from the first manuscript. The history of the *Canterbury Tales* is one of inclusiveness: it is not a matter of a few fragments being added to other early manuscripts. As there was a continuous process of accretion and editorial intervention, there will need to be strong arguments to show why some later pieces are genuine and others not. As the manuscript tradition itself provides no clue as to genuineness, the proof will be based on the literary excellence of some pieces as against the others. It must be admitted, however, that literary excellence is a subjective test. It is usually interpreted to mean pieces which fit into apparent gaps, which echo words or lines found already in Hg, and which are of a style worthy enough to be considered Chaucerian, though the merits of no passage have been argued in detail.

If we take Hg as our base we see that as regards material it differs from later manuscripts in two ways: it lacks complete tales and links, and in those fragments it does include it lacks passages of varying length. Four complete tales were added to the poem after Hg: CYT, Gamelyn, Beryn, and the Plowman's Tale. Hg also lacks many later links. The tales in Hg are often shorter than those found in El and other manuscripts. In WBP it omits five passages (D 44a–f, 575–84, 609–12, 619–26, 717–20); in MkT it omits the Adam stanza (B^2 3197–3204), which is added by another hand in the margin; it omits a long passage in NPP (B^2 3961–80); and it omits a variety of couplets from different tales. It occasionally has incomplete couplets, as at E

If each tale has a unique textual history, then each must have come to the scribes by different routes and thus circulated individually. This view seemed to find support from the apparently haphazard collection of tales in Hg.[6] Earlier scholars took the view that Chaucer had constantly revised the poem and that the different versions arose in this way.[7] This earlier view also presupposed that different versions were circulating in Chaucer's own lifetime since later manuscripts reflect this prior publication. A theory embracing prior publication allows for pieces not in the early manuscripts to be attributed to Chaucer since all authentic tales and links do not need to be gathered in one manuscript. It does not, however, provide any clue how to detect which pieces not in the early manuscripts are authentic. Taken to its logical extreme this theory implies that there was never a complete set of authentic fragments in Chaucer's possession which was used as the basis of a single manuscript, for no early manuscript contains all that is considered genuine. It also implies that the rather uncertain art of literary criticism is more reliable in reconstructing the poem than the authority of the earliest manuscript(s). Moreover the theory of prior publication (whether in individual tales or in authorial revised versions) is at variance with the assumption that changes made by Chaucer in his copy prompted scribes to different readings. For this assumption presupposes only one copy-text which was available to all (or most) later scribes, whereas the other presupposes there were many copies in circulation. The two assumptions are incompatible and both cannot be correct.

These assumptions have produced a double stance in *Canterbury Tales* scholarship which enables editors and others to take cognizance of early manuscripts without being bound by their evidence. At its simplest level this is seen in the division into

[6] Manly–Rickert, i. 266–83 and ii. 475–9. See also the description by A. I. Doyle and M. B. Parkes in the introduction to the Hengwrt facsimile (1979; henceforth *Facsimile*). I am indebted to Dr Doyle and Dr Parkes for their kindness in letting me see this piece before it was published.

[7] W. W. Skeat, *The Evolution of the Canterbury Tales*, Chaucer Society, 2nd ser. 38 (1907) and Brusendorff, op. cit., pp. 63–136.

groups/fragments. Current scholarship accepts ten. This division does not reflect the situation in either Hg or El. In Hg there are twelve fragments: A D MLPT SqT MeT FkT SNT ClT C B^2 H I. Groups E and F do not exist as entities in this manuscript. In El the rearrangement of the order resulted in the series A MLPT D E F C G B^2 H I. In this case, though, E and F clearly form one group and not two; the division between them is made in a speech by the Host. Indeed F as a group has no reality in any manuscript, for either SqT and FkT are part of a larger group as in El or else they are separated as in Hg. The division into groups E and F pays lip-service to the position in El while recognizing that there are differences in Hg; it is consequently unsatisfactory. The same is true of the text found in modern editions, for the assumptions mentioned above allow any piece to be included which an editor feels is genuine. It has not been necessary to explain why pieces not in early manuscripts were excluded by the scribes, for the theory provided a blanket explanation for all variations. As long as certain passages satisfied the editor's literary criteria of what was Chaucerian they were accepted. This situation could produce great diversity in what was included in the text; in fact early editorial decisions of what to include have largely been accepted and perpetuated. This uncritical reliance on earlier decisions made on dubious grounds is clearly unsatisfactory. Most readers of the poem accept this state of affairs because they have never seen an edition without these extra items, and editors have spent their time more in rearrangement of the links and tales than in justifying the inclusion of some.

In a recent article I criticized the assumption that there was prior circulation of the fragments of the *Canterbury Tales*.[8] There I sought to show that there was a system of arrangement in Hg, which presupposes that the scribe or editor had all the fragments before he started, and that El's order can be understood only as a development of Hg's. Since Mrs Dempster had

[8] N. F. Blake, 'The Relationship between the Hengwrt and Ellesmere Manuscripts of the *Canterbury Tales*', *Essays and Studies*, NS 32 (1979), 1–18.

On Editing the *Canterbury Tales*

————— ♦ ■—————

N. F. BLAKE

An editor of the *Canterbury Tales* has to face three major problems: what material in the extant manuscripts to include in his edition; in what order to arrange that material; and how to edit it. Although these are three interrelated problems, most scholarly attention has been devoted to the second, which is surprising for of the three it is the least important. It is also the one least likely to yield concrete results because it is agreed that the orders in the extant manuscripts do not reflect Chaucer's intentions. The neglect of the other two problems has meant that ideas about editing the *Canterbury Tales* have become so traditional that they are accepted without question. Two examples may illustrate this state of affairs. Firstly, the work by Manly and Rickert[1] on the poem's text has led to a general acceptance that Hg contains a good, perhaps the best, text. It is now used by some editors as their base manuscript and by others as an important manuscript against which to check the readings in El. The order of tales in El is still followed, though the relationship between the two remains unresolved. It has never been satisfactorily explained (indeed the question has rarely been asked) why one manuscript should have the best text and another the best order. Secondly, it is customary to include in editions of the poem passages which appear neither in Hg nor in El, though these are recognized as the two best manuscripts. While such additional pieces are categorized by many as

---

[1] J. M. Manly and E. Rickert, *The Text of the Canterbury Tales* (Chicago, 1940), particularly vols. i and ii. I have used the abbreviations of *Canterbury Tales* manuscripts and tales found in Manly–Rickert.

'indubitably genuine', the reasons for this description are less easy to determine. Consequently it is high time that the question of how to edit this important Middle English poem was reopened.

Two assumptions lie behind most current editorial practice. The first is that Chaucer altered passages within the poem by marking his copy-text so that scribes were uncertain of his intention or simply overlooked his instructions. Thus A. Brusendorff wrote of A 3721–2: 'The couplet is not found outside Ellesmere; probably it was added by Chaucer in the margin of his MS, and on that account was missed by most of the scribes.'[2] More drastically R. F. Jones suggested that in the Man of Law's endlink (B 1163–90) Chaucer kept changing his mind as to which pilgrim should tell the tale to follow. Each time he altered his plans he had to erase the name of the pilgrim at B 1179 and introduce a new one on the erasure. In the end the word became so illegible that only the initial capital S remained clear. Hence later scribes were uncertain which pilgrim was meant and so interpreted this S as they thought appropriate.[3] This type of suggestion is often justified on the grounds that Chaucer is known to have made alterations to his poem. It is believed, for example, that ShT was written in the first instance for the Wife of Bath.[4] But it must be emphasized that there is a difference between alterations which can be detected in the text and are found in all manuscripts and features suggested for the original copy-text because of variations in extant manuscripts. The former are authorial; the latter may be scribal.

The second assumption is that individual tales were circulated in Chaucer's lifetime and many were copied, probably without his permission or knowledge. This assumption rests mainly on Manly's investigations of the manuscripts, for he came to the conclusion that individual tales had different textual histories.[5]

[2] A. Brusendorff, *The Chaucer Tradition* (Oxford, 1925), p. 81.
[3] R. F. Jones, 'A Conjecture on the Wife of Bath's Prologue', *JEGP* xxiv (1925), 512–47.
[4] Manly–Rickert, ii. 350.
[5] Manly–Rickert, iii and iv, *passim*.

Hg's exemplar and he ignored it or that the revision was inserted in the copy-text after Hg was written. As the copy-text was presumably Chaucer's working copy, it is reasonable to assume that he did make alterations to it. But if we accept this hypothesis we have to assume that the scribe of Hg and El, who was careful and competent, chose to ignore the revisions in his copy-text. Since this reading is found largely in slightly later manuscript groups, such as *c* and *b*, it is more satisfactory to think that a fifteenth-century editor made the revision in the copy-text after the earliest manuscripts were copied. In the same way a later editor could have marked A 252ab for deletion after Hg was copied and this would explain why the lines are missing in most later manuscripts.

I would suggest, therefore, that the copy-text was constantly revised in the 'editorial office' and that it is this process of revision which explains the variant readings in the manuscript tradition. The revisions are not authorial. Naturally as more manuscripts became available scribes might start comparing the copy-text with early manuscripts and so produce mixed texts. Although this theory is one which cannot be proved in detail here, it seems more acceptable than Manly's hypothesis of prior circulation with authorial revisions, which is self-contradictory. That theory has produced the unsatisfactory modern editions, in which preferred literary readings can be accepted under its umbrella. It has been permissible to re-create Chaucer's text as we want it to be. The theory involving changes in the copy-text by editors enables us to account for most variants and perhaps to explain some puzzling features. For example, the Adam stanza in MkT (B² 3197–3204) is missing in Hg; it was included later in the margin in a different hand – a hand which is not that of the supervisor/editor. In some manuscripts, like Cp, Sɪ², and Mc, a gap is left for the stanza at the appropriate place in MkT, but the stanza was never added. Perhaps an editor wrote the stanza on a separate sheet and noted in the copy-text where it was to be inserted. It could be that this sheet (like the final folio(s) in MeT) was by mistake not sent to some scribes, though they knew there was an insertion from the marginal note. Therefore they left a gap for the stanza though they never received it.

The theory proposed here may also account for other puzzling features of the text. Dempster pointed out how strange it was that, although Hg was the earliest manuscript and had the best text, later manuscripts did not make use of this excellent text in Hg or its exemplar.[19] But if the exemplar (i.e. Chaucer's own fragments) was being constantly emended in the editorial office, the good text would gradually disappear under a host of corrections. If the original copy-text was being emended in this way to 'improve' it, there would be no incentive to use Hg as a copy-text since it would be considered too primitive by the members of the editorial office which organized the copying of the earliest manuscripts. On the other hand, the existence of the original fragments in separate fascicules may explain why Hg's Merchant–Franklin link (E 2419–40 with F 1–8) was rearranged as it was. I have suggested elsewhere that this link is spurious.[20] If so, it would have been copied on a single sheet and the sheet would have been inserted in the sequence between MeT and FkT. This link consists of two parts (as the modern numbering indicates): an endlink for MeT and an introduction to FkT. When the order was rearranged one might have expected the first twenty-two lines to go with MeT and the last eight to stay with FkT. In fact the whole link was moved and the references to the Franklin were replaced by those to the Squire found in El. This cumbersome editorial procedure is understandable only if we assume that the link existed as a single unit on a separate sheet which was treated as an entity in itself.

We may also accept that the original copy-text contained mistakes even though it was Chaucer's copy. There is nothing inherently improbable about this since Chaucer or his scribe (?Adam) could make slips as easily as anyone else. Thus in KtT at A 2037 the readings of the early manuscripts indicate that the copy-text read *sertres* for *sterres*, probably because an omitted

[19] *PMLA* lxiv (1949).   [20] Blake, op. cit.

prove there was only one copy-text, it does not prove that later scribes used Hg's exemplar rather than Hg. This may, however, be shown through other examples.

In Hg on fo. 151 the ink and writing show a marked change at E 2319, which Doyle and Parkes interpret as a sign the scribe was commencing to copy again after a short break, such as an overnight rest.[17] Since there is nothing in the text to make him pause at E 2319, it is probable that he did so because his exemplar started a new folio or quire there, since that would provide a suitable stopping place. Now as it happens manuscripts of group *c* end MeT at E 2318 and some include the explicit there because their scribes had no more text. The most reasonable explanation of this phenomenon is that their exemplar lacked the final folio(s) of the tale, which had inadvertently not been sent to the scribe of the archetype of *c*. Since Hg and El do not commence a new folio at E 2319 and since Hg's exemplar probably did, it is natural to assume that the scribe of the archetype of *c* used Hg's exemplar, i.e. the original copy-text. If he used it, others probably did so too, because most early texts were produced within the confined limits of London and Westminster.[18] A further indication of the use of the original copy-text is provided by the constant tinkering by the scribes of E and F. It seems probable that in the original copy-text each section was copied continuously without break between the tales. Thus later scribes would have no reason to change the order of tales in groups like A, B^2, and C because the copy-text would inhibit that kind of dismemberment as their tales were written without break. But sections consisting of single tales like SqT, MeT, FkT, and ClT would each be written as independent units and this arrangement would encourage scribes to reorder these tales. It would have been more difficult to

---

[17] *Facsimile.* Cf. also G. Dempster, 'On the Significance of Hengwrt's Change of Ink in the *Merchant's Tale*', *MLN* lxiii (1948), 325–30.

[18] A. I. Doyle and M. B. Parkes, 'The Production of Copies of the *Canterbury Tales* and the *Confessio Amantis* in the Early Fifteenth Century', in *Medieval Scribes, Manuscripts and Libraries: Essays Presented to N. R. Ker*, ed. M. B. Parkes and A. G. Watson (London, 1978), pp. 163–210.

rearrange these tales if Hg or El had been used, because in those manuscripts quire boundaries do not coincide with tale boundaries. It is because MeT formed a separate unit in the copy-text that in group *c* only the end of MeT is missing and not the beginning of the next tale as well.

The nature of the copy-text and its preservation are problems that an editor has to evaluate in deciding the usefulness of later manuscripts. If later scribes had access to the original copy-text it follows that they might have better readings than Hg, though as the scribe of Hg was careful this is not likely to happen frequently. Thus in Hg and some other manuscripts, at the end of the tragedy of Nero a line is repeated as the seventh line of two successive stanzas (B^2 3723, 3731): *For drede of this hym thoughte that he dyed.* In its first occurrence *dyed* rhymes with *espied, allyed,* and *cryed;* in its second it is spelt *deyde* and rhymes with *seyde, breyde,* and *preyde.* In other manuscripts the first of these two lines is replaced by *Tho wiste he wel he hadde hymself mysgyed,* the reading adopted by modern editors. The adoption of this reading is never defended, though the reason for its inclusion is probably literary. Equally it is not explained how Hg's reading arose. It is improbable that it is the result of anticipation, for *dyed/deyde* are spelt differently to match the two rhyme schemes and the rhymes are in different stanzas and thus some lines apart. Possibly some editors think Hg represents Chaucer's first version and other manuscripts his revised text; if so, we need to know why the revised version is preferred. Chaucer does use the same word in different forms, often in rhyme. The occurrence of *sik:seke* and *soote:swete* suggests there is nothing inherently unacceptable with *dyed:deyde.* Perhaps Chaucer intended them to form a word-play which the same preceding line would bring into focus. It is easy to understand that later scribes were disturbed by the repetition of the same line over two stanzas, particularly with a differing rhyme sound in the same word, and decided to do something about it. However, if we accept there is one copy-text, then we must assume either that the revised line was in

arranger was not familiar with the contents of all the tales. Hg's order is best explained as an editorial arrangement. Therefore in the light of our present knowledge it is safest to edit the poem following method (1), i.e. using Hg as the base manuscript and excluding anything not found in it, for the other methods seem unsatisfactory.

Once Hg is accepted as the base manuscript, the question of tale-order can be faced, though that now involves the twelve sections in Hg rather than the ten traditional groups/fragments.[16] It is unlikely that Chaucer reached any final order for these sections, as the nature of Hg indicates. The procedure so far has been to use El's order, but this is unsatisfactory because it means accepting links not in Hg. Indeed the use of El's order is precisely what has prompted the retention of spurious links in modern editions. One needs to avoid this dilemma if possible. Theoretically there are three arrangements which might be adopted. The first is to use some arbitrary principle such as an alphabetical arrangement of the initial letters of the teller of the first tale in each section. Though this would remind us that there is no authorial order, it would destroy the concept of the poem as an embryonic whole and upset some of Chaucer's arrangements, since PsT would not come last. This method is too drastic. The second is to do what all the scribes did and for the editor to reproduce the order which he finds most convincing. This would be an exercise in completing the poem, which could be justified if one makes clear what one is doing (i.e. making one's own order and not trying to reproduce Chaucer's) and if one uses only genuine segments of the poem. But not only could this procedure lead to great diversity in arrangements, it would also encourage the possibility of presenting the medieval poem in a modern structure. It too may be discarded. The third is to follow the order in the base manuscript, Hg. The principal danger here is that this order might soon come to be taken as

---

[16] In my article in *Essays and Studies* I suggested that MLP and MLT were originally independent fragments. As this is only a reasonable deduction it might be safer not to take it into account in an edition of the poem.

authoritative, though its non-dramatic system should remind us that it is scribal rather than authorial. The problem in using Hg is that it has a dynamic order which was modified as the manuscript was copied. One could thus put D after H, which is where it was originally meant to go. Or one might put D after MLPT where the scribe evidently wanted it to be, but could not put it there without breaking up his existing quires. Or one can follow the order of the tales as they stand in the manuscript (with the misbound quires reinserted at their proper place). This in the end appears the safest solution, since the other possible orders involve deductions which may later be proved wrong. Tinkering with the order found in the manuscripts has been for too long a favourite editorial pastime; it is time the manuscripts were allowed to speak for themselves.

That all manuscripts are ultimately dependent upon Hg's copy-text will guide editorial practice, for it presupposes that there was only one copy-text. The evidence suggests that this copy-text was used by most, if not all, early scribes. In Hg and a few other manuscripts the couplet that should fill E 1305–6 in MeT is incomplete, for only the first half of E 1305 is given: *And if thow take a wyf.* This was presumably the reading of the copy-text and no doubt Chaucer had not decided how to complete the couplet. In later manuscripts scribes react to this gap in various ways. Some leave out the half-line and pass directly from 1304 to 1307. Others complete the couplet, and there are at least seven readings for the missing part. If one manuscript was copied directly from the preceding one, once the couplet was abandoned or completed that version would become standard and later scribes would copy or adapt it. That they did not do so indicates they had access to a manuscript with the incomplete couplet or with a suggested reading in the margin, since the completion of the couplet is a response to that situation. The scribes could not otherwise have known that this couplet was any different from the others. It also confirms that there was only one copy-text, for Chaucer is unlikely to have issued MeT with a defective couplet. While this example may

that it rarely rises above the merely concrete.[13] Indeed the tale, though woven into the fabric of the poem, is different in several ways. In particular the distinction between prologue and tale is blurred, for the tale carries on in the same manner as the prologue even though the Canon's Yeoman is anxious to insist it is not about his master. The vindictive and brutal tone is also unlike anything else in the poem, partly because there is such a lurid exposure of an individual who had joined the pilgrims rather than of a class in society. Consequently the verdict on CYT by literary criticism is uncertain, and it would be a brave editor who inserted the tale only with that support. Moreover, the more praised CYT is as a literary work, the more difficult it becomes to explain why it was omitted in Hg.

The extra passages in WBP present a slightly different problem because they occur only in a few manuscripts and because even in those manuscripts not all passages are included. All are found in groups *a* and *b* and in Ch, Ii, Ry^1, and Se. Some, though in no consistent pattern, are found in El, Gg, Ad^3, Ha^2, and Ld^1. Within the manuscript tradition now posited for the *Canterbury Tales* it is possible only to assume that these pieces were in the margin of the copy-text, which has been the usual view. Editors who consider them all genuine have to accept that all these marginal additions were rejected by many scribes, including the earliest, and some by others. This presents the problem why scribes should have rejected what was in their copy. Thus we have no reason to think that the scribe of Hg was anything but meticulous and careful. And if some scribes rejected these passages, why should we accept them? It is more reasonable to assume that the pieces were added (not necessarily all at the same time) in the margin of the copy-text after the earliest manuscripts were written and that it was the knowledge of manuscripts without additions which led later scribes to omit them. Some may feel that literary excellence should carry more weight than the manuscript tradition, but literary excellence is

[13] C. Muscatine, *Chaucer and the French Tradition* (Berkeley and Los Angeles, 1957), p. 214.

difficult to prove in such relatively small passages and it is in any case a difficult procedure to vindicate. When all is said and done, those who want to include such pieces might well feel that method (2) of editing is less controversial. So let us consider that.

The palaeographical dating of manuscripts and the establishment of a textual tradition influence each other. At present Hg and El are dated just after 1400, partly because the former is explained as a compilation which could not have had the author's approval.[14] But both are in some respects old-fashioned and a pre-dating by five or ten years would not seem impossible paleographically. It is permissible to posit that both *could* have been written in Chaucer's lifetime. It would indeed be essential to assume that Hg at least was written then to allow for the possibility that they both represent authorial versions of the poem. It would, however, follow that these two manuscripts contain the earliest 'complete' editions and whatever was not in them (e.g. D 44a–f, B 1163–90) should be excluded from modern editions.

It is probably impossible to disprove that Hg and El do represent authorial revisions, but the balance of evidence is rather against it. The scribal insertion in Hg at the end of CkT, 'Of this Cokes tale maked Chaucer na moore', implies the author is dead. And the arrangement of Hg remains a considerable stumbling block.[15] Although there is a system in the ordering of the tales, it is not a dramatic one; it is an *ad hoc* order designed to accommodate all the fragments available. It is for this reason that previous scholars regarded Hg as disorganized. It is difficult to explain why Chaucer at a certain point in his life decided to arrange the fragments in a way that is contrary to the methods he used in linking constant groups. At best one might feel that he did so when he felt death approaching so that some order was provided. But this view would exclude El as a genuine revision, though it might alter out attitude over individual items such as CYT. Even this assumption does not account for the fact that the shifts of arrangement in Hg suggest that the

---

[14] *Facsimile*, p. xx.   [15] See Blake, op. cit. and *Facsimile*.

t was inserted above the abbreviation for *er* and scribes mistook its position. A few manuscripts like Ha⁴ do read *sterres*, but the readings in other manuscripts, such as *sere trees, septres, Ceres, certis*, indicate that their scribes did not understand their exemplar. Probably *sterres* in Ha⁴ is an emendation of *sertres*, just as *sere trees* and the others are; it differs only in being more intelligent.

If there were errors in the original copy-text, problems of a different nature arise. One is the question of justifying an emendation. Professor Donaldson suggested that in WBP where at D 117 Hg reads *And of so parfit wys a wight ywroght* the correct reading is *And of so parfit wys a wrighte ywroght.*²¹ This reading is supported by three late, and otherwise not reliable, manuscripts. By the theory of prior circulation correct readings could be preserved in late mauscripts with little authority. The emendation to Hg is also supported by the appropriate passage in *Epistola adversus Jovinianum*, which is Chaucer's source here. Donaldson believed with Manly that Hg's exemplar was a corrupt version of the poem and not Chaucer's copy. As Chaucer could make a mistake as well as another, this assumption is unnecessary. All editors like to feel that only a pure and perfect text left the author's hand, though many illogically also accept authorial corrections—a frequent cause of error. But common experience is quite against the assumption of an author's copy without any mistakes. Therefore, we do not need to agree with Donaldson that *wrighte* is 'what Chaucer must have written',²² though it may be what he meant to write. Later manuscripts may contain 'correct' readings through scribal emendation, as at A 2037, but we do not need to assume that the correct reading existed in the original copy-text and was handed down through some minor manuscript tradition which is otherwise unreliable. There is no harm in using later manuscripts when thinking of potential emendations, but they do not necessarily enshrine what was in Chaucer's own copy. We may

²¹ E. T. Donaldson, '*Canterbury Tales* D 117: A Critical Edition', in *Speaking of Chaucer* (London, 1970), pp. 119–30.   ²² Ibid., p. 127.

agree with Donaldson that *wrighte* is a good emendation—but it is so despite what was almost certainly in Chaucer's copy. The emendation is supported more by the source than by the occurrence of *wrighte* in late manuscripts. Late manuscripts may suggest emendations, but they in themselves cannot prove those readings to be correct.

In other words, an editor may correct what was in the author's own copy when his intentions are not fully realized there.[23] This is quite proper. Naturally, without external support such as a source, emendation is difficult because self-justifying assumptions could be made about Chaucer's intentions, language, and metre. This may be seen in ReT where the two undergraduates use Northern dialect forms. It is accepted that Chaucer was not consistent in his use of these Northernisms, for he wanted to give a Northern colouring to their speech, not to reproduce it accurately. Yet whenever El, for example, introduces a Northernism not in Hg it appears in modern editions. Naturally the scribe of Hg may have substituted Southernisms from time to time. But we do not need to assume that Chaucer was the only Londoner with some knowledge of a Northern dialect, and as there was constant scribal improvement in the poem some scribes may have tried to out-Chaucer Chaucer in his use of Northernisms.[24] At A 4027 Manly–Rickert accept that the original copy-text had *bihoves* which was corrected to *boes* by El,[25] for *bihoves* is found in most manuscripts including Hg. Here El reads *boes*, the *b* group *bus*, and one manuscript *bud*. Editors follow El here. But if the original copy-text read *bihoves*, we can emend only on the grounds that Chaucer meant to write *boes*, for El's reading has no textual

---

[23] The same holds true of the emendation *south* for *north* in MkT at B² 3657. By the same token at I 10 we might emend *the mones* to *Saturnes* because Libra was the latter's ascendant. We would not expect such an elementary mistake in astronomy from Chaucer, who elsewhere exhibits familiarity with the subject. See further Brusendorff, op. cit., pp. 116–18.

[24] This is true of Ha⁴; see J. S. P. Tatlock, *The Harleian Manuscript 7334 and Revision of the Canterbury Tales*, Chaucer Society, 2nd ser. 41 (1909), pp. 6–7.

[25] Manly–Rickert, iii. 443.

authority. El's reading has been accepted too readily, for it may provide evidence that the editors were replacing Southern forms with Northernisms. It is quite likely that both the substitution of Northernisms for Southern forms and Southernisms for Northern forms proceeded simultaneously. In cases like this where certainty is so difficult it is better to follow the lead in Hg simply because it was copied early and so antedates much editorial intervention in the original copy-text, even though one could not guarantee that it is an absolutely faithful copy of its exemplar.

Regrettably there will never be a complete edition of the *Canterbury Tales* because when Chaucer died the poem existed in a fragmentary state. The evidence suggests there was only one copy-text which was Chaucer's own copy. That is best represented by Hg because from the beginning there was considerable editorial intervention in the text by his 'literary executors' to present the poem in a more suitable dress.[26] While presumably Hg did not escape some of these attentions, as the earliest manuscript it may have avoided the majority. The improvements made by editors appear to have been added to the original copy-text, which was used by most scribes, especially the early ones. These revisions included new tales, new links, new tale-order and corrections of lines, words, and perhaps even spellings; the changes were entered in the margins or on new folios. The best an editor can do is to follow Hg closely. The testimony of later manuscripts cannot be ignored, but in view of the process of revision to the poem in the copy-text their evidence must be judiciously analysed. For the most part later manuscripts will suggest to an editor how Hg may be emended or corrected; their readings will not normally in themselves be proof of what the original copy-text contained.

[26] Cf. M. B. Parkes, 'The influence of the Concepts of *Ordinatio* and *Compilatio* on the Development of the Book', *Medieval Learning and Literature: Essays Presented to R. W. Hunt*, ed. J. J. G. Alexander and M. T. Gibson (Oxford, 1976), pp. 115–41.

Observations on the Text of *Troilus*

——————— ◆ ———————

DEREK BREWER

I

I first came to know Jack Bennett when I was an undergraduate returned from the war, and my acquaintance ripened when I began research in 1948. Research in English at Oxford in those bad old days was normally regarded, if at all, with derision, and it was tremendously heartening to be treated with kindness by one of the very few dons whom I ever came to know by his Christian name. Part of the benefit was to be introduced to the extraordinarily rich stores of a mind to which nothing in literature was alien. Jack Bennett's range of reading is immense, from Old English to modern American, and all that was read was savoured and tested by a judicious palate. From him, on country walks, in that college room crowded with treasured books, in visiting museums and art-galleries (how did he find the time?), and later in his house at Hinksey, I learnt something of the unity as well as the pleasure of artistic experience, and especially of English literature. I learnt too that characteristically Oxford love of the empirical particular. When as an undergraduate I read my weekly essay to him (as it happened, on those seventeenth-century devotional poets he especially loves—but it could have been on writers in any century) I rarely got to the end, for he sprang up continually to check a word in the dictionary—*the* dictionary—or to seek a book to bring in another line of fact. I can still hear him quoting with deep feeling those lines from Donne, 'O more then moone / Draw not up seas to drown me in thy sphere!', and thereby adding, for me, new dimensions to the poetry. As a reviewer of his latest

book has said, 'his ear for verse is pitch-perfect'. He likes to go
to the fountain-head. He once said to me, in later years, while
still living in Oxford, that when he wanted to consult Chaucer's
earlier poems he usually went along to Bodley and read MS Fairfax
16! For this paper, then, I propose to offer a series of comments
based on that same empirical observation of the text in the
manuscripts, and suitably tentative as to their conclusions.[1]

II

First let me examine in detail a series of representative lines,
which I happened on almost by chance, to illustrate some
editorial processes and to invite the agreement or disagreement
of the reader in a way impossible, for lack of space, in an edition
of such a big poem as *Troilus* surviving in so many manuscripts.
The process of comparison and decision seems to me fascinating.
Its minuteness is itself exemplary of the actual processes of
writing and reading. It is in the consideration of fine detail that
the connoisseur tests himself and his subject. Literary authenticity is here, if anywhere. Yet some general reflections may also
emerge.

Scribes differ over even very simple lines. Corpus 61 reads at
I. 502

> For which hym thoughte he felte his herte blede.

If this is what Chaucer actually wrote one would not expect it
to have offered much of a problem. There are seventeen witnesses
available for this line. Not one witness is identical with the

---

[1] I have also incurred other general debts in my turn to younger scholars that
I must acknowledge from the start. I have greatly benefited from reading the
Birmingham University MA dissertation (1964) by Miss Valerie Owen, now
Dr V. Edden, which consists of an edition of *Troilus*, I. 1–500; and from Dr
B. A. Windeatt's remarkable University of Cambridge doctoral dissertation
(1974), 'An Edition of Troilus IV and V'. Each of these is from all known
manuscripts. For more authoritative discussion of many of the points I raise
we must await Dr Windeatt's forthcoming edition of the whole poem from all
the manuscripts. I am also greatly indebted to Dr Ruth McQuillan for help
with the initial transcriptions, and to the Leverhulme Trust for a generous
grant to pay for research assistance on the text of *Troilus*, 1966–8.

Corpus text. The centre of controversy appears to be the simple word *which*. One manuscript has *such* (Campsall, now Pierpont Morgan Library MS 817). This reading is not to be rejected because it is in a minority of one, but because it is so inferior in sense and English idiom. The poet could not have written *such* when *which* was so obviously available. But did he write *which*? Six manuscripts read *that*, a reading followed by Root, though not by Skeat, Robinson, Donaldson, Baugh, Fisher, who all prefer *which*.

However three manuscripts, instead of *which* or *that*, read *that cause*, and in these we have

   a. For þᵗ cause hym thought he felte his herte blede
   b. For þᵗ cause he thoughte his herte blede
   c. For that cause he thougth his herte ded blede

(*a*: St. John's College, Cambridge, MS LI; *b*: Cambridge University Library MS Gg. 4. 27; *c*: British Library MS Harley 4912.) We may further note that one manuscript with *that* also reads *he thogt* (Bodleian Library Rawlinson poet. 163).

One of the great principles of textual criticism when confronted with variants is to ask oneself which version could have generated another. The version generated by the scribe will by definition naturally be in some way 'easier', that is, superficially more familiar, more immediately comprehensible, simpler, more emphatic, etc. It is interesting to see how difficult such a perception may be in practice. On this principle it would seem more likely that a scribe having *that* in front of him would clarify and emphasize (superficially) by adding *cause* than that a scribe having *cause* before him would omit it and stop short, even though scribes very commonly omit words. This impression is enhanced by seeing what happens in the rest of the line. The John's scribe gives a line that is metrically discordant. Other evidence shows that he recognizes, occasionally at least, the use of final *-e* in the metre; and if *herte* is disyllabic his line is 'mysmetred'. The scribe of Gg. 4.27 also recognized the use of final *-e*. Maybe he (or his predecessor, since the scribe of Harley 4912 is with him here) omitted *he felte* on metrical grounds, to mend the line. (The Harley scribe, who did *not* understand final *-e*, did not appreciate such mending, so uniquely added the feeble *ded*, to help out, though not far enough.)

There is another reason why *he felte* could have been omitted and it may be convenient to deal with that now, so that we may consider the line as a whole. Two manuscripts, as noted, omit *he felte*, and both of these read *he thoughte*, though in variant spellings, as do two other manuscripts, against twelve witnesses to *hym thoughte*. It is clear that *hym thought* is superior to *he thought*, in that it is older, grammatically more meaningful, more liable to be mistaken or misunderstood, than the easier reading. A mid-fifteenth-century scribe, if he found *he thought*, would be very unlikely to exchange this familiar and expectable phrase for an old-fashioned, unfamiliar *hym thought*. The earlier phrase also goes well with *he felte*, giving the admirably, poetically, precise plain information that 'it seemed to him that he felt', with its subtle distancing of poet from the character in the story. Chaucer must have written *hym thought*. Scribes who wrote *he thought* confused, like so many modern undergraduates (though not those trained by Professor Bennett) the forms, which in Middle English had fallen together, of the originally distinct Old English verbs *þyncan* and *þencan*. The scribes of Gg. 4. 27 and Harley 4912 either themselves, by coincidence, or drawing from some common predecessor, saw that a line which contained the expression *he thought* could only be weakened by the following expression, *he felt*. Such a line must either contain partial synonyms for a mixed process of intellection and feeling where each expression detracts from the other; or it must mean that *he thought*, that is, that he was not sure, that he felt that his heart was bleeding: as pretty an example of bathos as one could imagine, which Rawlinson poet. 163 alone does not shrink from.

Having decided thus we may conclude that the line originally read either

> For which hym thoughte he felte his herte blede

or

> For that hym thoughte he felte his herte blede.

We may then attempt a solution. There is a well-attested Middle English adverbial and conjunctive phrase *for that* (see *MED*), meaning 'because, in order that' which is clearly inappropriate here. But the phrase can mean, though it is much less frequently recorded in this sense, 'on that account', 'therefore', which would do, though it is not very satisfactory. There is no independent phrase *for which*, of course. We also get no outside help for the consideration of *which*. According to the usually reliable work by T. Mustanoja, *A Middle English Syntax* (1960), 'Most instances of *which* in Chaucer are to be found in his prose; in his poetry the occurrence of this relative is negligible' (p. 196). But of the 105 instances selected by the Concordance, only two are from the prose, so that the very opposite seems to be the case. We are back where we started.

If we invoke the principle of substitution, whereas it is easy to see that *For that* could generate the scribal emphasis *For that cause*, it is less easy to see which of *For that*, *For which* could generate the other. Mustanoja (loc. cit.) points out that *which* and *that* were rivals; that the dependent use of *which* became increasingly popular in the fifteenth century perhaps from a desire for greater clarity; and that *which* tends to be preferred in connection with prepositions. This does not help much. Chaucer might have been old-fashioned, using *that*, and later scribes might have substituted the more modern form, *which*; or Chaucer, so much in the *avant-garde* in vocabulary and attitude, might also have been so in syntax. Chaucer might have written the more modern *which*, while scribes might have preferred the older form, or have been unconsciously swayed by the occurrence of *That* as the first word in a previous line, or by the general prevalence of the phrase *for that*, which provides an 'easier' (but false) phrase implying causation at the beginning of the line. I prefer *For which* as apparently the more idiomatic form, referring to the whole situation which gives Troilus such pain. The difference is between this general reference and the stronger but vague sense of causation which lies behind what could be the plain relative use of *that*. But these same arguments could be used to justify *that*. Chaucer could have written one form first, then revised it to the other. In this case no solution is possible. Poetry does not depend on this kind of precision. There is a margin of uncertain authenticity.

III

Another simple line raises the question of revision in a more acute form. Corpus 61 reads at 1. 85

> The noise vp ros whan it was first aspied.

as do nine other manuscripts. But three manuscripts read differently: Harley 3943 (H2) reads

> Grete rumour gan whan it was first aspied.

Harley 2392 (H4) reads

> Gret rymour gan when it was first espied.

Phillipps 8250, now Huntington Library HM 114 (Ph) reads

> Grete rumour was whan it was first aspied.

We can easily dismiss the feeble and obvious *was* in favour of the fuller *gan* (noting meanwhile that the same scribe wrote both H2 and Ph here, though perhaps not from the same exemplar). If we had only these three manuscripts we could judge that Chaucer wrote *Grete rumour gan* etc. If we had only the other nine, we could judge that he wrote *The noise vp ros* etc. As it is, we have a choice. The printed texts do not help. Caxton omits *Grete*, then reads *noise vp ros* etc. Wynkyn de Worde reads *Grete noyse began* etc., as nice an example of conflation as one could hope for. Thynne reads *Great rumour rose* etc., which again beautifully conflates the two major manuscript variants, but does not help. By all principles of textual emendation our preference should surely go to the variant with *rumour*. It is a much less usual word, first recorded in English at this very period in Chaucer and Wycliffe. Chaucer himself uses it elsewhere only in his translation of the *Consolatio Philosophiae* of Boethius (singular at III, pr. vi.745–50 (probably the earliest recorded use); plural at II, pr. vii.555–60) and in *Troilus* at v.53 (where incidentally it caused no variants at all). On the other hand, in these other instances the word is used as in modern times to mean 'a hearsay report', whereas in the line in question it must mean 'Loud expression of disapproval or protest' first recorded elsewhere in 1400, of which the latest example is dated 1568. This latter sense, or the more general one of 'outcry' (first recorded 1440), is required by the meaning of the rest of the stanza, which tells of the anger of the Trojans when they heard that Calkas had deserted to the enemy. At this stage we may recall that Chaucer was frequently translating Boccaccio and we turn to Boccaccio's version, which reads *Fu'l romor grande quando fu sentito* (1.10). This is surely conclusive. Chaucer *must* have written *Grete rumour gan* etc.

Stow's edition of 1561 followed, as we might expect, Thynne's conflated *Great rumour rose* etc., and so did every subsequent editor (though Bell has *gan*) until Richard Morris's Aldine edition of 1866, which reads *The noyse up rose* etc. The reason is that, as Morris tells us (Preface, vol. i), he based his edition on Harley 2280 (H1) (which reads thus) collated with the other British Museum manuscripts, three Harleian and Additional 12044. It seems plain enough that Morris simply took the manuscripts that lay close to hand. Even so in the line we are discussing two of his five witnesses read *Gret(e) rumour*. It must have been a majority vote. There are no textual notes. From then on editors—Skeat, McCormick (in the Globe edition), Root, Robinson, Donaldson, Baugh, Fisher—have been as unanimous as earlier editors were in the *rumour* reading in preferring *The noise up ros* etc. Such a cloud of witnesses is impressive indeed. Root gives the rationale which it is to be doubted that Morris worked out. Root argues that the reading *Great rumour*

is indeed Chaucer's but that it was revised away by Chaucer.
The manuscripts in which the *noise* reading is found are often
grouped together to give a set of readings which Root considered
to be original but revised.

To remind the reader: our choice is between (accidents apart)
the now familiar

> The noise vp ros whan it was first aspied

and

> Grete rumour gan whan it was first aspied,

which is closer to the Italian.

My own conclusion is that *Grete rumour* is Chaucer's original,
and that the second is an intelligent scribal smoothing which
weakens, because it generalizes, the sense. If I am right, this
(and many similar instances) calls into question much of that
theory of revision of Root's which is nowadays accepted as fact.

IV

An example of Chaucer's 'commonplace' style which is not
nearly so commonplace when closely examined, and of how
scribes can fall into the trap of its real simplicity, so as to
become *really* commonplace and awkward, is offered by 1.458.
A close consideration of this line not only reveals aspects of
Chaucer's style but also shows how it has certain precise and
idiosyncratic usages that link up from work to work. Furthermore, in this line I would argue that no manuscript has preserved
the author's original, though the actual variation is minimal.

Troilus, having fallen in love, addresses Criseyde in his mind.
Corpus reads

> God goodly to whom serue I laboure.

The awkward metre suggests that something is wrong, but this
is how Root prints the line, noting the awkwardness but refrain-
ing from the Globe editor's 'tempting emendation', to which I

shall return, because it has no manuscript authority. There are
two difficulties: first, the word 'God'; and second, the syntax,
meaning, and metre of the last five words. The difficulties vary
independently of each other in the manuscripts, and are of a
quite different nature. The problem of whether to read *God* or
Good is primarily one of style and meaning, and may be taken
first. Ten manuscripts and two prints read *God* (Caxton and
Harley 1239 being 'out' here). Five manuscripts read *Good*, and
they are not manuscripts which exclusively run together in this
area. One of them is St. John's LI, which is normally close to
Corpus.

Kane and Donaldson have amply shown that in any given
line one cannot rely on 'good' manuscripts. We must examine
what we have, and the basic method must always be to assume
first that one of the versions is original, and to ask oneself which
version might have given rise to another. What objection or
difficulty in one version could have prompted a scribe, consciously
or unconsciously, to substitute an 'easier', which means a less
'meaningful', reading? If a scribe had before him *God goodly*
etc., why would he be tempted, or prompted, to change it to
'Good goodly' etc? As one looks at the phrase one begins to
see that although the variants are between *God* and *good* much
of the difficulty comes from the word *goodly*, which seems
more and more strange in this context. The Concordance
shows that it is used an exceptional number of times in
Troilus, and the spread of its usage in Chaucer's works as a
whole is rather curious. Manly-Rickert accept *goodly* (adverb)
against the common variant *gladly* in *Canterbury Tales*, I. 803,
and it appears twice as adjective in the *Nun's Priest's Tale*;
once (adverb) in the *Merchant's Tale*; once, as adjective
(*goodlich*), in the *Squire's Tale*; and *goodlich*, again as adjective,
once in the *Canon's Yeoman's Tale*; a total of 2 as adverb
and 4 as adjective, 6 in all. Then it appears no less than seven
times in *Melibeus*, 4 times as adverb and 3 as adjective, of which
2 are in the form *goodlich(e)*. So this is a total for the *Canterbury
Tales* of 13 instances, of which 7 come from *Melibeus*. If we

consider occurrences in other works the disproportion is even more striking. *Goodly* occurs four times in the *Book of the Duchess*, only once as adjective; then twice, both adverbs, in the *House of Fame*; then three times in the *Legend of Good Women* (adjectives); not at all in the Chaucerian part of the *Romaunt*; and *thirty-four* times in *Troilus*. This is a strange disproportion of usage in itself. In *Melibeus* and the *Book of the Duchess* the word normally qualifies speech, and never seems ironical. It evokes sincerity, grace, a deference to others, a desire to be agreeable. In *Troilus*, however, almost half, some 14 or 15 instances, are used in association with Criseyde, often spoken by Troilus, and there are only five uses in association with speech. Troilus himself is associated with four. There is a striking emphasis on Criseyde, and the force of the word is well illustrated at IV.409–11 (cf. Windeatt):

> If oon kan synge, another kan wel daunce;
> If this be goodly, she is glad and light;
> And this is faire, and that kan good aright.

To be *goodly* is different from being *glad and light*.

There are three other instances where Troilus addresses Criseyde using *goodly*: 'O goodly fresshe free' (III.128), 'O goodly myn Criseyde' (III.1473), and (in his letter of sad farewell) 'And fareth wel, goodly, faire, fresshe may' (V.1412, ed. Windeatt). *Goodly* is one of those words of general moral approbation that suffuse their glow throughout the poem, and Troilus's retention of it in this last use is an index of his steadfastness. It matches his first address to Criseyde, made only in his mind, at the line where we are still considering whether Chaucer wanted to make Troilus address her as 'God goodly' or 'Good goodly'. The final point to note is that *goodly* nowhere else in Chaucer appears as a noun.

Before coming to a decision, it will be useful to consider some stylistic aspects of Chaucer's uses of the words *God, good*. Both occur very frequently. For our purposes it may be enough to note, of *God*, that the word in *Troilus* is occasionally qualified by *blisful* or *myghty*, never by anything else. The gender is rarely needed, but possessives and pronouns in reference to *God* are invariably masculine. *God* is referred to in both pagan and Christian terms. It would seem highly unlikely that Troilus should refer to Criseyde as God (though Boccaccio in *Filostrato*, v.42 / 5 writes, 'e Criseida come suo Iddio'), and certainly if we read *Good* the whole line must refer to her. So the argument seems strong *against* the first word being *God*, not *Good*.

Good, on the other hand, is frequently used of people. *Good goodly* as an intensive phrase seems quite possible. Pandarus calls Criseyde *gode nece*, though Troilus never calls her 'good' (as opposed to *goodly*), and *good* is perhaps patronizing, as in modern English 'my good man' etc. There is an unexpected difficulty here. Whenever *good* is used in a vocative phrase (normally preceded by another word, for example a possessive) it is a disyllable, as for example Pandarus's expression *goode nece*, II.1203, cf. III.631, and other similar expressions (except when followed by a vowel or *h*: cf. III.264, 975, IV.1660, V.572, etc.). If the expression we were considering were 'good sweet' (as in V.572) it would undoubtedly appear as *gode swete*. Because *gode* in such use is a disyllable, with the stress on the first syllable, it is never, for obvious reasons, used as the first word in a line, and is always preceded by a single syllable word, or the vocative 'O'—unless we have such a case in the line under consideration. This grammatical and metrical argument must be very strong against *Good* if it is taken as an adjective, with *goodly* as a noun. If however we reverse their grammatical roles the difficulty disappears and we have *Good* as a noun, with *goodly* in its normal use in Chaucer as an adjective.

We may now summarize the arguments for and against each reading.

(*a*) *God goodly*. This is the harder reading. The locution is unusual. It is easy to imagine a scribe assuming that the phrase and line refer to Criseyde, and thinking that such a reference would be inappropriate, especially as Troilus expresses doubt whether Criseyde is woman or *goddess* a few lines earlier

(1.425). However, though Troilus's speech as a whole is directed in imagination to Criseyde, it would be possible to take this line in question as an address to the god of love, whom Troilus has already addressed (lines 422 ff.), although he says he serves Criseyde. Alternatively, Troilus might just this once call Criseyde his 'god'. But both these readings seem forced in meaning or syntax. Is the harder reading so hard as to be improbable?

(*b*) *Good goodly*. The reading is attractive, and the word *goodly* is strongly associated with Criseyde in this poem. It is an intensifying phrase, with some similarity to *manly man* (*CT* I. 167), and *wommanliche wif*, twice used in *Troilus* (III.103 and 1296) and only there, applied again to Criseyde. If *Good* is taken as a noun an unconscious substitution could be made of *God* for *Good* by an easy mechanical error of omitting one *o*, especially as the inflected form is often spelt with one 'o'. It could have been made coincidentally. (A comparable error, though made under the influence of a popular phrase, is made at this place in Harley 2392, which reads *Goode god* (!).) *Good goodly* must be the antecedent of the relative object 'whom' of the 'serve and labour' of the latter part of the line, and since Troilus has already expressed his 'service' of Criseyde, the natural meaning of the line, that he serves her, the 'good goodly', fits in very well. *Good goodly*, noun followed by adjective, is an inversion of normal word order due to the requirements of the metre but is grammatically sound and metrically acceptable. It suits the style of the poem and of Troilus, with its full plain easiness and yet a subtle and significant avoidance of cliché.

Balancing all this, it would seem that *Good goodly* must be the likelier reading.

What, however, of the Italian which is being translated? It is not close. The two preceding lines of *Troilus* are a close translation of the Italian—Troilus said to himself—then the speech begins (stanza 43),

O chiara luce che'l cor m'innamora
O Criseida bella, iddio volesse, etc.

The phrase 'iddio volesse' is translated correctly by Chaucer in his next line as 'wolde god', so does not affect the present argument. Boccaccio has none of the moral fervour nor expression of service. The 'chiara luce' which Chaucer turns to characteristic moral commendation is obviously an address to Criseida. The general sense of the Italian, therefore, supports, if it does not conclusively prove, the reading *Good goodly*. We should therefore abandon the reading *God* of Corpus and Root, and emend to *Good* with Robinson and others. But this is not the harder reading.

What of the rest of the line? Not only is it metrically clumsy, it is grammatically absurd in the received reading 'to whom serve I and labour'. This is essentially the accepted reading (with other minor variations) of five manuscripts and the two prints, although not of Corpus, which omits *and*. Another manuscript reads *in laboure*. The accepted reading is bad because the word-order gives the sense, when construed, 'I serve and labour to whom'. One does not, even in Middle English, *serve to* and *labour to*. *Every* manuscript (and the prints) reads *to whom*, but, as the Globe editor, Sir William McCormick, saw, the correct order must be *whom to*, with *to* as the marker of the infinitive *serve*. Then the metre is saved by the good Chaucerian form *seruen*. The authorial original must have read

> Good goodly, whom to seruen I laboure

which makes an admirable example, in sense and metre, of Chaucer's plain style. But it is the reading of not one single manuscript, and of only one, now unavailable, modern edition.

V

Another example of fine variation that nevertheless suggests important nuances occurs in 1.89. The stanza describes how the 'rumour' or the 'noise' about the treacherous flight of Calkas incensed the people of the town, who wished to be revenged—according to the general agreement of editors so far—

On hym that falsly hadde his feith so broken

which is the reading of Corpus 61. This does not seem a difficult line, yet it varies in detail so as to test our general sense of Chaucer's style and meaning. Digby 181 and Arch. Selden Supra 56, which in this neighbourhood frequently share variants, both begin the line with *Of*, with no obvious source for convergent variation, and are thus probably repeating an earlier manuscript and obviously wrong in this, though without further variation. Gg. 4.27 as so often gives us an excellent and solitary version of what classical scholars call *simplex ordo*, the prose or natural syntactical order,

On hym that hade falsely his feyt so broke.

(This, as will be noted, is the kind of variation that attests Chaucer's metrical concern by being obviously wrong and spoiling the metre.)

Out of the nineteen witnesses to this line, Additional 12044, Harley 3943, and a Huntington fragment omit *falsly* from the earlier position and insert it before *broken*. As these manuscripts are not normally associated in this area of text the likelihood is that this is a coincidental variation. Furthermore, Harley 3943 is normally associated with the former Phillipps MS 8250, now Huntington Library HM 114, each of these manuscripts being at this point written by the same scribe perhaps from the same exemplar, but Phillipps 8250 does *not* transpose *falsly* from the early to the late position. The number of manuscripts giving a particular reading is never a strong argument in itself for rejection or acceptance, as earlier examples have shown. Nor is any manuscript, however generally good, to be trusted in any single reading, since even good scribes, as will have been noted, can vary so unpredictably. The variation in the position of *falsly* should therefore be solved, once again, by attempting to account for it. The earlier position runs counter to *simplex ordo* more

obviously than the later position. It would therefore seem 'easier'
to omit it from the earlier position and place it later, when the
scribe was carrying, as seems normally to have been the case,
a single whole line in his head. If we agree on this point we may
then invoke as subsidiary argument the small number of manuscripts not otherwise associated, and the divergence between the
two associated manuscripts, to reinforce our decision. We may
then read

> On hym that falsly hadde his feith so broken.

Perhaps we can then invoke our judgement of the line as 'poetry',
to express our sense that the early position of *falsly* expresses
a nuance superior in meaning to the later position, which is less
emphatic and more of a cliché.

There is a moral here, which I hope has been emerging
throughout the discussion of these minuscule variations. The
poetry of the line is not merely to be found in these fine,
apparently subjective decisions, though they are important. The
poetry inheres also in the more 'objective' criteria previously
invoked, because they too concern the meaning. An inversion
of syntax from *simplex ordo*, extremely common in *Troilus*,
and in verse generally, for obvious 'practical' reasons, is a part
of the meaning, and in the end the only criterion of 'poetry' at
the verbal level is *fullness of meaning*.

'Fullness of meaning' implies a relatively high degree of
uniqueness of phraseology and sense. It is idiosyncratic, irregular,
with less in the way of repetition, or of the expectable, commonplace, familiar; with less, that is, of what is in the technical
linguistic sense 'redundancy'. The paradox here is that poetry
is made out of language, which is an instrument of communication, and communication depends on the exchange of units
which are already known, regular, subject to rules, highly
expectable, fully comprehensible. From a linguistic point of view
it would seem that the acme of language is the cliché, immediately
and fully comprehensible, a perfect message between sender and
receiver, *because* it tells us nothing we do not know already

— paradoxically tells us nothing because it tells us all. Poetry is the opposite, tending in essence, like so much modern verse, to the idiosyncratic, the unique, whereby it may become so full of meaning as to be totally original and completely incommunicable. Every period of our culture has to resolve this curious dilemma, poetry using language *against* itself in various ways. Perhaps we may say that whereas, for example, Dylan Thomas represents one pole of the axis somewhere along which poets must fix their tense compromise, the pole of virtual incomprehensibility (the poet as solipsist, drunk on his own words), Chaucer represents the other pole (the poet as social creature, a promiscuous flirt with a variety of commonplaces, not a drunkard but a tease). A poem is a compromise between 'language' and 'poetry'.

However, we are not yet finished with the possibilities of illustrating these matters, and of making them even more complicated, in the present line.

Although Harley 3943 and Phillipps 8250 (each, it will be recalled, written by the same scribe, perhaps from the same exemplar) diverge in their placing of *falsly*, they coincide in writing not of *feith* being broken, but *trouþe*. They are the only two manuscripts to do so, although Harley 2392 also omits *so* and alone writes neither *feith* nor *trouthe* but *surance*, which occurs nowhere in Chaucer (though first recorded *c.* 1300). This latter Harley manuscript has so lame and eccentric a line that we may leave it aside for the present purposes. *Trouthe* and *feith* are almost synonyms. Note for example, in the *Romaunt*, pretty certainly a very early work of Chaucer's, 'That feith ne trouthe holdith she' (ed. Robinson, l. 266), translating 'Qu'ele ne porte leauté' (ed. D. Poiron, Paris, 1974, l. 254). Each word may be used in an asseveration, like an oath, 'by my faith', 'by my truth'. Nevertheless, apart from such usages, which I have not examined closely, Chaucer's later work seems to discriminate at least between *breaking* of faith or 'trouthe'. The *Franklin's Tale* has two instances of 'breaking truth' (*CT* V. 1320, 1530); the *Parson's Tale* two of 'breaking faith' (*CT* X. 875–80). There are no other instances. The word *faith* is used in the sense of the act of religious belief; compare 'hooly chirches feith, in oure bileve' again in the *Franklin's Tale*, V. 1133. The word *trouthe*, on the other hand, refers either to 'the body of truth in which we believe', as in the *Second Nun's Tale*, 'Bileve aright and knowen verray trouthe' (VIII. 259), and 'Crist is verray trouthe' (the *Parson's Tale*, X. 590); or carries the more secular senses of 'loyalty', 'plighted word', for example Arcite's 'Have heer my trouth, tomorwe I wol nat faille' (the *Knight's Tale*, I. 1610). Although *faith* and *trouthe* are so closely linked, I do not think that one could substitute in Arcite's speech 'Have heer my *faith*' etc.

In consequence, when we return to the line in *Troilus*

> On hym that falsly hadde his feith so broken

as it appears in Corpus 61 and (more or less) in twelve other witnesses, we may well regard the variant of *trouthe* with *faith* as a real challenge. I would argue that 'to break faith' is an 'easier', because a religious and therefore likely to be a more familiar phrase to scribes, and that therefore *trouthe* is more likely to be the original word used by Chaucer. I would support this by arguing that *faith* in this secular context is a less Chaucerian usage. And finally I would point to the extreme importance of the word and concept *trouthe* in *Troilus*, by contrast with Boccaccio's poem, which incidentally has no comparable phraseology here. The word *trouthe* appears in *Troilus*, apart from the present instance, fifty-eight times, whereas *faith* appears (apart from the present line) only twelve times, five times in oaths. *Faith* is not indeed always used in a religious sense in the poem, but the rarity of its use, in contrast with *trouthe*, is striking. Another attraction of the reading *trouthe* is that it is a disyllable, and so avoids the empty filler *so*. It is interesting that the scribe of Harley 3943 blundered by writing *þus falsly*, even though when the same man wrote Phillipps 8250 he got the line correct (as I believe), writing

> On hym that falsly hadde his trouþe broken.

If I am right, and he was right, Phillipps 8250 is the *only* witness
out of a possible nineteen which preserves Chaucer's original
line. It alone preserves a tautness of metre and a subtle nuance
of meaning that are characteristic of Chaucer, and that are both
very near to and very far from a simple commonplace style.

My view is not so eccentric nor so solitary as I have allowed
it so far to appear. The interesting thing is that though all
editors follow Corpus 61 with *faith*, Root saw the reading with
trouthe as Chaucer's first version, later revised, as part of the
theory already touched on. This is not the place for a full
discussion of that theory of Chaucer's revisions of *Troilus*. It
has nowadays hardened into a general conviction that Chaucer
revised *Troilus* twice, giving versions labelled alpha, beta,
gamma. All I want to do here is to express the deepest scepticism
of this lately unquestioned article of faith (rather than truth).
It is clear that there was *some* revision; that, for example,
involving the insertion of Troilus's soliloquy in the temple
(IV.958–1082) and some consequent rearrangement of the lines
around. And there are a few other almost certain cases. But
most of the further instances of revision depend on line-by-line
instances such as the one under consideration; many of them
are just as doubtful as this one. Even if a revised version seems
likely, it probably amounts to no more than some incidental
and unsystematic tinkering by Chaucer with lines or passages
of a kind so very well documented even for modern poets like
Yeats and Auden. It is true that Phillipps 8250 was considered by
Sir William McCormick, who first devised the general scheme,
to be an 'alpha', i.e. a first version, manuscript all through, with
Harley 3943 running close till diverging early in Book IV. But
the general scheme of alpha, beta, and gamma manuscripts, and
their different relationships, variously arranged by McCormick,
Root, and Robinson, is vulnerable to many objections, of which
the line just discussed is an example. In that line it seems to me
highly unlikely that Chaucer himself substituted *feith so broken*
for *trouthe broken*.

The Punctuation of Middle English Texts

P. L. HEYWORTH

In his charming volume of recollections *The Weald of Youth* Siegfried Sassoon tells of dining with Edmund Gosse when the only other guest present (a minor novelist of considerable pretensions) raised 'the problem of punctuation'. Sassoon listened, as he declares, with modest alertness while his companions agreed that it was a matter to which many writers devoted far too little attention, and it was put to Gosse (by the novelist in waiting) that the use of punctuation was essentially personal. All this took Sassoon by surprise: he had never thought about it at all, had no aptitude for prose and assumed that poetry did not enter into the question.

I quote the ancedote for the discomfort of those of us who might be expected to know better than a young fox-hunting man on the wrong side of a quantity of Gosse's Hermitage.[1] For one cannot turn over many editions of Middle English texts without concluding that those responsible for them have, like Sassoon, too often not thought about punctuation at all. It may be that the explanation is in part to be found in the manuscripts that they edit: in the Middle Ages a vernacular manuscript in which any attempt has been made to introduce systematic punctuation is rare, and only occasionally is the punctuation of

---

[1] At Gosse's arch suggestion that he expected from his guests fullest appreciation of his hermitage Sassoon (puzzled at him referring to his house in Regent's Park as a hermitage and pronouncing the word with a sort of French accent) replied that it seemed to be a nice big one. 'Not unbecomingly large, I hope,' Gosse somewhat tartly replied, looking inquiringly at the bottle of Hermitage from which he was about to fill their glasses.

the medieval scribe at all helpful in elucidating the text.[2] This lack of awareness of punctuation-marks even as an aid to showing the relationship between the various parts of a sentence, together with the modern treatment of them as little more than a convenience in reading (and of which the reader has a very diminished consciousness), may account for present standards in editorial punctuation which would be tolerated in no other branch of medieval text-critical studies. For most of us will patiently examine the whole range of evidence bearing on a suspect reading and will give the fullest consideration to a detail of phonology, while allowing to pass without comment punctuation which gives at best forced or ambiguous meaning and which occasionally reduces a passage to nonsense.

Whatever the explanation, such perfunctoriness has two very damaging consequences. It may well (perhaps unconsciously) encourage quite unjustified editorial assumptions about the degree of a text's corruptness and, more seriously, in cases where the dislocation of meaning is not so marked as to suggest 'corruption' there will be a predisposition to accept a wholly false norm of style which may then be made the basis for defending uneasy (and perhaps corrupt) passages elsewhere in the text. In either case the editor is seriously handicapped in fulfilling his primary responsibility: the restoration of the text to the state in which as nearly as possible it represents that which the author originally wrote. I do not claim that the answer to perfunctoriness lies in elaborate statements of principle; punctuation does not, except in a very general sense, lend itself to codification. But what it is surely legitimate to look for is evidence that the editor of a medieval vernacular work has examined his text with some rigour, has fully considered all the

---

[2] Denholm-Young points out that the theory of punctuation was well understood by the writers on *ars dictaminis* though their views had little influence on contemporary practice. He cites MS Bodley 34 as a manuscript with helpful punctuation, referring to Tolkien, *Essays and Studies*, xiv (*Handwriting in England and Wales* (Cardiff, 1954), p. 77 and n. 5). As with spelling and the use of capitals it was left to the printers finally to restore order—and then not until the nineteenth century.

meanings latent in difficult or ambiguous passages, and has punctuated these passages so as to bring out as clearly as possible that sense he sees as most satisfactory.

Accusations of turpitude fall some way short of proof and my argument may best be made in examining particular examples from the work of two fourteenth-century authors, Thomas Usk and Chaucer. They are different in almost every way, which makes them, for present purposes, the more useful. Usk the amateur with a natural gift for intellectual confusion, the victim of a clumsy and congealed style; Chaucer the professional author, at all times the master of what he wishes to say, and with a facility for saying it in a deceptively lucid manner. Usk's *Testament of Love* extant in no manuscript and in only a single printed version and that version a model of corruptness, yet almost completely ignored by scholars; Chaucer's text rich in manuscript witnesses and refined by more than three centuries of text-critical activity.

I

The neglect of Usk's *Testament* is surprising in view of the unrivalled opportunities for censoriousness it affords. It survives only in Thynne's print of 1532, part of his collected edition of Chaucer. The work plainly baffled the printers, and the difficulties of its literary prose, which, in Krapp's pungent judgement, 'saved itself from being merely colloquial and natural by being unidiomatic and unintelligible',[3] are compounded by extensive corruption often of the most radical kind. After Thynne it appears in Speght's two editions (1598, 1602) and Harefinch's reprint (1687), in Urry (1721), and Chalmers (1810). The text deteriorates even further through this series of reprints and it was left to Skeat[4] to attempt for the first time serious

---

[3] G. P. Krapp, *The Rise of English Literary Prose* (New York, 1915), p. 31, quoted by Schaar.
[4] Who includes it in his volume of Chaucer apocrypha, *Chaucerian and Other Pieces* (Oxford, 1897).

text-critical work on it. He makes an energetic attack on the most obviously corrupt places but with mixed success. Corrections to Skeat were proposed and oversights in part remedied by Claes Schaar in 1950.[5]

II.x.99 f. Love urges the Dreamer not to set store by earthly goods and not to grieve when Fortune abandons him.

Ben these nat mortal thinges agon with ignorance of beestial wit, and hast receyved reson in knowing of vertue? What comfort is in thy herte, the knowinge sikerly in my service [to] be grounded? And wost thou nat wel, as I said, that deth maketh ende of al fortune? What than? Standest thou in noble plyte, litel hede or recking to take, if thou let fortune passe dying, or els that she fly whan her list, now by thy lyve?

Schaar accepts Skeat's emendation but believes this passage to be still not quite in order and citing the source of the passage in Boethius, II, pr. iii.99 f., attempts to put it right by introducing *not* after *Standest thou* in the last sentence. Neither emendation is necessary. (1) The sentence beginning *What comfort* is not a question but a statement; the sense is 'whatever comfort is in your heart, to the extent that it derives from the knowledge of virtue it is attributable to your service of me.' (2) The last sentence (beginning *Standest thou*) is not a question but an answer to the preceding *What than*? Earlier (78–80) the Lady has said, 'Me thinketh, thou clepest thilke plyte thou were in "selinesse of fortune"; and thou sayest, for that the selinesse is departed, thou art a wrecch.' She goes on to point out that in fact the Dreamer has misconceived his situation; he has lost his wealth, which was a source of wretchedness rather than happiness, and is therefore fortunate: 'If thou loke to the maner of al glad thinges and soroful, thou mayst nat nay it, that yet,

5 *Lunds Universitets Årsskrift*, N.F. Avd. 1, Bd. 46, Nr. 2 (1950), 3–45. In what follows I restrict myself to passages dealt with by Schaar. All the passages discussed are in the first instance printed from Skeat and reproduced with his punctuation; words within square brackets represent Skeat's emendations. A new edition of Usk by J. F. Leyerle is in preparation.

and namely now, thou standest in noble plyte in a good ginning'
(89–92). The last sentence of the present passage is a variation
on this.

Ben these nat mortal thinges agon with ignorance of beestial wit,
and hast receyved reson in knowing of vertue? What comfort is in thy
herte, the knowinge sikerly in my service be grounded. And wost
thou nat wel, as I said, that deth maketh ende of al fortune? What
than? Standest thou in noble plyte, litel hede or recking to take if
thou let fortune passe dying, or els that she fly whan her list, now
by thy lyve.

II.xiii.117 f. Love instructs the Dreamer about the nature of
virtue.

But the sonne is not knowe but he shyne; ne vertuous herbes, but
they have her kynde werchinge; ne vertue, but it strecche in goodnesse
or profyt to another, is no vertue. Than, by al wayes of reson, sithen
mercy and pitee ben moste commended among other vertues, and
they might never ben shewed, [unto] refresshement of helpe and of
comfort, but now at my moste nede; and that is the kynde werkinge
of these vertues.

Schaar argues against Skeat's *unto* in the last sentence and in
favour of reading in the same sentence *they might never ben*
more shewed, with refresshement of helpe. Rather omit both
Skeat's and Schaar's emendations and repunctuate.

But the sonne is not knowe but he shyne; ne vertuous herbes but
they have her kynde werchinge; ne vertue but it strecche in goodnesse
or profyt to another. Is no vertue than, by al wayes of reson (sithen
mercy and pitee ben moste commended among other vertues) and
they might never ben shewed, refresshement of helpe and of comfort,
but now at my moste nede. And that is the kynde werkinge of these
vertues.

The sense, confused in Usk's prose, is that virtue unless mani-
fested in action is no virtue; it cannot be passive, it must
'strecche in goodnesse or profyt to another'. Hence help and
comfort cannot reasonably be accounted praiseworthy unless

they are extended to someone (in this case the Dreamer) in the moment of his greatest need; mercy and pity (pre-eminent among virtues) dictate this.

II.xiv.78 f. The Dreamer is in despair and believes himself lost to his Margaret. Love comforts him.

Were thou not goodly accepted in-to grace? By my pluckinge was she to foryevenesse enclyned. And after, I her styred to drawe thee to house; and yet wendest thou utterly for ever have ben refused. But wel thou wost, sithen that I in suche sharpe disese might so greetly avayle, what thinkest in thy wit? How fer may my wit strecche? And thou lache not on thy syde, I wol make the knotte.

Schaar argues that it is 'deeply un-allegorical, un-medieval, un-Christian, to imagine Love endowed with wit', and believes *thy* for *my* in 'How fer may my wit strecche' to be inevitable. This is not so. Rather take the second *wit* in the sense 'practical talent, clever management' (*OED* under *wit* sb. II 5b) and understand it as a question imputed to the Dreamer by the Lady. That is, 'What are you thinking? Just how far my clever management extends?' The Lady answers in 87–8, 'Truste wel to me, and I wol thee not fayle.' Repunctuation makes it clear.

Were thou not goodly accepted in-to grace? By my pluckinge was she to foryevenesse enclyned. And after, I her styred to drawe thee to house; and yet wendest thou utterly for ever have ben refused. But wel thou wost sithen, that I in suche sharpe disese might so greetly avayle. What thinkest in thy wit? How fer may my wit strecche? And thou lache not on thy syde, I wol make the knotte.

III.ii.27 f. The Dreamer complains that there is no law which rewards such goodness as a guilty man may possess. The Lady replies.

Wherfore every wight, by reson of lawe, after his rightwysenesse apertely his mede may chalenge; and so thou, that maynteynest lawe of kynde, and therfore disese hast suffred in the lawe, reward is worthy to be rewarded and ordayned, and apertly thy mede might thou chalenge.

Schaar would delete *reward* and emend *is* to *art*. This is mere tinkering. The author's meaning is clarified if *reward* is allowed the rare sense 'estimation, worth' recorded by *OED* (under *reward* sb.[1] I 3) only in two texts from the fourteenth century, and the punctuation slightly modified.

Wherfore every wight, by reson of lawe, after his rightwysenesse apertely his mede may chalenge; and so thou that maynteynest lawe of kynde and therfore disese hast suffred in the lawe. Reward is worthy to be rewarded and ordayned, and apertly thy mede might thou chalenge.

That is, everyone may claim his reward to the extent that he has earned it by virtue of his goodness; so may the Dreamer, who has maintained nature's laws and suffered for his pains. Moral worth deserves to be rewarded and clearly the Dreamer is justified in claiming what is due to him.

III.ii.33 f. This follows immediately on the preceding passage.

'Certes', quod I, 'this have I wel lerned; and ever hensforward I shal drawe me therafter, in oonhed of wil to abyde, this lawe bothe maynteyne and kepe; and so hope I best entre in-to your grace, wel deservinge in-to worship of a wight, without nedeful compulsion, [that] ought medefully to be rewarded.'

Schaar rejects Skeat's emendation *that* and substitutes *and*. Neither is necessary. The Dreamer is here restating the law that the Lady has just enunciated: that by virtue of his goodness a man may claim the reward due to him (27–9); that worth ought to be rewarded (30–1). His restatement is: 'Wel deservinge in-to worship of a wight without nedeful compulsion ought medefully to be rewarded'. That is, merit in voluntarily doing honour to a person deserves to be rewarded. He is restating in relation to his own position as a lover the law that the Lady has (in 18–32) chiefly illustrated from political examples. The Lady provides a gloss on it in 39: 'good service in-to profit and avantage strecche'. Repunctuation helps to make the meaning clearer.

'Certes', quod I, 'this have I wel lerned. And ever hensforward I shal drawe me therafter in oonhed of wil to abyde, this lawe bothe maynteyne and kepe (and so hope I best entre in-to your grace): Wel deservinge in-to worship of a wight without nedeful compulsion ought medefully to be rewarded.'

II

It is reasonable to expect the case of Chaucer to be very different from that of Usk, and it is so to the extent that his text is free from the gross errors of the kind that disfigure the *Testament of Love*. But there are some places in Chaucer where the punctuation is clearly defective and many which invite more thought than has been given to them by editors. The treatment of punctuation in the major editions of Chaucer is disconcerting.[6] There is no suggestion that there are possible alternatives to (much less improvements of) the punctuation displayed in them; they show no recognition of the decisive importance of punctuation in controlling meaning; and they are mute in the face of the unsatisfactory sense that Chaucer's text has so often inherited from the wayward practice of their predecessors.

Collation of the editions leaves no doubt that punctuation became formalized at an early stage of modern Chaucerian textual studies and in most important respects survives unchanged in the latest and most authoritative editions. This is no bad thing where the meaning of a text is unambiguous and acceptable and the received punctuation clearly reveals it (although some simplification of the rhetorically orchestrated practice of the Victorians would be welcome). Where the

[6] Most disconcerting of all, in their monumental, eight-volume edition of the Canterbury Tales (Chicago, 1940), Manly and Rickert forgo punctuation altogether.

meaning transmitted by the punctuation is strained it is the editor's responsibility to seek ways of improving it; where it is impossible, to emend it as he would a corrupt reading. But, as the following examples show, there is little evidence that editors recognize the responsibility, much less accept it. No other conclusion is to be drawn from the perpetuation of erroneous or questionable punctuation and editorial silence concerning it.

Book of the Duchess, 611 f.[7] The Black Knight complaining at his desperate condition declares that he inhabits an upside-down world in which everything is turned into its opposite.

> My love ys hate, my slep wakynge,
> My myrthe and meles ys fastynge,
> My countenaunce ys nycete,
> And al abaved, where so I be;
> My pees, in pledynge and in werre.

The last line can hardly stand by itself. Chaucer uses a number of syntactical variations in the present catalogue (599 'My song ys turned to pleynynge', 602 'In travayle ys myn ydelnesse', 609 'To derke ys turned al my lyght', 610 'My wyt ys foly, my day ys nyght'), but 615 cannot be assimilated to any of them. Morris emends to read 'My pees is pledynge, and in werre' which recognizes the difficulty while making the syntax of the two halves of the line incompatible. Globe introduces a full stop at

---

[7] All the passages discussed are printed from Robinson's second edition (1957) and in the first instance reproduce his punctuation. It was with dissatisfaction at the punctuation of this edition that my interest in the subject began. Collation of other editions was undertaken to see whether I could find in them support for my attempts to improve on it. The following are quoted when they are relevant to the passage under consideration: Tyrwhitt (2nd edn., 1798), Morris (rev. of N. Harris Nicolas's Aldine edn., 1866), Skeat (1894–7), the Globe (1898), Root (1926), Koch (1928), Manly (1928), Robinson (1933), Donaldson (1958), and Baugh (1963). Morris, Skeat, the Globe, and Robinson print the complete works; Baugh prints all the major poetry, Donaldson most of it; Tyrwhitt prints the *Canterbury Tales*, Manly selections from them; Root prints the *Troilus*, Koch the Minor Poems.

the end of 614; Koch, Robinson, Donaldson, and Baugh follow
the punctuation cited. The uneasiness is resolved by taking *pees*
as the object of 614 *abaved* and punctuating:

> My love ys hate, my slep wakynge,
> My myrthe and meles ys fastynge,
> My countenaunce ys nycete,
> And al abaved, where so I be,
> My pees, in pledynge and in werre.

What the Black Knight holds to be destroyed is not his foolish
countenance but his peace, the victim of lawsuits and other
troublesome business.

Troilus, II.1289 f. Pandarus urges Criseyde to accept Troilus as
her lover, which she is reluctant to do.

> But theron was to heven and to doone.
> Considered al thing it may nat be;
> And whi, for shame; and it were ek to soone
> To graunten hym so gret a libertee.
> For pleynly hire entente, as seyde she,
> Was for to love hym unwist, if she myghte,
> And guerdon hym with nothing but with sighte.

Robinson's punctuation (adopted by Baugh without modification)
is completely at odds with the natural sense of this straightforward passage; yet it is an improvement on that of some earlier
editors. The first half of 1291 in particular gives trouble. Skeat
punctuates as Robinson. The Globe and Root (both with variant
speche for *shame*) 'And whi for speche?' Skeat and Globe
increase the confusion by assuming (different) parts of the stanza
to be in direct speech: Skeat 1293–5 ('For pleynly ... sighte'),[8]
Globe 1290–2 ('Considered ... libertee'). The obvious solution
lies in taking 1291 'And whi' as a rhetorical question which is
answered by what follows: 'All things considered it can't be

---

[8] But the inverted comma required before 1294 *was* to correspond with that
after 1295 *sighte* is omitted by Skeat.

done. And why not? Because modesty forbids it and such a concession would be premature.'

> But theron was to heven and to doone;
> Considered al thing it may nat be.
> And whi? For shame, and it were ek to soone
> To graunten hym so gret a libertee.

Morris in 1866 grasped the essential relationship between 'And whi' and what follows;[9] Donaldson rediscovered it in 1958.

If the case of *Book of the Duchess*, 611 f. illustrates the conservatism of editors, that of *Troilus*, II.1289 f. their eclecticism, together they confirm editorial reluctance to take thought about that which the practice of scholars (and not only editors) may, by default, be said to have sanctioned. They also emphasize the danger of allowing authority to accrue by silence; a tradition unquestioned may upon examination confess itself to be no more than a bad habit grown to a respectable maturity. And they reveal an alarming aptitude for misunderstanding straightforward passages. But they are disturbing in other ways. In *BD* 611 f. the emended punctuation was first supplied by Skeat in 1894 and is ignored by all subsequent editors; Morris in 1866 only just missed the correct punctuation for *TC* II.1289 f., it is then scrambled by editors in a variety of ways until Donaldson gets it right in 1958. But five years later Baugh reverts to the punctuation of Robinson. Such wilful neglect of the available aids is hard to understand. Perhaps the most charitable excuse is indifference.

Since indifference prevails where the question is one between correctness and careless or ignorant error, it is optimistic to look for more where it is between opposed views of correctness. Yet Chaucer's text offers us scores of places in which there are alternatives to the received punctuation and arguments for

---

[9] But punctuates eccentrically 'Considered al thing, it may nat be, / And whi? for shame; and it were ek to soone' etc.

preferring those alternatives on grounds of sense, usage, or
fitness to context, as the following examples show.

Book of the Duchess, 397 f. The Dreamer walking through a
wood on a spring morning is accosted by, and attempts to catch,
a small dog.

> And I hym folwed, and hyt forth wente
> Doun by a floury grene wente
> Ful thikke of gras, ful softe and swete.
> With floures fele, faire under fete,
> And litel used, hyt semed thus;
> For both Flora and Zephirus,
> They two that make floures growe,
> Had mad her dwellynge ther, I trowe.

The punctuation of 401 is found in all the editions. Yet it
impoverishes the passage in subtle ways. It allows *semed* to
modify only the idea of 'use', and restricts the allusion to Flora
and Zephirus to explaining why the path is *litel used*. Thus,
unjustified prominence is given to 'use' at the expense of the
much more characteristically Chaucerian idea of 'plenitude', the
fecundity of Nature represented by the thick grass and the
flowers, thicker on the ground (as Chaucer says later) than the
stars in the sky. Repunctuation gives a more satisfactory balance.

> And I hym folwed, and hyt forth wente
> Doun by a floury grene wente
> Ful thikke of gras, ful softe and swete,
> With floures fele, faire under fete,
> And litel used. Hyt semed thus
> For both Flora and Zephirus,
> They two that make floures growe,
> Had mad her dwellynge ther, I trowe.

Hyt refers to the plenitude of the woodland scene (further
described in 405 f.) and the plenitude is attributed, quite properly,
to Flora and Zephirus having their habitation there; that the
path is *litel used* is incidental.

Knight's Tale, 1572 f. Hiding in a grove after escaping from Theseus's prison Palamon overhears Arcite's account of his unhappy situation, an exile returned in disguise to Athens in order to be near his beloved Emily, but unable for fear of death to declare his love. At the end of his complaint Arcite collapses.

> And with that word he fil doun in a traunce
> A longe tyme, and after he up sterte.
> This Palamoun, that thoughte that thurgh his herte
> He felte a coold swerd sodeynliche glyde,
> For ire he quook, no lenger wolde he byde.
> And whan that he had herd Arcites tale,
> As he were wood, with face deed and pale,
> He stirte hym up out of the buskes thikke,
> And seide: 'Arcite ... [etc.]'

The punctuation of 1573 is found in all modern editions—Skeat (with the exception of semicolon for comma after *tyme*), Globe, Manly, Robinson, Donaldson, and Baugh—and they all begin a new paragraph at 1574. Tyrwhitt and subsequently Morris take a different view. They have semicolon for comma after *tyme*, no stop after *sterte*, and no new paragraph at 1574; Tyrwhitt begins his paragraph at 1572, Morris has no new paragraph.[10]

In such a passage punctuation must attempt to define clearly the stages of the action described and must be sensitive to its psychological and emotional implications. The three stages in the physical action are Arcite's collapse, his subsequent recovery, and Palamon's jumping out at him from the bushes. Of these the first is the most important. It is Arcite's trance which allows time for Palamon to realize the significance of what he has overheard; the revelation paralyses him until with Arcite's recovery paralysis gives way to anger and his own violent response. To reflect such a development a heavy stop must stand

[10] Brusendorff, *The Chaucer Tradition* (Oxford, 1925) draws attention to examples of Tyrwhitt's sensible punctuation in the course of a brief discussion (pp. 477–8) of some places where the received punctuation in Chaucer is open to question.

after 1573 *A longe tyme*, for in some sort it must imply both
Arcite's trance and Palamon's stunned revelation. Postponing
the heavy stop until the end of the line (then to compound it
with a paragraph break) destroys the dramatic structure of the
passage. In recognizing this Tyrwhitt's and Morris's punctuation
is surely right, although I would articulate the structure even
more clearly as follows:

> And with that word he fil doun in a traunce
> A longe tyme. And after he up sterte,
> This Palamoun, that thoughte that thurgh his herte
> He felte a coold swerd sodeynliche glyde,
> For ire he quook. No lenger wolde he byde.
> And whan that he had herd Arcites tale,
> As he were wood, with face deed and pale
> He stirte hym up out of the buskes thikke,
> And seide: 'Arcite ... [etc.]'

If a new paragraph is accounted necessary, Tyrwhitt's beginning
at 1572 is preferable to the orthodox division after 1573.

Clerk's Tale, 760 f. Walter summons his daughter and son from
Bologna where they have been cared for by his sister, Countess
of Panyk.

> But shortly if this storie I tellen shal,
> This markys writen hath in special
> A lettre, in which he sheweth his entente,
> And secreely he to Boloigne it sente.
>
>   To the Erl of Panyk, which that hadde tho
> Wedded his suster, preyde he specially
> To bryngen hoom agayn his children two
> In honurable estaat al openly.

Only Tyrwhitt runs on 763, substituting a comma for full stop.
It is not self-evident that the received punctuation is correct. The
comfortable defence that it respects the integrity of the stanza
is hardly compelling when neither the stanza before nor the one

after is end-stopped.[11] Running on allows the *Erl of Panyk* to stand as indirect object of 763 *sente* rather than the direct object of 765 *preyde*; this avoids the difficulty of requiring *preyde* to take the preposition *to*, which with a personal object it seldom does in Middle English.

> But shortly if this storie I tellen shal,
> This markys writen hath in special
> A lettre in which he sheweth his entente,
> And secreely he to Boloigne it sente
>
>   To the Erl of Panyk, which that hadde tho
> Wedded his suster; preyde he specially
> To bryngen hoom agayn his children two
> In honurable estaat al openly.

This also has the advantage of a more natural development of the sense: the first part of the sentence down to 765 *suster* deals with the sending of the letter and identification of its recipient, the second part discloses the message it brings.

III

The case for repunctuating Chaucer's text is unanswerable. But before it can be done intelligently punctuation must be recognized as deserving more attention than it usually gets in editions of early texts; it must be rescued from its reputation as the last tiresome chore of editorial housekeeping and dignified with a place in the canon of Middle English textual studies. This will come when editors are prepared to use punctuation as a tool for elucidating a text and for making clear their understanding of it, instead of treating it as something to be absent-mindedly distributed in typescript, tinkered with in galley, and desperately

---

[11] Although scarcely weighty evidence, it may be pointed out that in the editions there are proportionately more run-on stanzas in the *Clerk's Tale* than in most of Chaucer's poems in rhyme royal.

revised in page proof. For the most part satisfactory results will follow from the extension to questions of punctuation of the rigour customary in other branches of editorial scholarship and from a willingness on the part of editors to identify the hard places, to discuss the alternatives open to them, and to justify the punctuation they decide on.

The editing of the *Testament of Love*, for example, would demand no more than this, nor would the great mass of Middle English texts—of no great literary merit, seldom edited, and less often read. The case of the great authors—Chaucer, Langland, Malory, and the *Gawain*-poet—of some plays and romances, of certain religious prose works like *Ancrene Riwle* and *Ancrene Wisse*, and of a few other texts is different. Their importance (or their popularity) means that they have attracted the attention of generations of scholars and have been often printed. They have acquired as a result their own editorial histories and an editor will lay claim to respect to the extent that he takes account of them. It must be remembered that since the manuscripts afford so little help, the primary authorities in matters of punctuation are the editions of one's predecessors. And it is plain that much sensible punctuation is to be found in unfashionable places.[12]

Such authors and such texts demand more of the editor than intelligent address to questions of punctuation and open discussion of them. As we have seen, important points of interpretation may turn on how a passage is punctuated, and where this is the case students have a right to expect that the evidence which bears on the editor's decision will be fully displayed. The

[12] Some surprising conclusions emerge from my own limited collation of the major editions of Chaucer. In general: Tyrwhitt's punctuation is full of good sense and is always intelligent; Morris usually follows Tyrwhitt in the *Canterbury Tales* and is sensible elsewhere; Skeat is too rhetorical (as is Koch) and given to careless lapses; Robinson (the two editions are virtually identical) is mechanical and is heavily indebted to Skeat; Baugh is indistinguishable from Robinson. Only Donaldson of modern editors is consistently thoughtful and independent, although he is not always right. The different editorial hands in the Globe edition make it hard to generalize about it; I have not collated a sufficient number of passages in Root and Manly for a clear picture to emerge.

duty that this imposes is collation of the editions and the design of an apparatus for the citation of punctuation variants. There is only one precedent known to me: the edition of the Greek New Testament published by the United Bible Societies,[13] specially adapted to the requirements of Bible translators throughout the world. The punctuation apparatus incorporated in it sets out the evidence for some six hundred passages in which punctuation seems to be particularly significant for interpretation of the text. Because of the acute difficulties involved in comparing punctuation in different Greek editions and modern-language translations the editors settle for a relatively crude system which differentiates only between major 'breaks' and minor 'breaks', paragraphs, parentheses, etc.;[14] nevertheless, the essential evidence from fifteen editions is systematically and economically laid out and is easy to use.

A similar apparatus for a Middle English text, because free from the special problems associated with the New Testament, would allow much greater refinement than the system adopted by the Bible Societies' editors. One designed for Chaucer, for example, could encompass all important editions and list the precise details of the punctuation employed. It might look something like this.[15]

> And eek thise olde wydwes, God it woot,
> They konne so muchel craft on Wades boot,
> So muchel broken harm, whan that hem leste,   1425
> That with hem sholde I nevere lyve in reste,
> For sondry scoles maken sotile clerkis.
> Womman of manye scoles half a clerk is,
> But certeynly a yong thyng may men gye,
> Right as men may warm wex with handes plye.   1430
> Wherfore I sey yow pleynly in a clause,
> I wol noon oold wyf han right for this cause:

[13] Ed. K. Aland, M. Black, B. M. Metzger, and A. Wikgren (1966).
[14] For details see p. xxxvi of the United Bible Societies edition.
[15] Taken from the *Merchant's Tale*, *CT*, E 1423 f.; Robinson's text is followed but the punctuation is my own.

For if so were I hadde swich myschaunce
That I in hire ne koude han no plesaunce,
Thanne sholde I lede my lyf in avoutrye   1435
And go streight to the devel whan I dye;
Ne children sholde I none upon hire geten,
Yet were me levere houndes had me eten
Than that myn heritage sholde falle
In straunge hand. And this I telle yow alle,   1440
I dote nat—I woot the cause why
Men sholde wedde, and forthermoore woot I,
Ther speketh many a man of mariage
That woot namoore of it than woot my page.
   For whiche causes man sholde take a wyf?   1445
If he ne may nat lyven chaast his lyf,
Take hym a wyf with greet devocioun,
By cause of leveful procreacioun
Of children, to th' onour of God above
(And nat oonly for paramour or love)   1450
And for they sholde leccherye eschue,
And yelde hir dette whan that it is due;
Or for that ech of hem sholde helpen oother
In meschief, as a suster shal the brother,
And lyve in chastitee ful holily.   1455

1427 / clerkis. / G / ; / T²M°SR¹R²B / : / D   1428 / is. / T²M°SR¹R²
DB / ; / G   1440 / hand: / T² / ; / M°D /, / SGR¹R²B   1444 / page, /
T²SGR¹R²B // M°D   1445 / no para / all editions / wyf. / T²M°
SGR¹R²B / : / D   1450 / And … love; / all editions

The passage as punctuated differs from Robinson's text in nearly
two dozen places, but only in the seven cited is the interpretation
of the text sufficiently affected to require display of the evidence,
and only in two or three of these (1427–8, 1444–5, and perhaps
1450) would discussion be called for. Such an apparatus would
be a great service to the intelligent study of Chaucer's text, and
although the task of providing it would be onerous, it should
not be intolerably so.

   To conclude. If editors of Middle English texts can be

persuaded to take 'the problem of punctuation' more seriously than they presently do, what will follow? We can look for a much sharpened awareness of an author's language—something indispensable to text-critical study in all its branches —and a corresponding diminution of confident and misguided editorial assumptions that if a reading is right the sense will take care of itself. For there is no doubt that the airing of alternative interpretations deriving from different ways of punctuating a passage will favour the emergence of an author's intended meaning, and that it will encourage recognition that meaning is distinct from, and is not necessarily explained by, the form of words an author uses to express it. This in turn should lead to the reinvigoration of many passages long crippled by erroneous or inept punctuation. These are considerable benefits. It may even be that they will prove commensurate to the labour involved. I think few who have toiled in the thickets of Middle English textual criticism in the last fifty years would care, in their more sober moments, to claim so much.

'Noght in the Registre of Venus': Gower's English Mirror for Princes

M. A. MANZALAOUI

To choose Book VII of the *Confessio Amantis* as one's topic is to load oneself with the handicap of a subject most critics have found dull. True, we have become less prone today to dismiss as otiose the frequent departures in medieval narrative or expository structure from the straight and narrow path of post-Renaissance linearity; both medievalist scholars and our contemporary imaginative writers have accustomed us to non-sequential leaps from one realm of vision to another, to unfamiliar parallelisms, analogies, and ectypes, to unexpected and unauthorized bedfellows, long since revealed to be as common in the conceptual field of the Middle Ages as in the bed-sitters of modern fiction. But it is this particular excursus which has been found hard to accept, this summary of learning, ethics, and statecraft, interrupting the Lover's confession, and diminishing the impact of the main emotional exposition, the string of narrative *exempla*, and the texture of imagery and poetic language.

There is some justice in the complaints. But Gower has warned the reader early on that his *Confessio* is at least partly a work of advice for a ruler, while Book VII is not without its good narratives, such as the *exemplum* of the Pagan and the Jew, which derives from that Latin mirror for princes to which the Book is mainly indebted. Nor is this section without its true poetic touches. The theological exposition of the impulse of divine Pity which brought about the Incarnation is certainly not couched in dry or unmoving terms:

> It is the vertu of Pité
> Thurgh which the hihe Magesté

Was stered, whan His sone alyhte,
And in pite the world to rihte
Tok of the Maide fleissh and blod.

(VII.3107–11)[1]

In more sensory manner, the vignettes of the months, in the discussion of the Zodiac, are vivid verbal miniatures. So:

A monthe, whiche...
...The plowed oxe in wynter stalleth;
And fyr into the halle he bringeth
And thilke drinke of which men singeth;
He torneth must into the wyn;
Thanne is the larder of the swyn;
That is Novembre which I meene,
Whan that the lef hath lost his greene.

(ll.1159–68)[2]

Gower's cosmography serves as a reminder of the shared element in the medieval encyclopedic tradition and the poetry of Lucretius; thus, of the third 'Periferie' of the air:

such matiere as up is drawe
Of dreie thing, as it is ofte,
Among the cloudes upon lofte,
And is so clos, it may noght oute,—
Thanne is it chased sore aboute,

---

[1] I quote from G. C. Macaulay, *The Complete Works of John Gower*, 4 vols. (Oxford, 1899–1902), but I have departed from his policy over capitalization and the use of the acute accent. Henceforth, when lines from Book VII of the *Confessio* are quoted, the Book number is usually not indicated: for quotations from elsewhere in the poem, the number of the Book and, where helpful, the abbreviation *Confessio* are used.

[2] Macaulay punctuates:

And fyr into the halle he bringeth,
And thilke drinke of which men singeth,
He torneth must into the wyn ...

His reading takes 'must' as an auxiliary verb, and gives the meaning that November brings wine to maturity. I assume that 'must' means 'unfermented wine', and that the phrase forming the second of the three lines above is co-ordinated with the phrase in the first, as part of the description of the friendliness of an indoor autumn gathering.

Til it to fyr and leyt be falle,
And thanne it brekth the cloudes alle,
The whiche of so gret noyse craken,
That thei the feerful thonder maken.
(ll.298–306)

Awkwardly enough, it has become necessary today also to disengage Gower from the clutches of modern admirers who, in rightly stressing the clear-headed conceptual unity of his works, may have unduly homogenized their literary qualities.[3] Unquestionably, the *Mirour de l'Omme*, the *Vox Clamantis*, and the *Confessio* are complementary, and linked as a progression of movements in a study of man, his sins and virtues, the body politic, and the emotional life of the individual; unquestionably all share qualities of the encyclopedic *summa*. But they are as surely distinct works, each with individual qualities and a range of its own preoccupations, as the components of Malory's Arthuriad are (or, for that matter, the books of the Bible). However cerebral and abstract Book VII of the *Confessio* becomes, it does not fall back into the manner of the *Mirour* or of the *Vox*. It contains some *exempla* (non-allegorical and secular, unlike certain narrative sections of the *Mirour*), it parallels the Amans / Genius pair with its Alexander and his philosophical mentor, and it is concerned mainly with the education of a royal *individual* rather than addressing itself to the multiple estates of the social order. With one foot firmly, therefore, in the distinct structure which the *Confessio* is, Book VII arches over and connects it with the two other elements in the triple-pillared ambulatory of Gower's achievement. A similar linking-up has of course already been made in the Prologue to the *Confessio*, with its emphasis on the poem as a *speculum principis*.

---

[3] J. H. Fisher, *John Gower: Moral Philosopher and Friend of Chaucer* (New York, 1964; London, 1965): see Professor Bennett's (anonymous) review, *TLS*, 18 November 1965, p. 1022, and his 'Gower's "Honest Love"', in *Patterns of Love and Courtesy: Essays in Memory of C. S. Lewis*, ed. John Lawlor (London, 1966), pp. 107–21, esp. the opening paragraph.

In an illuminating phrase upon which he does not expand, Professor Fisher has helped us to see the connection between the erotic main theme of the *Confessio* and not only the statecraft of Book VII, but the view of humane learning and of the cosmos which it associates with it: 'The real context of the piece is not courtly love, but Empedoclean love, as a social cement' (p. 189). I assume that the phrase does not necessarily deny to the courtly love tradition the part which it does play, and that the descriptive word 'Empedoclean' does not imply any arcane line of influence descending from the philosopher. Gower himself gives no clear-cut explanation for the intrusion of the macrocosm and the body politic into a lesson in the discipline of the emotions. In a work which partly follows the model of the *Roman de la Rose* it is fitting that the Priest of Venus should also be court tutor and expositor of cosmic lore. In the anatomical exposition (ll.485–9) the heart is compared to a king, with reason accorded to it for 'governance'. In the body politic, Gower wishes a ruler to seek reason and wisdom in order to enrich and to control his personality.[4] The ideal in mind is not a philosopher-king, but a ruler with a wise man at his elbow. No two figures of Ruler and Sage were more common as medieval archetypes than those of Alexander and Aristotle. These are the pair in the *Secretum Secretorum*,[5] supposedly an encyclopedic letter from Aristotle to Alexander; these are the pair which, following the *Secretum*, Genius holds up as models. But the *Secretum* tradition is one in which successive translators, adaptors, and commentators view their own instructions as the ectype of this model one, and their own patrons as ectypes of Alexander.

Gower's view of his patron, and his presentation of it, are more than usually complex. The Mirror for Princes which is Book VII is part of an ethically unified corpus of moralizings on kingship, found in a number of discrete works: mainly the *Mirour*, the *Vox*, some of the minor Latin political poems, in

[4] See the rubric to Book VII and cf. *Mirour*, ll.26605 ff.
[5] For the *Secretum*, see below, n. 28 and pp. 169–80, *passim*.

particular the *Cronica Tripertita* and the 'O Deus Immense',[6] sections of the *Confessio* (particularly the 'envelope', that is the Prologue and Book VIII, ll.2940 to the end) together with Book VII, and, finally, *In Praise of Peace*. The earliest relevant passages seem to date from the mid 1370s, apparently before the accession of Richard; the latest stretch into Henry's reign and beyond Richard's death, to at least 1402.[7] During this quarter of a century, without shifting his basic ethical standpoint, Gower was impelled through changing circumstances to alter his views as to what it was most urgent to write about; he changed his mind about the character of Richard, making revisions and changing tack in the body of his poetry as he wrote it. Some general injunctions to kings (*Mirour*, 22225–23208) include disguised reproof of Edward II (ll.22801–23208, not later than 1377). The *Mirour* contains a warning (ll.26482–506) that injustice precipitates rebellion;[8] Book I of the *Vox*, written after the Peasants' Revolt of 1381, is a frightening picture of rebellion against monarchical authority. When the earliest form of the *Vox* was written (around 1380–1), there was no cause yet to criticize Richard: 'Stat puer immunis culpe' (VI.555*). In the final revision (after the first court tyranny of 1386) the King is given his share of blame over the mismanagement of the state: 'Rex, puer indoctus, morales negligit actus' (VI.555).[9] The first version of the Prologue of the *Confessio* represents the decision to write as being 'for King Richardes sake' (l.24*): the date appears to be 1390, the year after that in which Richard had claimed his right to rule as an adult. The early version already contains a dedication to Henry in the Latin *explicit* (Macaulay, p. 478): thus a new ectype is already lurking in the margins. The two revisions change the poem from one of appeal to Richard

---

[6] Macaulay, vol. iv, *Latin Works*, pp. 362–4: the rubric to the poem in All Souls College MS 98, as given by Macaulay, is 'Carmen quod Iohannes Gower adhuc viuens super principum regimine vltimo composuit'.

[7] Macaulay finds a reference to a comet of March 1402 in 'Presul ouile regis' (iv. 368 and 420). [8] Fisher, pp. 98 f.

[9] The same point is made by Eric W. Stockton, *The Major Latin Works of John Gower* (Seattle, 1962), p. 445.

to a rejection of him, and this within the space of a few months ('in anno quarto-decimo Regis Ricardi'),[10] and then to a final adoption in 'The yer sextenthe' (Prologue, final version, l.25) of Richard's reign (June 1392–June 1393) of Henry Bolingbroke as a new and more satisfying 'type' of the Prince,[11] while the poet now describes himself as writing the book 'for Engelondes sake'.[12] The later *Cronica Tripertita* and minor poems reinforce the validity of Henry as the ectype of kingship: one that requires only to be praised, and no longer to be besought in painful actuality to conform to the symbolic role. With symbols and actualities part identical and part distinct, political allegiance is changed but the poet's ideal remains unaltered.

The Aristotelian excursus outside the 'registre of Venus' (I take the words from ll.19–20) is more central to Gower's grand system of thought than is the main body of the *Confessio*. But in terms of artistic structure it is, of course, embedded in a lengthy dialogue on love in which the two interlocutors themselves clearly reflect the Tutor-Sage and Pupil-Prince. The transition from the major literary theme of the poem to the minor is achieved by means of a link passage in which we observe the literary device of using an 'avowed' structure to pursue an unstated thematic intention. In the *Confessio*, Nectanabus is the real father of Alexander. The tale of Nectanabus (VI.1789–2366) comes in as an illustration of the use of sorcery for sexual ends. In the course of the tale, the Confessor (ll.2274–9)

[10] Marginal note opposite VIII.2973: see Macaulay, ii.xxii and iii.468.
[11] The new dedication to Henry is in ll.86–9.
[12] Fisher (pp. 116–27) questions the date 1390 for the revised Prologue, adducing the events of 1392 as strong support for a later date for the revision, but produces no invalidation of the date 'in anno quarto-decimo Regis Ricardi' for the prayer for the state of England in the Prologue: one may surmise that if the reading in a prototype manuscript was 'anno xvi°', it may easily have been misread in a subsequent stage as 'anno xiv°'. Fisher also proposes a different interpretation of the process of revision, casting doubt upon the notion of an intermediary state, that is, the second of Macaulay's three steps, for the *exordium*. However, his argument (p. 120) assumes a process of revision during which the new form of the conclusion was produced, so that my notion of the evolving of Gower's feelings is untouched by Fisher's view of the publicly circulated forms of the *Confessio*.

mentions the education of Alexander by 'Calistre and Aristotle'; the Lover asks to hear more of 'Hou Alisandre was betawht / To Aristotle', hoping this may alleviate the pangs of love. The notion of a long lecture on higher education as a tranquillizer against erotic anxiety teeters on the brink of the absurd, but we are apparently being persuaded of an alternative opinion, that cerebral preoccupations can help in an emotional crisis. By the opening of Book VII, Genius has given the Lover's request a wider interpretation: he takes it that he has asked not only about the 'fare of Alexander'[13] but for a general survey of 'the scole ... of Aristotle' (ll.3–5).[14]

The mention of 'Calistre', i.e. Callisthenes, as an instructor of Alexander, makes Aristotle's nephew into an ancillary figure of the Sage.[15] Throughout the text these figures proliferate: we

[13] The *MED*'s definitions 4, 5, and 7 of the noun *fare*, and 5, 6a, 8a, and 11 of the verb *faren* can explain this use: see also the five other uses of the noun by Gower listed by Macaulay in his Glossary to the *Confessio*. Yet it seems plausible that the word is a calque upon the Latin *regimen*, as in the common title 'De regimine principum' for Mirrors for Princes, coloured in Gower's mind by the English use of *regimen* in the sense *fare* (attested *OED*, c.1400). Use of the noun *fare* for 'supply or provision of food' earlier than Gower is attested by *MED*, *fare* sb. 8a.

[14] A more solemn function is accorded to Gower's Nectanabus by Patrick J. Gallagher, *Love, the Word, and Mercury: A Reading of John Gower's 'Confessio Amantis'* (Albuquerque, 1975). Gallagher (*passim*, and esp. pp. 40–3) sees the seduction of Olimpias as a parodic Annunciation, 'an evil from which good flows', and one which gives the framework of 'an Annunciation' to the encyclopedic knowledge given in Book VII, which provides the formative influence upon King Alexander, the secular counterpart of the Saviour. One might also point out that similar 'parodic' birth-narratives are associated with Merlin and Galahad: evil intention, black magic, and adultery are, in spite of themselves, put to use for the setting up of good rule, and for the infusion of Grace.

[15] For an erroneous belief, found in ancient writers, that Callisthenes had been Alexander's teacher, see Dio Chrysostom, *Discourses*, LXIV.20 and the elder Seneca, *Suasoriae*, 1.5. These are mentioned by Truesdell S. Brown, 'Callisthenes and Alexander', *American Journal of Philology*, lxx (1949), 225–48; p. 228 n. 13.

Gower's authority must be a reference in a book which is one of his main sources for Book VII, Brunetto Latini, *Li Livres dou Tresor*, ed. Francis J. Carmody, University of California Publications in Modern Philology, xxii (Berkeley, 1948), hereafter referred to as Carmody. In I.xxvii, the *Tresors* say

have Claudius Ptolemy (Tholomeus, l.1043; the 'Almageste', l.739) and Abū Ma'shar al-Balkhī (Albumazar, l.1239) for astronomy, and Balaam for cunning strategy (ll.4406–31). Instruction in the natural magic (l.1301) of the knowledge of the fifteen stars with their corresponding stones and plants (VI.2276–9 and VII.1309–1433) is attributed to Nectanabus, as the machinery of the fiction requires, though, at the close (VII 1434–8), Gower steps out of the story and gives the true source, writings attributed to Hermes (ll.1434–8). Nectanabus has earlier used his display of astronomical learning and his black magic ('the craft of Artemage', l.1957) to seduce Olimpias. The teachings of the Sage in this Mirror for Princes are thus preceded and paralleled by the teachings and activities, 'deceipte and nigromance' (ll.217–19), of his negative counterpart, an evil counter-sage.[16] Is it also Gower's awareness of the ultimate lack of importance of worldly wisdom which causes him, in defiance of the tradition of the Mirror for Princes, to debase the chief exemplar of wisdom himself, and to do so in the subsequent and final section of the poem? Book VIII (ll.2705–13) mentions Aristotle among those wise men led to folly through infatuation for a woman: the lines are a sketchy repetition of the well-known anecdote in which Phyllis rides the philosopher as a horse.[17] Even the wisest must come to nothing, as much before the power of Venus as before the God of the final palinode: this minor retractation in fact echoes a phrase in that very passage in which Gower, in setting off, has stated

that Alexander 'avoit por sa metrie Aristote et Calistene'. The manuscript followed by Carmody abbreviates the latter name as 'Calistene', with the abbreviation sign for -ne; the form 'Calistre' presumably derives from a mistaken writing or reading of the abbreviation sign as the one for -re. The same chapter of Latini mentions that Alexander's mother declared that he was conceived by a god in the form of a dragon. It also mentions 'Nabucodonosre', who figures in the Prologue of the *Confessio* and elsewhere in it.

[16] Does this, *pace* Stockton, p. 234 n. 5, explain *Vox*, VI. 631 f.: 'Doctor Alexandri Magni prauos sibi mores / Primitus edocuit, dum puer ipse fuit'? Nectanabus' teachings are discussed in a similar manner by Gallagher, p. 148 f.

[17] See J. A. W. Bennett, *Selections from John Gower* (Oxford, 1968), note to ll.2689 ff., and the references cited there.

that he is to include a Mirror for Princes as part of his study of love:

> Whan the prologe is so despended,
> This bok schal afterward ben ended
> Of love, which doth many a wonder
> *And many a wys man hath put under*
> And in this wyse I thenke trete
> Towardes hem that now be grete,
> Betwen the vertu and the vice
> Which longeth unto this office.
>
> (Prologue, 73–80)

The debasing of Aristotle in the company of Solomon, Virgil, Plato, and others of the 'compaignie' of 'Elde' (VIII.2666f.) links him with Amans, whose elderliness has just been revealed to us (VIII, rubric iii and ll.2403 ff.). The passage reveals some wittiness in Gower, whose conceits here make a wry use of the terminology of Aristotelian logic and taxonomy, repeating some of the terms which have been part of the survey in Book VII, to give the verse texture an ironical and dismissive tone analogous to the spirit of *retraccioun*:

> in thilke time
> Sche made him such a *silogime*,
> That he foryat al his logique;
> Ther was non *art* of his *practique*
> Thurgh which it mihte ben *excluded*
> That he ne was fully *concluded*
> To love, and dede his obeissance.
>
> (VIII.2707–13)[18]

In mentioning this parodic passage now, my survey has put the tail before the horse. It is time to look at the structure of Book VII itself. The two halves of the exposition differ in construction both from each other and from the bulk of the poem. In the other Books, the formal framework of the confession and advice is Gower's own; the embellishments, that is

---

[18] The topic recurs in Book VII itself, ll.4292–6.

exempla, sententiae, and so forth, derive from earlier works. In Book VII the form, as well as the content, derives from the sources. Elsewhere, Gower is picking flowers; here he is relaying the flower-beds. In the first half of Book VII, which elucidates the threefold division of learning, Gower, as Macaulay has shown, is largely following Brunetto Latini's *Livres dou Tresor* for the broad lines of the classification of the branches of learning.[19] The learned debt of Latini is of interest to us: it has been shown that he depends, among other texts, upon the following: (*a*) the Latin version of Eustratius' commentary on the *Nicomachean Ethics*; (*b*) Hermanus Alemannus' thirteenth-century translation of an Arabic abbreviation of the *Nicomachean Ethics*, variously known as the *Translatio Alexandrina, Compendium,* or *Summa Alexandrinorum*;[20] (*c*) the treatise *De quatuor virtutibus* attributed to the sixth-century St. Martin of Braga; and (*d*) the *Rhetorica* of John of Antioch. Aristotle's *Meteorologia* has its influence, while a *Speculum Astronomiae,* or *De libris licitis et illicitis* has been used.[21] We have seen that Ptolemy[22] and Abū Ma'shar[23] are acknowledged sources (Ptolemy in fact being acknowledged even when he is not being followed), while the teachings of Nectanabus owe something to a *Liber Hermetis de xv stellis et de xv lapidibus et de xv herbis.*[24] The description of the jewels in the crown of the sun (ll.815–42) comes from Martianus Capella.[25]

The first hint of a return from *expositio* to the *Confessio's*

[19] One section of Book V (i.e. ll.747–1970) has similarly followed the *Vita Barlaam et Josaphat* in its treatment of the religions of the world.

[20] F. E. Peters, *Aristoteles arabus,* New York University Department of Classics Monographs on Mediterranean Antiquity (Leyden, 1968), pp. 52 f.

[21] Macaulay, notes to VI.1306 ff. and VII.1499 ff.; Carmody, p. xxvii. Abū Ma'shar's *Madkhal (Introductorium)* itself shows the influence of the *Meteorologica*: see Richard Lemay, *Abū Ma'shar and Latin Aristotelianism in the Twelfth Century,* Publication of the Faculty of Arts and Sciences, Oriental Series, no. 38 (Beirut, 1962), p. xxix and elsewhere.

[22] See Carmody, p. xxvii, for the use of the *Almageste.*

[23] See Macaulay's note to l.683. The *Madkhal,* or *Introductorium,* is the text which is meant.   [24] Macaulay, note to ll.1281 ff.

[25] George L. Hamilton, 'Some Sources of the Seventh Book of Gower's *Confessio Amantis',* *Modern Philology,* lx (1911), 323–46, esp. p. 345.

normal pattern of mixed precept and *exempla* comes in the passage on rhetoric, with two brief *exempla* linked by a passage of embellishment (ll.1558–1640). Then, with 'Practique', we come to a threefold subdivision into ethics, economics, and politics (Etique, Economique, Policie); the first two are dealt with briefly; as the exposition of the third, Gower gives the 'Five Points of Policy'. It is in this second half of the Book that *exempla* return to their normal prominence. As ever, the chief sources are the Old Testament, Ovid, and Valerius Maximus, with the use also of Seneca, Peter Comestor, and Godfrey of Viterbo, and with parallels to anecdotes in the *Gesta Romanorum*.[26]

The exposition seems to me to be of mixed derivation. Professor A. H. Gilbert shows the *Secretum Secretorum* to be a more important source than Macaulay supposed.[27] In a general fashion, the Five Points—Truth, Largess, Justice, Pity, and Chastity—can be found in the first three Discourses of the *Secretum*, Liberality in Discourse I, Truth, Pity, and Chastity in Discourse II, Justice in Discourses II and III. But Latini's compendium of the teachings of the *Nicomachean Ethics*, his section II.i–xlix, more clearly specifies particular virtues. These include Chastity, Largess, Pity, Truth, and Justice, which are Gower's Five Points. Latini, however, does not confine himself to these, but also lists Firmness, Magnificence, Magnanimity, Friendliness, and Constance, and, because he is conflating his sources, he deals with some of these virtues more than once.

The reader finds the same difficulty in this case as with Spenser's twelve virtues. The poet has found his way to a clear-cut classification, here apparently based on the *Secretum* and on Latini, where the rest of us can only see something considerably more amorphous: it is no easier to disentangle five clear and principal moral focuses in the teachings of the two distantly Aristotelian sources (and the Stoic strand woven into one of

[26] See Macaulay's notes to the *exempla* in the second section of Book VII.
[27] 'Notes on the Influence of the *Secretum Secretorum*', *Speculum*, iii (1928), 84–98 esp. pp. 86–93.

them) than it is to find a neat dozen in the original text of Aristotle's *Nicomachean Ethics*. It must be admitted that the interest of the text of this part of the poem is much less than the fascination of its synthesis (after a long and intricate transmission) of the *exemplum* tradition with versions of works that derive from the *Nicomachean Ethics*: Eustratius' *Commentaria*, the *Summa Alexandrinorum*, and the *Secretum Secretorum*,[28] of which the two last come into the Latin world from Arabic, while the whole comes together here to form a historiated everyman's digest, feudalized and Christianized, of Aristotle's political views.

The fivefold structuring of Gower's *Politique* indicates Latini as the closer model, especially as Gower has learned from Latini that this portion of his book consists of 'le livre Aristotle'.[29] But it is the *Secretum* which is specifically addressed to a king, as Gower's words are, while the *Tresors* is a treatise on general ethics for all men. When we turn to textual echoes, then, as Professor Gilbert has noted, it is the prose text of the *Secretum*

[28] The Arabic text of the *Secretum*, the *Sirr al-Asrār*, has been edited in A. Badawi, *Al Uṣūl al-yūnāniyyah lil-naẓariyyāt al-siyāsiyyah fil-Islām*, *Fontes Graecae doctrinarum politicarum Islamicarum*, Islamica 15 (Cairo, 1954). A modern English translation of the Arabic, by Ismail Ali, is found in an appendix to Robert Steele, *Opera hactenus inedita Rogeri Baconi*, fasc. v, *Secretum Secretorum* (Oxford, 1920), pp. 176–266. This volume contains Bacon's glossed recension of the Latin Vulgate text of the full translation by Philippus Tripolitanis, which is also found in Hilgart von Hürnheim, ed. Reinhold Möller, *Mittelhochdeutsche Prosaübersetzung des Secretum Secretorum*, Deutsche Texte des Mittelalters LVI, Deutsche Akademie der Wissenschaften (Berlin, 1963). A shorter version of the Latin, the so-called *Compendium*, is in an appendix in George B. Fowler, 'Manuscript Admont 608 and Engelbert of Admont (*c.*1250–1331)', *Archives d'histoire doctrinale et littéraire du moyen âge*, xliv (1977), 206–46. The more common Abbreviated form of Tripolitanus' translation is found in such early printed texts as that of Ther Hoernen, Cologne, *c.*1477 and such MSS as Paris, Bibliothèque Nationale 3029. A total of fifteen English versions translated between 1400 and 1702 can be studied in the following three volumes: R. Steele, *Three Prose Versions of the Secreta Secretorum*, EETS, ES 74 (1898); vol. ii of J. H. Stevenson, *Gilbert of the Haye's Prose Manuscript*, Scottish Text Society, 2 vols. (Edinburgh, 1900–14); M. A. Manzalaoui, *Secretum Secretorum: Nine English Versions*, vol. i, EETS, OS 276 (1977).

[29] Latini, II, introduction and rubric to Ch. i: Carmody, pp. 176, 224.

which is revealed behind the free versification of ethical principles. It is possible to tabulate some echoes of the
Secretum—both close and more distant—as noted by Macaulay,
Professor Gilbert, George L. Hamilton, Professor Fisher, and
myself, locating each in Gower's text and indicating the parallel
in the Latin *Secretum* and, for greater ease, in a fifteenth-century
English translation:[30]

Destiny, free will, and Grace	ll.314–18	B 61 / 27–62 / 3 ; *Ash* 47 / 11–21
Theory of correspondences	ll.366–84	B 60 / 21–62 / 16 & 119 / 3–120 / 2 ; *Ash* 46 / 10–47 / 35 & 66 / 35–67 / 22
Oaths	ll.1741–4	B 56 / 20–57 / 27; *Ash* 43 / 9–44 / 6
Largess	ll.2014–57, 2131–7, 2151–64	B 42 / 31–44 / 34; *Ash* 32 / 9–34 / 3
Honouring of law	marginalia at l.2694, & ll.2695–701	B 47 / 14–19 & 126 / 7–15; *Ash* 35 / 33–36 / 3 & 71 / 18–25
King's virtue and Justice	ll.2728–34	B 47 / 21–27 & 126 / 7–15; *Ash* 36 / 3–9 & 71 / 18–25
Mercy	ll.3075–91	B 47 / 21–27 & 54 / 28–55 / 20; *Ash* 36 / 3–9 & 41 / 31–42 / 14

[30] This table shows the line numbers of the sections of Book VII of the
Confessio, and the page and line numbers of the corresponding passages in
Steele's edition of Bacon's redaction of the Latin (here, and henceforward in
the text, referred to by the sigil *B*). For ease of reference, I also indicate
corresponding page and line numbers in text no. III, the 'Ashmole' version, in
my *Nine English Versions*: this version is referred to by the sigil *Ash* (the
complete volume is referred to henceforward as *9EV*). In one case, where *Ash*
contains no adequate equivalent, I take the parallel from text no. IV in *9EV*,
the translation by Johannes de Caritate, indicated as *Car*.

Mercy and Justice	ll.3125–9	B 47 / 21–48 / 17; Ash 36 / 3–27
Punishment	ll.3520–50 & 3851–9	B 52 / 24–34; Ash 39 / 34–40 / 11
Chastity	ll.4252–6	B 51 / 6–13; Ash 38 / 36 & Car 135 / 3–14
Chastity and beholding fair visages	ll.4210–14, with marginalia, & ll.257–61	B 51 / 6–13 & 82 / 23; Ash 38 / 36 & 59 / 31–32
Natural heat	marginalia at l.4560	B 81/20 & 88/5; Ash 59/6 & 62/8

The text is only occasionally very close to that of the *Secretum*: compare ll.2014–24 with *Secretum*, 42 / 31–43 / 11.[31] But at one point a rhetorical embellishment may inspire another of a different nature. The Octagon of Justice is a 'circle of virtues' with an interesting history in Arabic gnomologia:

Mundus est ortus seu viridarium, ejus materia uel species est judicium ... Judicium est dominator vallatus ... lego: Lex est qua rex regit regnum: Et rex est pastor qui defenditur a proceribus: Proceres sunt stipendiarii sustentati pecunia: Pecunia vero est fortuna que colligitur a subditi: Subditi autem sunt serui quos subjecit justicia: Justicia vero est que intenditur per se, in qua est salus subditorum.

(B 126 / 8–15)[32]

At Gower's hands it becomes a chain of four interlinking rhetorical questions:

What is a lond wher men ben none?
What ben the men whiche are al one
Withoute a kinges governance?
What is a king in his ligance,

[31] Badawi, p. 73; Ash 32 / 9–25. Badawi's Arabic text will henceforward be indicated by the sigil *Bad*.
[32] In the Arabic, the final item more clearly leads back to the first of the eight items: *Bad* 127 f.; B 126; Ash 71 / 18–25. For the Octagon, see M. A. Manzalaoui, 'The Pseudo-Aristotelian *Kitāb Sirr al-Asrār*: Facts and Problems', *Oriens*, xxiii–xxiv (1970–1), 147–257 (hereafter *FP*); pp. 185, 214, and 230.

Wher that ther is no lawe in londe?
What is to take lawe on honde,
But if the jugges weren trewe?

(ll.2695–71)

The revision of the *Confessio* brought in the only *exemplum* borrowed from the *Secretum*, the story of the Pagan and the Jew.[33] Used in the original in connection with the choice of a counsellor, Gower employs it to illustrate Pity, and prunes the story down to his usual calmly dignified proportions. He gives the story a definite setting in time and place, 'in a pas' on the road 'betwen Kaire and Babeloine, Whan comen is the somer heete' (3212*). It seems probable that 'Babeloine' comes from the same brief chapter in Latini from which Gower took Callistre.[34] The Magus of the *Secretum* becomes a 'paien', but one whose conduct is held up to praise, in contrast with the Jew's. Gower's historical sense, again guided by Latini's account, may have chosen Babylon as a place where Jew and pagan could have consorted as fellow-subjects of one empire; ironically, it has been supposed that the anecdote arose in the Persian empire which succeeded the Babylonian, in circles which disparaged Jews and favoured the official Zoroastrianism.[35] To Gower's complimentary view of ancient paganism I return later.

The *Secretum* is detectable in other parts of the *Confessio*. With the English throne as the ectype of Alexander's it is significant that Gower's apology in the Prologue echoes Aristotle's, and the ruler's right to demand instruction from a sage is reasserted: 'Hunc quidem librum composuit in sua senectute

33 *Bad* 140–42, *B* 144–6, *Ash* 81–3; *Confessio*, VII.3207*–3360*.
34 See above, p. 165 and n. 15. 'Babylon' was also the Byzantine name for the fortress which stood near the site of the later Cairo; hence it was sometimes the medieval name for Old Cairo. If Gower was familiar with this usage, he may have hazily conflated the cities on the Euphrates and the Nile; the journey would then uncertainly be either a suburban one of a few miles, or a trek along the caravan route linking Africa and Asia.
35 Professor S. Pines, of the Hebrew University, Jerusalem, private conversation: *FP*, pp. 183, 234.

et virtutum corporalium debilitate . . .' (*B* 36 / 14–15, and see also
40 / 17–20, 24–26).

> Thogh I seknesse haue upon honde
> And longe have had, yit woll I fonde
> To wryte and do my bisinesse...
> (*Confessio*, Prologue, 61–3, and see also 70*–75*.)[36]

Gower intrudes a reference to the 'symplesce of [his] wit', a
reminder that he does not claim Aristotle's profundity. But how
many readers notice that this echo of the *Secretum* spoken by
John Gower in his avatar as king's counsellor, in the envelope
of the poem, has already informed us of his advanced age, the
chief cause of sadness for John Gower as Lover, in the body of
the *Confessio*?[37]

These indications that Gower is at times following the text
of the *Secretum* closely as he writes the *Confessio* are supplemented by signs that he was familiar with that text throughout
his writing career. The statements in the *Vox* that moral
appearances should correspond to moral realities (*Vox*,
VI.1091–2; *B* 47 / 27–31) and that the king should respect the
law (*Vox*, VI.595 f., 613; *B* 47 / 14–19) are too platitudinous to
be taken as signs of a reading of the *Secretum*, but passages in
the earlier *Mirour* on man as microcosm (*Mirour*, 26929–34; *B*
143 / 27–28)[38] and on the respect due to humble men (*Mirour*,

---

[36] *Bad* 67 and 70; *Ash* 19 / 34 f. and 30 / 4–15.

[37] As another parallel with the *Secretum*, Fisher notes that the initial classification of the sins according to the five senses (Book I) echoes the stress in the
Secretum upon fivefold divisions (*B* 134–5).

[38] Gower here attributes the term 'le meindre monde' to Aristotle ('En un des
livres qu'il fasoit / Dont molt notable sont les vers'). The true Aristotelian use
of the term (see Macaulay's note to these lines) does not refer to man. The
similar comparison of man to other entities in the prologue to the *Confessio*
(ll.945–56) refers one to Gregory's *Moralia* (vi. 16), where man is not, however,
called a lesser world but 'universitas', and a knowledge of *Roman de la Rose*,
ll.19043 ff. ('vns petiz mondes nouveaus') is a moral certainty, yet the *Secretum*
seems equally to belong in this cluster of sources. Why speak of 'les vers' of
the *Secretum*? Did Gower know of a versified version, such as that of Pierre
d'Abernun of Fetcham (Anglo-Norman Texts 5, Anglo-Norman Text Society;
Oxford, 1944), or is he using *vers* in the generalized sense 'phrase'? (This sense
is recorded in Old and Middle English: *OED*, *verse* sb. 3.)

21997–22005; *B* 56 / 17–19, 137 / 33–34) make a knowledge of the pseudo-Aristotelian text almost certain.

In the *Confessio*, the *Secretum* plays some functional roles other than as a direct source. Sometimes there is a parallelism of content which suggests that the *Secretum* may not be far off. While the *Confessio* has no section on the system of hygiene for each of the four seasons,[39] it seems to imitate the *Secretum* in tagging lyric descriptions of the times of the year on to a series of technical passages: in Gower's case, accounts of the signs of the Zodiac, the month each governs, and the 'humour' of each. The lines quoted early on in this paper come from the account of Sagittarius.

Was Gower following any recension of the *Secretum* other than the 'Vulgate'?[40] There is nothing to suggest this. The systematizing of the ethical contents under five heads appears, as we have seen, to be his own, and to have been coloured by Latini's text. Gower may well have encountered the *Secretum* in conjunction with the *Tresors* in a single manuscript; this collocation of the vernacular *summa* and the Mirror for Princes is a known one: Paris, Bibliothèque Nationale MS 7068 contains Latini's text and a French version of the *Secretum*. It has been surmised that Gower used the rehandled French version by Jofroi de Waterford and Servais Copale.[41] The arguments for this on the grounds of common omission of material constitute no proof;[42] the parallels in the treatment of the humours in both authors are not close enough to sustain the argument;[43] the *exempla* used in common by both are in that section of Waterford which is a translation of John of Wales's *Breviloquium de quattuor virtutibus cardinalibus*.[44] Not only can this

---

[39] Cf. *B* 76–81; *Ash* 56–9.

[40] Steele, pp. xxii f.

[41] Hamilton, as in n. 25 above.

[42] Hamilton, p. 21.

[43] Hamilton, pp. 12 ff.

[44] Jacques Monfrin, 'Le *Secret des secrets*: recherches sur les traductions françaises suivies du texte de Jofroi de Waterford et Servais Copale', *Positions de thèses soutenues par les élèves de la promotion de 1947*, École nationale des Chartes (Paris, 1947), pp. 93–9. Monsieur Monfrin's text of Waterford is unpublished.

treatise have been used by Gower in its independent form, but it too is found in the manuscript tradition providing a 'Christianizing' complement to the *Secretum*.[45]

The *Secretum*, both in the Arabic and the Latin traditions, is a work which attempts to convey philosophical and scientific concepts to readers moderately well equipped by intellect and education to understand them. Gower's Book VII joins with the earlier work of Trevisa in providing the English language with some of its first attempts at the vocabulary and the prose of scholastic and of scientific exposition. Professor James Murphy has emphasized the interest it holds, however confused its teachings are, as the first discussion of rhetoric to be written in English.[46] Similarly, the book contains what seems to be the earliest approach to a sustained attempt at translating terms of scholastic Aristotelianism into English. Lines 91–104 contain the equivalent for *ens*, *res* (or perhaps *essentia*), *temporaneus*, *perpetuus*, and *sempiternalis*: respectively *beinge*, *thinge*, *temporal*, *perpetual*, and *sempiterne*. Earlier English uses of these words are in less precise senses: Gower's *perpetual*, of a thing which has a beginning but no end, is apparently unique in English. Gower seems to distinguish *kinde* (in the sense *species*) from *forme*:[47] he makes a similar distinction between *matiere* and *form* in his discussion of the consubstantiality of celestial and sublunary things (ll.633–6), and, more clearly than the *Secretum*, he implies that consubstantiality does not mean also having the same form.

Gower's verse rehandling of the matter of the *Secretum*

---

[45] In the manuscript of the *Secretum*, the property of Lord Brocket, sold at Sotheby's on 14 July 1952, the text is in the same hand as other treatises, including one, the *Ignorantia sacerdotum*, which contains instructions upon confession and the seven deadly sins. Could a manuscript collocation such as this one have acted as an ancillary contribution in causing Gower to include a section based on the *Secretum* in a poem with a framework derived from the pattern of the confessional?

[46] James J. Murphy, 'John Gower's *Confessio Amantis* and the First Discussion of Rhetoric in the English Language', *Philological Quarterly*, xli (1962), 401–11.

[47] Lines 339–41. We must read Macaulay's *fame* as *same*.

precedes the dozen or so prose translations of the text, the earliest of which dates from around 1400.[48] It is a characteristic of the prose versions that they prune, expand, and modify the text in order to fit the needs of their cultural environment, and the aims of the particular translators, each of whom often has his immediate patron in mind. Gower, basing himself on the Latin text (there is no sure sign of his employing one of the French versions already current), shows to the full an interpreter's independence in reusing the Mirror for Magistrates which he has inherited; he transmits its teachings in a form adapted to his own outlook, using them as the vehicle for a discussion of certain themes around which, as an English thinker and a 'public' Ricardian poet, his thoughts are running.[49]

Although the *Secretum* recommends that a ruler should win the hearts of his subjects,[50] it condemns undignified familiarity,[51] and even justifies rule through fear.[52] In the *exemplum* of Trajan (ll.3142–62), Gower reverses the two latter judgements, as Shakespeare was to do in building up his concept of the popular prince in the figure of Henry Bolingbroke's son.

On predestination, the *Secretum* attempts a reconciliation between divination, and Grace and free will: natural phenomena, though predetermined through a universality in nature, can be modified through efficacious prayer.[53] Gower commonly adheres to this: lightning and the thunderclap do irreparable harm 'wher ... thei descende, / Bot if God wolde His Grace sende' (ll.317–18). Thus the *Secretum* avoids falling into dualism: yet Gower goes his own way in one passage, which, in some contrast to the rest of the poem, puts forward a dualistic theory

[48] 9*EV*, pp. xxiv–xlvii.
[49] See Anne Middleton, 'The Idea of Public Poetry in the Reign of Richard II', *Speculum*, liii (1978), 94–114.
[50] B 53 / 5 f.   [51] B 49 / 9–21.
[52] B 52 / 24–9 and 53 / 13–15: the latter is a mistranslation of the Arabic (*Bad* 81 / 1) which is less stern and does not place reverence above love ('Let fear of you in their souls be sharper than your sword in a man's heart').
[53] B 61 / 7–62 / 3.

(ll.490–520). Nature purveys for Man's earthly life, God creates the soul 'in other wise', and although 'hir abydinge is conjoint / Forth with the bodi forto duelle' (ll.502–3) yet 'That on desireth toward helle / That other upward to the hevene' (ll.504–5). Balance can be achieved, however, by the governance of soul over body (ll.507 f.). Even though 'body' here includes the psychological inclinations caused by the 'complexions', something of a near-Manichaean concept has intruded. Elsewhere, the reconciling of faith and proto-scientific determinism is a more self-consistent synthesis. In the discussion of astronomy (ll.633–63), the opinion of the 'naturien' is that sublunary matter is governed by the planets (ll.633–50), and there is a specific application of this to Love (l.645). In antithesis, the 'divin' asserts the supremacy of virtue and wisdom (ll.651–7). The synthesis holds that uniformity can be broken through the intercession of a holy man (ll.658–63). The contrast with Roger Bacon is informative. Bacon, making use of the *Secretum*,[54] contends that the welfare of the world lies in the virtuous use by the scientist of the determined affinities and forces of the physical world. Gower, presumably expanding upon the two brief passages in the *Secretum* which make the same point, calls for a man both wise and good to restore the rule of will into the cosmic system, a thing made possible through the action of Grace:

> Lege planetarum magis inferiora reguntur,
> Ista set interdum regula fallit opus.
> Vir mediante deo sapiens dominabitur astris,
> Fata nec immerito quid nouitatis agunt.
>   (rubric preceding l.633)[55]

[54] Stewart C. Easton, *Roger Bacon and his Search for a Universal Science* (Oxford, 1952); M. A. Manzalaoui, 'The Pseudo-Aristotelian *Sirr al-Asrar* and Three Oxford Thinkers of the Middle Ages', *Arabic and Islamic Studies in Honour of Hamilton A. R. Gibb*, ed. George Makdisi (Leyden, 1965), pp. 480–500.
[55] Macaulay notes the development of this idea in *Vox Clamantis*, II.217–80,

The cerebral side of Gower enjoys the clarity and system of scientific teachings, the turning from the inchoate beliefs of 'the lewed poeple' to the explanations of the 'Philosophre' (ll.319–67). But his poetic side does not miss the opportunity to mention the 'fyrdrake' and gliding star into which fiery exhalations are shaped by the imagination of those who do not know of 'Assub' and 'Eges'.

Of those born under the sign of the sun, Gower does not say that they are suited to rule, but that they make good servants of the powerful, and are virtuous and wise men (ll.874–80). Such wisdom found its home in the past in Greece (l.887)—the seat, that is, of the power and wisdom represented by Alexander and Aristotle. Of a piece with this classicizing admiration of Greece is the use we have already noted of the epithet 'pagan' in a non-pejorative sense. The exposition of the faith of the Pagan in the *exemplum* reveals the finest quality of the older theism, the universal love which it shares with Christianity (ll.3222*–33*), as Trajan's Rome, 'Cité de la paiene gent', is praised in the *Mirour* (ll.22165 ff.) as the seat of good government. Interestingly, Gower's anecdote had entered the *Secretum* from the syncretizing writings of the Islamic group known as the 'Sincere Brethren', with their universalist ethic:[56] the English poet is echoing those views within Islamic philosophy which admired both latitudinarian humanism and that Greek love of learning which the *Secretum* holds up for praise.[57]

At a time when the English court[58] was asserting the King's

where an earlier version of the third of these four Latin lines is found, following upon the lines:

> Imperio iusti nequeunt obstare subacti
> Tortores baratri, set famulantur ei:
> Ac elementorum celestia corpora iustum
> Subdita iure colunt, et sua vota ferunt.
>   (ll.235–8)

[56] *FP*, pp. 175–84; Adel Awa, *L'Esprit critique des Frères de la Pureté* (Beirut, 1948).
[57] B 58 / 21–59 / 5, 64 / 28–31; Ash 44 / 33–45 / 10, 48 / 24–8.
[58] M. V. Clarke, 'The Lancastrian Faction and the Wonderful Parliament', in *Fourteenth-Century Studies* (Oxford, 1937), esp. p. 36; Anthony Steel, *Richard*

divine right, Gower incorporates into Book VII a theory of the development of monarchy for reasons of public convenience, out of primeval communism (ll.1991–2013), mainly to avoid economic chaos—hence it is (ll.2014–57) particularly important that a king should apportion rewards in fair-handed liberality. An evil king brings disaster upon his innocent nation (*Mirour*, 22825–36; *Vox*, VI.497–512; *Confessio*, 3927–35): the *Secretum* compares the king to the natural phenomena—rain, winds, heat, and cold—which can bring both good and evil upon humanity.[59]

There is a neat historical irony here. Gower saw in Richard's ways the destruction of the kingdom of England. The Arabic original of the *Secretum*[60] speaks of the excessive expenditure of the spendthrift kings of an unidentified people, the *Hanānīkh*,[61] just as the fourth clause of Haxey's petition of February 1397 spoke of Richard. In the manuscript edited by Steele (*B* 44/19) the Latin version calls the kingdom the 'regn[um] Caldeorum': hence Gower's reference (l.2031) to Chaldee as a warning example. An abbreviated form of the *Secretum*, common in Latin and French in the fifteenth century, had as a result of palaeographic slips changed the reading to make it end '. . . quod fuit causa destructionis regni *Anglorum*'. Although the prototype of this reading goes back earlier,[62] it is surely true that the fifteenth-century reader of the abbreviated *Secretum* would at this point have uppermost in his mind the fate of the king whom Gower rejected.[63] One recalls that, much later,

II (Cambridge, 1941), esp. p. 94; R. H. Jones, *The Royal Policy of Richard II: Absolutism in the Later Middle Ages* (Oxford, 1968).

[59] *B* 53/18–25, *Ash* 40/25–41/29.

[60] *Bad* 74, corresponding to *B* 44 and *Ash* 43 f.

[61] There are variants in the Arabic manuscripts, e.g. Hanākhikh, Hanānij: see Badawi, pp. 74 and 83, *FP*, pp. 206 f.

[62] The French-language MS Bibliothèque Nationale fonds français 5.71, produced for Edward III when still Prince of Wales, has a reading deriving from this: the intention in it is apparently to advert to the misrule and troubles of Edward II. The scribe may have had Edward II in mind.

[63] For the strong wind sent by God as a punishment upon the spendthrift kings, in the *Secretum* (*B* 44/24), one fifteenth-century English translation (BL Royal 18 A. vii; Steele, *Three Prose Versions*, p. 8) substitutes 'kyngis of vengeaunce'—presumably a reference to Henry IV.

Elizabeth was to say at the time of Essex's uprising, 'I am Richard II, knew ye not that?'

The *Confessio* itself continued to be read as a Mirror for Princes. It may lie behind the poem *De regimine*, contained in the Maitland Folio;[64] like the *Confessio*, this singles out for praise a specific number of royal virtues: they are four—Gower's five, less the more general virtue of chastity. Here too the past of Rome is extolled, and 'division' is given as the cause of its decay (cf. *Mirour*, ll.22158 ff.; *Confessio*, Prol. 839–64). The unifying conceit of the *De regimine* is the comparison of good rule to a harp with many strings. Gower had compared the harmony of a king's rule with a harp, in the *Mirour* (ll.22897 ff.).

It was as a substitute for the *rifacimento* of Gower's poem requested by his patron, Sir Giles Alington, that Alexander Barclay produced his *Mirror of Good Manners* in 1516.[65] While Alington had asked for an abridgement, rescuing the poem from its 'corrupte Englishe', it is little short of astonishing to find that Barclay excuses himself, not only because the poem is long and difficult, but because he thinks some may find it a 'thing wanton, not sad but insolent'.[66] He goes back in part to Latini's outlook, and to that of some adaptors of the *Secretum*, in substituting instead an English version of a treatise on the Cardinal Virtues.

But the most interesting of the possible influences are more shadowy.

It has been pointed out that Milton's allegory of Sin and Death has an antecedent in the *Mirour*.[67] For another speculation, we may turn from Book II to Books IV and IX, to Satan's rapid assuming of the bodies of a number of different creatures, as temporary habitations. Preparing for the seduction of

---

[64] *Maitland Folio Manuscript*, ed. W. A. Craigie, Scottish Text Society (1919–37), i. 115–25, ii. 72–91.

[65] Alexander Barclay, *The Mirrour of good Manners* (capitalized thus), published (in gatherings with independent signatures) together with *The Ship of Fooles*, London: John Cawood, 1570.

[66] Barclay, Dedicatory verses, sig. A2.

[67] Fisher, pp. 129 and 164 (with n. 56), and the works cited there. Milton's uses of Gower in his prose works are referred to in the footnote.

Olimpias, Gower's Nectanabus assumes in quick succession the forms of dragon, ram, and man (*Confessio*, VI.2058 ff.). Later, to impress Philip (ll.2177 ff.), he again sends (or himself assumes—the account is not clear) a figure which becomes in turn a dragon, an eagle, a pheasant, and a serpent. Although Milton has a sufficient antecedent in Du Bartas,[68] one may at least ask if Gower contributed a share to the shape-shifting in that first approach of Satan to Eve.

Gower follows Latini in illustrating the power of rhetoric (VII.1595–1628) with an *exemplum* derived from Sallust, comparing some funeral orations of two types.[69] One pair of them is rational and plain, another speech is emotive and embellished; the former is limited in appeal, the latter rouses its hearers in enthusiastic support of the speaker; the former are spoken against the reputation of a man in defeat, the latter in its favour. The occasion is the suppression of Catiline's conspiracy. The speakers of the first set are 'Cillenus' (Decimus Junius Silanus) and Cato; the opposing orator is 'Julius', that is, Caesar.[70] Gower only sketches the situation, which a greater imaginative writer would surely be eager to expand in its full dramatic possibilities. It is a well-known fact that Plutarch is not Shakespeare's authority in making Antony deliver his oration *immediately* after Brutus, and his work not an original for the dramatic collocation of two contrasting speeches. Shakespeare might

---

[68] Milton, *Poems*, ed. J. Carey and A. Fowler (London, 1968), n. to IV.402–8. In Du Bartas, the shapes assumed are those of horse, heifer, cock, dog, hart, peacock, and serpent; in Milton, they are cormorant (? 'Sat *like* a cormorant', IV.196), lion, tiger, toad, and serpent, besides the form of a mist (IX.75 reads 'involved *in* rising mist', but the headnote has 'returns *as* a mist by night').

[69] Latini, III.xxiv-xxxviii; Sallust, *Bellum Catilinae*, L.iv—LIII.i. The accounts by Sallust and Latini are considerably different from Gower's, and cannot be considered as alternative sources in making this supposition.

[70] Plutarch's 'Life of Caesar' places earliest Julius Caesar's speech in favour of showing clemency towards Catiline's followers; Caesar is succeeded and opposed by Cato and Catulus. In his 'Life of Cicero', Syllanus speaks first, then Caesar. In his 'Life of Caesar', after the assassination of Caesar, Brutus and his friends make public speeches, but there is no mention of Antony's oration. In his 'Lives' of Antony and of Brutus, Antony delivers his speech at Caesar's burial, which is some days after the speeches made by the conspirators.

conceivably have here derived an ancillary impetus from the Gower he uses elsewhere as a stage-speaker and a major source. More than that one cannot say: the apparition is truly intangible, but an impressionable reader of medieval Mirrors for Princes may well feel that there is an unseen presence upon the Elizabethan stage.

A Middle English Illustrated Poem

DOUGLAS GRAY

Devotional Pieces in Verse and Prose is a fine testimony to three of Jack Bennett's interests—in Middle Scots, in devotional literature, and in the visual arts and their relationship with the written word. It is the third of these—in a very particular form—which has suggested the following article. The manuscript which provided the bulk of his material, BL MS Arundel 285, is an interesting late example of a medieval illustrated devotional book. At appropriate places in the text seventeen woodcuts have been pasted in, to accompany the words of the devotions in a way which would have been familiar to readers of Books of Hours or of humbler devotional collections. He also printed from MS Harley 6919 a text—*The Contemplacioun of Synnaris*—which is illustrated with a number of pen and ink drawings, each of which 'occupies a leaf at the beginning of that section of the poem which opens with a description of the drawing'. This copy seems to have been designed as an illustrated devotional poem; as he says, 'the figures or illustrations on which it ostensibly depends make it a precursor of the emblem books'.

It seems appropriate to draw attention to a Middle English lyric based on the Litany, which is an example of this kind of illustrated poem (a kind that seems to have become popular in late medieval England), and which occurs in a particularly fine example of an illustrated devotional book, the 'Beauchamp Hours', now in the Library of the Fitzwilliam Museum.[1] The

[1] Surviving copies are listed in Brown-Robbins, *Index of Middle English Verse*, no. 914. A random and quite unsystematic search has unearthed four more

manuscript seems to have been made for Margaret Beauchamp, daughter of Richard Beauchamp, Earl of Warwick and a cele- brated 'flower of chivalry', probably for the occasion of her marriage to Sir John Talbot, later Earl of Shrewsbury, the famous English captain in the French wars. Like its companion book, the 'Talbot Hours', also in the Fitzwilliam, in which our poem also occurs, the 'Beauchamp Hours' has a full-page picture of the two with their patron saints, St. George and St. Margaret. Both books were produced in France. On a blank page in the 'Talbot Hours', a scribe has written a touching little verse prayer for his master's safe home-coming to England; as readers of Shakespeare know, 'brave Talbot' died on active service, in 1453. The poem also appears in a closely related manuscript belonging to Blairs College, Aberdeen, which accord- ing to N. R. Ker is an adaptation of a Talbot Book of Hours—but not copied from either of the manuscripts now in the Fitzwilliam Museum—made apparently in France for a member of the family of Bethune of Balfour.[2] A fourth illustrated copy is British Library MS Cotton Tiberius B iii, sadly damaged, but still impressive.

Among Middle English illustrated poems, that in the Beau- champ Hours stands out for the quality of its pictures. The fifteenth-century devotional illustrated book composed of

examples of it in *Horae* from the press of Wynkyn de Worde: (1510) BL C. 123 d. 32, (1519) BL C.25 f. 17, and two from 1526, *STC* 15947 and 15948. I have not been able to see the *Horae* in York Minister, nor the MS in the Huntington Library (the 'Bement' MS, a 'twin' of Longleat 30; see H.C. Schulz, *HLQ* xxx (1939), 443). I am especially grateful to the Marquess of Bath for permission to examine MS Longleat 30, to the vicar of Steeple Ashton for permission to examine the interesting manuscript bequeathed to the church as part of the library of Samuel Hey, vicar 1787–1828, and previously Fellow and President of Magdalene College, Cambridge (see C. Wordsworth, Surtees Society, cxxxii (1920), 161), and to the British Library and the Library of the Fitzwilliam Museum for allowing me to reproduce material in their possession.

[2] The two Fitzwilliam MSS are fully described by M. R. James in *A Descriptive Catalogue of the Second Series of Fifty Manuscripts ... in the Collection of Henry Yates Thompson* (Cambridge, 1902), pp.218–38, the Blairs College MS (now on deposit in the National Library of Scotland) by N. R. Ker, *Medieval Manuscripts in British Libraries*, ii (Oxford, 1977), pp. 113–18.

mainly or exclusively vernacular material is not usually produced as a presentation copy for members of noble families like the Talbots and the Beauchamps, and is consequently homely and vigorous rather than elegant.[3] Examples range from the Carthusian manuscript, BL Add. 37049, an extensive collection of prayers and devotional matter in verse and prose, a true 'spiritual encyclopedia of the late Middle Ages', and lavishly illustrated, to the tiny Bodleian MS Douce 1, in which English prayers are accompanied by small drawings. By some happy chance our poem found its way into the miscellaneous series of prayers and devotions in Latin and English which became part of a Book of Hours, and therefore found itself in what was—at least for the rich and powerful—the most common and often the most exquisitely made devotional book of the time.

The use of illustrations in the humbler vernacular devotional collections is usually fairly straightforward. They serve, above all, to concentrate the mind of the reader in his prayer or meditation upon a vivid 'speaking' picture. The verses may be explanatory, and, as in *The Contemplacioun of Synnaris*, closely linked with the image. A typically simple example is found in the *Arma Christi* of Douce 1, which begins with a figure of the 'veronycle'. This is immediately followed by the stanza:

> The veronycle I honour in worschip of The
> That made it through Thy preuyte...

The verse goes on to a brief devotional account of the incident at the Passion ('the clothe set over thy face...' etc.), and ends with a prayer, 'Shelde me, Lorde, for that in my lyue, / I haue synned with my wittes fyue'; the worshipper beseeches the Lord for forgiveness 'thrughe vertue of the figure that I here see'. The meditative structure of the stanza is obvious, and with its image it becomes a rudimentary kind of emblem. The relationship of image and words is a simple and a practical one: the image

---

[3] Cf. the illustrations in D. Gray, *Themes and Images in the Medieval English Religious Lyric* (London, 1972). MS Cotton Faustina B vi, Part II, offers a notable example of a talented artist at work with vernacular devotional material.

gives a visual focus for the reader of the words, and the words direct the eye of the worshipper to the image. There are sometimes more complicated arrangements. In Add. 37049, for instance, a verse complaint spoken by Christ on the cross to sinful man is given a more dramatic setting. The short poem is arranged in two parallel columns with an image of the crucified Christ between them, his outstretched arms above them. The intention is clearly to give the impression that the figure of Christ is speaking directly to the reader. Sometimes the figures in the picture have *tituli* which represent their words (as in the Middle English versions of the *Vado Mori*); sometimes the narrative or dramatic scene will be accompanied by explanatory verses. Sometimes there are mnemonic or didactic visual schemes. *The Desert of Religion*,[4] a poem on the contemplative life, is carefully set out in its manuscript copies. In one, for instance, there is on one page a column of text, with beside it a second column consisting of an illustration of some contemplative in prayer to the Virgin Mary or to some pious image, accompanied by various explanatory *tituli*, while on the facing page there is an allegorical tree-diagram exhibiting the various virtues etc., with their 'branches', that are touched on in the text. A combination of didactic and structural principles of visual arrangement is found in *The Contemplacioun of Synnaris*, which is organized around the days of the week, each marked off by an appropriate devotional image.

The illustrations to our poem have some structural, as well as devotional, purpose, in that they indicate each stage of the Litany, and each group of spiritual beings, saints, etc., to which the reader's prayer is directed. However, for all the intricacy and splendour of the total effect of the page in the Talbot books, there is no attempt at complicated visual arrangements. The simple pattern of image followed by words (one often found in illustrated prayers in the Books of Hours), is that of the *Arma Christi* and similar humble vernacular devotions. The effect is like that of the *memoriae* of the saints in the Books of Hours,

---

[4] *Index of Middle English Verse*, no. 672.

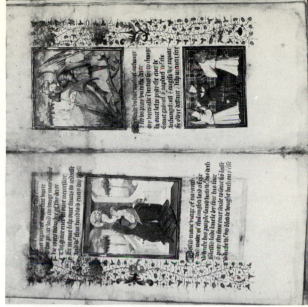

1b Fitzwilliam Museum, MS 41–1950, fos. 55^v–56.

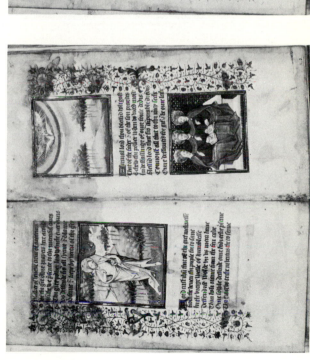

1a Fitzwilliam Museum, MS 41–1950, fos. 54^v–55.

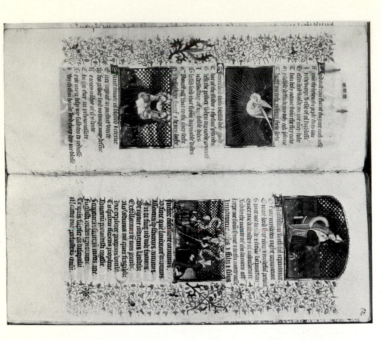

where each prayer (sometimes in verse) recalls the saint's deeds or his passion, and ends with a petition. The accompanying illustration—often of fine quality—has more artistic autonomy than the simple figures of a manuscript like Douce 1. It still certainly acts as a devotional focus for the eye of the reader, but—partly because of the demands of the traditional iconography of the scene, and partly because of the demands of the greater talent of the artists—the relationship between image and words is not so neatly reciprocal as in the *Arma Christi*. The relationship is a complementary one—each part exists in its own right, and illuminates the other—and is often rather more interesting because it is less schematic.

The arrangement differs in the four illustrated copies. The Cotton MS (cf Pl. 1d) adopts the simple and clear pattern of setting out on each page a single picture above its appropriate stanza. This allows the scribe plenty of room, and gives the artist more scope to produce a dramatic scene. The narrow, and rather long pages of the three Talbot books[5] encouraged the illustrators to squeeze more into each page. The result is a richer and more ornamental whole, but, as can be seen, it was sometimes more difficult to fit every illustration on to the same page as its appropriate stanza. Only the Blairs copy managed to achieve this throughout. There the script is very small, and it is possible to have three pictures and three stanzas on each page. This is consistently done except at the beginning and the end of the poem. On the first page (fo. 96) there are two pictures and two stanzas, but the first illustration—of the Cross and the Instruments of the Passion—is longer than the others, and adequately fills the space. This serves both to mark the importance of this scene in the devotion, and also—quite simply—to indicate the beginning of a new section in the book. On the last page (fo. 98[V]) there are again only two pictures with their verses, and here the final space after the end of stanza 16 is simply left blank.

[5] The tallest is the Fitzwilliam 'Talbot Hours' (275 × 115 mm); the 'Beauchamp Hours' is 50 mm shorter, the Blairs MS 224 × 90 mm.

As we should expect, the artists follow the traditional iconography of well-known figures or scenes (cf. our illustrations of
the Virgin and Child, of St Michael, and of two solutions to the
problem of the depiction of the Trinity which were common in
the fifteenth century). The traditional images are placed in their
appropriate places in the text—the illustrators did not devise
them specially from a careful study of the words of the poem.
Thus there is no attempt in the picture of the guardian angel to
illustrate literally that part of the stanza which prays for help
against the Seven Deadly Sins. The artists have expressed this
through the common idea of man's life spent between the
powers of a good and an evil angel.[6] The Cotton illustrator
gives the more dramatic evocation of the struggle, with the
praying figure defended by a militant good angel from the
clutches of a fearsome demon. Possibly the Beauchamp illustrator wished to avoid the repetition on the same page of an image
of a holy figure attacking a demon;[7] his conception, though
duller, catches something of the pathos of man's situation. In
the illustrations of the groups of apostles, martyrs, confessors,
and virgins, the artists have allowed several figures to be easily
identifiable by their attributes.[8] In two cases, the traditional
images of John the Baptist and St Michael have entirely banished
the patriarchs and the angels associated with them in their
stanzas. In fact, these two figures are singled out for special
mentions at the beginning of their respective stanzas, and their
images in isolation make a better focus for devotion than the
more heterogeneous groups.

The poem itself can hardly be claimed as one of the master-
pieces of the English religious lyric, but it is by no means devoid

[6] Cf. the illustrated poem on the ages of man's life in BL Add. 37049, fos.
28ᵛ–29.

[7] The Blairs artist does not seem to have been worried by this; he also has the
rather more dramatic scheme with the good angel (also on the right) defending
the praying figure by stabbing at the demon.

[8] That St George dominates the group of martyrs in the 'Beauchamp Hours'
may be as much due to the demands of his traditional image as to his
importance as Talbot's patron saint.

of interest. In the copies in the printed *Horae* it is described as 'a gloryous orysoun to the holy crosse and to all the sayntes of heuen'. It is an 'orysoun', but it is one which is based, quite closely, on the structure of the first part of the Litany of the Saints.[9] The first stanza, addressed to the Cross, does not have an equivalent in the Litany, unless it can be thought of as a devotional and visual equivalent of the opening *Kyrie*. However stanzas 2 (Father), 3 (Son), 4 (Holy Spirit), 5 (Trinity), 6 (Virgin Mary, as in the Litany *dei genitrix*, *virgo virginum*), and 7 (Michael, Gabriel, Raphael, and all holy angels and archangels) follow the order of the petitions exactly. The guardian angel to whom the whole of stanza 8 is devoted does not receive such prominent treatment in the Litany (although interestingly enough, he is mentioned in *The Golden Letany (Devotional Pieces in Verse and Prose*, p. 212): 'For þe administratioun of Sanct Micheall þe archeangell, and the haly angell þat is deput my keper...'), but with the following stanza to John the Baptist and the patriarchs and prophets we return to the Litany's order, and follow it through the groups of apostles (10),[10] martyrs (11),[11]

[9] It is not clear that the poet is following any particular use. Some of the saints listed are not frequently found in litanies, but most can be found (e.g. in the variations of Sarum, *Breviarum ad usum ... Sarum*, ed. F. Proctor and C. Wordsworth (Cambridge, 1879), pp. 250–9). 'Theophe' (l. 93) is obscure. She may represent a misreading of Cleophe (Maria Cleophe—i.e. Mary, wife of Cleopas—appears among the virgins in the litanies in the Fitzwilliam 'Talbot' and 'Beauchamp' Hours, as she does in 'a devoute prayer of al sayntis' in Bodleian MS Rawl. liturg. e. 3); this might explain the Balliol reading Cleothe. Alternatively, the form may be a corruption of Thecla (possibly in a vernacular spelling: 'saynt tecle' is in the English prose litany printed in W. Maskell, *Monumenta Ritualia Ecclesiae Anglicanae* (London, 1846–7), iii.99–110, as well as in Sarum).

[10] Barnabe, in our text, is obviously the correct reading against the 'Barnard' of some other manuscripts. Tadee (Thade) is Thaddeus, whose name appears often, though not always, in litanies.

[11] Our text's Geruais is clearly correct; the saint appears frequently (usually coupled with Prothase) in the litanies. 'Nicas' is presumably St. Nicasius, who is rare, but is found, for example, in Sarum (*feria tertia in Quadragesima*) and in a litany in a Book of Hours of the use of Rheims (Bodleian MS. Rawl. liturg. e.33). 'Nicholl', who replaces him in some manuscripts, must be an error.

and confessors (12). Stanza 13, with its list of various types of religious, is the poet's expansion of the single phrase 'omnes sancti monachi et hermite'. The virgins follow in stanza 14, and stanza 15 represents the 'omnes sancti et sancte' of the Litany.

There are relatively few English lyrics which could be called 'litanies'. Lydgate[12] has a more elaborate and rhetorical example, a series of prayers to ten saints, beginning

> Blessid Denys, of Athenys cheef sone,
> Sterre of Greece, charboncle of that contre ...

Each of the first five stanzas is a prayer to an individual saint (Denis, George, Christopher, Blaise, and Giles). After two stanzas of general prayer to all five, the second part continues with prayers to five virgins (Katherine, Margaret, Martha, Christina, and Barbara). Each verse prayer has a simple form. It recalls, as in the *memoriae* of the Books of Hours, the deeds or the passion of the saint and concludes with a request for prayer on behalf of the worshipper (the refrain lines in the first part all end with the word 'memorie'). Lydgate's poem is by no means unpleasing. The succession of single-stanza prayers suggests the movement of a litany without an over-insistent repetitive rhythm. Much less successful is a long and rather tedious verse litany[13] which occurs in two of the manuscripts containing our poem. It is much closer in form to the Litany, beginning with *Kyrieleyson*, and having as successive refrains the phrases '... miserere nobis', '... orate pro nobis', '... libera nos domine', '... te rogamus audi nos'. The order of petitions is the usual one, but unlike the other litany-lyrics, this poem continues with the second part of the Litany, into petitions for defence against the scourge of sword, hunger, and pestilence. At its best moments in this section it begins to sound a little like

---

[12] *Index*, no. 529; pr. EETS, ES 107, p. 120.
[13] *Index*, no. 1831; pr. Schulz, *HLQ* xxx (1939), 460–5. Another litany is found in the Vernon MS (*Index* no. 3027; pr. EETS, OS 98, p. 21).

Henryson's *Prayer for the Pest*. Another[14] is in the form of a carol with repeated burden:

> Prey we to the Trinyte
> And to al the holy compane
> For to bryng vs to the blys
> The wych shal neuer mysse.

It begins with a formulaic prayer, 'Jhesus, for thi holy name' (rather in the manner of our poem's invocation to the Cross), and then proceeds through the usual petitions. With surprising skill, the poet has converted the rhythms of the Litany into a song. As Professor Greene says, 'the repetitive nature of the carol form with its burden would make the words quite effective in performance, especially if a soloist sang the stanzas and an assembly the burden'. Perhaps the most attractive of the surviving 'litany-lyrics' is a little poem printed by Carleton Brown.[15] Again, the usual order of petitions is followed (in seven short stanzas); here the poet has given the repetitive form a genuinely lyrical ring, thanks largely to a simple repeated refrain, almost like the burden of a carol:

> Pray for me wyth our lady
> That Jesu on me have mercy.

The rather bald lists of parts of our poem are certainly tedious when they are read in isolation. Nevertheless the lyric as a whole has a simple and sometimes touching eloquence. The poet can handle a verse sentence; his syntax is clear, and the progression of the poem (though it is largely dictated by the shape of the Litany) is orderly and steady. At moments (as in stanza 6) his eloquence can rise to a genuine urgency. Above all, his unpretenious devotional verses make an ideal accompaniment for the images in the illustrated copies.

The version from the Beauchamp Hours which I print below

---

[14] *Index*, no. 1704; pr. Greene, *Early English Carols*, no. 309.
[15] *Index*, no. 2115; pr. Carleton Brown, *Religious Lyrics of the XVth Century*, p. 190.

(with a minimum of emendation[16]) is chosen for its interest as
a fine example of an illustrated poem rather than for its intrinsic
textual excellence. As will be seen from the textual notes, the
surviving copies show a good deal of variation. In some the
poem is incomplete,[17] and in most cases this is probably due to
accident. Once or twice, however, there is the possibility that
there may have been deliberate adaptation. The one clear case
is the first stanza of the version in Richard Hill's Commonplace
Book (MS Balliol 354), which is totally different from that in all
other copies. It may be—though it is far from certain—that the
shorter version found in the Fitzwilliam 'Talbot' Hours is an
adaptation. Here the poem is reduced to only stanzas 1–5 and
16; the consequent prominence of the final 'hol confession' lines
give the whole a distinctly more personal tone. It is no longer
a litany proper, but a simply devotional prayer to the Godhead.
It is also difficult to be sure whether the prayer to the guardian
angel (stanza 8) or the final 'hol confession' stanza (16) were
part of the original poem and have been lost in one group of
manuscripts or whether they were 'devotional' additions to the
pattern of the litany made at some stage in the transmission. It
must be said however that they fit easily and appropriately in
their places, and that there is no absolutely convincing evidence
that they were not part of the original.

The manuscripts fall into two groups. The three Talbot books
are very close indeed, and Cotton and Longleat (and its twin,
Bement) are related to them, as is Balliol 354 (though it has
more variations). The other group consists of the Steeple Ashton
MS, Sloane 1584, and the printed Horae. In some readings this

---

[16] The punctuation is editorial; i and j have been modernized.
[17] Cotton (the leaves of which are now out of order) does not have stanzas 1–2;
Sloane does not have the first five stanzas. In Steeple Ashton, stanzas 1–4 and
the first five lines of stanza 5 are missing; here the poem is found on the final
gathering now of only two leaves, and it seems very likely that two outer
leaves have been lost (the missing text would fit neatly into the first, and the
final leaf must either have been blank or have contained some other text; since
there is a gap after the final 'amen' on fo. 156ᵛ, it is clear that the version did
not have the 'hol confession' stanza).

second group seems inferior to the first. The third person singular forms in the rhymes (cf. 4, 81 *has*; 12, 101 *dures*; 23 *procedes*) might suggest a Northern origin for the poem. What is most striking, however, is the way in which the French origin of the Talbot manuscripts is reflected in the scribal spelling of these copies. The oddities are not, of course, limited to the text of this poem. The first scribe of the Fitzwilliam 'Talbot' Hours obviously had difficulty with the English spellings or letter-forms he found in his exemplar—in the rubric to the XV Oes, for instance, he writes *serye* for what was presumably *seiþe*, *ye ose* for *þese* or *þeose*, *dey* for *deþ*, and uses the Frenchified spelling *oroissounes*.[18] Similar errors can be found in the Fitzwilliam 'Beauchamp' and the Blairs manuscripts. These are interesting early examples of foreign spellings of English, of the kind we later come to expect at the hands of foreign printers—'at thy golg first eut of the hous vlysse the saynge thus'.[19] An early sixteenth-century translator of the *Calendrier des Bergers* complains about a predecessor:

Here before tyme this boke was prynted in Parys into corrupte Englysshe (and not by no Englysshe man) wherfore the bokes that were brought into Englande / the language of them was greately corrupte/imparfyte of good reason/and vnswete to parfy[t]e Englysshe men (and no meruayle) for it is vnlykely for a man of that cuntre / for to make it in good and parfyte Englysshe / as it sholde be...[20]

In the three Talbot copies, there are curious French spellings:[21] *glorieux*, *croix*, *vierge* (*virges*, *vierges*); French spellings of proper names: *Jaques*, *Marc*, *Luc*, *Gerosme*, *Marguerite*, *Barbe*, *Chartreux* (to rhyme with which the scribe apparently invented

---

[18] Further examples are given in the description by M. R. James.
[19] The title of an entertaining discussion by C. F. Bühler, *Studies in the Renaissance*, vi (1959), 223–7.
[20] *STC* 22411 (Douce K97; 1528); the Paris edition of 1503 is written in an extraordinary kind of Franco-Scots.
[21] Though not all (e.g. *parfait*) would have seemed strange to fifteenth-century English readers.

the odd form *recleux*), etc.; and French forms in *prestres*, *regnant*, and *saint* (adj.). The form *archange* (in rhyme, 43) is very remarkable, and is not attested in the dictionaries, but it is presumably a possible ME form (the *MED* records one possible case of *aunge*),[22] as is *creur* (9, found in both MS groups; cf. the ME verb *cree(n)*).

One final feature of the Fitzwilliam 'Beauchamp' text deserves note. In most cases the singular pronouns of the other copies (*prayth for me*, etc.) have become plural. The only comparable change in the other texts is a change to the plural in the last stanzas of Balliol. This virtually unique change to the plural seems to be a deliberate adaptation. It has not, however, been carried through consistently (*my vices* (45) occurs between plural pronouns, and in stanzas 13, 14, and 15 the pronouns are singular).[23] The purpose of this adaptation remains obscure. The easiest explanation is that the adapter was shifting his poem towards the more general, 'congregational' form which was common enough in religious lyrics (this certainly seems to be the reason for the switch to the plural at the end of Balliol); perhaps we might be allowed at least to entertain the more romantic possibility that he made the changes with his patron's wife in mind, so that she might include her spouse with herself in her prayers.

---

[22] Alternatively, if *archange* is a simple error for *archangel*, it may be that the original rhyme was imperfect (as in Cotton). It might be conjectured that Steeple Ashton etc. *repell(e)* is the *difficilior lectio*, but it seems to be used in a rather strained sense here.

[23] Possibly the occasional omission of pronouns in the Beauchamp text (cf. ll. 46, 63) is another result of this incomplete adaptation. It might be noted that one change (l. 55) to the plural 'vs that ar' implies a knowledge of English grammar which one suspects is superior to that possessed by the French scribe of the MS. In l. 24, *vs need most* may well be an error for *vs needis most*, but it may just possibly be a subjunctive form, or an early example of those *need* forms which (*OED*) became quite common in the sixteenth century.

Text

[Fitzwilliam Museum, Cambridge, MS 41–1950, fo. 54.]

(1)

[figure of the Cross with the Instruments of the Passion]

Glorieux croix, that wi*th* th[e] holi blod
Of Crist Jesu hallwid was by grace,
Glorieux crosse, so migthi and so good,
That all vertu by heuenli pouer ha[s],
Honowrid be thou this day yn eu*er*i place   5
In His worschip, whom Jwes crucified
With nailis thre, *and* for vs on th[e] died!

B: Blairs College.   Ball.: Balliol 354 (ed. R. Dyboski, in *Songs, Carols, etc.*,
EETS,ES 101)   C: Cotton Tiberius B iii.   L: Longleat 30.   S: Sloane 1584. SA:
Steeple Ashton.   T: 'Talbot Hours'.   W: Wynkyn de Worde print (*STC*
15947–8).

Stanza 1
L *has rubric* To þe holy cros; *in* W *headed* A gloryous orysoun to the holy
crosse and all the sayntes of heven.   1 glorieux] O gloryous W. the] TBL; thi
MS; *om.* W.   2 was] wast TB.   3 glorieux] O gloryous W.   4 has] TL; hace
B (?) W; hast MS.   6 in His worschip] To Hym be worshyp W.   7 the] TB
(?*faded*); ther MS; on the rode L; *and* for our sakes there deyed W.

(2)

[figure of God seated on a throne, giving blessing with
his right hand, holding an orb in his left]

Most blessid Fader *and* allmyghti Lord,
[fo.54ᵛ] Maker of heuene, creur of createurs,
Of Thi *g*race owre prayers here acorde,   10
Wiche we *p*resente to Thi merciful cures;
Thi gret power, Lord, whiche euer dures,
Vs deffende fro*m* all synne *and* blame,
Preserue *and* kepe by vertu of Thi [name].

Stanza 2
L *has rubric* unto þe fader (*similarly* Ball., W)   *In* Ball. *the stanza* (*which begins
the poem*) *is quite different from this version: see* Dyboski, p. 62.   10 owre]
my TBLW.   11 we] I TBLW. *p*resente] preserue W.   13 Vs] me TBLW.   14
name] TBW; by þe vertu of þi name L; grace MS.

(3)
[figure of Christ; *see Pl. 1a*]

Lord Crist Jesu, that of Thi gret meknesse   15
From the heuen thi puple for to saue
In the vierge, welle of [al] humblesse,
[Descende] wolde, [o]n vs merci haue;
Thin holi name from the feri cave
Oure sowle deffende, oure [b]odi eeke preserue;   20
Thi grace vs teche in vertus the to serue.

Stanza 3
L *has rubric* Unto þe sone (*similarly* Ball., W). 15 Lord Crist Jesu]
Lord Jhesu Crist W; O Lord Jhesu Crist that by thi gret grace an meknes Ball.
16 From the] Com fro the L; Com from hevyn Ball.   17 vierge] virgyn L; vergyn
Ball.; in a virgin W. al] TBC Ball.W; *om.* MS. humblesse] humblenesse L;
humblenes W.   18 descende] C; dyscende W; Dessend thou woldeste and Ball.;
descendest TB; deffendist MS; defendiste L. on] TBW; vn MS. vs] me TBC (?) LW.
have] to have W.   19 name] name, lorde W. feri] firy TB; Souereyn Lord of
the ever I crave Ball.   20 oure ... oure] my ... my TBCLBall.W. deffende]
to defende Ball. bodi] TBCLBall.W; hodi MS. eeke] also Ball.   21 in vertus ...
serue] in vertu *and* þe to serue L.; vertue W.

(4)
[figure of the Holy Spirit above a landscape; *see Pl. 1a*]

[fo. 55] Eternal Lord, Thou blessid Holi Gost,
That of the Fader *and* of the Son procedes,
Schew Thi power when vs need most
In deffassinge of oure foule dedis;   25
Blessid Lord, that from dampnable dredis
Conuoist all that to Thi mercy seche,
Oure deffautis forgif *and* be oure leche.

Stanza 4
L *has rubric* Unto the holy gooste (*similarly* Ball., W). 23 *and* of the Son] *and*
the son B; and sone L Ball.W   24 vs need] my ne(e)de is TBLC; me nedith
Ball.; I nede moost W.   25 oure] my TBC; all my W.   26 dredis] deedis L;
dedes Ball.   27 Conuoist] conueyest W; þat conveyest all them þat Ball.;
Counsceyl L.   28 oure ... oure] my ... my TBCLW; my sowle leche Ball.

(5)

[figure of the Trinity; see Pl. 1a]

[fo.55ᵛ]   Saint Trinite, all blessid and eterne,
Euer regnant in parfait vnite,   30
Whos pouer, Lord, no tonge may discerne
Ne joies nombre of Thy deite;
Thi grace euer in oure neccessite
Be in oure help oure fautis to redresse,
And with Thin hand, Lord, euery day [vs] blesse.   35

Stanza 5
L *has rubric* Unto þe trinite (*similarly* Ball., W).   29 Saint] Holy Ball. W. all]
om. Ball.   30 regnant] regnat C; regnyng LBall.; regnynge W (*STC 15947*
renynge).   31 Lord] *om.* L; hygh W. tonge] thynk Ball.   32 Ne joies] Ne the
joyes Ball.; nor W. deite] holy deyte W; dignite Ball.   33 oure] ych TB; eche
CLBall.W.   34 oure ... oure] my(n) ... my TBCLWSA; my socowr, my
Ball.   35 Thin hand Lord] þi holi hand euere SA; thy holy hande euery W.
vs] me TBCLBall.; *om.* SA, MS.

(6)

[figure of the Virgin Mary suckling her child; see Pl. 1b]

Blessid Marie, vierge of Nazareth,
And moder of thalmighti lord of grace
Whiche his peuple sauid hath with His deth
[From the peines of thinfernal place].
Blessed ladi, knele byfore His face,   40
And pray thi sone oure soule to saue from losse,
Whiche with His blod He bought hath on þe crosse.

Stanza 6
L *has rubric* Unto our lady seynt mary ((Vn) to our lady WSABall.)   36 Blessid
Marie] Blessid lady Ball.; Blessed lord (*marked for deletion*) Mari SA. vierge]
vierge] virgyn LBall. W; virgine SA; virgyne S.   37 of thalmighti] of almyȝty
(*variously spelt*) LCB; to þe myghte SA; to the myghty SW.   38 Whiche] that
SASW. with] by Ball. deth] graceʹ C.   39 *om.* MS (*supplied from B; so other
MSS*).   40 Blessid] Now blessyd SASW. byfore] afore L; tofore Ball.   41 pray
thi sone] pray to hym SASW. oure] my BLCSAW. soule...losse] to kepe me
from losse Ball.   42 blod he bought hath on] blode bought vs on LBall.; blod
hath bought vs on SASW; (?) me boght hath C (*faded*).

(7)

[figure of St Michael killing a fiend; *see Pl. 1b*]

[fo. 56]   Deffende vs, Saint Michael archange,
            And for vs pray vnto the deite,
            My vices alle *in* vertus for to change;   45
            In oure helpe [we] pray the euer be;
            Saint Gabriel *and* Raphael wi*th* the—
            Archangels all *and* angels we requere
            Be owre deffence *and* help in eueri fere.

Stanza 7
L *has rubric* Unto seynt michel archaungel (to þe angels SA; *similarly*
WBall.)   43 vs] me BLC; *om.* SAS. archange] archa(u)ngel CSALW   44 vs]
me BLBall.; for me repete SAW.   45 vertus] vertue L. for to change] for to
changes Ball.; to repell(e) SAW.   46 In] And in SAW. oure] my(n) BCSAW.
we] I BCSA; *om.* MS. pray the ever be] That þou my helpe I praye þe ever be
L; the beseche to be SAW; *and* þat you my helpers I pray you euer be Ball.   48
we] I CBall. SAW requere] pray(e) SAW. 49 owre] my BCLSAW; To be my
Ball. And help in eueri fere] and help me in L; and kepe me nyght and day SA.

(8)

[figure of a man between a good angel and a bad; *see Pl. 1b*]

[fo. 56ᵛ]   Saint angel, to wha*m* puissa*n*ce divine   50
            Vs geuyn has for to kepe *and* guyde,
            We the byseche, wi*th* all [th]ordres nyne,
            Help vs resist agayn ire, slouthe, *and* pride,
            And all the seuyn, that no*n* of tham abide
            In vs that ar of tender mater worght,   55
            For streng[t]h of flesche ys yoldin wi*th* a thoght.

Stanza 8
L *has rubric* Unto my gode aungell (Vnto þe propre angell Ball. *This stanza
is not found in all of the (more or less) complete versions*; W, SA, S *do not
have it.)*   50 saint] holy Ball.   51 Vs] me BLC; Is geven for Ball. for to kepe
and guyde] to kepe and to gide L; *and* me gwide Ball.   52 We] I BLCBall.
thordres] B; the ordres C; þe orderis L; ordres MS; with þe ordres Ball.   53
vs] me BLC; to help me Ball. agayn] *om.* Ball.   54 all the seuyn] all seuen L;
And of all seven Ball. tham] hem L; that non may Ball.   55 vs that ar] me that
am BLCBall.   56 strength] BL; strengh MS; fraylnes Ball.

(9)

[figure of St John the Baptist, with lamb and book, in a rocky landscape]

Blessid Jhon, that callid art Baptist,
Of Cristis lawe apreuid first wetenes,
Pray [t]o that Lord, whiche in thi moder ch[y]st
Of grace the inspirid *with* swetnesse,   60
Oure deffautes [with] his merci redresse;
Al patriarkis *and* saint prophetis ecke
Prayeth al so, humbly [we] you beseeke.

Stanza 9
L *has rubric* Unto Seynt John Baptist (*similarly* Ball.); To the patryarks SA (*similarly* SW).   57 that callid art] þat callyd is þe SA (*similarly* W); was Baptyst S.   58 apreuid first wetenes] preued LBall.; þat bare þe fyrst wytnes SA (*similarly* SW).   59 to] CSASW; tho BMS. that Lord] þe lord SA. whiche in] within LBall. thi] þe SA. chyst] BLSSAW; chest Ball.MS   60 the inspirid] t[h]e hath enspyred SA (similarly SW); þe enspire with switnesse L.   61 Oure] my BLCSASWBall. deffautes] defautes all SASW. with] BLBall.SASW; whiche MS. redresse] *om.* L; to dresse Ball.   62 Al] And Ball. saint] BL; (?) saintys C; *om.* SABall.W.   63 Prayeth ...] Pray you for me I you humbli beseche SAW (*STC* 15948 beseke); pray ye for me S; pray for me also mekly I you beseke Ball. we] I BLBall. SASW; *om.* C. (? *faded*), MS.

(10)

[fo. 57]   [figure of a group of apostles]

Petre apostle *and* doctor Paule we praye,
Phelip, Jacob, *and* Bartholomee,   65
Andrew, Jaques, Jhon, *and* Thomas ay,
Symon, Jude, Mathias, Mathie,
Barnabe, Marc, Luc, and Saint Tadee,
Wyth eueryche apostle *and* euaungelist—
Prayth for vs to the Lord of all, Crist.   70

Stanza 10
L *has rubric* Unto all the apostelis; to the apostles S (*similarly* WSABall.).   64 we] I BLCBall. SASW.   65 Phelip, Jacob] Philyp and Jacob SA (*similarly* S). and Bartholomee] et Bartholomew C; et sant Bartylmewe SA; and saynt

Bartylmewe W; and sant Bartholomew S. 66–8 Andrew ... Tadee] *texts diverge*: SA *has*

> Symon, Jude, and Thomas of Inde aye,
> Mathi, James, Thade, *and* holi Andrew,
> Barnard, Luke, Marke, *and* eke Sant Mathew

(*similarly* S, W (*with the insertion of* John *after* Jude)). Mathias, Mathie] Mathew *and* Mathie Ball. 68 Tadee] Thadee BL; Thadde Ball. 69 eueryche] ech(e) SASW. 70 Prayth for vs to] me B; my L; Pray for me Ball.; Pray to that Lord for in you is all my trist SA (*similarly* SW). Crist] BMS;(?) cryst, *possibly* tryst C (*faded*); trist(e), tryst LBall.SASW.

(11)
[figure of a group of martyrs]

[fo. 57ᵛ]   Steuyn, George, Cristofre, *and* Clement,
             Denis, Geruais, Laura*n*s, *and* Fabyan,
             Ni[c]as, Moris, Vrban, *and* Vincent,
             Eustace, Line, Thomas, Sebastian,
             Cornel, Sixte, Cosme *and* Damian,   75
             Victor, Lambart, oure sy*n*nis to defface
             Al martris praye vnto the Lord of *grace.*

Stanza 11
L *has rubric* Unto all martires; To the martyres S (*similarly* WSABall.). 72 Geruais] Jeruase L; Seruis SA; (?) Seruies S; Serueys W. 73 Nicas] BC(?); Nigas MS; Nicoll SA (*similarly* SW); Albon Ball. 74 Sebastian] and Sebastian SAS. 75 Cornel] Cornelis SABall.; Cornely W. 76 oure] my BLCBall.SASW. 77 Al] And all Ball. vnto] to Ball. the] thi C. of] for Ball.; All pray for me to thy Lordes grace SA (that Lordes grace SW).

(12)
[figure of a group of confessors]

             Siluester, Leo Marte[n], Benedigh[t],
             Gregoire, Austin, *and* Saint Nicholas,
             Germain, Julian that [herbers] by nyght,   80
             Ambros, Antoni that gret pouer has,
             Eduard, Lenard, Philbert, Thomas,
             Dunston, Gerosme, *with* al *c*onfessours,
             Prayght for [vs] to the Lord of all cures.

Stanza 12
L *has rubric* Unto all confessours; to the confessores S (*similarly*
WSABall.). 78 Marten] Marter MS. Benedight] B; Benedicte LBall.; Bene-
digh MS. 78–81 Siluester... has] *texts diverge*: SA *has*

> Sylves*t*er, Leo, Benedicte, and M*a*rtyn,
> Gregori, German, and Sant Nicholas,
> Julian thameur, and Sant Austyng,
> Ambrose, Antony, and Bonyface.

(*similarly* W, S (*with correct reading* Julyan thamener)). 80 herbers] BC; herbor-
neth L; harboreth at Ball.; brebris MS. 81 Antoni] MS. *possibly* Antoin. 82
Philbert] Philibert LBall.; Gilbert SASW. Thomas] *and* Bonefas Ball. Gerosme]
Jerone SAW. with] *and* Ball. 84 vs] vs *or* me *om.* MS; praieth for me B (*similarly*
LC); pray for me SAS; pray for us Ball. cures] socours SASW; Lord all owres
Ball.

(13)

[fo. 58]   [figure of a group of monks and other religious]

> Conuens of monks, can*o*ns, *and* Chartreux,   85
> Celestines, freres, and p*r*estres all,
> Palmers, pilgrems, hermites, *and* recleux,
> That stonde in g*r*ace holly here I calle;
> On yowre knees byfore owre Lord falle,
> With p*r*ayers help from synne me to deffe*n*de,   90
> That vnto blisse sewrly my sawle assende.

Stanza 13
L *has rubric* Unto all religious; Vnto all holy monkis and erimitis Ball.; to þe
orders SA (*similarly* SW). 85 Conuens] couentis LBall.; couentes SASW.
Chartreux] (?) Chartrus C; Charterhouses L; Charterhows Ball.; Charter*h*ous
SAW; channos of charthous S. 86 prestres] holi prestes SASW. 87 recleux]
(?) reclus C; recluses L; religious SAW; all religius Ball. 88 stonde] stondes
C (*similarly* SAW); standet S. in grace] in Gods grace SAW. holly] holi SA;
holy W; hole Ball. here I] to you I Ball. 89 On] upon SASW. byfore] afore
SASW. Lord] lady L. falle] to fall Ball.; ye falle SAS. 90 help] help me Ball.
deffende to þe fende C; L *omits* to. 91 vnto] into Ball. sewrly] MS *possibly*
(?) sewtly. SA *has* ... blys my soule may vp assend (*similarly* SW).

(14)

[figure of a group of female saints]

[fo. 58ᵛ] Blessed and meek Maudalaine Marie,
              Katherine, Anne, Marth, *and* Appoline,

Marguerite, Agath, with Theophe,
Egyptian, Anastase, Cristine,
Genoveve, Cicile, Barbe, Marine,   95
Elain, Agnes, Suzane, Bride, *and* Luce,
Prayeth for me in [y]owre most hum̃ble vce.

Stanza 14
L *has rubric* Unto all seyntes of wommen; To holy women and virgins SAW;
To the virgyns S (*similarly* Ball.).   92 Maudalaine Marie] Mari Mawdeleyne
SASW.   94 Margret, Agatha, Angnes and Elyne SA (*similarly* SW). Theophe]
Cleothe Ball.   95 Egyptian] Egypcian BLSA. Cristine] and Cristine SASW
Ball.   96 Cicile] Cecilie Ball. Barbe] MS *possibly* Berbe; Barbe BC(?); Barbare
L; Barbera Ball.; T(h)eodose and Marine SASW.   97 Barbara, Susan, Brygyt
and Luce SASW.   98 prayeth] pray SAW; Pray for me with entire humylitie
Ball. yowre] owre MS.

(15)

[figure of a group of saints]

Apostles, all martris *and* confesseures,
Euaungelistes, virges *and* innocens,   100
Praieth the Lord whos power ever dures
Of his grace forgif myn offens,
My sawle kepe from sy[n]ful pestilens,
And to his blisse that is celestial
Of mercy bring where lyf is eternal.   105

Stanza 15
L *has rubric* Unto all halowes; To all santes SA (*similarly* SWBall.).   99 all
martris] martyrs SASWBall. confesseures] confessours all SAS; confessour all
W.   100 virges *and* innocens] innocentes and virgins SASW.   101–2 SA *has*

Pray to that Lord wych is eternal
To pardon me as [he] al god begyns

(*similarly* SW).   101 the] that Ball. dures] indures Ball.   102 forgif myn offens]
to forgeve vs owr offens Ball.   103–5 SA *has*

And keyp my sal from al mortal syn[s],·
And in is blys, wyche is omnipotent,
He grant me grace for to be parmanen[t]

(*similarly* SW).   103 my sawle] owr sowles Ball. synful] symful MS; syn *and*
Ball.

(16)

[supplied from Fitzwilliam 'Talbot Hours', MS 40–1950, fo. 82]
[figure of scene of confession; *see Pl. 1c*]

[Hol co*n*fession with ful repentance
Of my mysdedes right reparacion
Grant, Lord, wit*h* *m*ercy *and* medeful pena*n*ce,
Space me tam*e*nde, *and* from da*m*pacion
Euer me deffende, *and* al tribulacion;   110
And for the merite of thi saintes all
Kepe me from synne, *and* to thi mercy calle.]

Stanza 16
Found also in BCLBall.   106 hol] Pray for hole Ball. with] and L.   107 of my]
And of owr Ball.   108 Lord with mercy] Lord mercy L. and … penance] *and*
I do penance Ball.   109 Space me tam*e*nde] spare me to amend L; Spare vs to
amend Ball.   110 Euer … *and* al] vs deffend from all Ball.   111 merite] meritis
Ball. thi] these L.

Arbor Caritatis

———————— ◆ ————————

PETER DRONKE

An eloquent chapter in Huizinga's *The Waning of the Middle Ages* is entitled 'Symbolism in its Decline'. Symbolism dwindled—into allegory:

Symbolism expresses a mysterious connection between two ideas, allegory gives a visible form to the conception of such a connection. Symbolism is a very profound function of the mind, allegory is a superficial one. ... The force of the symbol is easily lost in the allegory. ... Allegory seldom loses an air of elderliness and pedantry. Still, the use of it supplied a very earnest craving of the medieval mind.

In the later Middle Ages the decline of [the symbolic] mode of thought had already long set in. ... Symbolism was, in fact, played out.[1]

Huizinga's formulations clearly betray their descent from Goethe's sharp distinction between symbol and allegory, and reflect exactly Goethe's value-judgement.[2] Allegory is seen as

For reasons of space, the notes and references are strictly limited. Most of the texts discussed in the course of the essay (from Hermas to Pico) have a large secondary literature devoted to them, including much on which I should have liked to comment. Generally, however, I have referred only to secondary sources that are of special importance to my argument, or that offer extensive further bibliography in their subject.

[1] Penguin edn. (Harmondsworth, 1955), pp. 206–10. (The original Dutch edition, *Herfsttijd der Middeleeuwen*, was published in Haarlem, 1919; the first English version, *The Waning of the Middle Ages*, adapted and revised by the author, in London, 1924.)

[2] *Maximen und Reflexionen*, 749–50 (*Goethes Werke, Hamburger Ausgabe* (5th impr., 1963), xii.470–1). Like Goethe in these maxims, Huizinga associates symbolism with *Idee*, allegory with *Begriff* ('conception'). I have discussed Goethe's dicta in *Fabula* (Leyden–Cologne, 1974), pp. 120–2.

the anaemic, intellectually limited, unpoetic poor relation of symbolism.

In 1924, the year *The Waning of the Middle Ages* was published, Walter Benjamin was writing his *Ursprung des deutschen Trauerspiels*; it appeared three years later. In order to evaluate historically the overriding use of allegory in German baroque tragedy, Benjamin began by challenging the notion and the judgement that had remained virtual dogma since Goethe. Benjamin wanted to comprehend allegory rather than disparage it—to see it as a poetic language with its own existential validity:

Allegory ... is not a game with images, manipulating them, but a mode of expression, in the way language is expression, indeed in the way writing is.

Its antinomies must be analysed dialectically. ... Each person, each thing, each condition can signify any other. This possibility implies that the profane world ... is characterized as a world whose detailed features are not all that important. ... And yet ... as the necessary means of signifying and pointing to something other, these features win a power which allows them to appear incommensurable with profane objects, raises them to a higher plane, and can even sanctify them.[3]

Where Huizinga had seen as 'the general and essential tendency of the spirit of the expiring Middle Ages, that of accentuating every detail, of developing every thought and every image to the end, of giving concrete form to every concept of the mind',[4] Benjamin—here thinking primarily of baroque rather than late medieval allegory—stresses an element of fluidity and unpredictability:

Around the figural centre ... the whole mass of emblems groups itself. They seem capricious in their ordering: 'The disordered court'—the title of a Spanish tragedy—could be taken as indicating the scheme of allegory. The laws of this court are 'scattering' and 'gathering'. Things are gathered according to their signification; the lack of concern for their reality scatters them again. The disorder of

[3] W. Benjamin, *Ursprung des deutschen Trauerspiels* (Suhrkamp Taschenbuch, Frankfurt a. M., 1972), pp. 178, 193. On the period of composition, see ibid., p. 273.   [4] *The Waning*, pp. 278–9.

the allegorical scenery corresponds to that of the boudoir of the gallant.[5]

It is this 'disorder of the allegorical scenery' that I should like to examine more closely, by way of a motif particularly cherished in the later Middle Ages: the *arbor caritatis*. Here is a motif where one might expect an excess of schematization, 'of accentuating every detail, of developing every thought ... to the end', and indeed in some of the thirteenth- and fourteenth-century trees of love, both sacred and profane, this can be found, relentlessly. Yet there was also the possibility of disordered—or not rigidly ordered—scenery, and I believe that some of the finest poets and prose-writers saw this as a creative possibility and chose it consciously. For them Goethe's dichotomy between symbol and allegory was by no means necessary: what Goethe himself called 'true symbolism'—'the living momentary revelation of what is unanalysable'[6]—could and did occur in the midst of their allegories.

In the twelfth century Bernard Silvestris, discussing *figura* and *involucrum*, makes no demarcation between the realm of hidden inner meaning—all that is evocative, enigmatic, the dark utterances of the Sibyl—and that of explicitly distinguishable meanings, the realm of the allegorists.[7] For Bernard these were complementary and continuous—in his theory as in his own poetry. For him *involucrum* comprehended the whole spectrum of explicit and implicit meaning, allegory and symbol, concept and image. It is the interplay of these, and the continuities between them, that deserve special attention as we turn to some trees of love.

For English readers, perhaps the best-known instance is the tree of charity in *Piers Plowman*;[8] I shall take this as a point of

---

[5] *Ursprung*, p. 210.
[6] *Maximen und Reflexionen*, 752 (*Goethes Werke*, loc. cit.).
[7] See *Fabula*, pp. 119–26.
[8] *Piers Plowman: The B Version*, ed. George Kane and E. Talbot Donaldson (London, 1975). All my Langland citations are from this edition. For an account of the principal recent discussions of Langland's tree, see David Aers, *Piers*

departure for my reflections. I shall not be concerned here with
the place of Langland's tree in the vibrating web of the whole
poem. Every absorbed reader is aware of the seemingly unpre-
meditated interplay of vegetal notions throughout the poem,
and the constant interplay of echoes between the physical
and the spiritual worlds. There is the planting of seeds—whether
of corn or of virtues; the ripening of crops—of apples or of
humanity; the incursion of weeds and *wormes of synne*; the
hastening of the harvest of the world, which gives the poem its
urgency. I shall concentrate on certain fluctuations between the
abstract and the dramatic within the image of the tree itself.

As Passus XVI opens, the figure Anima explains to the poet-
dreamer that charity is a most steadfast tree; its root is mercy,
its trunk, pity. The next lines show Langland's characteristic
movement through different degrees of abstraction and reality,
different kinds of causal nexus: on the tree of charity, the leaves
are loyal words, the law of Holy Church; the blossoms are
gently acquiescent speech and looks; the tree is called patience
and the poor who are simple of heart; its fruit is charity, which
grows there through God and good men. Words, law, looks,
patience, poor people, charity, God, good men—all these are
conjoined, in effortless transitions, to convey aspects of the tree.

Next, the tree becomes microcosmic: it grows in a garden
fashioned by God—the human being. The root is of that stock
(the poet leaves open whether *þat stokke* is the human trunk or
the human race). The arbour of the garden is the heart, and the
land must be raked and weeded by free will—*liberum arbitrium*—under Piers Plowman. Later in the vision, *liberum
arbitrium* is interpreted as the Holy Ghost, active in human
beings as their principle of freedom: free will, proceeding from
the Father and the Son, *is þe holy goost of alle*[9]—a daring as

Plowman and Christian Allegory (London, 1975), pp. 79–109; to Aers's
bibliography I would add especially Morton W. Bloomfield, 'Piers Plowman
and the Three Grades of Chastity', *Anglia*, lxxvi (1958), 245–53; Pietro Cali,
Allegory and Vision in Dante and Langland (Cork, 1971), pp. 135–43.

[9] XVI.224. Whilst Donaldson (*Piers Plowman: The C-Text and Its Poet* (New
Haven, 1949), p. 189) quotes an extremely pertinent passage from Bernard of

well as difficult conception. Piers yields even less to a simple
allegoresis, yet he evokes an ideal of human life, whether as
realized by Christ in his time on earth, by Peter in his role as
trustee of salvation, or by any man or woman, at any time, in
so far as they incarnate that ideal form.

Now follows the dream within the vision, the *louedreem*, as
Langland calls it (20). Here Piers shows the dreamer the tree
supported by three props, so that it may stand upright against
the winds. The emissary of the first wind, the world, is
covetousness, who creeps among the leaves. Piers beats him
down with the first prop—the power of God the Father. The
second corrosive wind, carnality, Piers beats down with the
second prop, the wisdom of God, till he sees the tree to some
extent ripen and fill with fruit. Then the fiend tries to destroy
the fruit, shaking the tree's root and throwing up to the top
unkind neighbours, strife-brewing backbiters, and others, as if
they were so many sticks aimed at bringing fruit down. He sets
a ladder of lies against the tree, to fetch away Piers's flowers.
Piers's lieutenant, *liberum arbitrium*, hinders him for a while,
and at last, against a concerted attack, uses the third prop as a
weapon.

Once more these brief indications will suggest the strange
spectrum of realities: the wind of the world, creeping covetousness, human backbiters flung up at the tree, the fiend's ladder
of lies, the lieutenant *liberum arbitrium*, the three divine props.
The dreamer, his eyes fascinated by those props, questions
further, and Piers seems to give a purposely tantalizing reply:
I shall tell you at once, he says, what this tree is called. The
ground where it grows is called goodness. And I've told you the
name of the tree. It means the Trinity. As Piers looks at him
sharply, the dreamer stops himself from asking more about this.

Clairvaux, who sees free will as the aspect of man by which he is *imago dei*,
Langland's wording—*fre wille of hope* / Spiritus procedens a patre & filio
&c, / *Which is þe holy goost of alle, and alle is but o god*—suggests something
more radical: not an image of God but a 'human form divine', for which the
essential parallel, I believe, is to be found less in Bernard than in Joachim (see
esp. the passage from the *Concordia* cited in n. 19 below).

Yet through Piers's half-refusal to answer, alluding to his earlier
answer, the identity of the tree in the *louedreem* with that in the
framing vision is established.

From now on the transformations of concepts and images
become swifter and more insistent. The tree has three fruits: the
lowest, matrimony; the second, near the top, continence (later
called widowhood); the third, at the summit, maidenhood. The
dreamer asks Piers to pull down an apple for him, and Piers—like
the fiend previously—flings something to the top of the tree and
also shakes the tree. All its three fruits begin to cry lamentably.
As the fruits drop, they reveal themselves as human beings of
the pre-Christian world; they are gathered by the devil and
hoarded in limbo. Piers, in sheer rage at this, takes up *filius*—the
second prop—to hit out at the devil and get his fruit back. At
that moment *spiritus sanctus* spoke in Gabriel's mouth: *filius*
must dwell in Mary's chamber till the fruit of Piers flowers and
ripens; Jesus will have to joust, by judgement of arms, to carry
off Piers's fruit, if he wins his tourney against the fiend.

The dreamer's quest for the meaning of charity is crowned
by this enigmatic scene. To understand the charity that is
consummated in the incarnation and redemption—to win an
apple of the tree—it would appear, he must first understand
the condition of dying for which that charity is a remedy, he
must hear the death-cry of the fruits, and Piers must make the
fruits fall just as the devil does—though with another end in
view.

Later the poet, awake again, meets Abraham, or meets faith,
a herald of Abraham's house (this ambiguity is sustained also
in later Passus). The herald is looking for a knight whose blazon
is three equal persons in one limb. He explains: that there can
be three such persons, who none the less are one, is shown in
the threefold human condition—marriage, widowhood, and
virginity—which 'was taken out of one man', and which beto-
kens, respectively, Father, Son, and Spirit. Here, that is, the
conception of higher and lower fruits—marriage as the lowest,
virginity as the highest—which Piers, in conformity with ascetic

writers, had propounded earlier, is corrected: now each of the
three states signifies one of the three equal divine persons.

It is clear that these shifts and fluctuations are deliberate, that
the 'disordered scenery' was Langland's poetic choice. Moreover,
as I hope to indicate, the most memorable allegoric trees had
always been presented with the help of disordered scenery. The
processes of transformation—often as unpredictable, astound-
ing, or bizarre as some of the scene-changes required in Benjamin's baroque tragedies—had been, at least since the second
century AD, recurring features in the visionary tradition. What
we have in Langland, I believe, is less a toleration of inconsist-
encies than a number of instinctive contraventions of the norms
of allegoresis, in order to achieve a richness not fully explicable,
a whole that is greater than the sum of its explicit parts. It is the
new links—the logically unforeseeable ones—that are poetically
among the most profound. Thus for instance the transition from
the violent gesture of Piers, hitting out at the fiend with the
prop *filius* (by the will and generosity of Father and Spirit)—*To
go robbe þat Rageman and reue þe fruyt fro hym* (89)—to the
serene words

> And þanne spak *spiritus sanctus* in Gabrielis mouþe...

brings about a poetic fusion—fury and love, the divine prop
and the divine child, the human fruit of love, the theft that is
an act of love, even (if we insist on the bizarre) the third prop
of the tree becoming the angel's words—such as no purely
allegorical juxtaposition could have achieved. And it is not a
confusion but a flash of light.

Again, the comparison of the Son to the widow (or state of
widowhood)—itself a daring, original thought—is made luminous by the biblical text that is not so much a justification of
the likeness as a moving intuition, bringing disparate realms of
sorrow together for the first time:

> The sone, if I dorste seye, resembleþ wel þe widewe:
> *Deus meus, deus meus, ut quid dereliquisti me?*
>
>   (213–14)

None of the figurative elements that went to form these scenes in Langland is wholly new. An allegorical tree of charity is already used as something familiar by Augustine in his commentary on the first Epistle of John:

God finds the hearts of mankind like a field. .... There he wants to plant the tree: charity.

Let each of us test our action, to see whether it emanates from the vein of charity, whether, from the root of love, boughs of good works sprout forth.

Love and do what you will. .... If the root of love is within, nothing but what is good can come from that root.[10]

Again, the image of a tree with three fruits—marriage, widowhood, and virginity—had been widely expounded and presented pictorially, especially in the treatise *Speculum virginum*.[11] The twelfth and thirteenth centuries had seen the growth of a veritable forest of trees of virtues and trees of vices. From the late thirteenth century onwards, we find frequent homiletic and visual use of an *Arbor amoris*[12]—a tree of divine love, though there is also a profane counterpart, a tree of courtly love, in the *Romans du Vergier et de l'Arbre d'Amors*.[13]

[10] PL 35. 1993, 2020, 2033:

Quasi agrum invenit [deus] corda hominum ... Plantare ibi vult arborem: charitatem.

Opus ergo suum probet unusquisque nostrum, utrum de vena charitatis emanet, utrum de radice dilectionis rami bonorum operum pullulent.

Dilige, et quod vis fac ... radix sit intus dilectionis, non potest de ista radice nisi bonum existere.

Langland scholars hitherto have not, as far as I can discover, noted these vital passages.

[11] The *Speculum virginum* was composed c.1130–40 and diffused in nearly sixty MSS, including those of a Dutch and a Swedish translation. See esp. E. S. Greenhill, *Die geistigen Voraussetzungen der Bilderreihe des Speculum virginum* (Münster, 1962); Matthäus Bernards, *Speculum virginum* (Cologne–Graz, 1955); on Patristic sources for the three fruits of the tree, Bernards, pp. 40–4.

[12] *Arbor amoris / Der Minnebaum*, ed. Urs Kamber (Berlin, 1964). The *Arbor amoris* was popular in various Latin redactions from 1300 onwards, and later also in German ones. On some earlier, secular analogues in medieval German poetry, see H. J. Weigand, 'Arbor amoris', in *Essays on European Literature in Honor of Liselotte Dieckmann* (St. Louis, 1972), pp. 167–77.

[13] Ed. A. Långfors, *Neuphilologische Mitteilungen*, xxix (1928), 3–33. Långfors

The *Arbor amoris* gives a mystical interpretation of the tree
that Nebuchadnezzar saw in his dream (Daniel 4):

What is this tree if not the love of God? God planted his love at the
centre of the earth, wanting it to grow luxuriantly on every side. The
centre of the earth is the heart of man, from which the power both
of earthly and of heavenly action proceeds. And as the tree begins
on earth and, growing, tends heavenwards, so the love of God,
leaving earthly things, always seeks the heavenly.[14]

The beautiful, healing leaves are divine words; the fruit is
indescribable and unimaginable: the joy of divine union.

The courtly *Arbre d'Amors* was likewise planted in the
orchard of the human heart. Its root is *conoissance*, it is watered
by *volentés*; the branches are *loiautés*, *largesce*, *proësce*, and
courtoisie, and from each branch spring little twigs of further
qualities. The leaves trembling in the wind are the talk of
beloved and lover, the flowers are valorous deeds, the fruits,
honour and excellence. The crown of the tree is *mesure*—with
that, love becomes perfect.

As Langland's tree is threatened by *vnkynde
Neighebores, / Bakbiteris brewecheste, brawleris and chideris*,[15]
this *Arbre d'Amors* is attacked by all who are loveless or who
betray love:

> I vendront et mari jalous
> Et mesdisant et envious,
> Jangleour et losengeour,
> Cordelier et preechour,
> O fausses begines vendront,
> Et ipocrites i seront...[16]

Yet after the battles waged against these by true lovers, the tree
remains intact, victorious.

(p. 4) mentions the existence of two other poems on the same subject; I would
also signal the somewhat later ballade, 'J'ay ung arbre de la plante
d'amours / Enraciné en mon cueur proprement', which is generally printed in
the older editions of François Villon among the 'poésies attribuées' (though
without any serious grounds for the attribution).

[14] Ed. cit., p. 44.   [15] XVI.42–3.   [16] Ed. cit., pp. 19–20.

Such tree-allegories, however elaborate in their detail, are imaginatively simple compared with Langland's. And that there had been many crudely didactic tree-allegories in the century before *Piers Plowman* is undeniable. In this period, the art of preaching itself came to be likened to a tree. *Praedicare est arborizare*: the well-grown sermon must be rooted in a theme, that flourishes in the trunk of a biblical *auctoritas*, and thence grows into its branches and twigs: the divisions and subdivisions whereby the preacher extends his subject-matter.[17]

Yet subtler and more complex uses of the tree for image or analogy existed, especially in certain contexts where it came to be a figure of the Trinity. Joachim of Fiore, in the late twelfth century, depicted a tree of the Trinity in his *Liber figurarum*;[18] in his writings, on the other hand, he tends to speak rather of three trees growing each out of the other. In his *Concordia* he explains that this threefold tree means first the Trinity, and

---

[17] Urs Kamber, *Arbor amoris*, p. 73 (the phrase *praedicare est arborizare* itself, however, appears not to occur before the fifteenth century). The structural–homiletic use of a tree is also strikingly exemplifed in such a text as the prologue of Ubertino da Casale's *Arbor Vitae Crucifixae Iesu*, completed in 1305 and widely influential thereafter: see the facs. of the Venice 1485 edition, with introduction and bibliography by Charles T. Davis (Torino, 1961), fo.a iii.

An interesting range of material relating to allegorical trees is assembled by Leo Spitzer, *Essays in Historical Semantics* (New York, 1948), pp. 67–133, and by E. S. Greenhill, 'The Child in the Tree', *Traditio*, x (1954), 323–71. On the earlier Christian traditions, the bibliographies in the (collaborative) article 'Baum' in *Reallexikon für Antike und Christentum*, ii (1954), 1–34, in J. Flemming's article 'Baum, Bäume' in *Lexikon der christlichen Ikonographie*, i (1968), 258–68, and most recently in Manfred Lurker's *Der Baum in Glauben und Kunst* (2nd edn., Baden-Baden, 1976), pp. 163–70, are indispensable.

[18] The attribution of the *Liber figurarum* to Joachim himself has been cogently argued by M. Reeves and B. Hirsch-Reich, *The Figurae of Joachim of Fiore* (Oxford, 1972). The use of tree-imagery in connection with the Trinity can be found already at the beginnings of Christian Latin poetry, in Marius Victorinus' *Hymnus de Trinitate*, III. 87–90:

Semen,
Arbor,
Fructus,
          O beata trinitas.

(Ed. P. Henry and P. Hadot, Sources chrétiennes (1960), i.640.)

secondarily, by participation, mankind: mankind who progress from the first tree, of the ancient world, to the second—the incarnational world that grows out of it—towards the third, the world of the Holy Spirit. Here the affinity between Joachim and Langland seems to me closest—for to Joachim the world of the Holy Spirit is the world of free will and of charity:

The Holy Spirit manifests liberty, for it is love. Where there was fear, there was servitude; where there was teaching, there was discipline; and where there is love, there is liberty.[19]

The conjunction of the final tree, the Holy Spirit, both with liberty and with the Christian ideal of *amor*, which is charity, illuminates one of the most remarkable aspects of Langland's vision. Yet other parallels too are suggestive. In an Anglo-Norman bestiary of *c.*1210 a poet, Guillaume le

[19] *Concordia Novi ac Veteris Testamenti*, ii.1–4 (ed. Venice, 1519), fos. 19rb–20vb, with some corrections (in < > brackets) and modified punctuation:
　　Has, inquam, duas arbores sublimes et condensas ponamus ante oculos mentis: et sic in eis patrem et filium, quorum alius ex alio est, principaliter intelligamus—ut tamen cum eis genus hominum secundarie accipiamus, quia, etsi disiuncti sumus a bono deo conditione nature, gratie ipsius participatione coniuncti. . . .
　　In prima itaque cedro, de cuius medulla et ramorum vertice nata est arbor secunda, haud dubium quod similis ei populus ille antiquus intelligendus est, qui (sicut iam superius diximus) creatus est spiritualis ad imaginem patris, sicut et sequens populus ad imaginem filii. . . .
　　In tertia vero arbore, aliquid omnino simile, aliquid dissimile est. . . . Diximus primam arborem proprietate mysterii pertinere ad patrem; secunda⟨m⟩ ad filium; tertia⟨m⟩ ad spiritum sanctum. Et scimus quia primus ordo, qui institutus est primo, vocatus est ad laborem legalium preceptorum; secundus, qui institutus est secundo, vocatus est ad laborem passionis; tertius, qui procedit ex utroque, electus est ad libertatem contemplationis, scriptura attestante qu⟨e⟩ ait: 'Ubi spiritus domini, ibi libertas.' . . . Significat enim idem tempus tertium illum statum felicitatis extreme. . . .
　　Spiritus sanctus exhibet libertatem, quia amor est. Ubi enim timor, ibi servitus; et ubi magisterium, ibi disciplina; et ubi amor, ibi libertas.
On Joachim's tree-imagery, see M. Reeves, 'The *Arbores* of Joachim of Fiore', *Papers of the British School at Rome*, xxiv (1956), 124–36, and *The Figurae*, Part III, Chs. v–ix.

Clerc, presents the Indian tree, Peridexion, of the *Physiologus* tradition:[20]

In its branches dwell doves that feed to satiety on the tree's fruit[21] and rest in its shadow. A hostile dragon lurks to devour those doves that desert the tree, yet the dragon can never come within the shadow, or else he would die.

The tree is God the Father, the shadow is the Spirit, the fruit the Son. It was the Spirit that overshadowed Mary at the incarnation. The doves are all mankind, who can be saved by eating the fruit of the tree and never straying beyond its shadow.

The trinitarian trees both of Joachim and of the bestiaries might well have formed part of Langland's inheritance. Yet it is in mystical vernacular poets of the thirteenth century, whose work Langland could scarcely have known, that we perceive something approaching the speed of his own imaginative transitions and accumulations. Thus for instance in the *Revelations* of Mechthild of Magdeburg (*c.*1250), God in a dialogue says to the soul:

> I am in myself, in all places and in all things,
> as I was before all beginning;
> I am waiting for you in the arbour of love,
> plucking the flowers of sweet union for you
> and making a bed for you there
> with the delectable grass of holy intimacy...
> and there I bend down for you the highest tree
> of my holy Trinity,

---

[20] Guillaume le Clerc, *Le Bestiaire*, ed. R. Reinsch (1892; repr. Wiesbaden, 1967), vv. 2965–3104 (pp. 352–8). Reinsch edited the *Bestiaire* from twenty MSS (pp. 13 ff.). Guillaume's precise source here is not easy to determine. While much in the *Bestiaire*, as Reinsch noted, corresponds with ps-Hugh of St. Victor, *De bestiis et aliis rebus*, the Peridexion passage (III.39 in the printed text of ps-Hugh, *PL* 177. 99–100) is too garbled to ascertain whether Guillaume was using a better and fuller MS of this text, or other sources of *Physiologus* material. On ps-Hugh, cf. most recently N. Henkel, *Studien zum Physiologus im Mittelalter* (Tübingen, 1976), pp. 156–7.
[21] With Guillaume's expression, *saolez* (2979), compare Langland's *saulee* ('satisfaction of appetite', XVI.11).

and you will then pluck the green, white and red apples
of my madescent humanity,
and the shadow of my Holy Spirit shades you
from all earthly grief.[22]

Here the divine lover inclines the tree for Mechthild, to let her
take apples, whereas Piers brings the fruit down painfully at the
dreamer's request. The plucking of flowers and making a bed
in the grass echo moments of human love in songs of Walther
von der Vogelweide;[23] the tree of the Trinity, whose fruit is
Christ and whose shadow is the Spirit, must echo a divine
bestiary akin to Guillaume's. Yet this cannot account for the
particular fusion of images and allegories here, the fresh combinations—delectable grass of intimacy, apples rich with the sap
of Christ's human nature—or the tone of tender rhapsody.

In Italy around 1290 the Franciscan poet and mystic Jacopone
develops, in three of his *laude*,[24] tree-allegories with a compli-
cation and logical perplexity comparable to Langland's, though
his imagery can also be less controlled, his conceptual frame
less cogent. Thus in one (84), for instance, there are three
trees—faith, hope, and charity—and the branches of each tree
are at the same time three planetary heavens and three hierarchies
of angels. God commands Jacopone to mount his steed, so as
to climb the branches of the tree of charity. Jacopone takes

[22] Mechthild von Magdeburg, *Offenbarungen, oder Das fliessende Licht der
Gottheit*, ed. P. Gall Morel (1869; repr. Darmstadt, 1963), ii.25. With
Mechthild's expression *oepfel miner saftigen menscheit* (for the reading, see the
note in Margot Schmidt's translation (Einsiedeln, 1955), p. 403 n. 76), compare
Langland's image for matrimony (xvi.68): *a moiste fruyt wiþalle*.
  In the MHG treatise of the *Maibaum* (ed. A. Birlinger, *Alemannia*, viii.
109–17, xiii. 285 ff.), Christ on the cross is the May-tree, his body and limbs
the trunk and branches. His blood flows into the soil of the loving heart, that
it too may grow and bear fruit. The tree gives shade to all; a fountain of life
wells from its trunk. Birds—phoenix, eagle, nightingale, and parakeet—nest in
its branches, and human souls must fly after them: *Also vindet yeder vogel sein
genist in dem mayen*.
[23] Especially the songs 'Under der linden' and 'Nemt, frowe, disen kranz' (ed.
Lachmann-Kraus-Kuhn, 39,11 and 74,20).
[24] Iacopone da Todi, *Laude*, ed. Franco Mancini (Bari, 1974), nos. 77, 78, 84.

light as his shield and darkness as his lance, to joust against the vices as he climbs the branches of that tree.

We can see, then, that what is new in Langland's vision lies not so much in the components as in the movement and structure: within his *conjointure*, certain combinations of motifs and images are original, or have a dramatic force they had never had before. The scope of Langland's transgressions of known, systematic allegory, fusing traditional elements unpredictably, is startling. This is true also of Mechthild and Jacopone, though in rather different ways. Whether we view the transgressions as so many sins against an allegorical norm, or as imaginatively valid ways of stepping beyond that norm, is something each reader, in each context, must decide.

I should now like to consider a few instances of tree-imagery in greater detail. The examples, necessarily much restricted in number, have been chosen because they display some transformational processes comparable to those of Langland, and because they reach unusual heights of subtlety and intensity, especially, as we shall see, in the later Middle Ages. The texts are ones that show the imaginative potential of the 'disordered scenery'—where a writer, drawing on varied motifs and images, is aware of their power of transformation, not only into one another but also into the conceptual realm and then back into images again.[25]

[25] It is the nature of these complexities that is my concern here, not the establishing of specific historical relationships. I shall not, for instance, try to determine Langland's precise reading—even though, from what has been mentioned so far, it should be clear that Langland must have been aware of precedents not only for elements in his presentation of the *arbor caritatis*, but also for the remarkably fluid, multivalent mode of presentation.

Much in the tradition of visionary allegory, profane as well as sacred, could be illuminated if the influence of *Pastor Hermas* were studied in detail. As yet, no full recension of the numerous MSS of the 'Vulgate' translation has been published (cf. A. Siegmund, *Die Überlieferung der griechischen christlichen Literatur in der lateinischen Kirche* (Munich–Pasing, 1949), pp. 86–7). Among the texts discussed below, a direct influence of *Pastor Hermas* seems to me probable in the case of the sequence *Arbor eterna*, in Lambert's *Liber Floridus*, and in the writings of Hildegard and Joachim. It is noteworthy that Lefèvre d'Etaples, publishing the *editio princeps* of *Pastor Hermas* (Paris, 1513), edited

The first text, the *Pastor Hermas*—composed in Rome in the mid-second century—belongs to the beginnings of Christian visionary writing and helps to establish its poetic foundations.[26] The earliest Latin version of the Greek text, from the second century itself, survives so abundantly in manuscripts that we may be sure it was influential in making Hermas' gentle, tortuous, often puzzling apocalypse familiar to the medieval West. The two protagonists, the Shepherd and Ecclesia, who, in a series of visions, reveal truths to the narrator Hermas, are in their ways as richly elusive as Piers Plowman in Langland's poem. In Hermas' archaic theology, where Christ is called both Holy Spirit and highest of the angels, and human beatitude consists in becoming an angel, the Shepherd, who has been appointed by the highest angel to be Hermas' individual guardian from birth till death, is often also called 'the angel of repentance' (ὁ ἄγγελος τῆς μετανοίας).[27] Hermas does not recognize his

it along with Hildegard's *Scivias*, writings of Elizabeth of Schönau and Mechthild of Hackeborn, and the prophecies of a Dominican with Joachite affinities, Robert of Uzès (d.1296). Lefèvre dedicated the volume *Adelaidi virgini*—to the abbess of Hildegard's Rupertsberg; the letter of dedication shows that he was well aware of the features that linked these texts across the centuries. (On Hildegard and Hermas, see H. Liebeschütz, *Das allegorische Weltbild der heiligen Hildegard von Bingen* (Leipzig, 1930), esp. pp. 51–6.)

On the other hand, Hermas also exercised a considerable indirect influence: many of the texts, for instance, outlined in C. Fritzsche, 'Die lateinischen Visionen des Mittelalters bis zur Mitte des 12. Jhdts.', *Romanische Forschungen*, ii (1886), 247–79, iii (1887), 337–69, or in A. Rüegg, *Die Jenseitsvorstellungen vor Dante* (Einsiedeln, 1945), could be seen as testimonies to this. Whether Langland had read Hermas, or later texts in the Hermas tradition, is too large a question to broach here; none the less, certain features in the *Pastor* that are emphasized below should be particularly suggestive to readers familiar with *Piers Plowman*.

[26] For *Pastor Hermas* I have used Robert Joly's edition of the Greek (Sources chrétiennes, 2nd edn., Paris, 1968); there is a text of the Latin 'Vulgate' translation in *PG* 2. 891–1012, but for the passages cited below it seemed advisable to follow the Oxford, Bodleian MS Laud misc. 488 (s. xii½) rather than Migne. On one occasion I have corrected a phrase in this MS with the help of another, Cambridge University Library MS Dd.4.11 (s. xiii). References to the Migne text are given in parentheses.

[27] On Hermas' Christology and angelology, see R. Joly, ed. cit., pp. 31–3, 43, 49–50; the principal 'angel of repentance' passages are listed ibid., p. 369.

angel at first, but then the Shepherd's shape changes, and
Hermas realizes the Shepherd is his own guardian angel—for he
takes on the appearance of Hermas himself. The angel, we
might say, is Hermas' celestial image.[28]

But Hermas likewise meets with several womanly bringers of
revelation; chief among these is Ecclesia. Like Sapientia in the
Book of Proverbs, Hermas' Ecclesia is seen as the first-born of
creation, begotten before all things; for her, the Shepherd
declares, the universe was formed.[29] Thus at first she appears
to Hermas as a woman immensely ancient; then her face
becomes youthful, though she is still white-haired; and at
last, in a third vision, she is wholly young and beautiful, her
face noble, joyous, and serene.[30] Yet in two of the most elaborate
visions in the work Ecclesia is not only a woman but an edifice:
'The tower that you see being built, it is I, Ecclesia!' This tower
is four-sided ($\tau\epsilon\tau\rho\alpha\gamma\omega\nu\sigma\varsigma$), and is built with living, human
stones: it grows out of the terrestrial Church. Again, in the
vision that specially concerns us here, it is hard not to see the
immense tree that covers the whole earth and gives shade to all
the faithful as—at least implicitly—still another Ecclesia image.[31]

This tree, which the Shepherd shows to Hermas, is a willow
covering the fields and mountains. All who have been called in
the name of the Lord come into its shadow. A sublime angel
cuts branches from the tree and hands small twigs from the
branches to the people in the shade. Yet when the angel had
finished his cutting, the tree remained completely whole, as it

---

[28] *Vis.* V (ed. cit., pp. 140–5).   [29] *Vis.* II.4 (ed. cit., p. 96).
[30] *Vis.* III.11–13 (ed. cit., pp. 128–33).
[31] Hugo Rahner, *Greek Myths and Christian Mystery* (English edn., London,
1963), p. 303, goes further and, discussing *The Shepherd*, speaks of 'the Church
represented, with a wealth of development, as a green willow-tree'. But in
Rahner's account several surprising inaccuracies follow: e.g. 'And immediately
all are made to return their twig *which must be grafted anew on to the tree*,
and herein is shown the nature of penance, for *most of the Christians can only
give back a half-withered twig* ...' (italics mine). The two tower-episodes in
Pastor Hermas are *Vis.* III and *Sim.* IX (Ecclesia's characterization of herself
as tower, *Vis.* III.3, p. 106; the tower as tetragonal, *Sim.* IX.2, p. 292). The
willow-episode is *Sim.* VIII.

had been before. Each human being was then recalled by the angel, to hand back his twig.[32]

The condition of the returned twigs is elaborately described, by means of twelve distinctions: at one extreme are twigs arid and putrid and as if moth-eaten; others show varied proportions of greenness and dryness. But most people bring back their twigs as green as before, and this gives the angel joy. He is joyful too at seeing some whose green twigs have grown tendrils, and most joyful of all when he sees those whose twigs have borne not only tendrils but fruit. These last three groups are given crowns and shining robes, and are admitted into the beautiful tower.

The sublime angel then departs and leaves the scene to the Shepherd, who says to Hermas: Let us take all the other twigs and plant them, to see if they can revive.—My Lord, how can arid twigs grow again?—This tree is a willow, and forever it loves life. If the twigs are watered even a little, many will revive.[33]

As the Shepherd instructs Hermas, some aspects of the vision—such as the tree remaining whole after being cut—are left unexplained, but also new details emerge that make the

---

[32] *Sim.* VIII.1: Bodleian Laud misc. 488, fos. 55ᵛ–56ʳ (*PG* 2. 971–2):

Ostendit mihi salicem tegentem campos ac montes, sub cuius umbra venerant omnes qui vocati erant in nomine domini. Et iuxta eam salicem stabat nuntius domini valde preclarus et sublimis, et secabat cum falce magna de ea salice ramos, et populo illi, qui erat sub umbra salicis eiusdem, exiguas ac veluti cubitales virgas porrigebat. Postquam autem accepissent universi, deposuit falcem, et arbor illa integra permansit sicut antea videram eam. Quo nomine mirabar atque intra me disputabam. Ait ad me pastor ille: Desine mirari quod arbor illa tot ramis prescisis permanserit integra; hoc expecta, et tunc demonstrabitur tibi quid significet nuntius ille qui populo porrexerat virgas et rursus eas ab his reposcebat. Quo quisque istas acceperat ordine, eodem etiam vocabatur ad illum, virgamque reddebat (*sic* C, ad illam virgam que reddebatur O).

[33] *Sim.* VIII.2: fo. 57ᵛ (*PG* 2. 973–4):

Accipiamus ab omnibus virgas et plantemus eas, si possint reviviscere. Dico ei: Domine, iste, que sunt aride virge, quemadmodum possunt reviviscere? Ait mihi: Arbor hec salix est, semperque amat vitam. Si plantate ergo fuerint he virge exiguumque humoris acceperint, plurime ex hiis reviviscunt.

allegoresis more enigmatic than the vision it seeks to explain. Now the tree is said to cover not only fields and mountains but the whole of the earth: it is a cosmic tree, and it is called the law of God, which is given to the whole world. At the next moment, this willow becomes the Son of God. Whilst Hermas often calls the Son of God 'the sublime angel', here, mysteriously, the sublime angel is Michael, and is distinct from Christ.[34]

As Hermas and the Shepherd go, some days later, to look at the spoilt twigs they had planted, the twigs are again returned in diverse states. The Shepherd gazes at them and says: As I told you, this tree loves life: you see how many have done penance and won salvation. Once more each condition of a twig is seen to express, in meticulous detail, the condition of a soul. And then Hermas is sent by the Shepherd to proclaim the need for repentance throughout the world—for, even after these twig-testings, hope is still offered afresh to all mankind. The task that the sublime angel had handed over to the Shepherd is now entrusted by the Shepherd to Hermas, narrator of the vision.

Here at the dawn of Christian dream-allegory we already encounter some of that disordered scenery which was to be so versatile later. In Hermas' visions, events take place with an unhurried, magical, ritual solemnity: he has none of Langland's more insistent tempi, and little of his intellectual agility. Yet, as in Langland, there is an abundance of images and concepts that flout the logic of explanation. Where each of the twigs, for instance, has its meaning fixed and made explicit, the branches are never explained, the meaning of the tree itself undergoes several changes, and the Shepherd and the sublime angel, who preside over the episode, remain enigmatic: their precise place in the scheme of salvation is never spelt out. Most complex of all are the transformations of Ecclesia throughout the work:

[34] *Sim.* VIII.2: fo. 58ʳ (*PG* 2, loc. cit.):
Arbor hec magna que campos tegit atque montes totamque terram, lex est dei in totum orbem terrarum data. Hec autem lex filius dei est, predicatus in omnibus finibus orbis terre. Populi vero stantes sub umbra, hii sunt qui audierunt predicationes eius et crediderunt. Nuntius autem ille magnus et honestus Michahel est. . . .

first-born of creation, for whom the universe was made, young and beautiful guide, tetragonal tower of living stones, willow that covers the earth and protects the faithful.

Such transformations—and the imaginative processes that prompted them—have given vitality, I believe, to a number of visionary writings of the Latin Middle Ages. In a scarcely known classical sequence of *c*.900, copied in an insular hand and only once printed, in garbled fashion, a century ago,[35] a series of transformations is evoked that indeed reveals debts to Hermas, yet goes beyond the early Christian work in swift, flamboyant, lyrical language:

Arbor eterna,[36] diva, summa, / apostolorum pectora sonans...

[35] The sequence is copied on fo. 55^v of the Welsh Juvencus MS, Cambridge U.L. Ff.4.42. This MS contains both Welsh and Latin glosses (s. ix²–x¹), as well as later glosses (s. x / xi) in an English Caroline minuscule: the MS had been acquired by an English centre by the year 1000 (cf. T. A. M. Bishop, *Trans. Cambridge Bibl. Soc.* iv (1967), 258, and D. N. Dumville's O'Donnell Lectures, *England and the Celtic World in the Ninth and Tenth Centuries* (forthcoming)). The sequence was printed by A. W. Haddan and W. Stubbs, *Councils and Ecclesiastical Documents*, i (Oxford, 1869), pp. 622–3 (giving the MS pressmark as Ff.4.32). They did not recognize the classical sequence form, with syllabic parallelism between the half-strophes; they printed the entire text as a continuous *vers libre*. They also overlooked the contraction-sign to the upper right of the letter b in the first word, 'Arbor', and printed the opening phrase thus: 'Arbe terna', suggesting an emendation to 'Orbe terna'. Only one or two of their other misreadings are signalled below.

For knowledge of this text I am indebted to Michael Lapidge, who hopes to prepare a new edition shortly.

[36] Ecclesia is *arbor* at least implicitly in *Pastor Hermas* (see discussion above, and n. 31). In Patristic writings *arbor* is regularly used to denote the mast of the ship Ecclesia (see Hugo Rahner, *Symbole der Kirche* (Salzburg 1964), p. 363). In Gregory the Great's *Moralia* (xix.1, PL 76. 97), the risen Christ is the *arbor magna* that grew from the *granum sinapis*; the boughs of that tree are holy preachers, the birds that nest upon the boughs are blessed souls, who have flown aloft on wings of virtues. Here the allegory begins with the resurrection but is gradually transformed into the 'mystical body'. Scotus Eriugena unfolds an allegory of incomparable depth and splendour in *Periphyseon*, v.36 (PL 122.978–82), where the whole of human nature returns to paradise—its pristine state—to eat of the *arbor vitae* which is Christ, the centre of that paradise. Compare also the exposition of the tree of life by Scotus' early twelfth-century disciple Honorius, PL 172.276–8, and the image of the immense paradisal tree

Eternal tree, divine, supreme, echoing the heartbeats of the apostles, summit of the governable heaven[37] ... banquet of belief, queen of the East, whirling the courses of the stars: Ecclesia, the one mother, fourfold and undivided.

The opening phrases conjoin a cosmic image and a quasi-human one—an everlasting tree that none the less responds to the beating of men's hearts. This figure then becomes, allegorically, *fidei mensa*, yet at once, with *orientalis regina*, a human *figura*—the bride of the celestial Solomon—emerges again. We see her, like Sapientia at the creation, whirling the stars (*volvens sidera*), and then, identified as Mater Ecclesia, she is both fourfold and one—like Hermas' tower, and like the heavenly Jerusalem.

Near the close of the sequence the cosmic associations, as well as the allegorizing and Solomonic ones, yield to a human anguish:

11a Tandem derelicta   11b mater fugitiva,
12a quae peperit et   12b audita denique
     deflens pignora,   vox est in Rama...

At last the fugitive mother is abandoned, bewailing the children that she bore; at last a voice was heard in Rama...[38]

in the *Visio Tnugdali* (ed. A. Wagner, (Erlangen, 1882), pp. 50–51), which is explicitly *typus Ecclesie*: 'vidit unam arborem maximam et latissimam, frondibus et floribus viridissimam ... in cuius frondibus aves multe diversorum colorum et diversarum vocum cantantes et organizantes morabantur. ... Erant autem sub eadem arbore multi viri et femine in cellis aureis et eburneis, et ipsi sine cessatione laudabant et benedicebant deum. ... Anima autem, ad angelum conversa, ait: Que est arbor illa et ille, que sub ea sunt, anime? ... Hec arbor typus est sancte Ecclesie, et isti, qui sub ea sunt viri et femine, constructores et defensores erant sanctarum ecclesiarum....'

[37] I read *summa celi regnabilis* (the final word is rare: cf. Du Cange, s.v.); Haddan-Stubbs print *summa / Coeli regna, / Bi bis* (without elucidation).
[38] This part of the sequence, in my view, is indebted to Notker's renowned 'Rachel' sequence, *Quid tu, virgo* (ed. W. von den Steinen, *Notker der Dichter und seine geistige Welt* (Berne, 1948), ii.86); this sequence came to be used as the climax of numerous versions of the dramatic *Ordo Rachelis* (cf. Karl Young, *The Drama of the Medieval Church* (Oxford, 1933), ii.116 ff.).

Ecclesia, after embodying world-tree and allegoric banquet, cosmic principle and Solomonic queen, is the mother bereft—the Rachel of Matthew's gospel and Jeremiah's prophecy, helpless in grief as her innocents perish.[39] Concept and image, allegory, figura, and symbol are gathered—or swept headlong—in this stream of lyrical expression.

In the first years of the twelfth century Lambert of Saint-Omer, who completed his superbly designed *Liber Floridus* in 1120, drew a double tree-image, in which again a subtle inter-relation of images and concepts can be observed. To begin with, the good tree, *Arbor bona*, is the loyal Ecclesia, *Ecclesia Fidelis*; the evil tree—'autumnal, fruitless, doubly dead, uprooted' (*autumnalis ... infructuosa bis mortua eradicata*; cf. Jude, v.12)—is Synagoga, whose root had been cupidity (*Cupiditas, id est avaritia*).[40] But the root of the good tree is Karitas, as the inscription explains: 'just as many branches come forth from the one tree-root, so many virtues are generated from the one Karitas'. Each of the eleven virtues that sprouts from Karitas is

[39] Matt. 2: 17–18; Jer. 31:15; cf. W. von den Steinen, *Notker*, i.399–404.

[40] *Lamberti S. Audomari Canonici Liber Floridus* (facs. ed. A. Derolez, Ghent, 1968): *Arbor bona* and *Arbor mala* occur on fos. 231ᵛ–232ʳ, Derolez's transcription on pp. [102–3]. Derolez is the first scholar to transcribe the title *Ecclesia Fidelis* correctly. It had been misread as *Ecclesia fidelium* by many scholars (e.g. A. Katzenellenbogen, *Allegories of the Virtues and Vices in Mediaeval Art* (London 1939), p. 65; H. de Lubac, *Exégèse médiévale* (Paris, 1959 ff.), ii.2, 200; A. Grabar, C. Nordenfalk, *La peinture romane du onzième au treizième siècle* (Geneva, 1958), pp. 158–9, with the further misreading *cupiditas sive avaritia*). The point is of literary importance, as the correct reading marks Lambert's deliberate transition from image to concept, which is discussed below.

Nine further copies of the *Liber Floridus* were executed in the twelfth century (see esp. L. Behling, 'Ecclesia als Arbor bona', *Zeitschrift für Kunstwissenschaft* xiii (1959), 139–54; cf. also *Liber Floridus Colloquium*, ed. A. Derolez (Ghent, 1973). Notwithstanding the diffusion of the work, Lambert's tree, whose root is Karitas, has been strangely ignored by Langland scholars who have discussed the tree of charity. Thus for instance, to illustrate Langland's tree, D. W. Robertson, Jr. and B. F. Huppé, *Piers Plowman and Scriptural Tradition* (Princeton, 1951), pp. 192–5, use two drawings from a MS of Hugh of St. Victor's *De fructibus carnis et spiritus*. Yet this is not very apt, as the root of Hugh's tree is Humilitas; Caritas simply features on the trunk between Fides and Spes, and is not given any distinctive emphasis.

a distinct plant; the stem of the tree grows as holy hope (*Sancta Spes*).

So far the allegory might seem to be largely schematic; but a captivating range of associations is brought within the compass of the schema, by means of the diverse sacred texts inscribed on the illuminated page.[41] The tree is *Sapientia superna*, filled with good fruits; the fruit is the spirit; its guardians are a thousand peacemakers. Solomon says of Sapientia, 'her fruit is more precious than all riches'—and it is Sapientia the bride who replies to her lover: 'his fruit is sweet to my throat'.

At the foot of the page, the good tree is identified with the resplendent queen of Psalm 44:10, decked with many-coloured embroidery (*varietate circumdata*). She is at the right hand, not of the king anointed by God—as in the Psalm—but of God himself: *a dextris dei*. The image would again suggest Sapientia in her cosmic role, but instead Lambert now equates this queen with *fidelium ecclesia*. The change of expression (from *Ecclesia Fidelis* above) suggests that the image of the loyal bride has become the concept of the community of believers, just as the many-coloured bridal dress here becomes the diversity of virtues (*virtutum diversitate amicta*).

Three decades later, in Hildegard of Bingen's first visionary work, *Scivias*, completed in 1151, images and concepts act upon one another in more intense and less predictable ways. Here too a series of illustrations, prepared, it would seem, at Hildegard's direction, corroborates the visions and gives them greater immediacy, even though the illuminator cannot catch all the complexities suggested in the writing.[42]

[41] 'Iacobus de arbore bona dicit: Sapientia superna plena est fructibus bonis. Hinc Paulus: Fructus autem spiritus est; et dominus: Mille pacifici qui custodiunt fructus eius. David rex: Fructum suum dabit in tempore suo. Hinc Salomon: Fructus eius pretiosior cunctis opibus. Hinc Sapientia dicit: Fructus eius dulcis gutturi meo.'

[42] For the complete *Scivias*, one must still resort to the unreliable text in *PL* 197. 383–738. The illuminations from the *Scivias* MS Wiesbaden Nass. Landesbibl. 1, which today is lost, have been reproduced (from a twentieth-century copy made by the nuns at Eibingen) in Maura Böckeler's German translation, *Wisse die Wege* (2nd edn., Salzburg, 1954). For the extracts of *Scivias* newly

In the third part of *Scivias*, Hildegard, like Hermas, beholds a vast tower being built. This tower she calls 'the foreshadowing of the will of God' (*precursus voluntatis dei*). Its architecture is laden with mystic meanings. At the northward-facing corner of the tower—the North has for Hildegard connotations of the demonic and menacing—she sees a column of steely colour, vast and terrible to behold.[43] It was three-sided, each edge sharp as a sword. But from the edge facing East—the direction that suggests the burgeoning of the divine—boughs were growing out of that steely column, from root to summit. On the bough nearest the root Abraham was sitting, on the next, Moses, on the third, Joshua; each of the other patriarchs and prophets, too, has his own bough, in the order in which they had lived on earth. All were facing northwards, looking into the future. Between the edges of the column that faced East and North, it was smooth and round, as if lathed, but wrinkled like the bark of a tree at the places where shoots are wont to grow. A wondrous radiance shone out from the northern towards the southern face, and in the diffusion of light Hildegard perceived hosts of saints walking in joy. This third face of the column was shaped like an archer's bow, tapering at each end. At the summit of the column all was luminous; it was crowned by a dove with a beam of gold in its mouth. When I looked there, says Hildegard, I heard a voice from heaven reproving me, saying: What you are seeing is divine. At that voice I trembled so much that I dared not look further.

Throughout *Scivias*, such visions are followed by explanations, which Hildegard receives from the heavenly voice and edited below, the fundamental extant MS is Vat. Pal. lat. 311, which was copied in Hildegard's own scriptorium, on the Rupertsberg, within her lifetime (cf. M. Schrader and A. Führkötter, *Die Echtheit des Schrifttums der heiligen Hildegard von Bingen* (Cologne–Graz, 1956), pp. 44–5). I have also consulted for these passages the 'Riesenkodex', MS Wiesbaden Nass. Landesbibl. 2, prepared, again at the Rupertsberg scriptorium, in the decade immediately after Hildegard's death—1180–90 (Schrader–Führkötter, pp. 154–79)—though I adduce its readings only on the very rare occasions when the text of Vat. Pal. lat. 311 is faulty or doubtful.

[43] The passages discussed from here onwards are edited in the Appendix below.

records. The column shows the mystery of the divine word, in which all justice, of the New Testament and the Old, is fulfilled. Justice is the key concept in the allegoresis here. The first face of the column looks eastward—towards the dawn that precedes the perfect day of total justice. The second looks to the North, where—despite gospel and precepts—all injustice begins. The third, southward-looking face is the wisdom of the saints, strengthened by justice—the saints who showed in the gospels the bud that they made fruitful, both in good works and in the perception of hidden meanings.

The allegory then becomes more complex. The boughs on the eastern edge of the column show the ages of the patriarchs and prophets, because the sharp column of divinity extended those ages from root to summit—from the good that begins in the minds of the elect to the summit that manifests the Son of Man, who is total justice. In the exposition of the tree-imagery that follows, inner moral meanings, concerning aspects of justice, are constantly interwoven with Old and New Testament allusions, which themselves are related figurally to one another. Thus for instance Moses, on the second bough, shows the act of planting that God inspired, by beginning that law-giving which was fulfilled in the Son of the most high. In the age of each patriarch and prophet, God breathed upwards towards the height of his laws, a height that—by a succinct metaphor —Hildegard calls 'the unique bud of each age'. On the northward-looking face of the column, the patriarchs and prophets see the future: the incarnation, but also Christ's battle against Satan, the ruler of the North. The smooth bark, with wrinkles where new shoots will sprout, shows the whole process of prefiguring, that culminates in 'the most just bud' (*rectissimum germen*) of the incarnation.

Hildegard called her poetic and dramatic work a 'symphony of the harmony of heavenly revelations' (*symphonia armonie celestium revelationum*);[44] so too, truly to convey the texture of

---

[44] I have discussed Hildegard's *Symphonia* in *Poetic Individuality in the Middle Ages* (Oxford, 1970), pp. 150–92 (texts with melodies, ibid., pp. 209–31), and

her visionary prose, one would have to dwell on its symphonic aspect. Only a few hints, with reference to her tree-imagery, can be ventured here. The arboreal aspects of the column, for instance, which contrast surrealistically with its steely sharpness,[45] are already adumbrated in the preceding vision, the description of the tower. Later visions in *Scivias* depict another column—'secret and mighty and purple-black in colour' (III.7)[46]—the column of the Trinity, and then (III.8) a shadowy column, *obumbrosa* (the word seems to be Hildegard's coinage)[47]—the column of Christ's humanity, with rungs like a ladder reaching from top to bottom. On the rungs all the powers of God, or virtues—the *virtutes dei*—descend and ascend again, laden with stones, having 'a keen desire to complete the task of building' the edifice, the heavenly Ecclesia. (Here an echo of Hermas seems to me unmistakable.)[48]

To suggest Hildegard's symphonic use of language here: the

in the essay 'The Composition of Hildegard of Bingen's *Symphonia*', *Sacris Erudiri*, xix (1969–70), 381–93.

[45] For other images of trees with metallic characteristics, see C. G. Jung, 'Der philosophische Baum', *Verhandlungen der Naturforschenden Gesellschaft in Basel*, lvi (1945), 411–23 (esp. pp. 412, 418, 420–1).

[46] Vat. Pal. lat. 311, fo. 150va:

⟨D⟩einde vidi in angulo occidentali demonstrati edificii mirabilem et secretam atque fortissimam columpnam, colorem purpuree nigredinis habentem, eidemque angulo ita impositam, ut et intra et extra ipsum edificium appareret. Que etiam tante quantitatis erat, ut nec magnitudo nec altitudo ipsius intellectui meo pateret, sed quod tantum miro modo planissima absque omni ruga fuit. Habebat autem in exteriore sui parte tres angulos calibei coloris, a pede usque ad cacumen ipsius velut acutissimus gladius incidentes, quorum unus contra affricum respiciebat, ubi plurimum putridi straminis ab eo succisum et dispersum fuerat, et unus contra chorum, ubi multe pennule per illum discisse ceciderant, atque medius contra occidentem, ubi plurima putrida ligna ab ipso desecta iacebant—hec singula ab eisdem angulis propter temeritatem ipsorum succisa. . . .

[47] *Obumbrosus* is not attested in *TLL*, in the *Novum Glossarium*, in A. Blaise's *Dictionnaire latin–français des auteurs chrétiens*, or in his *Lexicon Latinitatis Medii Aevi*.

[48] In particular, the *virtutes* as maidenly figures carrying the living stones for the building of Ecclesia offer a striking resemblance to the 'blessed spirits', the maidens in *Pastor Hermas*, Sim. IX.4 (cf. my discussion in *Eranos-Jahrbuch*, xli (1972), 62–4).

first of these *virtutes*, Humilitas, both in her emblematic costume
and her words, recalls a tree:

The first image wore a gold crown on her head, with three branches
reaching higher, flashing with the beauty of precious stones, green
and red, and with white berries. On her breast she wore a lucent
mirror, in which appeared, with wondrous brightness, the image of
the incarnate Son of God. She said: I am the column of lowly minds
... for whoever, when ascending, catches hold of the highest bough
of the tree first, most often falls by sudden accident. But he who,
wishing to ascend, starts from the root, cannot fall easily....
    I was roused to anger in heaven when Lucifer bit himself and be-
yond himself [again the expression—*semetipsum transmomordit*
—is an arresting coinage], in hate and pride. ... But when man was
formed—O O O the noblest seed, O O O the sweetest bud—the Son
of God was born, for man's sake, at the end of ages, a human being.[49]

    If a certain heaviness and repetitiveness is at times felt in these
developments, if the concepts seem an anticlimax after the stark,
intense images, the tree-pillar, together with its exposition and
relation to the cognate visions, none the less shows how little
Hildegard's way of writing proceeds in terms of known quantities. Her allegoresis can give rise to wholly unforeseen complexities, and also at moments to daring new metaphors that
are not themselves explained. Each of Hildegard's visions can
be seen as a totality embracing several modes: it is a divine
image with temporal significance, or an earthly image that
carries a reflection of the divine; but it also always becomes an
image of virtues, seen both as 'powers of God', descending the
rungs of the pillar or tree, and as human qualities capable of
ascending. Through this, Hildegard's images of the divine realm
become at the same time reflections concerning the human

---

[49] Text below, p. 249. So, too, *Gratia dei*—another of the *virtutes*—continues
this vein of imagery (Vat. Pal. lat. 311, fo. 160vb):
    Nam bona arbor ut fructum ferat irrigatur, circumciditur, atque circumfo-
ditur, et ab ea vermes, ne fructum eius comedant, abstrahuntur. Quid est hoc?
Bonus scilicet homo non sit durus nec malivolus ad iusticiam dei. ... Sed tamen
antequam homo sentiat me in cogitatione sua, aut intellectus ipsius intelligat
me intra se, sum ei caput et plantatrix fructuositatis.

knowledge by which the divine can be reached and known. This is something that the images alone could scarcely have achieved.

In 1298 another mystic who, like Hildegard, was both poet and cosmologist—Ramón Lull—wrote his *Tree of the Philosophy of Love*.[50] He dedicated the Latin version, in Paris that year, to the king, Philippe le Bel, and a vernacular one—not his own Catalan text but, it would seem, a French adaptation which today is lost—to the queen, Jeanne de Navarre.[51] The *Tree*, he tells us, was made in order to exalt lady Amor (the love whose

[50] *Arbre de Filosofia d'Amor*, ed. Jordi Rubió, in *Ramon Llull: Obres Essencials* (Barcelona, 1960), ii. 9–84. All references below are to this edition.

[51] *Arbre*, pp. 23, 79; cf. also J. N. Hillgarth, *Ramón Lull and Lullism in Fourteenth-Century France* (Oxford, 1971), pp. 108, 154. It would seem to me plausible to see Ramón's *Arbre* as in some respects a rejoinder to the *albre d'amor* described by Matfre Ermengaud a decade earlier in his *Breviari d'amor* (composed 1288–92). For Matfre's prose description of his tree, see the excellent edition of the Provençal, Catalan, and Castilian versions by P. T. Ricketts, in *Hispanic Studies in Honour of Joseph Manson* (Oxford, 1972), pp. 227–53. Dr Ricketts has in progress a new edn. of the entire *Breviari* (Leyden, 1976 ff.), which will eventually supersede that of G. Azaïs (Béziers, 1862–81).

What Matfre wanted to depict by means of his tree was the whole of love, sacred and profane. Thus, 'In the topmost circle of the tree God is inscribed and figured, from whom is born all that is, has been, and will be good. In the next circle, descending from the first, is Natura, whom God appointed to govern all creatures' (ed. Ricketts, art. cit., p. 235). From Natura descend two kinds of law, natural and human. From each of these are born two kinds of love: from the natural come sexual love and love of offspring, which are common to all creatures; from the human come love of God and one's neighbour, and love of earthly goods. Each of these four branches of the tree of love bears its own fruit: love of God and neighbour bears the fruit everlasting life; the fruit of loving earthly goods is pleasure, that of sexual love is children, that of the love of children, joy. The leaves, flowers, and roots of this tree are likewise specified. Like Langland's tree of charity, it is a threatened tree: beside each of its branches stands a figure with iron implement, trying to cut a branch down. At the summit is a lady called Universal Love—*Amors generals*—who comprehends all the loves in herself.

Matfre's allegory, though elaborate, does not go beyond a schematic structure; yet it is a scheme of extraordinary inventiveness, in that it brings concepts into new configurations. To establish his hierarchy of values and their interrelations, Matfre draws on the humanism of twelfth-century Chartrain thought: the relation he depicts between God, Nature, and *Amors generals* shows affinities with Alan of Lille's *De planctu Naturae*; the two branches of law, that of nature and that of man, take up a profound distinction first made by

form is *caritat*) and the beloved (*amat*), who is God. The lover (*amic*) is the human being who loves God. Like the trees in Ramón's other writings, this one is analysed in every aspect of its roots, trunk, branches, twigs, leaves, flowers, and fruit. To begin with, there are eighteen roots, each showing one of the attributes of love: its goodness, greatness, duration, power, wisdom, and many others. Only two of the roots have a negative potential: *contrarietat* and *menoritat* (contrariness and less-love).

How was it possible for Ramón to transform such diagrammatic artifice into a means of conveying intense emotional experience? I suggest, by way of all that is unpredictable, even deliberately inconsistent, that he introduces. Thus for instance, when Ramón defines the form of love, the first part of the tree-trunk, we see the *amic* suffering from his too-great longing for the beloved:

'Contrariness,' said the lover, 'could you help me against greater loving?' Greater concord-of-love overheard this, and related it to greater goodness, duration and power, and to lady Love; and all together bound and captured the lover, and punished him—with loving more.

The lover sighed, lamented, wept, and railed at lady Love, who was killing him with loving. Contrariness and less-love heard his plaints and weeping; but the other roots of love refused to listen, and as much as they could they tortured the lover with loving.[52]

Roots that punish and refuse to listen are strange enough, yet their role soon becomes far more mysterious (or, if you will, illogical) than that. To illustrate by at least one motif: in an interlude set between the leaves and the flowers of the tree, the lover, mortally sick, asks lady Love for a doctor. Yet all the doctor does is done deliberately to inflame the lover more. After

William of Conches (see S. Gagnér, *Studien zur Ideengeschichte der Gesetzgebung* (Uppsala, 1960), esp. pp. 226–46); as in William, Matfre's two branches are still seen as springing from both God and Natura. Where Matfre attempted a subtle integrative synthesis, Ramón devised an *Arbre* from which—at least overtly—all human love was banished.

[52] *Arbre*, p. 31.

taking the patient's pulse and examining his urine, the doctor concludes: this man needs a medicine that will make him mad! The medicine is compounded of the roots of the tree of love—all save contrariness and less-love. A moment later, however, these roots have been transformed into lady Love's page-boys (*donzells d'amor*)—the two treacherous ones, contrariness and less-love, abetting the lover's escape from the sick-room into a forest, the others pursuing, fighting, and at last leaving him imprisoned.

The beloved wants to condemn the runaway lover to death, and a trial takes place. Love-life is appointed as the lover's advocate, love-death is retained by the beloved, so that the lover's rights may be established. And here Ramón makes explicit: 'The rights of love are the roots of love.'[53]

The beloved consults these roots: should the lover die? Only two—contrariness and less-love—say that he should live. Then, to bring about the lover's death, the roots are commanded to take him through the world and show him all those who dishonour the beloved. Then he will die of sorrow:

Love's pages brought the lover to see the poor, who die of hunger, thirst, disease and cold, who ask alms of greedy, rich, vainglorious men. ... Then the lover felt great sorrow for the poor, for his beloved was little loved by the rich and greedy; and through that sorrow his sickness multiplied....

'Love-death,' said wisdom, 'tell the pages to bring the lover to Jerusalem: let them take him through the entire holy land, show him the temple of David and the temple of Solomon, and show him where Jesus Christ was born and died. Then shall the lover die of love!' ... When the lover saw the holy land ... and remembered the passion of Christ, his loving multiplied so greatly ... that by force of love he cried: 'Ah holiness, ah lady Love, ah loving! Forgive Love's pages, who have brought me to this land to die!'[54]

So swift an outline of certain moments, while it cannot do justice to the poetic excitement of the text, at least makes clear that Ramón's is an extreme case of disordered scenery—or better, of disordered drama, as it is the characters themselves

[53] *Arbre*, p. 56.   [54] *Arbre*, p. 63.

who are constantly changing form and function. The roots of
the tree of love, who had begun as abstractions, turn into
ingredients of a love-philtre, then into messengers, then fighters,
and back into a more abstract sphere as the rights of love. Then
they become a jury deciding on the lover's fate, and at last one
of the roots, *saviea* (wisdom), seals his fate, by showing him the
death of Christ and making him echo Christ's dying words
('Father, forgive them ...') in his own moment of death. The
paradox is this: all that goes to make these roots of love logically
incoherent is also what gives them imaginative life. The consistent schema is impaired over and over again, every detail
fluctuates, and in these fluctuations the febrile experience is
accurately portrayed. The imaginative splendour of Ramón's
Arbre is inseparable from his numerous and conscious transgressions of allegorical norms; at the same time, the work presupposes those norms and would have been inconceivable without
them.

In Ramón Lull's writings, every aspect of knowledge was
depicted and analysed in terms of trees and their structure; in his
vast *Arbre de Sciencia* Ramón devised no fewer than sixteen
such trees, from the elemental tree to the divine. In the words
of Pico della Mirandola two centuries later, Ramón's was an
ars combinandi, and because of this Pico honours it as a *cabala*,
a counterpart *apud nostros* of the Jewish cabbalistic works.[55]
In 1486 Pico—still only twenty-three years old—included two
groups of 'cabbalistic' theses among the 900 *Conclusiones* that
he set up as a challenge for public disputation in Rome.[56] The
previous year he had come in contact with a converted Sicilian
Jew, who had assumed the magnificent name Flavius Mithri-

---

[55] *Apologia* (*Giovanni Pico della Mirandola, Gian Francesco Pico: Opera
Omnia*, Basle, 1557–73, repr. Hildesheim, 1969) i.180.
[56] Giovanni Pico della Mirandola, *Conclusiones*, ed. B. Kieszkowski (Geneva,
1973). Kieszkowski, however, bases his edition on the Erlangen MS, which,
according to Chaim Wirszubski, 'is a copy and not the original of the *editio
princeps*' ('Francesco Giorgio's Commentary on Giovanni Pico's Kabbalistic
Theses', *Journal of the Warburg and Courtauld Institutes*, xxxvii (1974), 145
n. 1).

dates. Flavius translated a corpus of cabbalistic writings for Pico, from Hebrew into Latin; his autograph manuscripts survive, unpublished, in the Vatican Library today.[57] One of the works Pico mentions by name in his *Conclusiones* is the book *Bahir*:[58] this is the oldest extant cabbalistic text; it was composed or redacted in Provence *c.*1167–80, and translated by Flavius in 1485–6. It is a text pervaded by images and allegories of a mystic tree, as vivid as they are enigmatic. Since this tree not only shows striking affinities with the more complex mystic trees of Christian tradition, especially those of Hildegard and Langland—though naturally there is no question of a direct relationship—but also takes us forward into the thought of one of the most brilliant humanists, it offers an appropriate concluding illustration.

Once more the transitions among diverse imaginative modes are remarkable. For all its daring innovations, the *Bahir*, in Scholem's words, 'preserves or imitates the literary form of the *Midrash*—questions to elicit the meaning of difficult or contradictory verses in the Bible'.[59] And indeed the first appearance

[57] On Flavius, see especially Chaim Wirszubski (ed.), *Flavius Mithridates, Sermo de Passione Domini* (Jerusalem, 1963). On the relations between Flavius and Pico, see G. Scholem, 'Zur Geschichte der Anfänge der christlichen Kabbala', *Essays presented to Leo Baeck* (London, 1954), pp. 158–93; F. Secret, 'Nouvelles précisions sur Flavius Mithridates maître de Pic de la Mirandole', in *L'opera e il pensiero di Giovanni Pico della Mirandola nella storia dell' umanesimo* (Florence, 1965), ii.169–82.

[58] Ed. Kieszkowski, p. 78. None the less, as Scholem (art. cit., p. 167) showed, Pico's reference is in fact to fo. 331[v] of the MS, Vat. Ebr. 191—that is, to a series of passages appended to the *Bahir* proper, of which the translation finishes on fo. 326[r]. These additional passages follow the *Bahir* in several of the Hebrew MSS, and were not distinguished from it in the Latin translation. Pico's allusion naturally implies that he had read the work itself as well as the 'appendices'. On the *Bahir*, see the admirable translation and commentary by G. Scholem, *Das Buch Bahir* (Leipzig, 1923), and his more recent discussion in his *Ursprung und Anfänge der Kabbalah* (Berlin, 1962), pp. 29–70. On the possibility of an earlier direct influence of the *Bahir* on European thought, in Catharist circles in southern France, see Shulamith Shahar, 'Le catharisme et le début de la cabale', *Annales Economies Sociétés Civilisations*, xxix (1974), 1185–1210. The *rapprochements* are not decisive, however, and the author is appropriately cautious in her conclusions. [59] *Ursprung*, p. 46.

of the tree in the *Bahir* comes in the midst of a learned discussion
of when the angels were created, an exegesis of Psalm 104:3–4:[60]
'All admit that the angels were not created on the first day—lest
it should be said that Michael extended in the southern part of
the firmament and Gabriel in the north and the holy and blessed
God in the middle.' To counter this, a verse from Isaiah (44:24)
is adduced: 'But I am the Lord, creating all things, extending
the heavens alone, making fast the earth—who could have been
with me?' Then suddenly, from exegesis and biblical *auctoritas*,
we move into a myth, such as can be paralleled in Gnostic
writings of the second and third centuries AD:[61] the text
continues:

I indeed, when I planted this tree, so that the delight of the whole
world might be found in it, called it by the name *chol*, that is, 'all',
for all things hang on that tree and all things proceed from it, all
stand in need of it, all gaze through it and hope in it; from there the
souls fly forth. I was alone when I made it, nor can any angel strut

---

[60] The texts discussed from here on are edited in the Appendix below, from
Flavius' autograph. I am deeply grateful to the late Professor Wirszubski for
checking my edition of these passages, and for giving me his expert advice
about the Hebraisms in the Latin text.

[61] The principal relevant text is the cosmogonic myth of Simon Magus, as
expounded in Hippolytus' *Refutatio*, VI.9–18 (ed. P. Wendland (Leipzig, 1916);
cf. G. Scholem, *Ursprung*, pp. 63 ff.). On the cosmic tree in myth and religion
there is a vast literature: in addition to the article 'Baum' in *Reallexikon für
Antike und Christentum* (see above, n. 17), I have found the following
treatments of the mythologem in diverse cultures particularly illuminating: Z.
Ameisenowa, 'The Tree of Life in Jewish Iconography', *Journal of the Warburg
and Courtauld Institutes*, ii (1938–9), 326–45; R. Bauerreis, *Arbor vitae*
(Munich, 1938); E. A. S. Butterworth, *The Tree at the Navel of the Earth*
(Berlin, 1970); A. K. Coomaraswamy, 'The Inverted Tree', *Quarterly Journal
of the Mythic Society*, xxix (1938), 111–49; C.-M. Edsman, 'Arbor inversa:
Heiland, Welt und Mensch als Himmelspflanzen', *Festschrift Walter Baetke*
(Weimar, 1966), pp. 85–109; Uno Holmberg, *Der Baum des Lebens*, Annales
Academiae Scientiarum Fennicae B XVI (Helsinki, 1922); E. O. James, *The
Tree of Life* (Leyden, 1966); G. Lechler, 'The Tree of Life in Indo-European
and Islamic Cultures', *Ars Islamica*, iv (1937), 369–416; H. de Lubac, 'L'Arbre
cosmique', *Mélanges E. Podechard* (Lyons, 1945), pp. 191–8; O. Viennot, *Le
culte de l'arbre dans l'Inde ancienne: textes et monuments bràhmaniques et
bouddhiques* (Paris, 1954).

on it and say 'I was there before you'. And when I made fast the earth in which I planted and rooted this tree, and gave them joy and rejoiced in them[62]—who could have been with me to whom to reveal this secret?

Immediately afterwards we are back with the exegetes: Rabbi Emorai says, this then implies that God created the necessary things of the world even before the heavens. And the Rabbi who had just evoked the grandiose Gnostic myth replies in a different mode. As the narrator in Langland has a dream within a dream, in which the tree of his outer dream is expounded and enriched with new concepts, so here the myth of the cosmic tree is extended by a parable, which none the less continues the myth conceptually. To explain how God could have created the *necessaria mundi* before creating the heavens, we are now told:

It is like a king who wanted to plant a tree in his garden. He searched the whole garden to find out if it had a spring that would keep the tree alive, and did not find one. Then he said: I shall dig for water and bring forth a spring, so that the tree can survive. He dug and brought forth a spring welling with living water, and then planted the tree. And the tree stood firm and bore fruit and prospered in its roots, because men watered it continually by drawing water from the spring.

Here we are not far from the willow of *Pastor Hermas*, which, because it is by the water, forever loves life and brings new life forth.

The next appearance of the tree in the *Bahir* again begins with cosmological—and now, it would seem, astrological—images.[63] Yet soon these too are transformed into allegories: the

[62] The reference here is presumably to tree and earth together. These passages are sects. 14–15 in Scholem's translation. The other passages, in order of citation below, are from sects. 66–7, 71, 85.

[63] See the Latin text in the Appendix below: 'The holy and blessed God has a tree traversed by twelve world-boundaries: north-east, south-east, the east of height and depth, north-west, south-west, the west of height and depth, the north of height and depth and the south of height and depth. They are extended and they reach as far as the immeasurable, and they are the arms of the world, and within them is the tree. And in all the world-boundaries there are prefects,

tree whose arms are the twelve boundaries of the world, presided
over by a series of astral rulers, becomes a tree of justice, a tree
of Israel, whose actions are seen as determining the course of the
universe; at the same time it is a microcosmic tree, whose heart
is the human heart and whose stem is the human spine:

As Rabbi Rehamai said: Unless there were holy and pious Israelites
who exalt me (God) over the whole world through their merits, by
whom the heart is nourished and the heart nourishes them, there
would be no world;[64] for they are all holy forms, who have been set
over every people and race, and saints of Israel have occupied the
body of the tree, or rather its pillar and its heart. For as the fruit is
the beauty of the body, so Israel has received the fruit of the beautiful
tree called citrus; as the palm-tree has branches all around and its
heart is at the centre, so Israel has received the beauty of this tree,
which is its heart, and corresponding to that beauty is the spinal
column in the human being, the central part of the body....

In a later passage we learn that what Flavius here calls *citrus*
is that 'fruit of the fairest tree' which is mentioned along with
the palm in Leviticus 23:40, in the instructions for plucking
festive branches for the Feast of Tabernacles; then the citrus is
allegorized as the feminine principle, without which the world
cannot subsist; its glory is celebrated in words that are used of
the bride in the Song of Songs, and the conjunction of citrus
and palm is seen as a *hieros gamos*. In the earlier moment,
however, it is the saints of Israel who are the palm and who
receive the fruit of the citrus. It is inwardly, in the saints, that

corresponding to prefects or governors, and they are twelve. Again, within the
(celestial) sphere there are twelve prefects, these ... (making) thirty-six in all,
including those of the world-boundaries.'
    Here a lacuna in the MSS, even in the early MS from which Flavius was
translating, makes understanding difficult. Scholem (*Das Buch Bahir*, pp. 64–9)
would see in the numbers a complex symbolism in which the prefects are
celestial powers operating in the cosmos, like the rulers of the thirty-six decans
in astrology, and in which the twelve directions correspond to the twelve tribes
of Israel, and the twofold series of thirty-six prefects matches the seventy-two
names of God.

[64] Here Scholem (*Das Buch Bahir*, p. 70 n. 2) postulates another lacuna; but
Flavius translates the sentence without a break.

the primordial union of the two trees is re-enacted. As in Hildegard, the cosmic tree is also a column: it is the arboreal trunk, and the spinal column in the human being, and, some twenty lines later in the *Bahir*, it becomes both the world-axis and a moral allegory of justice:

It is said there is a pillar reaching from the earth to the firmament, and it is called *Sadic*, after the just. And when there are just men in the world, it is augmented and grows strong; otherwise it grows feeble. And it supports the whole world, as is written (of the just man): 'foundation of the world'. When it is (completely) enfeebled, it can no longer support the world. So, even if there were only one just man in the world, he can sustain it.

As in Hildegard's vision, the cosmic and moral and inner law are apprehended simultaneously. Where in Hildegard the just are perched on branches growing out of the steely pillar, here they constitute the pillar itself.

In still another modulation, which again recalls Hildegard, the tree grows in layers that are the *virtutes dei*; it is watered by

wisdom, the soul of the saints, flying from the spring to the great duct, ascending and joining the tree. Through whose hands does that soul leap? Through the hands of Israel: when there are just and good men, the indweller (Shekinah)[65] dwells in their midst and in their works.... And justice is that (divine) indweller....

In the diverse moments concerning the tree in the *Bahir* Scholem would see diverse strata of composition: there are 'old fragments' that preserve an archaic myth of the cosmic tree, a younger layer, where the tree has become a figure of the human organism, and a final redaction in Provence, after 1167, in which Israel becomes the trunk or heart of the tree whose fruits are souls.[66] However valid this may be as a historical perspective, I would suggest that imaginatively the most vital aspect of the

[65] On Shekinah, see especially G. Scholem, *Von der mystischen Gestalt der Gottheit* (Zürich, 1962), Ch. IV (pp. 135–91).
[66] *Ursprung*, pp. 64, 66, 68–70.

Bahir tree is precisely the synthesis, the complex interplay of myth and allegory, of image and concept, that one—presumably late—author, relying on disparate sources, achieved. Whoever devised those complex transformations of the tree was no ordinary redactor or compiler, but had an exceptional power of giving cohesion of a new kind—the kind that depends on the 'disordered scenery' of medieval allegorical visions.

When Pico, within a year of receiving Flavius' translation, came to write his *Conclusiones*, he formulated several of his 'cabbalistic' theses in arboreal terms:

4. The sin of Adam was the truncation of the kingdom from the other plants.

36. The sin of Sodom came about by the truncation of the ultimate plant.

42. Joseph was buried in bones and not in body, because his bones were the powers (*virtutes*) and host of the tree on high called *Sadic*, flowing to the earth above.[67]

These cryptic sentences imply a vision of the world as a living growth, that can be impaired by sin and sustained by even one just man. As in the *Bahir*, Sadic, the pillar of the just, is also the mystic tree; the bones of Joseph the just become the celestial *virtutes*, which are the layers of that tree; and the expression 'flowing to the earth above' recalls the numerous *Bahir* images of the watering of the tree, so that it may bear fruit. Why did Pico, a rhetorician with marvellous powers of conceptual explication, here adopt such compressed, riddling language, full of suggestiveness yet not rationally ordered? It would seem that both the matter and the manner of the *Bahir* had stirred a response in him.

The complexities that we glimpsed with Langland's tree of

---

[67] Ed. Kieszkowski, pp. 51–3. To cite at least one suggestive parallel to the uses of the pillar-tree in Hildegard, the *Bahir*, and Pico—Henri de Lubac, in his 'L'Arbre cosmique' (see n. 61), says of the *stûpa* of Sanchi: 'Ainsi cette sculpture du *torâna* nord de Sanchi nous offre, unis jusqu'à l'identification, un homme, un arbre, un pilier. Considéré dans son essence suprême, le Bouddha est en même temps le pilier cosmique et l'arbre de la vie.'

charity can lead us to perceive comparable imaginative and conceptual processes in many works of different kinds in different centuries. But whereas to Huizinga these processes seemed regressive, a phenomenon typical of a time of waning, a decline from an age when symbolism had been fresher and more direct, to Benjamin the same phenomenon was elemental: in the baroque tragedies 'the disordered court' of allegory could still become an authentic community, could express complex perceptions, which might scarcely have been conveyable any other way. In the late Middle Ages there are, to be sure, many allegories that tend to the mechanical and make one think Huizinga was right. At the same time, a heritage that includes Hildegard and Mechthild, Jacopone, Ramón Lull, and Will Langland, and later the translation that Flavius made for Pico, lends profound support to Benjamin's reassessment of allegory's nature and worth.

Additional note: Since this essay was dispatched for publication, a new edn. of Hildegard of Bingen's *Scivias*, ed. A. Führkötter and A. Carlevaris, has appeared (Corpus Christianorum, Cont. Med. xliii–xliii A, Turnhout, 1978). While substantially superior to that in Migne, it still offers a normalized and not always well-chosen text (cf. my discussion, 'Problemata Hildegardiana', *Mittellateinisches Jahrbuch* xvi, forthcoming). An important study of the *Liber Floridus* MS has also appeared: A. Derolez, *Lambertus qui librum fecit* (Brussels, 1978). An essay by G. B. Ladner, 'Medieval and Modern Understanding of Symbolism: a Comparison', *Speculum* liv (1979), 223–56, includes fine discussion of medieval tree-symbolism, though not specifically of trees of charity. To my pages on Mechthild, finally, I should like to add cross-references to Gertrude of Helfta, *Legatus* iii.15 (*De arbore amoris*; cf. also iii.17), ed. P. Doyère, Sources chrétiennes 143, pp. 62 ff.; and to Marguerite d'Oingt, *Les oeuvres*, ed. A. Duraffour, P. Gardette and P. Durdilly (Paris, 1965), pp. 144–7. Such tree-visions, it seems, became something of a constant among thirteenth-century women mystics; but there is already a striking use of the tree of charity motif in Dhuoda's *Liber manualis* for her son William (composed 841–3), ed. P. Riché, Sources chrétiennes 225, pp. 268–70.

APPENDIX

1. From Hildegard of Bingen's *Scivias* (on the manuscripts,
see above, n. 42)

127vb

Quarta visio tercie partis.

⟨E⟩t deinde, ultra predictam turrim precursus voluntatis
dei, sed cubito uno infra angulum qui respicit ad septentrionem, vidi quasi / columpnam calibei coloris, pre-
fate lucide parti muri eiusdem edificii exterius appositam,
valde terribilem aspectu, tanteque magnitudinis ac alti-
tudinis, ut mensuram eius nullomodo discernere possem.
Et eadem columpna tres angulos habebat, ab imo usque
ad summum quasi gladium acutos, quorum primus
respiciebat ad orientem, secundus autem ad septentrionem, et tercius ad meridiem, exterius ipsi edificio
aliquantulum coniunctus.

Ex angulo autem qui respiciebat ad orientem proce-
debant rami a radice usque ad cacumen eius, iuxta cuius
radicem vidi in primo ramo Abraham sedentem, in
secundo vero Moysen, et in tercio Iosue, ac deinde
reliquos patriarchas et prophetas, ita sursum singulos in
singulis ramis ordinate sedentes, secundum tempus quo
in hoc seculo sibimet successerant—qui se omnes con-
verterant ad angulum eiusdem columpne qui respiciebat
ad septentrionem, admirantes ea que in spiritu futura
viderunt in ipsa.

Sed inter hos duos angulos, unum scilicet vergentem
ad orientem et alterum ad septentrionem, erat—ante
facies ipsorum patriarcharum et prophetarum—eadem
columpna ab imo usque ⟨ad⟩ summum¹ quasi tornatilis
et rotunda, plenaque rugarum, ut de arboris cortice solet
germen pullulare. A secundo vero angulo, respiciente / ad
septentrionem, exivit splendor mire claritatis, se exten-
dentis et reflectentis ad angulum qui respiciebat ad
meridiem. Et in eodem splendore, in tam magnam
latitudinem se diffundente, conspexi apostolos, martires,
confessores et virgines, atque alios plurimos sanctos, in

¹ usque summum V usque ad summum W

Margin references: 128ra 128rb

magno gaudio deambulantes. Tercius vero angulus, qui
respiciebat ad meridiem, erat in medio latus et extentus,
in imo autem et in summitate aliquantulum gracilior et
constrictus, secundum modum arcus qui extenditur ad
sagittas iaciendas. In cacumine autem eiusdem columpne
vidi tantam claritatem luminis, ultra quam humana
lingua effari possit, in qua apparuit columba, habens in
ore suo radium aurei coloris, multo fulgore in eandem
columpnam radiantem. Cumque illuc aspicerem, audivi
vocem de celo, magno terrore me redarguentem, et
dicentem: 'Quod vides, divinum est.' Ex qua voce ita
contremui, ut amplius illuc aspicere non auderem.

128vb ... 'Quapropter et hec columpna, quam ultra predictam turrim precursus voluntatis dei vides, designat inef-
fabile misterium verbi dei, quia in vero verbo, id est in
filio dei, impleta est omnis iusticia novi et veteris testamenti...

129ra 'Est quoque valde terribilis aspectu, quoniam iusticia
in verbo dei metuenda est humane scientie...

129rb 'Et primus angulus respicit ad orientem, qui est primus
ortus inceptionis cognoscere deum in divina lege, ante
perfectum diem omnis iusticie. Secundus autem ad septentrionem, quoniam, post inceptionem bone et institute
operationis, evangelium filii mei et alia precepta in me
patre surrexerunt: contra partem aquilonis, ubi omnis
iniusticia orta est. Tertius vero ad meridiem, exterius
ipsi edificio aliquantulum coniunctus, qui est roboratis
operibus iusticie profunda et exquisita sapientia prin-
cipalium magistrorum, per calorem spiritus sancti, qui
obscura in lege et prophetia aperuerunt, et qui in evan-
geliis ostenderunt germen quod fructuosum fecerunt ad
intelligendum, tangentes exteriorem materiam scriptu-
rarum in opere bonitatis patris, et suaviter ruminantes
in ea misticam significationem.

129va 'Quod autem / ex angulo qui respicit ad orientem
procedunt rami a radice usque ad cacumen eius, hoc est
quod in ortu cognitionis dei per legem iusticie—quasi in
angulo orientali—apparuerunt rami: tempora scilicet
patriarcharum et prophetarum, quia illa acuta columpna

divinitatis hec omnia extendit ab initio radicis—id est bone inceptionis in mentibus electorum suorum—usque ad cacumen eius, quod est usque ad manifestationem filii hominis, qui omnis iusticia est. Unde etiam iuxta eius radicem vides in primo ramo Abraham sedentem, quia per acutissimam divinitatem exspirabatur hoc tempus, quod primitus ortum est in eodem Abraham, cum quieta mente reliquit patriam suam obediens deo; in secundo vero Moysen, quoniam deinde plantatio surrexit inspiratione dei, in initio date legis per eundem Moysen, in presignificatione filii altissimi; et in tercio Iosue, quia ipse postmodum habuit spiritum hunc a deo, ut consuetudinem legis dei confirmaret robustiorem in precepto divino.

'Ac deinde vides reliquos patriarchas et prophetas, ita sursum singulos in singulis ramis ordinate sedentes, secundum tempus quo in hoc seculo sibimet successerant: quoniam, in unoquoque tempore subsequentium patriarcharum et prophetarum exspiravit / deus sursum ad altitudinem preceptorum suorum—uniuscuiusque singulare germen—cum ipsi in diebus suis disposite et ordinate in ostensa sibi iusticia quiescebant, divine maiestati fideliter subiecti, ut in temporibus suis venientes erant.

129vb

'Et hii omnes convertunt se ad angulum eiusdem columpne qui respicit ad septentrionem, admirantes ea que in spiritu futura vident in ipsa, quia omnes, admoniti spiritu per spiritum sanctum, se verterunt et viderunt ad evangelicam doctrinam fortitudinis filii dei, diabolo repugnantis—de incarnatione eius loquentes, et admirantes quod ipse, veniens ex corde patris et de utero virginis, in magnis mirabilibus se ostendit in suo opere et sequentium se, qui ipsum in nova gratia mirabiliter imitantes caduca conculcabant, et ad eternorum gaudia fortiter anhelabant.

'Sed quod inter hos duos angulos, unum scilicet vergentem ad orientem et alterum ad septentrionem, est ante faciem ipsorum patriarcharum et prophetarum eadem columpna ab imo usque ad summum quasi

130ra

tornatilis et rotunda, plenaque rugarum, ut de arboris cortice solet germen pullulare—hoc est quod inter binas summitates, videlicet inter manifestatam cognitionem meam et subsequentem doctrinam filii mei, latuit per tipum prefigurationis in animabus / antiquorum patrum, in legibus meis commorantium, unicum verbum quod est filius meus, a primo electo usque ad ultimum sanctum, in mistica tornatura circumornatus: quia ipse omnia instrumenta sua bene composuit ac limavit, scilicet per volubilem gratiam omnibus se pium manifestans, ut prefigurabatur in rugis circumcisionis, que fuit umbra futurorum in appositis significationibus per austeritatem legis, in se habentis rectissimum germen latens, summe et sanctissime incarnationis.'

156ra

Octava visio tercie partis.

⟨E⟩t deinde, in plaga meridiana in prefato lapideo muro demonstrati edificii, ultra predictam columpnam vere trinitatis, item vidi quasi columpnam magnam et obumbratam, intra et extra idem edificium apparentem, que scilicet visui meo tam obumbrosa apparuit, ut nec magnitudinem nec altitudinem eius cognoscere valerem. Et intra columpnam hanc atque columpnam vere trinitatis, erat interruptus locus longitudinis trium cubitorum, vacuusque absque muro, ut superius ostensum est, fundamento ibi tantum posito. Hec ergo umbrosa columpna in hoc ipso edificio in eodem loco stabat ubi desuper in celestibus misteriis, coram deo, illum magnum et quadratum lucidissimique candoris splendorem prius

156rb

videram, qui, secretum superni creatoris / designans, in maximo misterio mihi manifestatus est—in quo etiam alius splendor velut aurora, in se aeriam in alto purpuree lucis claritatem habens, fulgebat, per quem mihi in mistica ostensione misterium incarnati filii dei demonstratum fuerat.

In columpna autem ista, ab imo usque ad summum eius, in modum scale ascensus erat, ubi omnes virtutes dei, descendentes et ascendentes, oneratas lapidibus, ad opus suum ire videbam, acutum studium idem opus

156va

perficiendi habentes. Et audivi lucidum illum qui sedebat in throno dicentem: 'Isti fortissimi operarii dei sunt.'...

Prima imago portabat coronam auream capiti suo impositam, tres ramos altius extantes habentem, atque preciosissimis lapidibus viridis et rubei coloris et albis bacis multo fulgentem ornatu. In pectore vero suo habebat speculum lucidissimum, in quo mira claritate imago incarnati filii dei apparebat. Et ait: 'Ego sum columpna humilium mentium, et interfectrix superborum cordium. In minimo incepi, et ad ardua celorum ascendi. Lucifer erexit se sursum super se, et corruit sub se deorsum. Quisquis me vult imitari, filius meus esse desiderans, si me matrem sitit amplecti, opus meum in me perficiendo, hic tangat fundamentum, et leniter ad alta sursum ascendat. Quid est hoc? Ipse primum carnis sue vilitatem inspiciat, et sic sursum de virtute in virtutem suavi et leni animo gradatim proficiat—quia qui summum ramum arboris primum apprehendit ad ascendendum, repentino casu sepissime cadit. Qui autem, volens ascendere, a radice incipit, huic non est tam

156vb

facile / cadendum, si caute incedit....

'Ego ad indignationem in celo provocabar, cum Lucifer semetipsum odio et superbia transmomordit. Sed o o o, humilitas hoc tolerare noluit. Propter quod etiam ille ruina magna deiectus est. Formato autem homine, o o o, nobilissimum granum, et o o o, dulcissimum germen, filius dei propter hominem in fine temporum natus est, homo.... O virtutes, ubi est / Lucifer?

157ra

In inferno est. Surgamus ergo omnes, ad veram lucem appropinquantes, atque edificemus maximas et fortissimas turres in provinciis, ut, cum venerit dies novissimus, plurimum fructum et in spiritalibus et in carnalibus apportemus.'

2. From Flavius Mithridates' version of the *Bahir*: MS Vat. Ebr. 191 (1485/6)

290^r

Dixit Rabi Johanan, 'secunda die creati sunt angeli, ut scribitur, "qui trabificat in aquis ascensus suos, vel edes

Ps. 104:3–4 suas", et scribitur, "qui facit angelos suos spiritus, ministros eius ignem urentem.'"

290ᵛ Dixit Rabi / Levitas, filius Tiberie,[1] 'omnes concedunt, et concedit etiam Rabi Johanan, quod aque iam erant, sed in secundo "trabeficavit in aquas ascensus

Ps. 104:3 suos, vel edes suas". Quisnam?—"Qui posuit nubes currum suum". Quisnam hic?—"Ille qui ambulat super pennas venti". Legati[2] tamen non fuerunt creati nisi usque ad diem quintam.

'Et concedunt omnes quod non fuerunt creati die prima, ne diceretur quod Michael extendebat in parte meridionali firmamenti et Gabriel in septentrionali et deus sanctus et benedictus ordinabat in medio. "Sed ego dominus, faciens omnia, extendens celos solus ego,

Isa. 44:24 firmans terra⟨m⟩, mi mecum existente?*

'"Ego quidem, quando plantavi hanc arborem ut delectatio totius mundi in ea esset, et firmavi in ea omnia, vocavi nomen eius chol, idest omne, quia omnia pendent in ea et omnia ab ea exeunt, et omnia indigent ea, et per eam speculantur et in ea sperant, et inde volantes anime sunt. Ego solus fui quando feci illam, nec superbiat aliquis angelus in ea, dicere 'ego preveni te'. Etiam quando firmavi terram in qua plantavi et radicavi arborem hanc, et letificavi ea simul et letatus sum in eis—mi mecum existente* cui revelavi hoc secretum?'"

Dixit Rabi Emorai, 'A verbis tuis discimus quod necessaria huius mundi creavit deus sanctus et benedictus ante celos.' Dixit ei etiam, paradigmaticos, 'Res similis est regi qui voluit plantare arborem in horto. Consideravit totum hortum ad sciendum si haberet fontem aquarum subsistere illam[3] facientem, et non invenit. Dixit "Fodiam aquam et educam fontem, ut possit subsistere arbor." Fodit et eduxit fontem scaturientem aquam vivam, et postea plantavit arborem. Et stetit arbor et fecit fructum, et prosperavit in radicibus suis, quia aquarunt eam continuo hauriendo a fonte.'

* mi mecum existente = quis mecum existebat

[1] Tiburie MS   [2] vel nuntii MS (*in margin*)   [3] illum MS

301ʳ   Arborem enim habet deus sanctus et benedictus, in qua sunt duodecim termini diametrales: scilicet terminus orientalis septentrionalis, terminus orientalis meridionalis, terminus orientalis celsitudinis, terminus orientalis profunditatis, terminus occidentalis septentrionalis, terminus occidentalis meridionalis, terminus occidentalis celsitudinis, terminus occidentalis profunditatis, terminus septentrionalis celsitudinis, terminus septentrionalis profunditatis, terminus meridionalis celsitudinis, terminus meridionalis profunditatis.

Et ampliantur et eunt usque ad 'adead', et sunt brachia mundi, et intus eos est arbor. Et in omnibus his diametralibus sunt prefecti e regione prefectorum, sive comissarii, et su⟨n⟩t duodecim. Etiam intus in spera sunt duodecim prefecti, hi¹ ⟨...⟩ triginta sex quidem cum

301ᵛ   diametralibus. Et / unicuique est unus, ut scribitur, 'quia
Eccl. 5:7   alcior altiore custode custos est'.

302ʳ   Ut dixit Rabi Rahamai, 'nisi essent sancti et pii Israelite qui sublevant me super toto mundo per suos meritos, a quibus alitur cor et cor alit eos, mundus non esset—nam omnes sunt forme sancte que prefecte sunt super quemcumque populum et gentem, et Israel sancti ceperunt corpus arboris, seu cippum eius et cor eius. Quemadmodum enim fructus est decor corporis, sic Israel acceperunt fructum arboris decore que dicitur citrus; quemadmodum arbor palme habet ramos circumcirca et cor eius in medio est, sic Israel acceperunt decorem huius arboris, qui est cor eius, e cuius decoris regione est filus spine dorsi in homine, qui est principale corporis.'...

303ʳ   Traditum est, una columna est a terra usque ad firmamentum, et vocatur Sadic, nomine iustorum. Et quando sunt iusti in mundo, augetur et roboratur; sin autem, debilitatur. Et sustinet totum mundum, ut scribitur,
Prov. 10:26   'fundamentum seculi'. Quando enim debilitatur, non

---

¹ *Lacuna after* hi (cf. G. Scholem, *Das Buch Bahir*, p. 66 n. 3); triginta duo *deleted before* triginta sex MS

potest sustinere mundum. Ideo, quamivis in mundo non esset nisi unus iustus, potest substentare seculum.

307ʳ   Quenam est ⟨radix⟩ arboris quam dixisti? Dixit ei, omnes virtutes dei sancti et benedicti sunt una super alia, et similes sunt arbori. Quemadmodum arbor hec per aquas educit fructus suos, sic deus sanctus et benedictus per manus aquarum multiplicat virtutes arboris. Quenam sunt aque dei sancti et benedicti? Sapientia est, et hec est anima sanctorum que volat[1] a fonte ad magnum syphona, et ascendit et coniungit se in arbore. Et per manus cuius volat? Per manus Israel: quando sunt iusti et boni, habitatrix habitat in medio eorum, et habitat in operibus eorum ... Et iusticia est habitatrix ...

317ʳ   Quidnam est latus tabernaculi? Aut, numquid latus in eis est? Dixit quidem, 'latus est in eo tabernaculo paradigmaticos. Res similis est regi qui cogitavit in corde suo plantare novem arbores masculas in paradiso suo, et erant omnes palme mascule que dicuntur dacalim. Quidnam fecit? Dixit, postquam sunt tantum unius speciei, non poterunt durare. Igitur in medio eorum plantavit citrum, et est una de illis novem que ascen-

317ᵛ   derant in cogitatione sua / ut essent masculi. Et quenam est citrus? Equidem citrus femina est, et hoc quod

Lev. 23:40   scribitur, "fructus arboris gloriose et palme palmarum". Quidnam est fructus arboris gloriose? Equidem ut dicit glossa Chaldaica, "fructus arboris citri et palmarum cordis". Quidnam gloriose? Quia gloria omnium est, et est hec illa gloriosa que dicitur in cantico canticorum,

Cant. 6: 10   ubi scribitur, "que est zoth* que oritur ut aurora, pulchra ut luna, clara ut sol, venerabilis ut turmate?" Et hoc quidem e regione femine est, et secundum nomen suum capta est femina ab Adam, quia inpossibile est mundus tam superior quam inferior permanere sine femina.'

Quare igitur vocatur femina Hebraice necheba, idest perforata? Quia poros habet et foramina lata, et habet etiam plura foramina quam habeat vir. Quenam

---

* zoth (Hebr.) = ista
[1] volant MS

sunt?—sunt quidem foramina uberum et matricis et loci
receptionis. Quidnam est illud quod dixisti, quod canticum canticorum est gloriosum? Equidem gloriosum
est omnium voluminum sanctorum. Sic enim dixit Rabi
Johanan: 'omnes libri textus sunt sancti, et lex etiam
sancta, sed canticum canticorum est sanctum sanctorum.'...

Quidnam est hoc sanctum?—est quidem citrus, que
est gloria omnium. Quare vocatur gloriosa, idest
hadar?—Equidem quia hec hadar est citrus que est
gloria omnium, separata scilicet a fasciculo cordis palme.
Non preceptum cordis palme adinpletur nisi per eam,
et ipsa citrus connexa est in eo cum omnibus, quia cum
omnibus unum est, et cum omnibus simul est cor palme.
Quemnam representat cor palme?—filum scilicet spine
dorsi. Et ita est 'folium autem arboris myrthi'. Quemnam
representat?/ ⟨...⟩ Quia scilicet oportet ut folium
arboris myrthi habeat folia coperiencia maiorem partem
sui. Si enim folia non coperiunt maiorem partem sui,
nihil est. Quare? Paradigmaticos: res est similis homini
habenti brachia quibus protegit caput suum; sunt quidem brachia duo, et cum capite tria, et sic sunt hic folium
ad sinistram, myrthi vero ad dextram, arbor vero in
medio. Quare dicta est arbor?—quia est radix arboris.

Lev. 23: 40
318ʳ

Commoners and Kings: Book One of More's *Utopia*

EMRYS JONES

At a first reading, Book One of *Utopia* can seem a rather
shapeless piece of work, an uneasy mixture of purposeful
argument and unashamed digressiveness. What is never in any
doubt is its vitality. Once Raphael Hythlodaeus and Thomas
More are settled in Peter Giles's garden and their talk gets under
way, the first Book never relaxes its hold. This dialogue, with
its continuation at the end of Book Two (the 'peroration' and
'conclusion', to use Professor Hexter's terms), shows More at
the height of his literary powers, writing with an intensity and
economy he was never again to match (though the best passages
in *Richard III* run it close). None the less, although a reader
may feel intuitively confident in More's authorial control, he
may not at first reading, or even at second or third, be very
clear as to what plan More is following, what structural
principles have decided that this should come before that, or
indeed whether More has any firm formal ideas at all. Most of
the scholarly attention given to *Utopia* has come from political
historians or historians of ideas, comparatively little from literary
critics, mere readers of books, people interested in the reading
experience itself and predisposed to thinking about literary
works in terms of the shapes they assume. Certainly More in
Utopia is a man of ideas, and historians of political theories
have every right to their interest in him, but in *Utopia* he is also
a literary artist, a man of imagination for whom form and effect
are inescapably important. To an imaginative artist, of course,
the shaping *is* the thinking. In Wilson Knight's formulation, 'A
poet doesn't think thoughts; he makes them.' And More, in
Utopia, is fundamentally a poet.

To call the author of *Utopia* a poet is nothing new, though it has become less common to do so than it was in the sixteenth century. According to Erasmus, More was a poet even in his prose, and Tyndale, though with no favourable intent, followed Erasmus. But it was Sidney in the *Defence of Poetry* who most memorably praised *Utopia* as the work of a poet. For Sidney, More was, like Plato, a poet in the only sense that mattered: he was a 'maker'; he brought into being new forms for the mind to contemplate. And for Sidney, as for Erasmus, it was no disqualification that More's chief writings were in prose. *Utopia* is a poem in the same sense that the *Aeneid* is a poem: it emanates power; it illuminates and enlarges the mind of the reader, and like all works of imagination it invites and repays innumerable readings—for although it uses arguments, its chief purpose is not to argue a position but to communicate a vision. It works upon its reader in a thoroughly traditional literary way.

Something of the literary and even 'poetic' nature of *Utopia* can be glimpsed from the process of its composition. All the indications are that More did not in some real sense 'know' what he wanted to say until he had said it. He discovered what it was only as he wrote. Indeed the different sections of what we now refer to as the two Books of *Utopia* came to him in a quite different order from the order in which we now read them. He wrote most of the second Book before most of the first—a fact which Erasmus in very general terms disclosed in a letter of 1519. And, pursuing the implications of Erasmus's remark, Professor Hexter has demonstrated, convincingly for the most part, the probable order of composition of the chief sections of *Utopia*.[1] The introduction and the description of Utopia itself (now in Book Two) came first. The Book One dialogue, called by Hexter the Dialogue of Counsel, followed some months later, along with the peroration and conclusion of Book Two. Also late in the process of composition came the episode set in Cardinal Morton's court, which now forms part of the dialogue in Book One.

[1] *Utopia*, ed. Edward Surtz, SJ, and J. H. Hexter (Yale, 1965), pp. XV–XXII.

Utopia is therefore a work of accretion: it grew into its present shape in ways which More could probably not have foreseen. He went on modifying its nature by inserting material into it, in so doing, perhaps, achieving that special literary quality of thickness and opacity which it shares with many other works of imagination. But if *Utopia* in its final shape—text, prefatory epistles, printer's map, and all—is a genuinely literary work, a poem in Sidney's understanding of the word, it needs far more literary study than it has so far received.[2] A properly literary study of *Utopia*, however, is unusually difficult. The study of More's Latin style is still only in its infancy: few are competent to analyse or describe it with any sensitivity. In the meantime something can be said about the work's shaping, its internal disposition into parts, the order of the topics discussed by its speakers, and something too about the working of More's images, not only the smaller figures of speech at one extreme but the fuller descriptions at the other, one or two of which are likely to stay with the reader quite as vividly as the social and political arguments. I want to look here at only one or two features of Book One, with a view to ascertaining their expressive value, and I do so because a glance at some recent accounts of *Utopia* suggests that this aspect has been in some respects misunderstood.[3]

The first of these is the Cardinal Morton episode, which comes early in the conversation between More, Raphael, and Peter Giles. Peter Giles, who is acting as host, contributes very

---

[2] Apart from J. H. Hexter's Yale Introduction and his earlier book *More's 'Utopia': The Biography of an Idea* (Princeton, 1962), some notable contributions have been made by the following: H. A. Mason, *Humanism and Poetry in the Early Tudor Period* (1959); David Bevington, 'The Dialogue in *Utopia*: Two Sides to the Question', *SP* lviii (1961); and R. C. Elliott's chapter in *The Shape of Utopia* (Chicago, 1970).

[3] I quote throughout from Paul Turner's Penguin translation (Harmondsworth, 1965), which seems to me unquestionably the best in English. (The version included in the Yale edition is of mediocre literary quality.) Turner's is the only one to give any sense that *Utopia* is, as H. A. Mason rightly insists, a 'work of wit'; it is certainly the only one I know which can be read through with pleasure.

little to the dialogue, but he is given the honour of opening the discussion: 'My dear Raphael, I can't think why you don't enter the service of some king or other.' And at once an argument develops for and against an intellectual like Raphael becoming a king's counsellor. Raphael is against it, More (the speaker) for it. And Raphael's main point, which he now begins to elaborate in a long monologue, is that most people hate new ideas; they prefer the status quo; they don't want to be bothered or disturbed; so that radically innovative—and at the same time widely travelled and experienced—thinkers like Raphael himself would be wasting their time. Suppose you're in a council chamber, he says, and

you suggest a policy that you've seen adopted elsewhere, or for which you can quote a historical precedent, what will happen? They'll behave as though their professional reputations were at stake, and they'd look fools for the rest of their lives if they couldn't raise some objection to your proposal. Failing all else, their last resort will be: 'This was good enough for our ancestors, and who are we to question their wisdom?' Then they'll settle back in their chairs, with an air of having said the last word on the subject—as if it would be a major disaster for anyone to be caught being wiser than his ancestors. And yet we're quite prepared to reverse their most sensible decisions. It's only the less intelligent ones that we cling on to like grim death. I've come across this curious mixture of conceit, stupidity, and stubbornness in several different places. On one occasion I even met it in England.

And at this point Raphael embarks on his account of a high-table conversation he had while staying at the court of Cardinal Morton in England. This was in the reign of Henry VII, nearly twenty years before.

This episode at Morton's court is one of the chief features of Book One, yet it has received curiously little comment. In his excellent introductory essay in the Yale edition, Professor Hexter says this about it: 'With one digression—a dialogue within a dialogue—to describe the condition of English society, the latter (the Dialogue of Counsel) is a tight-knit exploration of the problem of counseling princes in sixteenth-century Europe.' I have no quarrel with Hexter's suggestion that the episode was conceived late in the process of composition and was inserted into a Book One which was otherwise more or less as we have it. It helps to explain the sheer oddity of the structure at this point—the Chinese box effect—which is otherwise hard to account for. What is less acceptable, however, is the term 'digression'. It makes it seem that at this point we turn aside from the Book's chief concern (the problem of Counsel, according to Hexter) for a quite different topic, an exposure of the social ills of England. Hexter has perhaps allowed his interest in the process of composition of *Utopia* to obscure his sense of the final product and the full imaginative effect it has on an unprejudiced reader. At any rate he does an injustice here to More's artistic conception.

We need to recall Sidney's description of *Utopia* as a poem and to remember that, in closely organized imaginative writing such as this, individual details of whatever kind will be likely to have more than one function. Connections will be made, so to speak, in several directions at once. For the work will not progress in a single linear uni-directional way, like a philosophical argument; it will have instead a spatial dimension—we may well be required to recall the beginning when we reach the end and will do so effortlessly, matching like with like, and with equal lack of effort noting significant points of difference and contrast. The impulse to make meaning-patterns which enact and dramatize intellectual distinctions will be felt throughout.

That this is the situation here can be argued from Professor Hexter's own account of the process of composition. The reversed order of writing itself suggests something of the creative effort which *Utopia* cost More. It is not the product of coolly premeditated thought, pushing an argument through from beginning to end, but essentially the work of emotion playing on the materials of his reading, conversation, and experience of life. *Utopia* was rapidly written, thrown off, in a concentrated effort of the whole mind. It fused ideas, themes, even forms and genres, which had previously been separate; and this synthesizing activity is the task of the imagination, controlled by what seems uncontrolled, the unconscious mind. It is no surprise that the result has the quasi-three-dimensional solidity and roundness which is so often found in works of the purest imaginative power (one might instance *A Midsummer Night's Dream* and *The Tempest*), works which furnish us with great mental images, mental *forms*, rather than with carefully worked out sequences of argument. And like these other works, *Utopia* engages the attention in different ways and on different levels—it makes many abrupt transitions between different kinds of discourse, all of which contribute to the complex, many-layered, essentially poetic address it makes to the reader.

To return to the Morton episode: Raphael has raised the subject of human resistance to reason and thought. This is of course a leading theme of *Utopia*, which receives its first statement here and recurs at key points right to the end of the second Book. It is here stated in the form 'Why don't you become a king's counsellor?', and is later elaborated in these specifically curial terms; but More presumably intends us to understand it as having a much wider application. He means it to involve the use of reason and intelligence not only in the courts of princes but in any situation in life. More was always keenly interested in the various ways people both resist and resent the appeal to reason; the subject abuts on his Erasmian interest in folly. So it is here: 'I've come across this mixture of conceit, stupidity, and stubbornness in several different places. On one occasion I even met it in England.' And we switch from the garden in Antwerp to the Cardinal's court in England.

But the talk is not at first about 'conceit, stupidity, and stubbornness', or not in an obvious way, but about something quite different: thieves. An opinionated lawyer was present, who 'was speaking with great enthusiasm about the stern measures that were then being taken against thieves'.

'We're hanging them all over the place,' he said, 'I've seen as many as twenty on a single gallows. And that's what I find so odd.

Considering how few of them get away with it, why are we still plagued with so many robbers?'

Raphael is at once provoked into giving him the answer: poor people find it impossible to stay alive without becoming criminals. And he embarks on a quick survey of some of the salient features of English society. In his view, the chief breeding-ground for thieves is the feudal system itself which encourages great households to man themselves with whole platoons of retainers and servants:

Well, first of all there are lots of noblemen who live like drones on the labour of other people, in other words, of their tenants, and keep bleeding them white by constantly raising their rents. For that's their only idea of practical economy—otherwise they'd soon be ruined by their extravagance. But not content with remaining idle themselves, they take round with them vast numbers of equally idle retainers, who have never been taught any method of earning their living. The moment their master dies, or they themselves fall ill, they're promptly given the sack—for these noblemen are far more sympathetic towards idleness than illness, and their heirs often can't afford to keep up such large establishments. Now a sacked retainer is apt to get violently hungry, if he doesn't resort to violence. For what's the alternative? He can, of course, wander around until his clothes and his body are both worn out, and he's nothing but a mass of rags and sores. But in that state no gentleman will condescend to employ him, and no farmer can risk doing so—for who could be less likely to serve a poor man faithfully, sweating away with mattock and hoe for a beggarly wage and a barely adequate diet, than a man who has been brought up in the lap of luxury, and is used to swaggering about in military uniform, looking down his nose at everyone else in the neighbourhood?

With great economy on More's part, we are made to feel for a moment what it is like (for instance) to be a small tenant-farmer who can't take the risk of employing a sacked retainer because he has already had reason to fear his tyranny. A complex social situation, at once specific and representative, is imagined from the inside. Nor does More exclude sympathy for the petty bully now in need of a job: 'a sacked retainer is apt to get violently hungry, if he doesn't resort to violence'—though here More's Latin is neater and more ruthless in pressing the stark alternatives: 'interim illi esurient strennue, nisi strennue latrocinentur' (Yale, p. 62). Throughout the entire passage we are brought up against the friction of believable human cases; there are no bland generalities. More's strategy is to stress the human cost of bad government.

Raphael goes on to another crying abuse, as he sees it, of English society, and the new topic is signalled by an abrupt change of tempo and a startling figure of speech:

'But that's not the only thing that compels people to steal. There are other factors at work which must, I think, be peculiar to your country.'

'What are they?' asked the Cardinal.

'Sheep,' I told him. 'These placid creatures, which used to require so little food, have now apparently developed a raging appetite, and turned into man-eaters. Fields, houses, towns, everything goes down their throats...'

A second rapid survey follows, this time of the evils of the large-scale conversion of arable land to pastoral, with the consequent evictions of the peasantry. For a few moments he dwells on the dispossessed tenant-farmers and their families:

... hundreds of farmers are evicted. They're either cheated or bullied into giving up their property, or systematically ill-treated until they're finally forced to sell. Whichever way it's done, out the poor creatures have to go, men and women, husbands and wives, widows and orphans, mothers and tiny children, together with all their employees —whose great numbers are not a sign of wealth, but simply of the fact that you can't run a farm without plenty of manpower. Out they have to go from the homes they know so well, and they can't find anywhere else to live. Their whole stock of furniture wouldn't fetch much of a price, even if they could afford to wait for a suitable offer. But they can't, so they get very little indeed for it. By the time they've been wandering around for a bit, this little is all used up, and then what can they do but steal—and be very properly hanged?

As with the dismissed retainers, the entire social process is unsparingly imagined—from loss of lawful occupation to vagrancy to theft and so to execution. For all the brevity of the account, however, the process is seen to be a complex one, and any number of variations are allowed for. But it comes to the same thing in the end. Raphael's survey of English society has become a speech for the prosecution: 'Get rid of these pernicious practices...'

You allow people to be brought up in the worst possible way, and systematically corrupted from their earliest years. Finally, when they grow up and commit the crimes they were obviously destined to commit, ever since they were children, you start punishing them.

And so to the final punch-line:

In other words, you create thieves, and then punish them for stealing!

Or in More's even terser Latin: 'quid aliud quaeso quam facitis fures, & iidem plectitis?' (Yale, p. 70).

The whole of Raphael's speech is a brilliant rhetorical declamation, which is brought to an expertly managed climax. But what is its subject? It ends as it began: with the hanging of thieves. But its true concern is misgovernment, the mis-ordering of society. Its subject forms in fact the second of the two chief themes of *Utopia*, for if the first was the possibility of applying reason to life ('Why don't you become a king's counsellor?'), the other is how to organize society, or (to use the title More himself gave to his *libellus*) 'concerning the best state of the commonwealth'. The topic of the hanging of thieves is a kind of synecdoche, a part for the whole: it serves Raphael (and More) as a convenient means of entry into his real subject, the corrupt institutions of society, with their staggeringly unjust distribution of wealth and property. This is why Raphael's diatribe takes off from the mention of thieves and returns to thieves at its close. The essential point, in terms of More's larger strategy in *Utopia*, is that the topic of thieving (appropriating the property of others) anticipates the ultimate remedy for this social evil, which is not simply abolishing the death penalty and substituting forced labour, which is Raphael's intermediate solution, but the remedy discovered by him in Utopia: the abolition of property as such, the sharing of all things in common so that theft is simply not possible. The entire topic of theft and of what to do about thieves sets up one half of an antithesis the other half of which is later supplied by the idea of communism. Abolish property and you abolish theft.

If the Morton episode, or this part of it, is taken in this light, it follows that it is quite misleading to refer to it, as Professor Hexter does, as 'a digression on the condition of England'. It is not a digression at all. It is not a digression because it has an essential function in the imaginative and rhetorical working of *Utopia*. But to see why this should be, we must glance at the end of Book Two.

When Raphael has completed his description of Utopia, we return in imagination to Christendom. This is one of the great moments of the work. The description of Utopia has ended with a moving account of the Utopians' version of the Lord's Prayer, and it is with (so to speak) the sounds of their solemn religious music still in our ears that we come back to Europe, back to the world as it is—and as it has been evoked in Book One. The impersonal voice of the author-narrator is now changed for the very personal tones of Raphael Hythlodaeus. He at once begins the long summing-up or peroration, which C. S. Lewis called 'this magnificent rebuke of all existing societies'.[4] Everything that went before it in *Utopia* leads up to this. But previously, and particularly in the long description of the island which fills Book Two, More's satire on the social order in the old world has been either indirect or directed to *specific* abuses. Only now does he make a direct assault on the entire system. The effect, coming as it does at the end of the work, is one of great energy being released.

[4] *English Literature in the Sixteenth Century Excluding Drama* (Oxford, 1954), p. 169.

In the course of this peroration, Raphael's praise of Utopia becomes simultaneously a dispraise of Europe:

Everyone gets a fair share, so there are never any poor men or beggars. Nobody owns anything, but everyone is rich—for what greater wealth can there be than cheerfulness, peace of mind, and freedom from anxiety? Instead of being worried about his food supply, upset by the plaintive demands of his wife, afraid of poverty for his son, and baffled by the problem of finding a dowry for his daughter, the Utopian can feel absolutely sure that he, his wife, his children, his grandchildren, his great-grandchildren, his great-great-grandchildren, and as long a line of descendants as the proudest peer could wish to look forward to, will always have enough to eat and enough to make them happy...

—a good example, this last, of More's expressive shaping of sentences, here pursuing consequences into the far future through several generations. And finally, after dwelling on the lives of the exploited poor in Europe, he reaches what has since become the most famous sentence in *Utopia* (which I shall quote in the Tudor English of Ralph Robinson):

Therfore when I consider and way in my mind all these commen wealthes, which now a dayes any where do florish, so god help me, I can perceaue nothing but a certein conspiracy of riche men procuringe theire own commodities vnder the name and title of the commen wealth.

I am arguing that this peroration and Raphael's diatribe in Morton's court belong together. They are two parts of one conception, one device; the two arms of a pincer-movement. The Morton episode can of course be enjoyed on its own, but it contributes vitally to the effect of the peroration, for in the peroration Raphael picks up points he had made earlier, and by implication now answers earlier questions. The sentence about the 'conspiracy of riche men' ('quaedam conspiratio diuitum') gains force from the account Raphael had earlier given of the rich dispossessing the poor and of the travesty of a judicial system which punishes with the death penalty people who are forced into crime in order to stay alive. Similarly the sentence I have just quoted about the Utopian's freedom from anxiety ('Instead of being worried about his food supply ...') is all the stronger if we recall, as we probably will, the description of the evicted families on the road. They are worried to death about their food supply; some of their members may well be hanged for trying to secure it. In fact Professor Hexter's theory of the composition of *Utopia* might perhaps be emended so as to make the Morton episode not a separate 'digression' on the condition of England but the essential half of a two-part conception, all of which was planned and composed at the same time. The obtuse lawyer, talking about the problem of thieves, had asked: 'Considering how few of them get away with it, why are we still plagued with so many robbers?' The full answer is reserved for the peroration: 'For obviously the end of money means the end of all those types of criminal behaviour which daily punishments are powerless to check: fraud, theft, burglary, brawls, riot' and so on.

Raphael's diatribe occupies only the first half of the Morton episode. The remaining part further dramatizes the themes already treated—the application of reason to life, and how to order a commonwealth—and is finally rounded off with a farcical incident of quarrelling between an irresponsible wit and an irascible friar. The incident is, as Edward Surtz observes, a *reductio ad absurdum* illustrating human folly and divisiveness, a kind of *scherzo* on the previous themes: mere flippant irresponsibility on the one side and pugnacious touchiness on the other, quite the reverse of the solicitude and concern shown by Raphael and More himself in the rest of the dialogue.[5]

The scene at Morton's court is one of the best things in

---

[5] Yale *Utopia*, p. cxlv. I can see no justification for the view that the irresponsible wit (the 'parasitus', i.e. 'hanger-on' as the Yale translation has it, or 'professional diner-out' as Paul Turner calls him) is a self-portrait of More himself. See Alison Hanham, *Richard III and his early historians 1483–1535* (Oxford, 1975), p. 156. R. C. Elliott (op. cit.) suggests that the incident derives from Horace (*Satires*, I.vii); in view of More's use of Horace's phrase 'perfusus aceto' this is possible, though More's treatment is very remote from Horace's.

Utopia, though there is admittedly a slight oddity, even clumsiness, about a dialogue of such length inserted so frankly into another dialogue. Yet the net result is curiously effective, suggesting art rather than mere chance. For it undoubtedly adds to Raphael's reality as a character; it endows his past life with solidity and credibility. And by making him a friend of Cardinal Morton, More's own esteemed and loved patron, it establishes a profound alliance between Raphael and More (the speaker), suggesting even an ultimate likeness if not identity of attitude between them. Of course from another point of view, one outside the fiction altogether, we can say that Raphael *is* More, not Raphael's interlocutor but the author of *Utopia* and as such quite as much More the author as More the speaker is. We can go further and say that this evocation of Morton's court obscurely adumbrates the dual nature of *Utopia* as an act of imaginative discourse—its peculiar status as both an objective fiction and a subjective inner dialogue, with Raphael as both antagonist to 'More' and as a projection of the other More, Utopia's creator.

At this point the episode is wound up, and we return to Raphael talking to More and Giles in the garden in Antwerp. And there follows a kind of pause. The Book now enters its second movement. For the whole of this Book One dialogue falls into two parts, each of them opening with the same question: Should one (should Raphael) become a king's counsellor? That was how Peter Giles opened the first part; now More says the same: 'I still can't help thinking that if you could only overcome your aversion to court life, your advice would be extremely useful to the public.' In other words: Why don't you enter a king's service? And we start on the second phase of the dialogue, which has the same themes as the first—human resistance to reason, and the state of the commonwealth.

But this time the dialogue is conducted in a rather different manner. The first part was vividly dramatic: Raphael's diatribe, especially, had at times a painful immediacy; it powerfully evoked the actuality of life in a misgoverned state. This second phase will be more discursive, more removed from ordinary life, although some lively fables will be worked in to show how other countries visited by Raphael have solved their problems of government. More important, the Morton episode had looked at government from the viewpoint of the governed, the people themselves, or rather the lowest rank of the people, the poor and destitute. This second part, by contrast, will turn its attention to the governors, and in particular kings. Indeed it is only now, looking back at the Morton episode, that we will notice the peculiar absence of kings from it. Morton is said to be the king's right hand ('at the time of my visit the whole country seemed to depend on him'), but the atmosphere of his court is not particularly royalist ('I never hesitated to speak freely in front of the Cardinal'). Only now, in the second part, does More confront that unignorable feature of the society of his time, the monarch.

Raphael starts with a brilliant imaginary account of a council-meeting at the French court:

... just imagine me in France, at a top-secret meeting of the Cabinet. The King himself is in the chair, and round the table sit all his expert advisers, earnestly discussing ways and means of solving the following problems: how can His Majesty keep a grip on Milan, and get Naples back into his clutches? How can he conquer Venice, and complete the subjection of Italy? How can he then establish control over Flanders, Brabant, and finally the whole of Burgundy?—not to mention all the other countries he has already invaded in his dreams. ... And now for the knottiest problem of all—what's to be done about the English?

This is the first of the two royal councils imagined by Raphael. And in order to bring out the tight shape and urgent rhythm of this phase of Book One, it is essential to see how these councils are contrasted with each other with an effect of mounting climax. The Yale co-editor, the late Fr. Edward Surtz, obscures this rhythmical arrangement by running together the Morton episode with these two scenes: 'Through three dramatic scenes (at Morton's table, at the French King's meeting, and at an anonymous ruler's council), Hythlodaeus shows how his salutary advice would be resisted. ...'[6] This fails to clarify More's real structure: the Morton episode stands on its own, and deals with the governed; the other two are meant to be taken together and deal with kings. Moreover the talk at Morton's court is said by Raphael to have actually occurred; the other two are imagined by him, and are therefore more frankly fabulous, even fantastic, in their tone and treatment.

This phase of Book One is the most daringly anti-royalist part of *Utopia*. It is not about (what would have been conventional enough in More's time) how kings can govern their subjects, but about how subjects can control their kings. Since this was at the very least a delicate topic, the writing here shows More using some circumspection, yet without in any way pulling his punches. Indeed he is never more sardonically incisive. The first council, set in France, deals with foreign affairs; the second deals with home affairs. The first shows a king's aggression against other countries; the second, a king's aggression against his own subjects. The first is therefore a satire on the power-politics of early sixteenth-century Europe as it concerns the pursuit of national aggrandisement. The second exposes the avarice and greed of a king who manipulates the laws of his realm in order to extort money from his subjects. While the first council was set in France, however, the second was set in an unnamed country, with the anonymity of the king working as a broad hint: the extortionary policies so scathingly detailed by Raphael allude to the fiscal policies of Henry VII—who had died only seven years before the publication of *Utopia*.

Each of Raphael's little illustrative fables pointedly puts kings in their place. In the first, the land of the Achorians ('Nolandia' is Turner's name), the king's desire to rule two kingdoms at once—to the severe disadvantage of his own people—is finally checked by the ultimatum given him by his subjects. He must choose one kingdom or the other. 'So that exemplary monarch was forced to hand over the new kingdom to a friend of

[6] Yale *Utopia*, p. cxxviii; though later Surtz observes some of the oppositions between the two royal councils (p. cxxix).

his—who was very soon thrown out—and make do with the old one.' In the second, the land of the Macarians (Turner's 'Happiland'), the king is required to swear at his coronation not to keep in his treasury more than a thousand pounds of gold or silver. He is therefore prevented by statute from amassing wealth in the manner of Henry VII.

This coolly irreverent attitude to kings runs through the whole of *Utopia*, and to forestall any possibility that an exceptionally inattentive reader might miss it his attention is repeatedly called to it by the marginal comments which were added to More's text. (They were probably by Erasmus and Peter Giles.) One such passage deals with the vileness of hunting as a sport, and the marginal note reads: 'Yet this is today the art of the superior beings at court' ('At haec hodie ars est deorum aulicorum'). Similarly the remark about dicing which is worked into the account of Utopian recreations—'Dice and that kind of foolish game they are not acquainted with'—has the marginal note: 'Yet now dicing is the amusement of kings' ('At nunc alea principum lusus est'). However, the very first sentence of *Utopia* had referred to Henry VIII and Charles in the hyperbolical language conventional at the time: 'There was recently', More begins, 'a rather serious difference of opinion between that great expert in the art of government, His Invincible Majesty, King Henry the Eighth of England, and His Serene Highness, Prince Charles of Castile.' Only retrospectively, perhaps, in the course of reading the work, will a reader find a certain mischievous hollowness in those large epithets.

To Raphael Hythlodaeus (whose name of course means 'purveyor of nonsense', so we need not take him seriously), kings are not much better than tiresome nuisances. They are obstacles to good government, self-important bores, whose egoistic and infantile desires have somehow to be got round, deflected and nullified so that as little harm as possible is done. But in the world of *Utopia*, kings are both menacingly present, sinister looming shadows, and at the same time exhilaratingly absent—absent, that is, to the imagination that dares to project a future without them. Indeed one might say that for the reader of *Utopia* kings have been reduced to being mere ideas in the minds of their subjects. For what is ultimately powerful is not force but thought, not the capacity to coerce obedience but the capacity to envisage the possibility of change, to realize that what seems here and now an absolute necessity is perhaps only a temporary state of affairs. Accordingly, *Utopia* leaves us at its close with an image not so much of kings, courts, and councils as of men arguing about them. It is the power of thought that finally matters.

Utopia is an act of imagination on the part of its author which also urges the exercise of imagination upon its reader. It continually asks him to put himself into other people's situations, to adopt a different point of view and so become a little more flexible of mind. The implied injunction to the reader to *imagine*, to let the mind play over a situation in a controlled fantasy, becomes almost a leitmotif of *Utopia*. It is in fact one of the recognizable features of Raphael as a character: 'Suppose ... you suggest a policy that you've seen adopted elsewhere ...'; 'What do you suppose would happen if I started telling a king to make sensible laws ...?'; '... just imagine me in France ...'; 'Now let's imagine another situation ...'[7] These expressions of supposing, imagining, and putting the case shade off into others which similarly describe acts of creative thinking: '... when I think of the fair and sensible arrangements in Utopia ...; when I consider all this, I feel much more sympathy with Plato, and much less surprise at his refusal to legislate for a city that rejected egalitarian principles'. And finally: 'You're bound to take that view, for you simply can't imagine what it would be like ...' Raphael's vignettes of the dismissed retainers

[7] One or two of Turner's phrases containing the word 'suppose' or 'imagine' are free renderings of conditional clauses in More's Latin. But elsewhere More does use words meaning 'suppose' or 'imagine': e.g. 'An non me putas, si apud aliquem regem decreta sana proponerem' (Yale, p. 86); 'Age finge me apud regem esse Gallorum' (Yale, p. 86). *OED* quotes More as an early authority for 'imagine' meaning 'suppose': 'Imagine your self in the same case...' (*Four Last Things*).

and the evicted farmers work to the same end: they too are the fruit of a mind which has closely observed the world and is yet not overcome by the assumption that nothing can be different, that radical change is unthinkable. For More, as for Erasmus, it was thinkable.

To this I may add a brief postscript. The anonymous Elizabethan play called *The Book of Sir Thomas More*—which survives only in manuscript—contains a scene thought by many good judges to be in Shakespeare's hand. It is a curious coincidence, if nothing else, that it should be composed in a style in some ways very like More's own style in *Utopia*. In this scene, Shakespeare's More is trying to win away the London rioters from their fury against the immigrant workers ('the strangers'). At one point he speaks almost in Raphael's voice:

> Grant them removed and grant that this your noise
> Hath chid down all the majesty of England.
> Imagine that you see the wretched strangers,
> Their babies at their backs, with their poor luggage,
> Plodding to th'ports and coasts for transportation...

He tells them to use their imagination; more than that, he makes them use it. And in doing so he succeeds in pacifying the rioters by bringing them to a more humane sense of the plight of the immigrants.

Shakespeare's More speaks with a voice modified by Elizabethan assumptions: he is more sonorously monarchical than the real More would have been. For all that, it is tempting to think that, in writing this scene, Shakespeare recalled not only the person of More himself but the characteristic strategy of More the mental traveller and the creator of Utopia. Indeed, as a man supremely endowed with imagination himself, Shakespeare could hardly have failed to respond to that intensely serious play of mind which distinguished More from all his English predecessors: 'Imagine that you see...'

Playing 'The Resurrection'[1]

MEG TWYCROSS

This essay is about the performance of a medieval English mystery play, and what it showed me, the producer, about the way in which these plays seem to work dramatically. The play was the York Carpenters' pageant of *The Resurrection of Christ*, performed in March 1977 in the Nuffield Theatre Studio of the University of Lancaster. Here I attempted to re-create the effect of a pageant-waggon staging in a street-shaped space, with a standing and potentially mobile audience. I have documented the details, and the historical evidence for my reconstruction, elsewhere.[2] I want here to concentrate on what happens to the play in performance: how the physical circumstances of production seem to me to have been exploited by the playwright, and especially how the audience is implicated in the play.

Let us start with the most obvious feature. With this kind of staging, actors and audience are very close to each other. There are of course no footlights. There is not even a respectful gulf of open space marking the divide between them: even in the widest urban street, there is no room for one. The actors may even have to walk into the crowd. Entrances and exits are of course made through the audience, but from the script of *The Resurrection* it is clear that several speeches, in certain cases

[1] I should like to thank Miss Sarah Carpenter of the University of Edinburgh, and Miss Helen Phillips of the University of Lancaster, who played the Magdalen, for their invaluable help and encouragement during the writing of this essay.
[2] 'The Flemish *Ommegang* and its Pageant Cars', *Medieval English Theatre*, 2 i and ii, especially pp. 19–33, 83–4, 88–9.

even whole scenes, are played at some remove from the waggon.
The Centurion, for example, begins to speak out of earshot of
Pilate:

> [To] oure princes and prestes bedene
> Of this affray,
> *I woll go weten*, withouten wene
> What thei can saye.[3]   (45–8)

The Maries see the Angel from a distance:

> Sisteris! a ȝonge child, *as we goo*
> *Makand mornyng*,
> *I see it sitte wher we wende to*,
> In white clothyng...   (225–8)

so they presumably play their whole scene of lamentation in the
street. In our production, even on the nights when the audience
tried to keep their distance, they were never more than three
feet away from the actors.

This physical closeness made the audience very much an
active factor in the performance, and to us an unpredictable
one. We did not know until they were actually there on the first
night how we, as well as they, were going to react in these
unfamiliar 'medieval' circumstances. It was not just that we did
not know where they were going to stand, or whether they
would move out of the way at the right time, or whether the
action we had rehearsed at street-level would be at all visible:
they presented an active physical presence which had to be
reckoned with. They might be responsive, or they might be
inert, but they were *there*. In an open-air, close-up form of
theatre like this, it is impossible, no, fatal, to pretend they are
not. You cannot sustain the familiar darkened-auditorium illusion, that the audience are eavesdropping on a private conversation. The actors can solicit their attention, or they may
pointedly ignore them, but they must acknowledge their presence.

[3] Quotations are from *The York Mystery Plays*, ed. Lucy Toulmin Smith (1885,
repr. New York, 1963), slightly adapted.

Because we approach these plays from the other side of the three hundred years of the proscenium arch, we find it difficult to get this relationship in perspective. Critics tend to feel that the medieval theatre must have been either extremely naïve, or extremely radical. In fact it is neither. The deliberate audience-involvement that we notice is not approached in the embarrassingly self-conscious way of some modern theatre. It is just accepted that the audience is there, and that the characters can talk to them. There is a certain self-confidence in the handling that precludes embarrassment.

This does not mean that the characters become 'part of' the audience, or that they are 'the same as' them. It is difficult, of course, to tell how far the fact that our characters were wearing fifteenth-century clothing marked them out as peculiarly separate; but the effect would have been the same in the original productions, because it is not primarily a matter of costuming, but that the actors belong to a different world, and that they are in charge of the action. Meeting the Magdalen face to face in the crowd was rather like seeing the Queen 'as near as I see you' in a Jubilee celebration—if one can imagine seeing the Queen in tears.

Despite the lack of physical separation, the actors are still inhabitants of the world of the play, the audience still onlookers. The illusion is not 'broken'.[4] But the playwright uses this physical closeness to extend as it were the terms of the contract between them. The characters (not merely the actors) are made to acknowledge the audience's presence, and to make use of it.

This operates within strict limits. The audience have no independent hand in the action. They cannot control the course of events, nor is it ever suggested that they might. (Sometimes

---

[4] R. C. Johnson, in an otherwise very interesting article on 'Audience Involvement in the Tudor Interlude', *Theatre Notebook*, 24 (1969–70), 101–10, makes this assumption, which seems common to writers on this kind of drama: it is a much too simplistic view. The best discussion on the topic I have found is in J. W. Robinson, ' Medieval English Dramaturgy', Ph.D. Thesis, Glasgow (1961), pp. 279–81, though this is based entirely on scripts, not performance.

it is suggested that they *might have*, but that is a different kind of game.) They may occasionally be given the role of 'crowd', say as spectators at the *Via Dolorosa*, but this is not extended to full participation in the action; they are used as spectators because they *are* spectators, no more. Most of the time, if they have a role, it is the role of audience: a willing ear, sympathetic to lamentation, attentive to instruction, cheerfully submissive to bullying. But they have consented to be an audience more actively implicated than we are used to. The characters seem to be saying, 'We know you're there, and we intend to use you.' The audience respond, 'We're willing to be used, and we'll answer to any role you like to cast us in, friend or enemy. But we are still both aware that we're playing a game.'

This relationship is thus as much part of the dramatic illusion as the more obvious forms of stagecraft. The interesting thing is that this appears to be recognized openly. This is part and parcel of what seems to be in medieval theatre a heightened consciousness of the whole fact of dramatic illusion. This is partly due, no doubt, to the use of distinctly non-naturalistic stage props, like the Chester *Noah* animals on boards, and, for example, the use of masks. Far from trying to pretend that these things are real, the playwrights underline the lack of naturalism, as when Noah remarks on how smoothly his Ark-building is going.[5] It is also partly due to the medieval sense, particularly in religious matters, of the 'figural view of reality', which produces a drama where it is quite natural for one character to hand another a symbol to commemorate a real but many-layered event: 'This beest, John, thou bere with the ... John, it is the lamb of me'.[6] The effect it seems to have in our present context is that the audience are invited into a kind of complicity with the players, in which they behave as if they were taking the illusion for reality, while at the same time reserving the right to remember that it is only illusion. But there would be no point in this game if it were not also accepted that the illusion

[5] Wakefield *Noah*, 283–8 and throughout the speech.
[6] Wakefield *John the Baptist*, 209, 211; stage direction *hic tradat ei agnum dei*.

represents a historical and spiritual reality which is vitally important to both actors and audience.

The play does not always, of course, operate on this intimate level of audience-recognition. There may not be a natural 'footlights' line of demarcation, but there is always the opportunity of withdrawing from acknowledged contact with the audience. When the actor climbs up on the stage, the height, and the fact that he has entered a frame, give him a certain distance which he can choose to use or ignore. Pilate can look down on the audience and hector them, or he can enter into a 'private' conversation with Annas and Caiaphas (though even this illusion of privacy can be manipulated by the playwright, as we shall see).

The extreme of distancing comes when the 'framing effect' of the waggon posts and fascia is exploited so that the playwright, in the midst of events, suddenly resolves the action into a familiar picture—the Annunciation, the Crucifixion, Pentecost. The contrast between action and image, the sudden shift of focus, can be emotionally extremely powerful; at one moment the characters are talking to the audience, at the next they are part of a venerable icon. This suddenness of contrast seems also to be part of the playing with illusion: 'Now you see it, now you don't' in reverse. But even on a less striking level, the playwrights seem conscious of their ability to exploit the contrasts between different distances, different depths of focus.

The writer of the York *Resurrection* is particularly good at these shifts. He is also particularly adept at manipulating the actor–audience relationship which we have been looking at. In part this is due to the theme of the play itself. I should like now to analyse his use of this relationship, starting off with some of the simpler and more familiar instances of audience-involvement, and gradually complicating things.

The comic effects are probably the most recognizable exploitation of the relationship, rather like circus or music-hall; the Soldiers threaten the audience with their swords, the audience shriek, knowing that the Soldiers are not really going to attack them, but thinking that those swords are sharp and dangerously close, all the same. Here we are only a step away from the circus clown with his hosepipe or bag of flour. We had planned for this in rehearsal; what we had not reckoned on was the way in which the playing to the audience would extend itself. What had in rehearsal been private conversations became public boasts or threats: 'And sone we schall crake his croune Whoso comes here' (185–6) became 'Don't any of *you* try anything on while we're asleep'. Audience-involving 'business' blossomed: the First Soldier, coming round after a stolen nap, found himself moved to exchange a luxurious stretch and self-satisfied smile with the audience before realizing, with a mighty double-take, that the body had gone.

This did not only happen with comedy, however. We found the whole balance of what we had read on the page and prepared in rehearsal as private deliberation, voice-over on which the audience were to be permitted to eavesdrop, shifting in performance. Suddenly there was no such thing as a private soliloquy. The Centurion's opening speech, 'A! blissid lorde Adonay!' (37) is ostensibly addressed either to himself or to God, but he found himself sharing what had read like private bewilderment with the audience among whom he was standing—'What may thes mervayles signifie?' (38), and thus calling on them to sympathize with his perplexity. But here something else is happening. The audience *know* what the marvels signify. They cannot tell him, because he is a character in the story, and they are not; but they want him to realize what has happened, and then they want him to convince Pilate and the Bishops.

Because the audience are not coming to the play cold (indeed, in some ways they are already better informed than the characters), the playwright can use their superior knowledge to engage them emotionally. A 'good' character who doubts, or is mystified, or who gets things unwittingly wrong, and 'soliloquizes' about it, is in this kind of staging actively calling on the audience for help. (This technique is particularly striking in plays about 'Joseph's Doubts'.) The audience respond with a feeling of active support, and if, as here, the situation leads into a debate with agents of the 'other side', a feeling of definite partisanship. What they do not realize is that in drawing out this support, the playwright is making them give emotional consent to their own convictions—'strengthening their faith'.

In the debate with Pilate, in fact, the Centurion talks to persuade; his speech is as much an emotional appeal as a factual one. Taking up the 'all creation wept' theme found in the commentaries,[7] he gives the inanimate world emotions:

> All elementis, both *olde and ʒing,*
> *In ther maneres thai made mornyng*
>   In ilke a stede,
> And *knewe be countenaunce* that *ther kyng*
>   Was done to dede.
>
> The sonne *for woo he waxed all wanne;*
> The mone and sterres of schynyng blanne;
> The erthe *tremeled,* and *also manne*
>   Began to speke...   (86–94)

Against this, the logical replies of Pilate and Caiaphas

> ʒe wote oure clerkis the clipsis thei call
>   Such sodayne sight:
> Both sonne and mone that sesonne schall
>   Lak of ther light   (99–102)

sound like rationalizations. The Centurion has to use this kind of language because he is talking about something outside nature; the audience accept it, because they know that something outside nature has happened, and because by this time they want the unbelievers to realize it too.

It is characteristic of debates in medieval drama that they are there for the audience rather than for the characters. It does not matter if the Centurion fails to persuade Pilate, though of course we would like him to, provided he has persuaded us. It is a

---

[7] *Glossa Ordinaria*, PL 114. 176, 348: Ludolphus de Saxonia, *Vita Jesu Christi* (1878), pp. 119 and 131, who quotes Chrysostom, Pope Leo, Anselm, and Augustine.

form of didacticism, but a more subtle one than straightforward assertion. The debate's function is to lay out both sides of the case for the audience to consider. To quote from a completely different context:

> If you put a superior thing side by side with an inferior, for the sake of comparison, that is, in this case, the virtue over against the vice, you will get a firm understanding of their important and distinctive qualities. For when you compare the qualities of contrary things, you should be immediately and clearly able to assess which are the better ones. So when you have surveyed these roots, branches, and fruits of ours, it will be up to you to choose which one you want.[8]

There is never any doubt about the eventual outcome; of the green tree and the dry, which would you choose? but the demonstration, against suitably strong, if suitably venal, opposition, is necessary, in order to confirm with you that your choice is the right one. The playwright manœuvres you into partisanship with the right side to make quite sure that you give your emotional as well as your intellectual consent to it.

We have been concentrating on the evidence of the play in performance. The most striking example in the *Resurrection* of the use of the audience is almost invisible in the script, and yet it comes over very powerfully in performance to reinforce the theme of the play. It plays with the two worlds of involvement and illusion by first acknowledging the presence of the audience, and then pretending that in fact they aren't there, that there really is a private stage-world in which the characters can't be overheard. Then, in a final sleight of hand, this too is shown up to be an illusion.

Let me elucidate. The *Resurrection* is an extended *Quem Quaeritis*; it goes to some trouble to make this quite clear. It is not particularly concerned with expressing the cosmic, triumphal aspects of the Resurrection; this has been done already, in the preceding pageant of the *Harrowing of Hell*. Like the *Quem Quaeritis*, which takes its essential character from an earlier age,

[8] Pseudo-Hugh of St. Victor, *De fructibus carnis et spiritus*, PL 176. 997, my translation.

it concentrates on the theme of bearing witness to the event, true witness and false witness. The evidence is scrupulously displayed, both by the Maries and the Soldiers: the empty tomb; the sudary; the angelic message; the portents that surround the actual moment of Christ's rising. At the end, the epigraph could be

> Credendum est magis soli Mariae veraci
> quam Judaeorum turbae fallaci.[9]

But it goes beyond the *Ludus Paschalis* in giving the actual ocular proof: dressing up an actor as Christ, and making him emerge from the tomb in the sight of all. The audience are also made witnesses.

The end of the play thus rests on an immense dramatic irony. It seems to show Pilate and the Jews successful: they have bribed the Soldiers to lie, the scandal has been swept under the carpet. But they have not succeeded, because the audience know the truth: they have seen it with their own eyes. Once the audience is there, the argument is no longer about fooling some hypothetical 'people' of first-century Jews and Romans: *they* are 'the people'. They were swept into the role in this play when Annas said

> *The pepull*, sirs, *in this same steede*
> Before ȝou saide with a hole hede
> That he was worthy to be dede
>   (19–21)

At the end of the play, Pilate and the Bishops are plotting to keep from them the truth of an event they have just witnessed with their own eyes. Caiaphas says, 'We nolde, for thyng that myght befall That no man wiste' (405–6); the reaction is, 'Well, that's a bit late, because *we* know'. The playwright plays off the fiction that Pilate, Annas, and Caiaphas are having a private

---

[9] *Victimae Paschali Laudes*, v.6. This sequence was frequently incorporated into the *Ludus Paschalis*: see K. Young, *The Drama of the Medieval Church* (Oxford, 1933), i. 273 ff.

conversation (which is reinforced visually if they draw together inside the 'walls ' of their waggon while the Soldiers remain outside) against the real-life fact that the audience can hear everything they are saying.

This would not work if the play had not consistently implicated the audience and made them conscious of their own role in the drama. As it is, they are again in the familiar position of being one jump ahead of the characters (not only have they seen Christ, they have been privy to the Soldiers' desperate fabrication of a story). The playwright then points this up by making the characters openly despise the audience. Pilate sums up:

> And *to the pepull* schall we saie
> It is gretely agaynste oure lay
>   To trowe such thing.
> *So schall thei deme*, both nyght and day,
>   All is lesyng.   (444–8)

'The people' can be easily fooled. The audience are probably made more aware of their own separateness because the characters have antagonized them: there would be no reason to feel that way if they were in agreement.

We then get a curious two-layer effect. Pilate ends the play with a piece of 'confession' moralizing, half-stepping out of character:

> Thus schall the sothe be bought and solde,
> And treasoune schall for trewthe be tolde
>   (449–50)

and an ambiguous remark, addressed ostensibly to Annas and Caiaphas,

> Therfore ay in youre hartis ȝe holde
> This counsaile clene   (451–2)

To the Jews, this would seem to mean 'Keep quiet about this'; to the audience 'Remember what you have seen and think about it'. On one level, the cover-up conspiracy is going on here and now, aimed at the audience, who are, however, not fooled by it; thus, 'The Jowis and thair errour ar confoundit'. At the same

2a *Mary Magdalen*: Of ilke a myscheve he is medicyne [195] The 'affective' mode in action. Note also how the sleeping Soldier is completely forgotten: he belongs to a different world.   Photo: Ivor Dykes

2b The Resurrection. The familiar icon is created in the frame of the pageant-waggon.   Photo: Joe Thompson

2c   *Pilate*: And to þe pepull schall we saie
                     It is gretely agaynste oure lay
                     to trowe such thing [446]
A more conventional situation: an apparently 'private' conversation. The
soldiers are, however, on the level of the crowd, which opens out the picture.
Photo: Les Stringer © *Times Higher Education Supplement*

time, we are watching a historical event, with the valid 'story-line' observation that 'this saying is commonly reported among the Jews to this day' (Matthew 28:15). This double time-focus, and its implications, is more usually commented on with reference to the 'anachronism' of, say, the Wakefield *Second Shepherds' Play*; but the presence and involvement of the audience make it an ongoing thing throughout the Cycles. The difference between this and ordinary anachronism is that, as here, one lens may show quite a different picture from the other, not the same one made contemporary.

To move to what may seem a completely different part of the play, both in style and technique, it may come as a surprise to the reader to be told that the three Maries and their lamentation were engaged in the most intense form of audience-involvement in the play. On paper, they look remote from this. Their role is about as far from naturalistic drama as can be imagined. A modern audience, used to the convention that grief is inarticulate, and to whom the vocabulary of lament is unfamiliar, finds the whole concept of public, ritualized mourning alien, the thought that they might actually be touched by it unimaginable. In the type of production that invites the audience to observe the Maries at a distance, as private persons undergoing an emotional crisis, they become tedious; we listen to them out of good manners, or because we feel we ought. Set them down in the audience, on their level, 'as we goo Makand mornyng' (225–6), and their role suddenly becomes quite different. They are almost agitators, inciters to emotion.

They are down among the audience partly because of the dictates of staging (they have a journey to go before they can see the Angel), partly because the audience seem to be rather more emotionally vulnerable to figures in their midst. (For some of them, perhaps, it is the shock of finding themselves close to the source of the magic.) There seems to be a certain intentional correlation of 'togetherness' with the characters who start off down in the street (the Maries, the Centurion, the Soldiers), and of distance, though not necessarily hostile, with those who put themselves up at a height, on stage (Pilate and his boasting, Christ and the Resurrection).

So far we have been looking at emotion as the unacknowledged handmaid of argument. We now see emotion almost as a goal in itself: 'Who cannot wepe, come lerne at me'. The writer's aim is that of popular affective piety: the techniques he uses are borrowed from the vernacular lyrics and meditations. But the drama does part of the job of imagination for us. Typically, in the meditations we stir up our own sorrow at the death of Christ by focusing it on the figure of one of those near to him; but here we do not have to imagine their sorrow, as we can see it before us. As the Christ from the York *Crucifixion* is a devotional image come to life, so the Maries are the figures from the meditations made visible, embodiments of mourning.

We are not, however, to stop at contemplating them. They share the techniques of affective piety in that they are there to engage us in activity; we are to use them as channels through which to direct our emotions. They describe their suffering, drawing the audience to share in it, because they are not asking for sympathy for themselves, but for the sufferings of Christ.

They are not even lamenting over a present scene, but a remembered one; Magdalen, in the meditative tradition, visualizes the crucified Christ: 'Allas! *that I schulde se* his pyne!' (193); Mary Jacobi suggests a meditation on the Five Wounds, 'Allas! who schall my balis bete *Whanne I thynke on* his woundes wete?' (199–200) A literature which was devised to help the late medieval reader imagine the emotions of being at the Crucifixion is being used to provide the techniques for representing those emotions in characters who are supposed to have just come from the Crucifixion. If the audience was at all familiar with this kind of aid to meditation, and it seems likely that they were, they would presumably recognize their own role in it, and the end to which it was working.

Because the Maries are used as conductors for this emotion, we are not particularly interested in the individuality of their feeling. The stress in the script on '*my* sorowe', '*my* balis', '*my* mone' makes it look as if their lamentations are personal and private: but when you hear them, the very fact that they echo each other makes them already part of a group emotion. Their laments are formal in shape, almost operatic; the three voices chime in one after the other, weaving variations on the same pattern, three in one. (It also ensures that though they are down among the audience, and so not visible to all of them and therefore harder to hear, nothing of the content of their lament is really lost, as it is repeated three times.) From the point of view of the story, this shows their unity of love and purpose. As in the liturgical drama, from which the over-all shape though not the detail of the scene seems to come, this is emphasized by their shared verbal patterns. But they are also urging the audience to join in their feeling. These shared patterns are also the familiar rhetorical patterns of language traditionally used to stir emotion in the hearers: repetition: 'Allas! ... Allas! ... Allas!', 'is dede ... is dede ....'; concatenation: 'Withouten skil ... Withowten skil ...', 'Sen he is dede ... Sen he is dede ...'; and audience-involving exclamations and rhetorical questions: 'Allas! to ded I wolde be dight!' (187), 'To whome nowe schall I make my mone?' (209).

It is a familiar observation that the 'I' of affective piety is meant to be the 'I' both of the (imagined) speaker and of the reader. Affective meditation calls on the individual to respond, but with those emotions which he shares with everyone. When he is set down in a crowd, and then spoken to in the same way, he is responding as an individual still, but he will find himself doing it at the same time and to the same stimuli as everyone else; and to a certain extent, he will surrender his individuality to the movement of the group.

Audiences are, it should be remembered, vulnerable to each other's emotion. Standing in an open-air crowd, you cannot isolate yourelf and your reactions from those of your neighbour. If you feel moved to weep (and some members of our audience did, mostly old women and small girls), you cannot hide it in the protective darkness of your cinema seat. I also got the impression that by joining such an audience, you had consented to share in the group emotion, as you would nowadays with a crowd watching a sporting event. Emotions, both grief and laughter, become catching.

This works in an interesting way to neutralize any disadvantages there might have been in setting scenes in the street. When the actors are on the waggons, they are perfectly visible even from the thick of the crowd. This is not so when they are on the ground. Then only a few people can see the actors perfectly, but they can all hear, and oddly enough, seem to *feel* the reactions of the people closest to the actors. Laughter or sensations run like a ripple through the crowd to the outside edge. The actual joke or appeal may have been indistinct, may even have been a visual one, and so lost, one would think, to any but the people standing next to the actor, but the mood manages to transmit itself through the crowd. Thus not only does the audience never lose concentration, but there is very much the sense of taking part in an occasion, rather than 'merely' being spectators to a play.

It is noticeable how quickly an audience like this can be shifted *en bloc* from one emotion to another, and how adept the playwrights are at such sudden contrastive shifts. It seems characteristic of the plays in performance that they turn out, many of them, to have been constructed in blocks, each with one ruling emotion or mood, which is then played almost to the limits of its capacity, but with a very sure sense of just how much the audience can take before the mood has to be switched.

In a way, particularly with comedy and lamentation, this exploitation of one particular mood is part of the awareness of artifice of which I have been talking. A scene of lamentation will not just show characters displaying a normal (certainly not a restrained) amount of distress, it will show distress itself, formalized and orchestrated to operatic heights. Comedy will wring the last ounce of laughter out of the audience. Both can thus be placed without incongruity alongside presentations of cosmic or symbolic acts, because they seem themselves to be aware that they too are representative. This does not mean that they are stylized to the point of being remote or unnatural. They are still true to life, in the sense that each emotion is perfectly recognizable, and evokes its proper response; it is just pushed as far as it can properly go.

I am not saying that every scene is so intense, or that there are no gradual movements from one emotion to another. But quite often one is aware that there has just been a complete switch of mood, precisely when one was ready for it. This often seems to operate more on instinct than on any logical basis. It can even run directly counter to narrative probability. In the *Resurrection*, the Magdalen's second lamentation seems completely illogical. Why, having just accepted the news of the Resurrection with delight, should she suddenly turn back to weeping? But it is emotionally and thematically necessary, as I shall hope to show, and at the time, nobody questions it.

This switch is most effective where it seems most daring, in the way in which the most serious episodes in the plays are often juxtaposed with scenes of high comedy. A riotously comic scene, which exhausts the audience with laughter, will be replaced—it is as distinct as that—by an act of immense seriousness, which grows out of the silence following the dying away of that laughter. In the *Resurrection*, the laughter that accompanies the setting of the watch fades as the Soldiers fall asleep, to be replaced by the earthquake, the plainsong, and the Resurrection itself. The new seriousness neither discredits the laughter nor is discredited by it; the laughter wipes away all potential restlessness, and enhances the seriousness of what follows.

This change of mood is often accompanied by a change of mode, a shift of verbal and dramatic style. This has been noticed in such plays as the York *Crucifixion*.[10] Here Christ speaks only twice, and each time the stage picture has suddenly been resolved into a familiar devotional icon: the 'Christ seated on the Cross',

[10] See J. W. Robinson, 'The Late Medieval Cult of Jesus and the Mystery Plays', *PMLA* lxxx (1965), 508–15.

and the Crucifix itself. Each time what he says, and how he says it, comes from a completely different tradition than the noisy jibing of the Soldiers. He is a living version of the devotional images illustrated by Woolf and Gray;[11] his words belong to the kind of lyric that accompanies them in the manuscripts. We would probably consider this a non-dramatic tradition, but the playwright has no qualms about using it, and is completely justified by the results.

The plays use a much wider variety of literary and dramatic traditions than is perhaps recognized: the over-all pattern of the verse-forms tends to obscure this fact. This may partly be due to the kind of eclecticism that has never heard of the unities. We cannot know how much it is a matter of deliberate choice, and how much a matter of taking what was there. But in competent hands the effect is unmistakable. As the playwright moves from one tradition to another, he produces this sense of shifting focus, in time, and in nearness and distancing, that we have noticed.

The *Resurrection* is a particularly rich example of this. The subject itself has a complex literary and dramatic history. It was the earliest piece of liturgical drama and the playwright seems to realize its antiquity. Besides this, partly because of what the Bible leaves unsaid, and partly because of changes of emphasis in what was felt to be important about it, it has acquired more of apocryphal embroidery and of commentary than most other episodes. Our play attempts to give the fullest possible account of the event, and as a result each episode and each batch of characters belongs to a different tradition: the Soldiers, Annas, Caiaphas, Pilate, and the Centurion to the narrative apocryphal writings like the *Northern Passion* and the vernacular *Gospel of Nicodemus*; the Maries, and especially the Magdalen, from the tradition of popular affective meditation and romantic hagiography; the Resurrection itself, and the *Quem Quaeritis*,

[11] Rosemary Woolf, *The English Religious Lyric in the Middle Ages* (Oxford, 1968), Plates 1 and 2; Douglas Gray, *Themes and Images in the Medieval English Religious Lyric* (London, 1972), Plates 1, 2, 3, and 5.

to religious iconography and liturgical drama. Each of these has its own style and preoccupations, which the playwright mirrors. In effect, the theme of the Resurrection is played over four times—as itself, by the Maries and in the *Quem Quaeritis*, by the Magdalen, and lastly by the Soldiers. Each time we are given a different reaction to the event (the 'witness' theme), and each time we see it in a different focus, so that by the end of the play we have experienced it through a fairly complex variety of emotions.

Let us trace these through, starting with the Resurrection itself. Seen soberly, it is an outrageous thing to have to present on stage, especially an open-air stage with no possibility of dimming the lights, or doing any of the other things which, in a modern theatre, denote the supernatural. This word has been devalued; it is an event so cosmic and mysterious that in fact none of the liturgical plays actually attempt to enact it. Instead they represent it, either by some variant on the Easter Sepulchre ceremony, in which the Cross or the Host stands for Christ, or by having the Angels sing a Resurrection anthem.[12] But the York playwright is committed to impersonation. He solves the problem by drawing on the audience's experiences of the sacred; he presents them with an icon of the Resurrection, and he uses singing to remind them of the Liturgy. Apart from this, the whole scene takes place in silence.

Because in the script the whole scene is limited to the laconic stage direction *Tunc Iesu resurgente*, it is possible for the reader to underestimate its dramatic effect. In practice, it took some three minutes of extreme tension to play through, heralded by the thundering of the earthquake, and acted in silence, while the Angel chanted its Easter Sepulchre anthem *Christus resurgens*.[13]

---

[12] See Rosemary Woolf, *The English Mystery Plays*, (Oxford, 1972), pp. 274–5; Young, *Medieval Church*, i. 408, 423, 435, 439. Only a few plays even include the Soldiers and the setting of the watch; usually they start with the *Elevatio Crucis* or *Hostiae*, and then slip into 'drama'.

[13] The marginal stage direction *Tunc angelus cantat Resurgens* is a later addition but seems genuine; in Wakefield we have *Tunc cantabunt angeli* '*Christus resurgens*', *& postea dicit ihesus*; in Chester *Tunc cantabunt duo angeli*

The pictorial effect was stunning. Within the frame of the waggon, the red of Christ's cloak seemed to fill the stage; the banner extended his height, which was enhanced by the fact that everyone else on stage, except for the young Angel, was either sitting or lying. He really seemed to be bursting the bonds of something confining. How much more powerful this must have seemed to an audience who were actually familiar with the traditional image.

For a modern audience, too, the singing of *Christus resurgens* was merely an appropriately unearthly accompaniment. In the fifteenth century, anyone who went conscientiously to his parish church on Easter Sunday at dawn must have been strongly reminded of his emotional response to the Easter Sepulchre ceremony.[14] At the same time, being referred so strongly to a *ceremony* is a way of reminding the audience that this too is representational, that what they are seeing is only a shadow of something real. The actual emergence of a Christ-figure from the tomb must at first have seemed like the ritual come to life. Where there is usually a cross or a wooden figure, now there is a human being, with the wounds painted on him. The actual physicality of the actor playing Christ is almost shocking, especially since the audience has to watch the whole process of

'*Christus resurgens a mortuis*' etc.; *et Christus tunc resurget*; *ac postea cantu finito, dicat ut sequitur.*

[14] The singing of this anthem was a traditional part of the Easter Sepulchre ceremony in parish churches as well as in religious houses: see *Manuale et Processionale ad Usum Insignis Ecclesiæ Eboracensis*, ed. W. G. Henderson, Surtees Society, lxiii (1875), pp. 170–1. Henderson also cites a version from a MS *Manual* of *c*.1405, where *Christus resurgens* is sung even closer to the Sepulchre, and the Sarum *Processional* for the same ceremony. The *Ordinal and Customary* of St. Mary's Abbey, York, also provides for it, with procession (ed. The Abbess of Stanbrook and J. B. L. Tolhurst, Henry Bradshaw Society, lxxv (1937), p.298. No permanent stone Easter sepulchres have survived in York city churches, but records of bequests show that almost every one had a temporary sepulchre, presumably of wood, which was erected for Easter. See Angelo Raine, *Medieval York* (London, 1955), pp. 37, 125, 161, 191, 214, 231, 235, 250, 254, and 295. A wooden sepulchre, formerly in the church of Cowthorpe, west of York, and now in Temple Newsam House, Leeds, is illustrated in F. E. Howard and F. H. Crossley, *English Church Woodwork* (London, 1927), p. 143.

resurrection, not just contemplate, safely, a posed, two-dimensional, triumphal moment. Yet no one for a moment believes that this is really Christ: he is a representation of Christ.

The first sense of shock was succeeded by silence, awe, and amazement. The mood was so powerful that the only thing one could do, it seemed, was to break into it in some way. The playwright does this with the unexpected cry of anguish from Mary Magdalen. The focus is changed; there follows the canon of lamentation from the Maries, a complete shift of mood, tone, and distance. We are now to get the first of the replays; we are going to see the Resurrection through their eyes.

As far as the story is concerned, of course, they do not know what has happened. The audience do, and they might be expected to have some sort of 'superior knowledge' attitude towards the lamentation. In fact the lamentation is so intense the audience are swept into it. It is psychologically necessary for them that they should be. They have been stunned by the Resurrection: they now have to start realizing it. The Maries' ignorance of what has just happened enables the playwright to go back in time, to a situation when Christ is still dead. The Maries then talk the audience through the whole experience of Easter, starting with loss and lamentation, ending with realization and joy.[15]

We have seen already how they engage the audience in their grief. They then have to engage them in their joy. This transition is very difficult to handle; it was in fact the most difficult part of the play to work out in rehearsal, because it was in no way naturalistic. The Maries do not react like the Soldiers. They have to witness in a different way, a formal, liturgical way: they

[15] This is similar to the narrative meditative exercises of the pseudo-Bonaventure, *Meditationes Vitae Christi*, ed. A. C. Peltier, *Opera Omnia*, xii (Paris, 1868), Ch. 87, p. 617, and of Ludophus de Saxonia, *Vita Jesu Christi*, Part 2, Ch. 71. p. 4, 'Cogitationes mulierum, dum veniunt ad sepulchrum', p. 184. The women going to the Tomb are made to retrace the Via Dolorosa, recalling the incidents of the Stations of the Cross, and pause by Calvary itself to recall the Crucifixion and Deposition: an emotional recapitulation to enable the reader to experience the full contrast of the Resurrection.

are given the angelic message, are shown and display the evidence, the empty tomb, the sudary; they believe, they rejoice, they go off to obey the command *Ite nunciate*. In terms of naturalistic psychology, this scene does not work. It is too sudden. They have no time to get over the shock, to reassemble the picture. The Soldiers' reaction is much more plausible: they merely have to cope with the fact that the body has gone, and immediately they fasten on the one small part of it that seems to affect them, 'Witte sir Pilate of this affraye We mon be slone' (309–10). They then talk themselves into accepting the situation. The Maries are not even allowed to talk: they must react in silence.

It is in fact too big a thing to take in naturalistically. Tradition demands that they should accept it without question. (The Gospels are more naturalistic, and the 'Appearances' plays deal with the problem of acceptance at more length.) Two things operate to make the audience accept the Maries' acceptance. One is the fact of their own superior knowledge. They have actually seen Christ rise. (They also accept the way in which the Soldiers, reporting to Pilate, describe things which, if they were 'slepande whanne he 3ede' (318), they cannot possibly have seen.) The other is the very stylization of the acceptance, which refers them again to the ancient patterns of liturgical drama, and the familiar icon.

Again, the change of mode is accompanied by a physical distancing. The Maries have been lamenting in the street: Magdalen sees the Angel from a distance and they go up to him—'Nere will we wende' (232)—on the waggon. They thus enter the frame and complete the picture, the 'Holy Women at the Sepulchre', and the Angel engages them in the ancient dialogue.

This is so deliberate a translation of a *Quem Quaeritis* that it comes as a shock to find that no direct source has yet been discovered.[16] It echoes the liturgical drama so strongly that it

[16] No liturgical Resurrection play-texts survive from the Yorkshire area: there are references to performances, e.g. the famous one at Beverley in the thirteenth

calls for a completely different style of acting. We found that the only way to make it work was to make it an accurate copy of the stylized gestures of the early *Quem Quaeritis*:

Quo viso, deponant turribula quae gestaverunt in eodem sepulchro, sumantque linteum et extendant contra clerum ... veluti ostendentes quod surrexerit dominus, etiam non sit involutus ...[17]

The displaying of the *sudarium* is an important feature of the *Ludus Paschalis* from its beginnings. Here, they display it while the Angel is saying 'He is resen and wente his way' (245), thus combining the angelic witness with the visible evidence: *Angelicos testes, Sudarium et vestes*. Here we get a curious historical reversal. In the early *Quem Quaeritis*, the displaying of the cloth was the high point of audience involvement. Instead of being spectators to a ritual which was being enacted for but not by them, the congregation were suddenly caught up into it, the evidence was being shown to *them*. Here, the showing had quite a different quality: it was being shown as part of a ritual. It remained curiously distant, high and dry on an ancient historical beach-head of drama.

The Maries then rejoice, embrace, and go off, still in unison and silence, until the Magdalen breaks abruptly into the mood with the declaration that she intends to stay behind. As soon as they go, she starts to lament again.

This new section seems, as I have said, illogical. Why, having heard of the Resurrection, and accepted it with joy, should she suddenly start to weep? Why should the audience be made to

century, and the account (1522) from the Earl of Northumberland's palace, just north of Beverley, of rewards to 'them of his Lordship Chapell and other, if they do play the play of Resurrection upon Esturday in the morning in my Lords Chapell' (E. K. Chambers, *The Medieval Stage*, ii (Oxford, 1903), pp. 339, 375. For further speculation, see W. van der Gaaf, 'Miracles and Mysteries in S.E. Yorkshire', *Englische Studien*, xxxvi (1906), 228–30. York Minster had a *Stella*: see *Records of Early English Drama: York*, ed. A. F. Johnston and M. Rogerson (Toronto, 1979), i. p.1. The 1343 Constitution printed on the same page seems to forbid drama, rather than suggest that any is going on in the Minster.

[17] Young, *Medieval Church*, i.249, the *Regularis Concordia* version.

weep with her? It does not really help to be told that here the
author was faced with an uncomfortable hiatus in his sources,
which were trying to reconcile the Gospel according to St. Mark,
which provided the *Quem Quaeritis*, with the Gospel according
to St. John, which provided the *Hortulanus*, the next pageant.
True, he has to provide a bridge to the next play. But it is not
until we look at the actual content of her lament that the main
reason for it becomes clear. In naturalistic terms this is bewildering, as she goes back to the Crucifixion again:

> Allas! what schall nowe worthe on me?
> Mi kaytiffe herte will breke in three
> Whenne I thynke on that body free
>   How it was spilte.
> Both feete and handes nayled tille a tre,
>   Withouten gilte.   (270–5)

The words 'Whenne I thynke on that body free' shows us where
we are. The shift of mood is also a shift from the liturgical
mode, which seems to be proper for the presentation of great
events, back to the meditative, affective, personal mode. The
audience have seen the Resurrection, they have been called on
to live through the appropriate cycle of emotions, now they are
to pause and consider what it means to them personally. It is
reminiscent of the structure of those meditative works where
each narrative section is followed by a prayer which brings the
historical events to the here-and-now of the reader.[18]

She stands before the audience as the Mary Magdalen of
tradition, the beautiful, the rich, the emotional, the ex-courtesan,
the great sinner, the penitent, whose 'sins, which are many, are
forgiven, for she loved much' (Luke 7:47). Though on paper she
seems to speak in first-person terms,

> The woundes he suffered many one
>   Was for my misse;
> It was my dede he was for slayne,
>   And nothyng his   (278–81)

---

[18] For example Ludolphus, *Vita Jesu Christi*, p. 191.

every member of the audience is meant to take them personally. She is speaking for Every Sinner.[19] She leads the audience through the stages of affective meditation—compassion, tears (the audience may be stirred to weep in sympathy), love; even her exit lines, which have a purely narrative linking function, express the devout longing of the soul for God:[20]

> Ther is no thing to that we mete
> May make me blithe. (286–7)

Her lamentation dies away, and we wake up to the ordinary, short-sighted world of the Soldiers. I hesitate to mention the words 'comic relief', but this is how it seems to work; it provides a sudden release of tension from high serious emotional involvement into laughter, but also directs the laughter away through another set of people, with a different set of values, a new change of focus.

A young member of the audience said, when consulted, that she thought the Soldiers were there 'to restore our faith in human nature', and one can see what she meant. The high emotion of the centre part of the play has to be anchored to the everyday world: we cannot stay on the mountain peak. To a certain extent the audience are laughing at themselves, as they might have behaved in a situation that is just too big for them: even when the Soldiers confess the truth to Pilate, it becomes 'I was a-ferde, I durst not loke' (393). They even laugh in

[19] There is even an independent morality tradition of her as an Everyman figure, seduced by the World, the Flesh, and the Devil. See the Digby *Mary Magdalene*, in *The Digby Plays*, ed. F. J. Furnivall, EETS, ES 70. A later morality by Lewis Wager (ed. F. I. Carpenter, *The Life and Repentance of Mary Magdalene*, Chicago, 1904) is even more allegorical. Her role as the Lover makes her a favourite figure in popular affective meditation, a subject on which I intend to write further. Helen M. Garth, *Saint Mary Magdalene in Medieval Literature*, Johns Hopkins Studies in Historical and Political Science, 68.3 (1950), pp. 68–74, writes of this role, but does not explore the spiritual implications. Victor Saxer, *La Culte de Marie Magdeleine en occident* (Paris, 1959), is mainly interested in the cult at Vézelay, and the liturgical aspects.

[20] For this idea, see especially the homily *De beata maria magdalena* attributed to Origen (ed. London, 1504), fo. 9^{r-v}.

recognition when the Soldiers accept the bribe with such unbe-coming alacrity: 'That's how things are', 'Thus schall the sothe be bought and solde' (449).

Yet somehow it is not reductive laughter. This is possibly because the Soldiers lack malice (and at the end, even Pilate dissociates himself from his role, and turns into an actor commenting on it); possibly because they have in fact borne witness to the event by accepting it in front of the audience even though in the story they are too cowardly to stand up for their acceptance; possibly also because their betrayal does not actually make any difference to the outcome, for the audience are by now secure in their own knowledge. But the laughter is something more positive and simpler than these explanations might suggest. I have been talking about a play in performance, where the sense of mood often seems to override logic, and also where the effects are often simpler than literary criticism might like them to be. Here what came over most strongly was that the Soldiers were eventually 'on our side' because they were funny. We weren't even aware of anything complicated about accepting the shortcomings of human nature; rather it was as if the playwright had sensed that the play should end with laughter; the Resurrection is a joyful thing, and on the everyday level to which we had returned, comedy is the appropriate expression of this. *Haec dies quam fecit Dominus: exultemus et laetamur in ea.* 'This is the day which the Lord hath made: we will rejoice and be glad in it.'

Angelus ad virginem: the History of a Medieval Song

JOHN STEVENS

Many of Jack Bennett's most memorable contributions to medieval studies have come in the form of extended textual commentary: they have arisen from an assiduous curiosity about the words on the page and what they really mean. 'Meaning' in his enquiries may come to embrace a whole field of knowledge belonging to any particular term, not merely a limited context. The essay that follows similarly tries to embrace a field of knowledge. It may be admitted at the outset that the enquiry will not cast any startlingly new light on one of the most famous musical references in Chaucer. It will, however, digest for the reader all the information at present known to me about the song, its sources, its verbal texts and musical settings. Very few medieval non-liturgical songs are as well documented as 'Angelus ad virginem', and this short study will, I hope, prove to be an interesting case-history, ranging as it does over two centuries and more. For musicians the perpetually changing presentation of the song has its own fascination and raises questions which are assuredly not new but which are still awaiting their answers.

The song and its sources

Early in the *Miller's Tale* the Miller describes the 'poure scoler', otherwise known as 'hende Nicholas', his well-scented lodging, his equipment ('astrelabie' and 'augrym stones') and his musical skills. On top of his 'presse' was a psaltery, an instrument of the harp family and sometimes mentioned with it: it was often triangular or trapezoid in shape, played against the chest or on the lap and plucked with quills—a good instrument, in fact, with which to accompany one's own singing as Nicholas evidently did.[1]

> And al above ther lay a gay sautrie,
> On which he made a-nyghtes melodie
> So swetely that all the chambre rong;
> And *Angelus ad virginem* he song;
> And after that he song the Kynges Noote.
> Ful often blessed was his myrie throte.
> (I(A) 3213–18)[2]

'Angelus ad virginem' belongs with hundreds of other Latin poems honouring the Virgin.[3] Its form, genre, and function(s) will be considered later; its content could be paralleled in almost any collection of medieval Latin devotional verse. Dreves placed it in volume viii of his *Analecta Hymnica*, a volume entitled *Sequentiae ineditae: Liturgische Prosen des Mittelalters*.[4] This title begs a question but was justified in the particular instance since Dreves took his text from the Cluniac Missal of 1550 (Source *e* (ii) below). The continuing popularity of 'Angelus ad virginem' over the centuries seems to show that the simple paradoxes and mystery of the Annunciation pleased as surely in the sixteenth century as they had two or three hundred years before. Perhaps part of its enduring appeal rested, in fact, on the strong narrative element and comparative absence of wit and word-play. We find *parata sum parere* (3.11) and the inevitable *concipies et paries intacta* (1.7–9), but basically the poem is not much more than the Vulgate story versified, extended to include the cross-as-sword image (4.11–12) and

[1] See Mary Remnant, *Musical Instruments of the West* (1978), pp. 27–8.
[2] Text from F. N. Robinson, ed., *The Works of Geoffrey Chaucer* (2nd edn., 1957), p. 48.
[3] There are, moreover, at least two other separate Latin poems beginning with the same three words: (i) 'Angelus ad virginem a te destinatur' (Chevalier, *Rep. Hymn.*, no. 1065) and (ii) 'Angelus ad virginem, Christe, destinatur' (ibid., no. 1066).
[4] G. M. Dreves, *Analecta Hymnica*, viii (1980), no. 51. Nos. 49 to 51 are, all three, De Annunciatione BVM, the first two being true sequences. Dreves does not give the liturgical context of the poems he prints.

concluded with a prayer. It is a fairly fresh poem and not unduly laden with the clichés of Mariolatry—*porta celi, medela criminum* (1.11–12) and the rest.

The sources of the song 'Angelus ad virginem' are as follows:

a. London, British Library, Arundel MS 248, fo. 154: Latin text with music for one voice and translated English text, 'Gabriel fram evene king', underlaid below the Latin text.[5]

b. London, British Library, Cotton MSS frag. xxix, fo. 36^v (mounted): Latin text with music for two voices.[6]

c. Cambridge, University Library, Additional MS 710 (The Dublin Troper): three versions:

   (i) fo. 127: Latin text with music for one voice;

   (ii) fos. 130–130^v: incomplete Latin text with music for three voices;

   (iii) fo. 130^v: music for three voices, differing slightly from (ii), without words.[7]

---

[5] Arundel 248 is fully itemized in the British Museum catalogue of 1834; there appears to be no modern study of the manuscript as such. The contents include theological and devotional writings, an index of Scriptural passages for use on Sundays and feast-days, an *oratio academica*, a treatise on verbal synonyms. The songs are in two groups: (i) fos. 153–5, eleven pieces in English, Latin, and French (reproduced in facsimile, *Early English Harmony*, ed. H. E. Wooldridge, Plainsong and Medieval Music Society (1897), vol. i, Plates 32–6); (ii) fos. 200^v, 201^v, two Latin items. The MS is briefly, and the polyphonic items more fully, described by G. Reaney in *Repertoire Internationale des Sources Musicales* (*RISM*), vol. B IV^1, p. 491. The MS is usually dated 14th century (? first half).

[6] The volume is described by Reaney, *RISM* B IV^1, p. 494, as a nineteenth-century miscellany of burnt fragments which escaped the Cottonian fire in 1731. The folio in question (fo. 36) was apparently a fly-leaf in Cotton Titus A.xviii. As Reaney observes, the date 1349 occurs in a document at the bottom of the recto. The MS probably came from Addle in Yorkshire. The music on the recto is a two-part motet *Veni mater gracie / tenor* without words (identifiable from elsewhere as an English song 'Dou way robin'; see *New Oxford History of Music*, iii. 111).

[7] CUL Add. MS 710 is the Dublin Troper reproduced in facsimile by Dom Hesbert, *Le Tropaire-Prosaire de Dublin*, Monumenta Musicae Sacrae, iv (Rouen, 1966). The MS is to be dated *c*.1360. The 'Angelus ad virginem' is one of four Latin songs which follow the group of Marian sequences. Dom Hesbert discusses the song, pp. 105–10.

d. Cambridge, University Library, MS Gg.1.32, fo. 5^v: Latin text without music.[8]

e. (i) *Missale ordinis Cluniacensis* (Paris, 1523);
   (ii) *Missale secundum usum celebris monasterii Cluniacensis* (Paris, 1550): Latin text without music in both cases.[9]

f. *Missale ad usum insignis ecclesie Silvanectensis* (Paris, 1524): Latin text without music.[10]

g. Munich, Staatsbibliothek, MS cgm 716, fo. 18: Latin text, with substantial variant, and music for one voice differing completely from the standard melody.[11]

h. Metz, Bibliothèque de la Ville, MS 535, fo. 163: Latin text with music for one voice. [This MS was completely destroyed in the last war.][12]

---

[8] A collection of theological tracts made in the 15th century by various hands (see *Catalogue of MSS*). The poem is preceded by two metrical meditations, 'Thynke man qware off thou art wrought' and 'Salamon sat and sayde' (*Index of Middle English Verse*, nos. 3567, 3069), on fos. 3–4.

[9] Three copies of the printed Cluniac Missal (1523) survive; a fourth was burnt in a fire at Arras, Bibl. Municip., in 1915. Through the kindness of the libraries concerned, I have been able to see photocopies of those at the Abbaye Saint-Pierre de Solesmes and the Bibliothèque Mazarine, Paris. The song is on fo. 22 (D ij) in both copies, which are nearly but not precisely identical (e.g. in their capitals). I have not been able to see a copy of the 1550 Missal, of which five Continental exemplars are recorded in W. H. J. Weale, *Bibliographia Liturgica* (1928).

[10] Weale (see n. 9 above) records four surviving copies of the Senlis Missal (1524), and I am grateful to the librarian of the Bibliothèque Sainte-Geneviève, Paris, for sending me a reproduction of fos. 21^v–22 of his copy.

[11] The Munich MS is a voluminous collection of music for devotion and edification probably compiled between 1415 and 1443 and associated with the monastery at Tegernsee in Bavaria since about 1430. It contains metrical Alleluias, *cantiones*, sequences, a musical treatise, Marian songs in German, processional songs, single voice-parts from polyphonic motets, etc. (see J. A. Emerson, 'Über Entstehung und Inhalt von MüD [Munich Staatsbibl., cgm 716]', in *Kirchenmusikalisches Jahrbuch*, xlviii (1964), 33). I am grateful for help with this item to Professor Karl Reichl and Mrs Janthia Yearley.

[12] This MS before its destruction was described by: P. Meyer, in *Bulletin de la Société des anciens Textes*, xii (1886), 41; A. Långfors, 'Notices des manuscrits 535 de la Bibliothèque Municipale de Metz ...', in *Notices et extraits*, xlii (1933), 139; and, the fullest musical account, by F. Ludwig, *Repertorium organorum recentioris et motetorum vetustissimi stili*, Bd. I, Abteilung i (Halle

i. Oxford, Bodleian Library, Digby MS 147, fo. 151ᵛ: Latin text without music.[13]

j. Oxford, Bodleian Library, Bodley MS 786, fo. viiᵛ: Latin text without music.[14]

k. Oxford, Bodleian Library, Douce MS 302, fos. 24–24ᵛ: English translation, 'The angel to the vergyn said', without Latin text or music.[15]

In addition to the above, the song is mentioned, by title only, in:

l. Cambridge, St. John's College, MS D.27, fo. 50ᵛ (Ordinal of St. Mary's, York);[16]

a/S., 1910), p. 339, from which we learn that 'Angelus' was the only purely Latin piece in the whole MS and that it was notated in neumes on a lined stave. The MS contained devotional tracts, sermons, religious poems in French, etc., and the ten religious songs (fos. 161–70). I have not been able to trace any transcription, published or unpublished, of the music. The destruction of the MS is not referred to by H. Spanke in *G. Raynauds Bibliographie des altfranzösischen Liedes* (1955), p. 6, or by Hesbert (n. 7 above). The date seems to have been late 13th or early 14th century; and the MS belonged to the monastery of St. Arnulf in Metz. (Ludwig, however, dated the MS to the second third of the 13th century).

[13] A large miscellany, dated 14th century, containing tracts on a wide variety of subjects from agriculture and alchemy to metrics and human anatomy; the 'Angelus' precedes a version of Alanus's *De planctu naturae*. The MS belonged at an early date to the church of 'Sancte Marie de Mertone' in Surrey. See *Catal. Codd. MSS Bibl. Bodl.*, ix (1883), cols. 144–6.

[14] A collection of medical treatises, with a calendar 'apparently written in some Cistercian house in the west of England between 1228 and 1244' (*Summary Cat.*, no. 2626). Two *obits* were added to the calendar in the 14th century, and the same hand, perhaps, added the 'Angelus' beneath the calendar entry for November and December; it is written as prose, is rich in abbreviations, and is squeezed into the right-hand margin.

[15] The manuscript is well known to scholars; it contains the poems and carols of John Audelay, and it was edited by E. K. Whiting, EETS, os184 (1931), who presents the contents entire except for one religious allegory in prose and the Latin poem *Cur mundus militat*. The fact that item 21, in Whiting's numbering, is a close translation of 'Angelus' was first noted, I believe, by myself in *Music and Poetry in the Early Tudor Court* (London, 1961), p. 40. The MS was compiled in the second quarter of the 15th century.

[16] The manuscript is an early 15th-century Ordinal of St. Mary's Abbey, York, and has been edited by the Abbess of Stanbrook and J. B. L. Tolhurst, *The*

m. Aberdeen (*Fasti Aberdonenses*).[17]

Latin texts and English translations

Of the complete versions, Latin text with music, the earliest are sources *a* (Arundel) of xiv century (? early), *b* (Cotton) late xiii / early xiv century (?), and *h* (Metz) middle or late xiii century (?). Of these, Metz no longer exists and the Cotton fragment is in a badly damaged state. The Arundel MS, on the other hand, is complete and well preserved. I use it therefore as a base text, giving the variant readings of the other MSS and PB's (Sources *b*, *c*, *d*, *e*, *f*, *g*, *i*, and *j*). To my knowledge a comparative edition of 'Angelus ad virginem' has not previously been published; the apparently scholarly text in Dom Hesbert's edition of the Dublin Troper (*c*) turns out on closer inspection to be quite unreliable. Purporting to be a transcription of the Dublin version, his text is actually closer to Arundel (*a*) than to Dublin and contains at least one reading (2.3: confringerem) which does not exist in any source. In his text the italicized syllables are not manuscript abbreviations but rhyme-syllables.

The transcription below is from BL Arundel MS 248 (Source *a*). Manuscript abbreviations have been expanded. The manuscript punctuation, here omitted, is confined to an occasional stop at the end of a line seeming to serve an entirely formal purpose. The only dubious reading is in stanza 3, line 7 *consensciens* : ? *consensiens*.

Ordinal and Customary of ... St. Mary's York, Henry Bradshaw Society, vols. lxxiii, lxxv, lxxxiv (1936–51). 'Angelus' is listed as a sequence on fo. 50ᵛ.

[17] F. Ll. Harrison, *Music in Medieval Britain* (1958), p. 169, states that at St. Mary's College, Aberdeen, in the first half of the 16th century, regulation required that 'Every evening at six between Vespers and supper, all the members of the college were to sing *sollemniter cum organis et cantu*, in the intervals between the strokes of the great bell, the three antiphons *Salve regina, Angelus ad virginem* and *Sub tuam protectionem*'. Harrison gives as his authority *Fasti Aberdonenses*, ed. C. Innes, Spalding Club Publications (Aberdeen 1854), p. 60; the precise reference is to p. 63. The printed text there reads *solempniter* for *sollemniter*.

1. Angelus ad virginem
    subintrans in conclave
    virginis formidinem   3
    demulcens inquit ave
    Ave regina virginum
    celi terreque dominum   6
        concipies
        et paries
        intacta   9
    salutem hominum
    tu porta celi facta
    medela criminum.   12

2. Quomodo conciperem
    que virum non cognovi
    qualiter infringerem   3
    quod firma mente vovi
    Spiritus sancti gracia
    perficiet hec omnia   6
        ne timeas
        sed gaudeas
        secura   9
    quod castimonia
    manebit in te pura
    dei potentia.   12

3. Ad hec virgo nobilis
    respondens inquit ei
    ancilla sum humilis   3
    omnipotentis dei
        tibi celesti nuncio
        tanti secreti conscio   6
        consensciens
        et cupiens
        videre   9
    factum quod audio
    parata sum parere
    dei consilio.   12

4. Angelus disparuit
   et statim puellaris
uterus intumuit   3
   vi partus salutaris
   quo circumdatur utero
   novem mensium numero   6
     post exiit
     et iniit
     conflictum   9
   affigens humero
   crucem qui dedit ictum
   soli mortifero.   12

5. Eya mater domini
   que pacem reddidisti
angelis et homini   3
   cum christum genuisti
   tuum exora filium
   ut se nobis propiçium   6
     exhibeat
     et deleat
     peccata   9
   prestans auxilium
   vita frui beata
   post hoc exilium.   12
  Amen.

In the following list of variants reference is to stanza and line number. The reading of the base text (Arundel) precedes the colon when it is needed for identification; the reading of the source in question follows the colon.

Source (*b*) BL Cotton frag. xix.
1.1 Angelus: ngelus (*space for initial*) / 1.4 demulcens: demulc[?] / 1.6 terreque: *second* e *inserted above* / 1.10 salutem: salut[?] / 2.1 quomodo: ? / 2.1–2: conciperem que: *pasted over in repair* / 2.2 cognovi: agnoui / 3.3 ancilla: seruula / 3.4 dei: *omitted* / 3.5 celesti: celestis / 3.6 conscio: concio / 3.7 consensciens: consentiens / 4.2 puellaris: *gummed over but legible* / 4.5: cum circumdatus / 4.5–6 *badly damaged and almost illegible* / 4.7 post: hinc / 4.10: affligens / 4.10–11: *badly dam-*

aged or missing; *one can just read* humo ... cru / 5.2 reddidisti:
[?]ddisti / 5.3 homini: ho[?] / 5.4: [...] christum peperisti / 5.9 peccata: ? / 5.10 prestans: [?]stans

Source (*c*)(i) CUL Add. 710, fo. 127.
1.4: inquid / 3.3 ancilla: seruula / 3.6: concio / 3.7: consenciens / 4.3
intumuit: intumut / 4.7 post: hinc / 4.9 conflictum: afflictum / 4.10:
affligens / 4.11 qui: qua / 4.12 soli: hosti / 5.2: que christum credi-
disti / 5.4: que pacem reddidisti / 5.6 se: sit.

Source (*c*)(ii) ditto, fos. 130–130ᵛ.
*The underlaid text breaks off at 1.8 pari[es] at the bottom of fo. 130
and is not continued on the verso.*

Source (*c*)(iii) ditto, fo. 130ᵛ; *no words.*

Source (*d*) CUL, Gg. 1. 32.
1.4: inquid / 1.12 criminum: crinimum / 2.8 sed: set / 3.2: inquid / 3.3
ancilla: seruula/3.5 nuncio: nūcō/3.6 secreti: scerti (?)/3.7: consenciens / 4.1 disparuit: *very unclearly written* / 4.5 quo circumdatur: qui
circumdatus / 4.7 post: hinc / 4.12 mortifero: tantummodo / 5.2: christum peperisti / 5.3 et homini: hominibus / 5.4: dum pacem reddidisti / 5.10: auxillium.

Source (*e*)(i) Cluny Missal, pr. 1523.
Headed: Alia prosa. (The following variants are taken from the copy
in the Abbey of Solesmes.) 1.2: conclavi / 1.4 ave: ei / 2.3: infrig-
erem / 2.11: menebit / 3.3 ancilla: seruula / 3.7: consentiens / 4.4 salutaris: virginalis / 4.5: qui circumdatus / 4.7 post: hinc / 4.10: affligens
(NB. *In the Mazarine library copy corrected by erasure to*
affigens) / 4.11 qui: qua / 4.12 soli: hosti / 5.3: angelo / 5.9 peccata:
reata.

Source (*f*) Senlis Missal, pr. 1524.
Headed: Alia prosa. (The following variants are taken from the copy
in the Bibliothèque Ste. Geneviève, Paris). The Senlis Missal has
the same variants as Source (*e*)(i) in the following instances:
1.2 / 1.4 / 3.3 / 3.7 / 4.5 / 4.7 / 4.12 / 5.3 / 5.9. *Additional variants*: 4.4:
in partu virginali / 4.11 qui: qua *preceded by colon.*

Source (*g*) Munich, cgm 716.
1.5 virginum: filium / 1.6: celi que terre / 1.9: in tacta. *After* 1.9 *the
text deviates completely, reading*: Vt sit salus in periculis pauperibus

et in uinculis solamenque peccantibus iuuamen disperantibus Appareas aufer mundi varias tristicias angarias O maria. *Rubric*: secu*ntur* alie *antiph*one sole*n*nes.

Source (*i*) Oxford, Bodl., Digby 147.
1.2: subinstrans/1.11 facta: pacta/2.2 que: cum/3.3 ancilla: seruula / 3.6: concio / 3.7: consenciens / 4.4 salutaris: virginalis / 4.5: qui circumdatus/4.7 post: hinc/4.10 affligens/4.11 qua:quam/ 4.12: *After stanza 4 an extra stanza is inserted*:

> 4a.   Virgo prolem genuit
>   castum seruans cubile
>   homo deum aluit
>   corpus lactans seruile
>   O quam beata vicera [*sic*]
>   O quam beata vbera
>   que faciunt
>   et nesciunt
>   quo iure
>   fiunt hec opera
>   fit contra ius nature
>   virgo puerpera.

5.4   christum: deum / 5.12 Amen *has decorative extension touched in in red.*

Source (*j*) ditto, MS Bodley 786.
1.6: celi que terre/2.2 que: cum/2.5 Spiritus: *erased and rewritten* / 3.2: inquid / 3.3 ancilla: seruula / 3.6: concio / 3.7: consenciens/3.10 factum: verbum/4.7: hic ? vicijt ? et exiit (*the reading of the second word is uncertain*) / 4.10: affligens / 5.2: reddisti/ 5.4 cum: dum / 5.6 se: sit.

The variant readings indicate a relatively stable text. If the Digby poem is in fact of the mid-thirteenth century, it shows that a human preference for the 'easy' reading set in early in the song's history. The tempting *affligens* (4.10), a predictable response to the *crucem* (4.11), is surely inferior to *affigens*; and in one copy at least of the *Missel de Cluny*, 1523, we find that nearly 300 years later someone was sharp enough to spot and correct the printer's error. The end of that same verse seems to have caused trouble, and the reading of the Arundel and some other early MSS *soli mortifero* ('the only deathbringer') seems to have been dropped for the more obvious *hosti mortifero* ('the death-bringing enemy'). By far the most interesting 'occurrences' in the history of the text of 'Angelus ad virginem', however, are (i) the extra, unique stanza 4a of the Digby MS,[18] and (ii) the total and extraordinary deviation of the Munich MS after the word *intacta* in stanza 1 (line 9). The Digby stanza adds nothing to the narrative; it simply draws out some favourite paradoxes of the Nativity—*homo deum aluit* and *fit contra ius nature / virgo puerpera*—sugaring them with favourite exclamations of joy: O *quam beata vi[s]cera ... ubera*! The stanza comes a little oddly since the narrative has already taken us through to the Crucifixion. On these grounds alone it looks like an addition to an already established text rather than something which was originally part of the poem and later fell out. The Munich 'deviation' (properly so called, I think, since it is a deliberate rewriting—by creative addition—of the well-known song) is alto-gether more mysterious. The musical repetitions, which will be discussed later, make it certain that the new conclusion to stanza 1 *is* verse not, as it might appear, prose. Lineated, it reads:

> Angelus ad virginem
> Subintrans in conclave
> virginis formidinem
> demulcens inquit ave
> Ave regina filium   5
> celique terre dominum
> concipies
> et paries
> intacta   9
> Ut sit salus in periculis
> pauperibus et in vinculis
> solamenque peccantibus
> iuvamen desperantibus   13

---

[18] See below, p. 310, for the occurrence of this stanza in one English translation (Source *k*).

> Appareas
> aufer mundi varias
> tristicias angarias
> O Maria   17

(The purpose clause, *ut sit*, takes up the *filium* of line 5—'that he may be ...'. Lines 14–16, though awkward, seem to mean, 'Appear, take away the manifold sadnesses, tribulations, of the world!') Whatever the precise significance and function of this new version of the text, there can be no doubt that, like the music which goes with it, it is highly contrived and purposed. The new ending is not confused with any half-recollections of the standard versions.

Part of the interest of the 'Angelus ad virginem' and further evidence of its popularity is the survival of two Middle English translations of it. The earlier one, from the Arundel MS, is well known, since it accompanies the Latin song in that manuscript.[19] The later (Source *k*) has no ready means of identification; it appears in the Douce MS labelled simply, and ungrammatically, *Hec salutacio composuit Angelus Gabrielus.*[20] There is considerable difference between the two English versions, as a comparison of the first two stanzas of each will make clear.

Arundel MS

> Gabriel, fram evene-king
>   sent to þe maide swete,
> broute þire blisful tiding
>   And faire he gan hire greten:
>   'heil be þu ful of grace a-rith!   5
>   for godes sone, þis euene lith,
>   for mannes louen
>   wile man bicomen,
>   and taken

---

[19] See Wooldridge, op. cit. (see n.5 above), vol. i, Plate 34. The English text is taken from *English Lyrics of the 13th Century*, ed. Carleton Brown (Oxford, 1932), p. 75, no. 44.

[20] See n. 15 above. The text is taken from Whiting's edition, p. 159, no. 21.

fles of þe maiden brith,   10
   manken fre for to maken
   of senne and deules mith.'

Mildeliche im gan andsweren
   þe milde maiden þanne:
'Wichewise sold ichs beren   15
   child with-huten manne?'
      þangle seide, 'ne dred te nout;
      þurw þoligast sal ben iwrout
      þis ilche þing,
      war-of tiding   20
      ichs bringe,
      al manken wrth ibout
      þur þi swete chiltinge,
      and hut of pine ibrout.'

Douce MS

The angel to þe vergyn said,
   Entreng into here boure,
Fore drede of quakyng of þis mayd,
   He said, 'haile!' with gret honour,
      'Haile! be þou quene of maidyns mo,   5
      Lord of heuen and erþ also,
Consayue þou schalt, and bere with ale, þe Lord of myзt,
   Hele of al monkyn.
He wil make þe þe зate of heuen bryзt,
   Medesyne of al our syn.'   10

'How schuld I consayue and gete?
   No syn neuer I knew.
How schuld I breke þat I haue forehete
   Of þoзt stedfast and trewe?'
      'Þe grace al of þe Hole Gost   15
      Schal bryng ale forþ without boost;
Ne drede þou tak, bot ioy þou make, serten and sere.
   Þis message He send to þe,
To dwel withyn þe ful pere
   Þroз myзt of His Fader fre.'   20

The Arundel version is little more than a loose paraphrase of the Latin: there is not a single line in the first stanza that really conveys the literal sense of the original. John Audelay's poem, on the other hand, represents the pith of the Latin text in almost every line; he gets stumped occasionally ('Fore drede of quakying of this mayd' is somewhat awkward for *formidinem demulcens*), but to have got so much of the Latin into an uninflected language whilst preserving almost intact the complicated metrical and rhyming scheme is quite an achievement. The Arundel version is flaccid by comparison; its freedom is not earned by any particular felicities.

There is one respect in which the Arundel English text scores slightly: it is more consistently close to the metre of the Latin. The latter depends essentially on syllable-count (a matter to be discussed shortly), though stress plays a part in it. John Audelay seems occasionally to have swallowed more syllables than are good for him, as for instance in stanza 1, where *tu pórta céli fácta* (7 syllables with three stresses) is rendered 'He wil máke þe þe ʒáte of héuen brýʒt' (? 10 syllables with four stresses). The conventions of fitting words to music in the fifteenth century could accommodate a few extra slack syllables; but the fact that the ninth line of *each* of Audelay's stanzas has four syllables instead of three makes one wonder whether he had in his head a slightly different version of the melody. That he was writing a *contrafactum* to the melody, there can, I think, be no reasonable doubt.

The most curious feature of Audelay's translation has yet to be mentioned. He omits the whole of stanza 3 of the standard Latin version, the stanza that contains the Virgin's humble acceptance of her divine mission—a very odd thing for him to do—and he inserts between stanzas 4 and 5 of the original an extra stanza which turns out to be a close translation of the stanza unique to the Digby MS, *Virgo prolem genuit* ... (see above).

Music: the monophonic and polyphonic versions

Musically, 'Angelus ad virginem' is well worth study, since it is not common for a song, as distinct from a fully liturgical piece out of the 'official' repertory, so to speak, to survive in so many varied versions in *English* sources. Discounting the lost version, of which no transcript is known, there are two monophonic versions of the standard melody, one monophonic version of a quite different character in the Munich MS, and three polyphonic settings using the standard melody. Let us consider the monophonic songs first.

Both Arundel and Dublin present the standard melody as a song for one voice; yet it is obvious at a glance that the Arundel version (Musical Example I) implies a different rendering from the Dublin (Musical Example II). The latter presents the song in a straightforward 'square' notation on a four-line stave.[21] The layout is the most typical of those used for monophonic songs in the thirteenth and fourteenth centuries—that is to say, music is written out in full for the first verse, the words of which are underlaid. (In actual fact, the words were normally written first and the notes added above afterwards; the careful insertion of the G for the last syllable of *dominum* (6.8) between the *-um* and the *con-* of *concipies* suggests that this may have been the procedure here—a music scribe writing first would have placed the note further to the left?) The notational symbols used are: the *virga* (the square or squarish notehead has a tail down to the right varying in length from the barely visible to 3/16″); the *punctum* (normally a square note-head without tail but in this and other British sources often rhomboid in shape—see 1.2 *angelus*); the descending and ascending two-note neumes (*clivis* 3.7 and *podatus* 7.8); and the *plica* (a liquescent neume, the simplest form of which, 4.2 and 4.4, consists of a note-head with two downward tails—the main note has a written pitch, the *plica*-ed note which follows it is lighter and of indeterminate pitch and often goes with an *n*, *l*, *r*, or other sounded consonant).

[21] Hesbert, op.cit. (n. 7 above), Plate 186.

Although the *virga* and the *punctum* may resemble the *long* and the *breve* of mensural notation, there is no sign in the manuscript that they have mensural significance; they are undifferentiated as temporal symbols.

The Arundel version of the same melody has a more unusual layout and a more complicated notation.[22] Whereas in the Dublin MS the subsequent verses are written out as prose at the end of verse 1, in the Arundel MS no less than ten lines of words are underlaid to the melody (five of Latin, five of the English translation). The notation, on a five-line stave, is of the same basic type—a square notation—but in this case the comparative variety of symbols used suggests a flexibility of melodic style; the notation appears closer to the neume-systems from which it derives, systems which, as the history of Gregorian chant-notation shows, *lost* subtlety, sophistication, and nuance at the same time as they developed clarity in pitch indications.[23] In the Arundel song *virga* and *punctum* are again undifferentiated and there are the same basic ligatures (12.4, 5). The main variety is achieved through *plica* combinations. The downward *plica* is normally attached to a double main note (1.1, 6), perhaps suggesting the lengthening of the main note; this is supplemented by an upward *plica* (1.2, 3.2, 5.1, etc.) on a single note and by *plicas* attached to two- and three-note neumes (9.1, 11.5).

I have dwelt on the technicalities of the notation in order to dispel the all-too-easy assumption into which we may fall that monophonic means musically 'primitive' and simple, and in order to question, as one must, the still predominant view that the notation was inadequate to express what was meant. It is only if we think that all monophonic songs of this period were sung metrically (i.e. in clearly measured long and short notes like contemporary polyphony) that we shall regard the notation

[22] The Arundel songs are not consistent in this respect; but, for example, the very next song, 'Þe milde lombe' (*Index MEV*, no. 3432), employs a similar notation. See Wooldridge, op.cit., for facsimile.
[23] Some of the most recent developments in the understanding of Gregorian neumatic notations are summarized by Dom Eugène Cardine in his *Semiologie Gregorienne* (n.d., pr. Coconnier, Sable).

as hopelessly wanting in precision. Of course, all musical notations are inadequate to some degree or other, not least our own modern system; but almost all older systems have something to tell us that a modern transcription cannot convey.[24]

The question then is: how was 'Angelus ad virginem' performed in the circles from which the Arundel and Dublin versions arose? Before attempting to answer this we should consider the other versions. The earliest of the polyphonic versions is evidently the badly damaged one in the Cotton MS (Source *b*). It has proved possible to decipher most of it, and since it has not been published I give it here in its entirety (Musical Example III).[25] It is written on three sets of red four-line staves with a red line between the staves; the words of stanza 1 are underlaid to Voice II, the lower of the two parts, though the tune is in the upper voice. The notation is non-mensural: *virga* and *punctum* are not differentiated as long and short notes, though some have long tails and some have not. The notation, then, resembles in its general features the monophonic ones already described, except that it employs frequently an oblique form of ligature (compound neume) not used much in monophonic notations—it is a descending ligature with or without a left-hand downward tail.[26] As with the monophonic notations, the most striking feature of this Cottonian notation is its *syllabic* nature: each syllable has a note or group of notes attached to it (the groups are always 'bound' together, the ligature having the function of a modern slur) and there is never any ambiguity about the underlay. For the same reasons, supported by the fact that the polyphony is written 'in score', there is no difficulty in fitting the two voices together; both

---

[24] I have attempted to discuss the notational subtleties of some secular sources in 'The Manuscript Presentation and Notation of Adam de la Halle's Courtly Chansons', *Source Materials and the Interpretation of Music: a Memorial Volume to Thurston Dart*, ed. I. Bent and M. Tilmouth (Stainer and Bell; forthcoming).   [25] No facsimile available.

[26] Trouvère MS R (B.N. fr. 1591) is an exception in this respect; but the observation must remain a tentative one until the notations have been more systematically analysed.

parts are syllabic and their notes and note-groups are precisely governed by the text. Voice I sticks fairly closely to the standard melody as established by Arundel and Dublin (i), but has more melodic 'in-filling' than the latter. Harmonically, there are strong hints of the tenor-and-discant style of the fourteenth and fifteenth centuries, consisting of progressions in parallel sixths (lightly disguised by ornamentation in lines 2 and 4 for instance) moving towards a cadence on unison and octave. Some passages also recall the style sometimes anachronistically called 'gymel' and thought to be particularly English; it involves parallel thirds and the interweaving of voices (see lines 10 and 12). Finally, and this is important, there is no need to assume that the Cotton two-part version was necessarily sung metrically. The traditional argument that the growth of polyphony stimulated the development of mensural notation for obvious practical reasons must in general be true but clearly need not apply to 'syllabic' polyphony such as this. Synchronization in so simple a note-against-note style presents no problems.

Both the other polyphonic settings are in the Dublin MS (Source *c* (ii) and (iii)); they are close but not identical. They appear to be certainly written by the same scribe, whose upward tails are very long, usually longer than the height of the roughly drawn four-line stave, and whose flats likewise have a very long ascender. The style of the notational penmanship is crude compared with that of the rest of the manuscript, even compared with that of the new section beginning on fo. 128; and the same may be said of the literary text, written in a more cursive, less formal hand than the earlier scribes employed (this scribe always uses the deep v-shaped form of r, for instance). Nevertheless the scribe (or his model) has a perfectly sound grasp of the notational system which he is using. The notation is the usual 'black full' mensural, in use in England in the fourteenth and fifteenth centuries when it was gradually replaced by the 'void' notation. The implied metre is ⊙ (*tempus perfectum cum prolatione perfecta*), as is indicated by the frequent 'imperfection' of the breve and the 'alteration' of the semibreve, and, for the lower values, by the occasional 'imperfection' of the semibreve in groups such as *s m s s*. On notational grounds these two polyphonic settings could well be half a century or more later than the main part of the manuscript, assuming a date for that of *c*.1350.

In each setting the well-known tune is placed in the middle voice.[27] The two settings are both in the same style and may well represent two attempts by the same person to achieve a satisfactory result. They are both homophonic and rhythmically straightforward; the text is set syllabically and, when it is supplied, is underlaid to the third voice (the tenor) not to the melody itself. Both are written in score. All these (except the placing of the tune in Voice II) are features of the 'old style' *conductus* and are found in the English fifteenth-century polyphonic carol. 'Angelus ad virginem' could not, however, be mistaken for a carol since it not only has a quite different form but also lacks the distinctive rhythmic idioms which give the carols their vitality. Few carols, moreover, employ the ⊙ metre (modern 9 / 8 time-signature) which was already becoming old-fashioned by the mid-fifteenth century.[28] The two settings are almost identical in the last 15 measures or so; but before that the different 'harmonizations' show, I think, at least that no single tonal scheme ought to be felt to belong inevitably to this catchy major melody. Particularly, however, as the cadence-points are approached, the 'fa-burden' progressions (i.e. parallel $\frac{6}{3}$ chords) characteristic of the period tend to take over completely.

A principal interest of these two mensural polyphonic versions to anyone studying the whole history of 'Angelus ad virginem' is that they, and they only, provide clear directions for a metrical interpretation of the melody. They agree that it should be sung in triple time, that the penultimate syllable of a line with a weak ending ('... in conclâve') should occupy a whole measure, that

[27] The setting of the *cantus firmus*, usually plainsong of course, in the middle voice was standard practice in the style known as 'English descant'. See F. Ll. Harrison, op.cit. (n. 17 above), p. 152 and *passim*.

[28] See, however, *Medieval Carols*, Musica Britannica, vol. iv (2nd edn. rev., 1958), nos. 1 and 25.

certain first syllables should do likewise (lines 5, 6, 7, 11), and that otherwise each measure should accommodate two syllables—one strong on the first beat, one weak on the third beat. To put it shortly, the measured version of the melody brings out the strong metrical 'swing' which we feel to inhere in the words. But whether this means that all the surviving versions of the poem were sung in the same strongly lilting way is another matter. To the problem, then, of the earliest, the monophonic, versions we must now return.

'Angelus ad virginem' is not unique in raising the issue of rhythmic interpretation. Indeed, in the long-standing and unresolved dispute over the proper interpretation of the thousands of surviving medieval monophonic songs (of the troubadours, trouvères, Minnesinger and many others), the existence of a few later mensuralized versions alongside unmeasured ones in far greater numbers and often of earlier date has proved a bone of contention. One party has argued that the mensuralized versions clearly demonstrate how the songs should be, and always were, sung; the other party, with increasing persuasiveness, that these versions simply reflect the taste of a later age and have no more authority than, say, Malory's interpretation of the Grail has in the early history of that symbol. The problem of the rhythmic interpretation of monody is far too vast and intricate to enter upon here. I can only record my personal conviction, borne out in this case by the evidently subtle notational style of at least one of our sources (Arundel) discussed above, that sometime during the thirteenth and fourteenth centuries a whole rhythmic tradition of flexible, sophisticated, non-metrical singing (analogous to traditions still surviving in Oriental music) was lost, to be replaced by a mensural and indeed metrical one more familiar and thence more persuasive to most modern ears.[29]

[29] For the scholarly controversy over the right rhythmic interpretation of the monophonic repertory, see, most recently, Bruno Stäblein's magisterial work, *Schriftbild der einstimmigen Musik*, Musikgeschichte in Bildern, Bd. III, Lfg. 4 (Leipzig, 1975); and, in English, Hendrik van der Werf, *The Chansons of the Troubadours and Trouvères* (Utrecht, 1972).

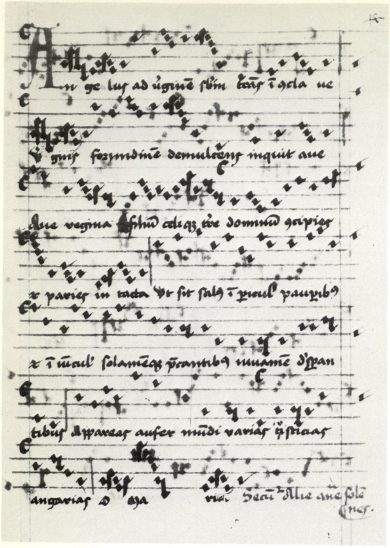

3 This second melody to 'Angelus' is reproduced, by kind permission, from the
unique source, Munich, Staatsbibliothek, MS cgm 716, fo. 18 (xv century)

That the text of 'Angelus ad virginem' was not *of itself* thought to require the strongly pulsing melody with which we are all too familiar is very happily demonstrated by the survival of the Munich version which up to now I have omitted from the discussion. It is time to see what it is and what can be learnt from it.

In the German source, previously unpublished, which I give in full (Musical Example IV),[30] the standard text breaks off after the short ninth line of the stanza, *intacta*, and continues freely with an otherwise unknown ending which turns the angelic announcement into a congregational prayer, a petition to the Virgin to help us in the trials and tribulations of this world.

Ut sit salus in periculis
pauperibus et in vinculis
solamenque peccantibus
iuvamen desperantibus
Appareas
aufer mundi varias
tristicias angarias
O Maria

Amongst the other changes there seems to be one in the rhythmical style of the verse, which loses its clearly stress-governed character and approximates rather to the style of syllable-counting verse. It is hard to see, for instance, how the first two, nine-syllabled lines of the addition can be stressed the same: *páupĕríbŭs* will not do, and *Ŭt sít sălús* is little better.

Musically, the two halves are clearly differentiated but not at all in the way one would expect. The 'lilting' verse of the first half is set to a quite florid melody in which four- or five-note neumes are common; the more 'syllabic' second half, on the other hand, receives more-or-less single-note treatment until we reach the final O *Maria*, which is again florid. Nevertheless, despite the internal contrast of florid and simple setting, the

[30] No facsimile available. The notation is in the distinctively German style of Gothic neumes, the so-called *Hufnagel* notation.

melody was clearly designed as a whole: the melodic material, for instance, of line 17, O *Maria*, derives from phrases in lines 1–2; and one of these motifs (on *Ma*-) is partly anticipated in lines 12 to 16. It is a wholly integrated melody. I have not yet been able to identify its source, if it has one. Phrygian-mode (E-mode) melodies are rare, it seems, in the music for the principal feasts of the Virgin; and Bryden and Hughes record only one melody which has a similar opening figure (it is in a different mode).[31] The familiar musical form A-A-B (lines 1–2; 3–4; 5–16) suggests a *cantio*, a 'Latin chanson';[32] but the strictly parallel phrases of lines 10 and 11, 13 and 16, are more reminiscent of sequence or Latin *lai*.

Apart from confirming the observation already made, that a rhythmically emphatic text does not require a rhythmically emphatic melody—an observation which is important when considering how the standard melody may originally have been performed—this Munich version contributes little to our understanding of the main tradition of 'Angelus ad virginem'. It remains an interesting and slightly baffling oddity. There is, however, nothing here to support the supposition that the strongly lilting, metrical melody with which we are familiar must inevitably represent the style in which 'Angelus ad virginem' was first conceived and sung. An altogether freer and not precisely measured style may have been the basis of the earliest performances—the style suggested, in fact, by the notation of the Arundel version.

Form and function

Questions of form and function are very closely bound up together in medieval music. Indeed, to find an answer to the question, nearly always an essential one—what was this song written for?—it is usually necessary to consider (*a*) what form it has taken, and (*b*) what company it keeps in the manuscripts

[31] J. R. Bryden and D. G. Hughes, *An Index of Gregorian Chant* (Harvard, 1970).
[32] For *cantio*, see n. 37 below.

which preserve it. My purpose in this section is to attempt an answer to these questions. The 'standard' text (i.e. the text of all the sources apart from Munich) is a strophic poem of five stanzas with 12 lines to the stanza, rhyming

$$a^7 \ b^{6+} \ a^7 \ b^{6+} \ c^8 \ c^8 \ d^4 \ d^4 e^2 \ c^6 \ e^{6+} \ c^6$$

The superscript numbers indicate the syllables per line, the plus-sign standing for the extra 'weak' syllable at the end of a line: *concláve*, *intácta*, etc. The metrical form is repeated precisely from stanza to stanza; each stanza has precisely 74 syllables and the same rhyme-scheme though not the same rhyme-sounds. There is nothing in the form which dogmatically declares what it is. The three main alternatives are hymn, sequence, and *cantio*.

'Hymn' is favoured by several modern editors and cataloguers, but this is not borne out by any source (not that this would be decisive, since medieval nomenclature is often loose and self-cancelling). Moreover, the majority of hymns are formally simpler, the commonest form being a monorhymed quatrain.[33] It is quite otherwise with the 'sequence' (or 'prose'), which may have a quite elaborate formal structure: its characteristic form is A B B¹ C C¹ D D¹ ... X (freer, however, in many early examples).[34] 'Sequence' is the term used most often by scholars to describe 'Angelus'; they take their tip perhaps from Dreves, who, as noted above, included the text of 'Angelus' in a volume of *sequentiae ineditae*. This description is authorized by several of the original sources. In the Missals of Cluny (1523) and of Senlis (1524) the text appears, without music, in sections of the Missal labelled respectively *De Beata* and *De beata per aduentum*. In each case the song is headed *alia prosa* and occurs with sequences such as 'Missus Gabriel de celis' (Cluny), 'Mittit ad virginem non quemvis angelum' (Cluny and Senlis), 'Mirandum commercium virginis in gremium' (Senlis). Moreover, it

---

[33] For a recent concise discussion of hymn form, see K. H. Schlager, in K. G. Fellerer, ed., *Geschichte der katholischen Kirchenmusik* (Kassel, 1972), i.282–6.

[34] On the sequence see, amongst many studies, Stäblein, op.cit., 256, Index s.v. 'sequenz'; R. L. Crocker, 'The Sequence', in *Gedenkschrift Schrade*, ed. W. Arlt *et al.* (Berne and Munich, 1973), pp. 269 ff.

takes the normal liturgical position of a sequence, after the Alleluia of the Mass and before the Gospel. However, this only establishes the suitability of 'Angelus ad virginem' to be treated as a sequence, not that it was originally conceived as such. Formally it permits of such an interpretation, since stanza 1 could be regarded as the initial introductory and separable unit, while stanzas 2–3 and 4–5 form double versicles (B B¹ C C¹); but the case is hardly a strong one. Several of the manuscript sources rather bring the 'Angelus' into association with the sequence than define it as such. Thus, in the mid-fourteenth century, the Dublin Troper.

The Dublin Troper (Source *c*) contains first a troper to the *Kyriale* (Kyries, Glorias, etc.), then a liturgical sequentiary or 'proser', then more tropes (Sanctus and Agnus Dei), then a new series of sequences, all addressed to the BVM, to which are appended in the same hand and style and without break four songs in Latin: 'Omnis caro peccaverat' (a Latin *lai*), 'Angelus ad virginem' (monophonic version), 'In ecclesiis' (a strophic song on the vices of the clergy), and 'Scribere proposui' (a song, strophic again, on the vanities of this world). To have placed 'Angelus' in the middle of this group in effect emphasizes its difference and separation from the Marian sequences, while allowing it, so to speak, into good company.

The Cotton fragment poses a more difficult problem. The volume that contains it is a nineteenth-century miscellany of burnt fragments of Cottonian manuscripts which escaped the fire in 1731. The leaf that preserves the two-voice 'Angelus ad virginem', apparently a fly-leaf from Cotton Titus A.xviii, contains the date 1349 and had some connection with Addle in Yorkshire. It has been described as a leaf from a sequentiary, but the evidence is inconclusive. The recto is occupied by a piece '[V]eni mater gracie / [Dou way robin]' which has been described, on the basis of a concordance, as 'the first and so far the only known motet with English words'.[35] The text

---

[35] M. Bukofzer, in *New Oxford History of Music*, iii (1960), p. 112.

in the upper voice is apparently a sequence, but musically it is not set as a sequence, for there is virtually no melodic repetition.

Other terms which appear in the sources, referring to 'Angelus', are *antiphona* and *cantilena*. It is the Munich source that uses the term *antiphona*; but this does not help our enquiry much, first because of the altogether unique form of text and melody in this manuscript, and secondly because the term is used throughout the collection simply as a synonym for song. The scribe does in fact occasionally use other terms, including *prosa* in its technical sense. *Cantilena*, or rather *cantalena* as the scribe spells it, occurs frequently in Audelay's MS (Douce 302)—e.g. *Hic incipiunt decem precepta in modum cantalene*; it is not specifically applied to 'The angel to the vergyn said', which is headed simply *salutacio*.

Finally we may consider the evidence of the lost Metz MS. The manuscript, which at an early date belonged to the monastery of St. Arnulf in Metz, was a collection of meditations, treatises, exhortations, prayers, and poems to Christ and the Virgin Mary. It contained (fos. 161–70, written in the same hand as the rest) ten religious songs, all monophonic and notated in Messine neumes. Nine were in French, 'chansons pieuses', and one was in Latin, the 'Angelus ad virginem'. If Ludwig's dating 'second third of the thirteenth century' was correct, then we have lost with the loss of this manuscript probably the earliest musical version of the song.[36]

What is especially interesting about the Metz transmission of 'Angelus' is that this single Latin song appeared in the midst of a group of French songs, chansons including rondeaux and a pastourelle (a devotional *contrafactum* of the well-known 'L'autrier estoie montez'). It is to the category of the chanson, Latin *cantio*, that 'Angelus ad virginem' surely in the first instance belonged. Formally, it has a basic resemblance to the standard chanson (Dante's *canzone*) A (lines 1–2) A (3–4) B

[36] See n. 12 above.

(5–12, the *cauda*) but with the significant difference that there is more patterned repetition in the *cauda* (5 ≃ 6; 10 = 11). It is an elaborate strophic song, a Latin *chanson pieuse*.

The different types of *cantio* are well described by Schlager, who observes that the genre is distinguished from the sequence or 'prose' by being strophic and from the hymn, its nearest relation, by the absence of a doxology and by the occasional presence of a refrain (not the case with 'Angelus' however).[37] Schlager describes how various types of *cantiones*, by definition non-liturgical, were 'legitimized' as part of the liturgy: some were associated with the 'Benedicamus-domino' (the versicle which normally ended the services of the Hours), some were adopted as *conductus* (rhythmical chants used in liturgical movement, processions, the escort of reader to lectern, etc.). It seems evident that 'Angelus ad virginem' achieved respectability in the same sort of way: it began life simply as a song, though not a simple song, and because of its popularity was adopted into the company of Marian sequences, finding by the sixteenth century an official place in Masses of Our Lady during the Advent season especially.

The changing status and function of the song are confirmed by the evidence of manuscripts not so far considered in this part of the discussion. The Arundel MS is, broadly described, a theological and moral miscellany containing material as diverse as Latin verse, a Tree of Virtues and Vices, sermons, proverbs, a *speculum misse*, treatises on the love of God, an academic oration on methods of teaching and disputation.[38] On the face of it a clerical, not purely monastic, milieu seems indicated. The songs appear as a group and include a French, or Anglo-French, chanson, a sequence on Mary Magdalene based on the *Laetabundus* melody, English songs, a Latin *cantus de domina post cantum Aaliz* with French alternative text, and so on—a real

---

[37] Schlager, op. cit., pp. 286–93; he defines *cantiones* as follows: 'Lieder mit geistlichem Text, die dem liturgischen Gesang im engeren Sinne nicht angehören, werden im 14. und 15. Jahrhundert als Cantiones bezeichnet ...' (p. 286).
[38] See n. 5 above.

miscellany without, it need scarcely be said, any liturgical function.

By the fifteenth century 'Angelus ad virginem' had already begun its liturgical career: the Ordinal of St. Mary's Abbey, York (Source *l*), lists it in the rubric, *Missa familiaris sive de Domina ... ad altare beate Virginis celebretur In Adventu Domini officium* [i.e. introit] *est 'Rorate celi'* ; *Kyrie cum versibus* [i.e. troped] ... *Sequencia: 'Missus Gabriel' vel 'Angelus ad Virginem', 'Verbum bonum'* ... But another Cambridge manuscript of the same century (Source *d*) contains the Latin text scribbled on to a blank page and keeping company with verses on the Holy Blood, a hymn (*Jesus ex deo genitus*), and various jottings; the main business of the manuscript is theological and ascetical tracts. It is likely that a song as well loved as 'Angelus' evidently was was never lost from popular circulation, never completely taken over by liturgical officialdom.

Conclusion

This short history of a medieval song, well known not only in England but evidently in various parts of Europe also, has, I hope, some interest in itself, especially in so far as it indicates the shifting and (*vis-à-vis* the liturgy) ambiguous status such a song might have. Whether it casts new light on the passage in the *Miller's Tale* is open to question. The most one can say is that if the 'Angelus ad virginem' had already begun its liturgical career by the 1380s, Nicholas's singing of it, whilst doubtless dreaming of some other 'virgo', gains an additional piquancy and point.[39]

MUSICAL EXAMPLES

In the following examples, all of which are presented in the sources in non-mensural notations, I have adopted a syllabic style of transcription. As in the manuscripts themselves, each syllable is

[39] See Beryl Rowland, *Chaucer Review*, v (1970), 140–6.

accompanied either by a single note or by a group of notes joined together in ligature. The single note of the manuscripts appears as a crotchet in the transcription; the notes in ligature appear as groups of quavers. A quaver with a broken stem (see, e.g., Musical Example I, line 1, syllable 2, second note) represents a *plica*, i.e. a liquescent. The songs should be sung in a free 'isochronous' style: that is to say, the syllables should be roughly equivalent in length, but naturally a four-note group may take longer than a single note. The transcriptions are set out in such a way as to make the phrase-units and thence the stanza-pattern clear.[40]

[40] I regret that the edition, *Medieval English Songs*, by E. J. Dobson and F. Ll. Harrison (London, 1979), did not appear in time for me to consult it in the preparation of this article.

Song I

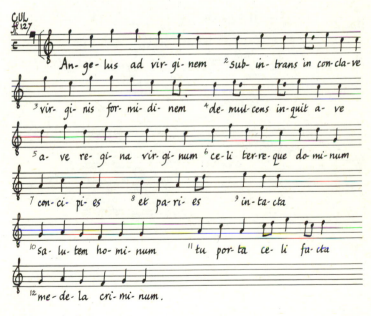

Song II

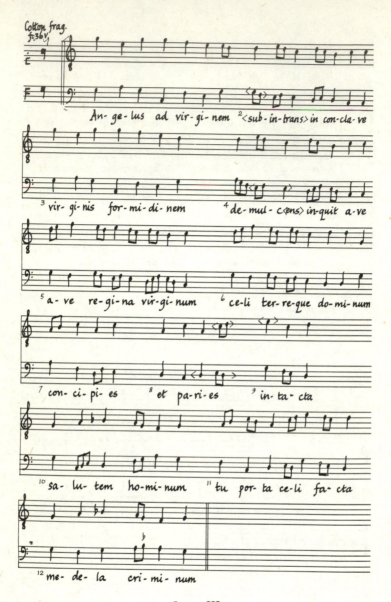

Cotton frag.
fo 36 v

An- ge- lus ad vir- gi- nem ²‹sub- in- trans› in con- cla- ve

³ vir- gi- nis for- mi- di- nem ⁴ de- mul- c‹ens› in- quit a- ve

⁵ a- ve re- gi- na vir- gi- num ⁶ ce- li ter- re- que do- mi- num

⁷ con- ci- pi- es ⁸ et pa- ri- es ⁹ in- ta- cta

¹⁰ sa- lu- tem ho- mi- num ¹¹ tu por- ta ce- li fa- cta

¹² me- de- la cri- mi- num

Song III

An- ge- - lus ad vir- gi- nem ²sub- in- trans in con- cla- ve

³vir- gi- - nis for- mi- di- nem ⁴de- mul- cens in- quit a- ve

⁵A- ve re- gi- na fi- li- um ⁶ce- li que ter- re do- mi- num

⁷con- ci- pi- es ⁸et pa- ri- es ⁹in- ta- cta

¹⁰Ut sit sa- lus in pe- ri- cu- lis ¹¹pau- pe- ri- bus et in vin- cu- lis

¹²so- la- men- que pec- can- ti- bus ¹³iu- va- men de- spe- ran- ti- bus

¹⁴Ap- pa- re- as

¹⁵au- fer mun- di va- ri- as ¹⁶tris- ti- ci- as an- ga- ri- as

¹⁷O___ Ma- - - ri - a

Song IV

Notes to the musical examples

Reference is by line and syllable (in musical terms, by phrase and note-group). In Song III roman numerals refer to the voices.

Song I. 7.2–4: written as a separated-out *conjunctura* taking 3 syllables in place of the normal single syllable.

Song II. None.

Song III. This shrivelled manuscript is not easy to read. Conjectural restorations of text or music are enclosed in ⟨ ⟩ brackets. In such instances something survives—a tail or a note-head—to provide evidence. The small roman numerals in the notes indicate the stave (i.e. voice) referred to / 3.3 (ii): an E punctum seems to follow this note / 5.1–2 (ii): pasted over in repair; apparently joined in ligature / 5.3.4 (i): apparently joined in ligature / 10.3 (i): flat *follows* the note at the beginning of a new stave, 10.4 / 10.4 (ii): pasted over / 11.1 (i): clef change / 12.3 (i): flat precedes 12.1 / At the end of the song, the music starts again with precisely the same notational symbols in voice i and nearly the same in voice ii, so far as can be seen; the music stops at 2.1. The MS is clipped but the first word of verse 2, *Quomodo*, can be made out. / In this song some words have been erased under voice (i); they are now illegible.

Song IV. I have not seen the MS and the transcription is from photograph (reproduced as Plate 3). There is a good deal of 'show-through' from the verso but no ambiguity. / 3.3: line from note to syllable indicates precise underlay / 3.5: cf. 1.5; such slight discrepancies are not uncommon in repeated phrases / 6.3–5: there is some uncertainty about the division of the groups; ? divide CDB (*que*) CB (*ter-*) AG (*-re*), but cf. 8.1 ff. for the melodic figure.

Language in Letters from Sir John Fastolf's Household

NORMAN DAVIS

In his new castle at Caister near Great Yarmouth, in which he took up residence in 1454 and lived until his death five years later, Sir John Fastolf maintained a large staff of household servants and clerks who administered his estates and often wrote his letters.[1] The names of a number of them are known, from references by Fastolf and letters written and signed by them, and the handwriting of others still unidentified can be seen to recur in numerous documents.[2] The most important of these men was William Worcester, who in addition to his work for Fastolf wrote a Latin *Itinerarium* and notes on many subjects, composed *The Boke of Noblesse*, and translated Cicero's *De Senectute*.[3] Fastolf's household included also his stepson Stephen Scrope, who translated *The Dicts and Sayings of the Philosophers* and *The Epistle of Othea*;[4] but as far as we know his work was literary and not secretarial. These writers, minor as they are, have received some attention; other members of the household

[1] See especially K. B. McFarlane, 'William Worcester: a preliminary survey', in *Studies presented to Sir Hilary Jenkinson*, ed. J. Conway Davies (Oxford, 1957), pp. 196–221, particularly p. 199; and 'The Investment of Sir John Fastolf's Profits of War', *Trans. Royal Hist. Soc.*, 5th ser. vii (1957), 91–116 (p. 105 on the cost of Caister).

[2] For example *Paston Letters and Papers of the Fifteenth Century* [P.L.P.], ed. N. Davis (Oxford, Part i 1971, Part ii 1976), nos. 520, 536. Most of the letters mentioned below are printed in this edition; references to them, by number, are given in parentheses. Letters not in this edition are referred to by the numbers of the text or abstract in J. Gairdner's editions of *The Paston Letters* of 1901 and 1904, marked G.

[3] See, in addition to McFarlane's study cited in n. 1, *Paston Letters and Papers*, i.lxxviii.

[4] Both ed. C. F. Bühler, EETS, os 211 (1941) and os 264 (1970).

concerned with merely practical affairs also deserve notice. They were less mobile than Worcester, and exemplify a more usual type of estate employee—a type, whether in orders or lay, which must effectively have managed the day-to-day operation of large households all over the country, and have used their 'business English' to do it.

Many papers concerning Fastolf's estate business survive. The largest collection is in Magdalen College, Oxford, to which the greater part of his lands eventually came; but of these only part is in English and few are letters.[5] Many others are among the Paston papers in the British Library, where there is also a distinct group of Fastolf documents in MS Add. 39848, formerly Phillipps 9735. Fastolf's letters to John Paston I in this manuscript have been printed in *Paston Letters and Papers*, Part ii; those to his own servants were abstracted in Gairdner's editions. Some relevant documents are in the Bodleian Library, one of them of special interest because it was acquired as recently as 1971. It is a brief letter in Fastolf's name, MS Eng. lett. c.291, fo. 95. The hand is so far unidentified, but it is clear that the subscribed name John Fastolf is in the hand of the text and not Fastolf's autograph, which is very distinctive. It is addressed to 'my right trusty and weelbeloued frende John Lynford, my styward of my courtes', asking him to inspect some property at Sisland in Norfolk. The letter was written at Caister, dated only 5 March without year. An unknown modern hand has pencilled '6 Henry VI' on the manuscript, but there is no evidence for this and so early a date (1428) is improbable: Fastolf was in France for much of the time from 1422 until about Michaelmas 1439.[6] Most of his surviving letters up to 1451, though written in various hands, have autograph signatures (not *P.L.P.* no. 457 of September 1450); but from

[5] I am obliged to the President and Fellows of Magdalen for allowing me to consult these documents and publish some of them, and especially to the Librarian, Dr G. L. Harriss, for his help.

[6] McFarlane, 'Fastolf's Profits' (see n. 1), pp. 96, 104. F. Blomefield, *History of Norfolk* (2nd edn., 1805–10), x.67, records that Fastolf granted an annuity to John Lyndford of Stalham on 28 April 6 Henry VI, and this may well be the source of the note on the manuscript.

July of that year, beginning with the letter abstracted by Gairdner
as 168 / 202 (MS Add. 39848, fo. 19), the subscriptions are all in
the hands of the clerks. Since there are thirty-eight letters from
July 1451 onwards, and none of them has an autograph signature, it seems likely that by then Fastolf was unable or disinclined
to sign his name—he says in G.169 / 203, 'Item, blessid be God
of hise visitacion, I haue ben right soore seeke'; and though he
adds that he is 'weel amendid' this need not mean complete
recovery. If this is right, the letter should be dated later than
July 1451. Indeed it is likely to be no earlier than 1454, since it
is dated from Caister, where he went to live permanently in that
year (no. 83); but it might have been written during an earlier
visit. Lyn(d)ford appears occasionally in Blomefield's *History of
Norfolk* and in public records. He was collector of a tax in
Norfolk in 1449, and his will was proved in 1457.[7] He is
mentioned in Fastolf's will of June 1459 as a former member
of his household (G.332 / 385). Whoever the scribe of this
letter may have been, it is linguistically unremarkable for its
date.

Other servants of Fastolf's show more individual writing
habits. There are four worth special attention: Thomas Howys,
John Russe, William Barker, and John Bokkyng. Though Russe
is the most interesting of these because of his later career, Howys
was more prominent in Fastolf's affairs for many years and it
is unfortunate that very little of his own writing survives. He
was a priest, from 1445 rector of Castle Combe in Wiltshire,
where Fastolf held one of his many widely dispersed properties,
and later of Blofield, Mautby, and Pulham in Norfolk.[8] Fastolf
chose him and John Paston I to assume on his behalf the
wardship of Thomas Fastolf of Cowhaugh in Suffolk,[9] and
again—at any rate according to Paston's version of events—to
act as the only executive administrators of his estate among the

[7] *Cal. Fine Rolls 1445–52*, p. 129; *Index of Wills proved at Norwich* (Norwich
Record Soc. xvi.2), p. 238.
[8] *William Worcestre, Itineraries*, ed. J. H. Harvey (Oxford, 1969), p. 252 n. 1.
[9] *Cal. Fine Rolls 1452–61*, pp. 92–3 (6 June 1454), and *P.L.P.* no. 886.

ten named executors (no. 54, ll. 128–48). The will propounded by Paston was challenged by William Yelverton, Justice, another executor; and this led to a long inquiry in the Archbishop of Canterbury's court of audience. Howys at first maintained his association with Paston, but he later changed sides, and in 1467 wrote a long statement 'for the discharge of his conscience'. In this he claimed that immediately after Fastolf died he saw Paston with 'a littyll scrowe of papyr in his honde of hys owne wrytyng yn Englyssh' which purported to contain an agreement made by Fastolf for the sale of all his Norfolk and Suffolk property to Paston for four thousand marks, and the nomination of Paston and Howys as administrators. Paston later, he said, caused alterations and additions to be made: 'Water Shypdam, an avditour of the seyd Fastolf, wrote a part of hyt, Frere Brakeley, John Russe of Jermuth another parte, and Richard Calle, a seruaunt of the seyd Paston, wrotte also parcell of the forseyd maters to the said scrowe' (no. 901 B)—a remarkable confirmation of the practice of employing a number of clerks on a single piece of writing, such as can be seen in some surviving drafts of legal documents.[10] Howys died on 4 February 1469.[11]

In addition to the statement about the will there are six letters signed with Howys's name, and another signed jointly by him and John Paston I (no. 53). One of the signatures differs from all the others, and is evidently by the same hand as the body of the letter (no. 516), which appears to be that of John Russe. The other six signatures are in the same rather coarse, angular hand; but only one of the letters is in that hand throughout. This must be Howys's own. Of the others, two are in Worcester's hand (nos. 53 and 507), two apparently in Russe's (nos. 510 and 511), and one in Barker's (no. 662). It may seem strange that a household servant of Howys's rank should be able to call on others to write his letters, but there is no escaping it; and it is significant that Barker, in writing a letter to John Paston I in 1459 (no. 578), added below the subscription 'per mandatum

[10] Examples of multiple drafting are *P.L.P.* nos. 42, 63, 900 A.
[11] Magdalen College, Fastolf Paper 90.

T.H.', which can only refer to Howys. He would appear to have had considerable authority in the administration.

John Russe first appears in the Paston papers in late 1454, when a letter undoubtedly in his hand, unsigned and unaddressed but evidently intended for John Paston I, gives an account, with some reported speech, of a court that he and his colleague Bartholomew Elys had attended at Cowhaugh in Suffolk in consequence of the grant of the wardship of Thomas Fastolf to Paston and Howys, in the interest of Sir John Fastolf (noted above, p. 331. Elys objected to the holding of the court by 'Long Bernard', the representative of the opposing interest of Sir Philip Wentworth; and when Bernard refused to yield he said he would sit beside him and record the proceedings. '"Nay", quod Bernard, "I wyl suffre you to sytte but not to wryte." "Well", quod Bertylmev, "thanne forsybly ye put vs from oure pocession, whiche I doute not but shalbe remembryd you anothir day"' (no. 508). Several letters written for Fastolf show Russe engaged in this kind of estate business, often together with other household officers such as Howys or Geoffrey Sperlyng (who later acquired greater merit as scribe of the Hunterian manuscript of the *Canterbury Tales*). After Fastolf's death he continued to be concerned with the estate. John Paston told his wife Margaret in June 1460 that he had asked Russe and Calle for information about the tenure of Fastolf's properties, and an inventory of goods at Caister drawn up in June 1462 recorded that the items listed were delivered by Howys 'be the handes of John Russe' to Calle, to be handed over to Paston (nos. 55, 64). Margaret Paston in November 1461 reported to her husband that 'Syr Thomas Howys and John Rus schall make an end of all thyngys aftyr yowyr intent as myche as they can do ther-in þis wek' (no. 163). At the inquiry into Fastolf's will Russe gave evidence in favour of Paston, and the opposing side accused him of corruption. A series of notes in English, written in a clerk's hand with additions by William Worcester (who adhered to Yelverton in the dispute), claims that John Russe, Robert Cutler vicar of Caister, and Friar Clement Felmyngham were 'falsly corrupted and waged' and gave an untrue account of Fastolf's health on the last day of his life; also John Osbern, William Pykeryng, and John Heydon, 'corrupted and hyred falsly', said that Osbern had seen Russe at Caister that day, whereas 'the trouth ys that John Rus from the begynnyng of vij in to the last endyng of xj at clok the said Saturday and that Robert Hart, porter of the place, from the houre of vij almoost to x afore noone from the seid manere, halle, cloyster, and chamber of Castre were absent, and at Jermuth personally present, iij mile from Castre'.[12] Russe wrote to Paston in 1462, 'I calle my-self a servaunt of yourez, and soo wil do, if it plese you', and he asked Paston to promote his nomination to the post of controller or searcher in the port of Yarmouth. Whether or not this helped his candidature, he was in fact appointed collector of customs and subsidies in July 1463, and the appointment was repeatedly renewed as late as 1485. He became a bailiff of Yarmouth in 1466 and was several times reappointed, and was elected to parliament for Yarmouth in 1467–8, 1472–5, 1478, and 1483. He was on commissions of various kinds in 1477, 1478, 1487, and 1488, and was made deputy butler, under Anthony Woodville, Lord Scales, in 1479.[13] These public offices are mostly later in date than his surviving letters, but they confirm the strong connection with Yarmouth that he had from his Caister days onwards. Unfortunately there is no information about his birthplace or education. At the inquiry in 1464 he was described by a hostile witness as illiterate and unable to understand Latin;[14] but he was amply literate in English, writing in three somewhat differing styles.

As early as 1461 Russe had begun to extend his activities to trade. Richard Calle wrote that he and Robert Glover were sending a ship loaded with corn to Flanders, where the price of malt was said to be good (no. 650). These trading ventures later

---

[12] Magdalen College, Fastolf Paper 85 (1).
[13] Blomefield, *History of Norfolk*, xi.325, 326; J. C. Wedgwood, *History of Parliament, Biographies* (1936), pp. 730–1; *Cal. Pat. Rolls 1476–85*, pp. 49, 112, 167; *Cal. Pat. Rolls 1485–94*, pp. 213, 239; *Cal. Fine Rolls 1461–71*, pp. 95, 270, etc.; *Cal. Fine Rolls 1485–1509*, no. 36, etc.
[14] Bodl. MS Top. Norfolk c.4, abstract in G.488 / 565.

led to requests to John Paston for payment, for example of 'the lytil syluir whiche fore serteyn thyngys delyuerid to youre vse is dewe to me', and of £19, as reported by Paston, 'for diuers parcelles whech he seith he shuld haue deliuerid in-to myn hows' (nos. 671, 675). Though the former of these occurs in a letter that cannot be dated firmly, the general contents so closely resemble those of no. 688 that it is probably to be placed in the same year, 1465. Paston was then in London pursuing his dispute with Yelverton, and Russe wrote urging him to come to terms: 'Ser, at the reuerence of Jesu laboure the meanys to haue peas, fore be my trowth the contynwaunce ⟨of thys⟩ trobyll shall short the dayez of my maistresse and it shall cause you to gret losse.' Later in the letter, in a passage incomplete because of damage to the paper, he taxed Paston with 'wylfullnesse, whyche men sey ye ocupye to excessifly', and continued, 'It is a dethe to me to remembre in what prosperite and in what degre ye myght stonde in Norfolk and Suffolk and ye had peas and were in hertys ease'. This is strikingly like the expressions of no. 671, 'Ser, I prey God bryng you onys to regne amongys youre cuntremen in love, and to be dred ... Men sey ye will neythere folwe the auyse of youre owyn kynred nore of youre counsell, but oon⟨ly⟩ youre owyn wylfullnesse ... God betir it and graunt yow onys hertys ease, fore it is half a deth to me to here the generall voyse of the pepyll, whiche dayli encreasyth.' In a letter the chief purpose of which was to ask Paston to intervene with the Lord Treasurer on his behalf, Russe's admonitions are surprisingly freely expressed; it is no wonder that in no. 688 he felt it prudent to add, 'Ser, I beseke youre maistirshyp fore-yeue me that I wryte thus boldly and homly to you.'

After John Paston I's death Russe maintained an association with the Paston family. At one time he was embarrassed by owing £9. 16s. 8d. to Margaret Paston, but tempered his apology with some scepticism: 'In as goodly haste as I can youre maistresship shal haue it, with euyr my seruise and preyere, fore ye do a meritory dede. It hathe sauyd my pore honeste and gretly auayled me, where as if it had leyn in youre coferys, as

I doute not a m^l li. more dothe, no profit shuld haue growe to ony man' (no. 725). John Paston II approved of the evidence Russe gave in the later stages of the Archbishop's inquiry: 'Also sende John Russe worde þat he hathe don in the best wyse, and þat hys deposicion and þe examynacion in Canterbury cort acorde in the best wyse' (no. 240, 1469); and he mentioned him in passing in a letter of 1473 (no. 274, ll. 3, 15). His last appearance in the letters is in November 1477, in a letter from William Pecock, a family servant, to John Paston II: 'I sold yet no barly nere non can a-bove xiiij d. þe comb, as I sen word in a leter be John Russe' (no. 779), which shows that he kept in touch with the Pastons at least up to that time. He died in 1492.[15]

William Barker, though less well represented by his surviving work than John Russe, appears in the documents earlier and his last known writing is later. He is first heard of in the address of a long letter from Fastolf, in Worcester's hand but with autograph signature, dated at London on 15 October 29 Henry VI, that is 1450: 'To my ryght trusty freende Ser Thomas Howys, parson of Castellcombe, beyng at Castre, and William Barker in haste at East yn by Jermuth.' This letter is BL MS Add. 34888, fo. 49, which Gairdner printed as no. 115 / 144 but, following Fenn, very imperfectly—he gave only a small part of it, and included an opening sentence that is not in the original. In 1454 a letter from Fastolf to John Paston I mentions Barker and Bokkyng together (no. 509), and they are often associated in this way, sometimes with other members of the household as well; for example in 1456 by Worcester, who disliked Barker: 'it ys ymagyned of me when I wryte lettres to London to Bokkyng or Barker that yn such materes as please hem not then it ys my doyng; yff it take well to theyr entent, then it ys her doyng. And yn gode feyth so it was ymagyned of me and othyrs that wrote by my maister commaundment to Castre, to the parson of Blofeld, Geffrey Spyrlyng, and othyrs. ... I am eased

---

[15] *Cal. Fine Rolls 1485–1509*, no. 443.

of my spyrytes now that I hafe expressed my leude menyng because of my felow Barker, as of such othyr berkers ayenst the mone, to make wysemen laugh at her folye' (no. 566). Barker was described in a petition to parliament in 1459 by Sir Philip Wentworth as 'de Norwico, gentilman', but in his own declaration made many years later he called himself 'late of Blofeld in the cownte of Norffolk, clark', and added at the end the note 'Predictum Willelmus Barker capellanus manu propria scripsit' (nos. 886, 925). There he said he was 'late howshold servaunte be the space of xxj yere wyth Syr John Fastolf, knyght, dyssesid, and had wedded Annes, late dyssesid', who was Thomas Howys's sister. If his period of service is taken back from the date of Fastolf's death, it must have begun in 1439, the year of Fastolf's return from France.

John Bokkyng seems to have been of much the same standing among Fastolf's servants as Barker. His father was Fastolf's receiver-general,[16] and he had a room of his own in Caister Castle (no. 64, l. 181). He first appears in the documents in 1450, in a letter from Fastolf dated at London on 15 September 29 Henry VI to Howys at Caister: 'Now that John Bokkyng ys in that parties he shall and can to you and to my councell all myne entent concernyng that mater.'[17] He was addressed by Yelverton, already a judge but not yet a knight, in November of the same year in terms which imply that he was thought to have some influence on Fastolf's actions: '... and also for to meve hym for that we may haue a good shereve and a good vndershereve that neythir for good fauore no fere wol returne for the Kyng ne betwix partie and partie non othir men but such as are good and trewe and in no wyse will be forsworne' (no. 878). He was associated with John Paston I in handling legal business for Fastolf, who wrote of him as 'my ryght trusty seruaunt' (no. 457); but after Fastolf's death he was said by William Paston II to be 'rythe euyll disposyd' to Howys and Paston. He was described as 'gentleman' in the record of a gift by Worcester in

---

[16] McFarlane, 'Worcester', p. 199.
[17] MS Add. 39848 fo. 8, abstract in G.110/138.

1460, and when appointed collector of a tax in 1468.[18] He was dead by 1478 (no. 782, l. 48).

These four men, Howys, Russe, Barker, and Bokkyng, were constantly in touch with each other, and with Worcester, and might be expected to share most of their linguistic habits. The incidence of their surviving letters varies a good deal. The complexity of Howys's secretarial arrangements has been noticed above. Eight letters survive written by Russe in his own hand and signed by him, all to John Paston I except for one to John's widow Margaret: nos. 551, 643, 666, 671, 675, 676, 688, 725, ranging in date from 1456 to 1466. Another, no. 508 of 1454, is not signed but is in Russe's hand, and also evidently to John Paston I. No. 643 is dated from London, nos. 671 and 688 from Yarmouth; the others give no place, but the content shows nos. 508 and 551 to have been written in Norfolk, nos. 666 and 676 in London. Russe also wrote a letter for Fastolf (no. 514 of 1455, from Caister), and one, unsigned, in the Paston interest to Master Rothwell about 1464 (no. 894). There are also three letters (noticed above, p. 332) among the total of eight which bear the name of Thomas Howys, the handwriting of which seems to be Russe's though it differs in some details from his usual style. These are nos. 510 and 511 of November 1454—they are dated by the regnal year, from Caister—and no. 516, of 1455, probably March, the place not stated but evidently again Caister. They are thus some five years earlier than all but two of Russe's own letters, but it cannot be said that there is a distinct change of style at any particular time; rather it appears that Russe used three more or less distinguishable styles, and to some extent associated certain linguistic forms with each.

William Barker's earliest known letter on his own account is one written to Fastolf on 3 November 1454, from Wroxham in Norfolk (G.221/265, MS Add. 27444, fo. 28). Four other documents were written and signed or initialled by him: nos. 578 (1459) and 667 (1462), letters from Norwich to John Paston I, 718 (1462) to Margaret Paston, and 925, a formal statement

[18] *Cal. Close Rolls 1454–61*, p. 475; *Cal. Fine Rolls 1461–71*, p. 234.

of uncertain date but undoubtedly much later than the rest, perhaps about 1485. In addition four letters written in Barker's hand for Fastolf, and signed by Fastolf, are preserved in MS Add. 39848: fos. 3, 13, 14, 15, abstracted in G.79 / 104, 133 / 164, 141 / 171, 142 / 173, from London in 1450 and 1451, and three others, all to John Paston I from Caister, were written by Barker and signed by him with Fastolf's name: nos. 518 of 1455, 553 and 589 between then and 1459. There is also one letter in Barker's hand signed by Howys (no. 662, 1462), and another signed by Barker with the name of James Arblaster (no. 702, not after 1466).

John Bokkyng's earliest known letter on his own account is to William Wayte, dated from London on 2 January, evidently 1451 (G.140 / 169, MS Add. 34888, fo. 62). The next is to Fastolf at Caister, apparently from Southwark ('your place') in February 1456 (G.275 / 322). Four to John Paston I (nos. 548 from Southwark, 549 from Caister, 552 from Horsleydown, and 565 again from Southwark) follow in the same year; then G.315 / 366 to Fastolf from London in 1458, and two more to Paston (no. 584 from Coventry in 1459 and no. 590 from Caister of uncertain date but before Fastolf's death). All these are signed, most of them with initials only, by Bokkyng. There is another short letter in Magdalen College (Fastolf Paper 94) addressed to the 'rent gaderer of Sir John Fastolf renters in Southw⟨erk⟩ by Batell brigge in Beremondsey strete by London'. The man's name is lost except for the first two letters *Ro* and the last three *ton*, because the rest was evidently written on the sealing tape. Since Wainfleet assumed administration of Fastolf's will in February 1470 (no. 248), the September of the date is probably that of 1469. Bokkng's 'Norffolklyk' patriotism is notable; his language is not conspicuously regional. The text of the letter is as follows:[19]

Right welbeloued frende, I commaunde me to you and pray you and charge you in myn vncle Yeluertons name that ye goo to my lord of

---

[19] Punctuation and capitals are editorial; abbreviations are expanded in italics; the angle brackets mark a small hole in the paper.

Wynchestre, or sum man of his for you, and recommaunde hym vnto his lordship and pray hym þat he wole nought refuse to take
administracion vp-on hym for myn maister Fastolfes goodes as thei
were accordid, ner þat he discharge hym nought þerof in noo wise
til myn vncle may speke with his lordship þerjnne, for many grete
causes of proffite and wele þat shal growe þerjnne to þe plesance of
God and þe sowle, what þat ony man haue enformed hise lordship
of þe contrarie. Ther come tidynges from Worcestre þat my lord
was discoragid þerjnne, and þerfore myn vncle prayd me to write
þus to you. If ye see Maister Tilney or John Gilberte þei may doo
þis for you, or your silf oþer. And recommaunde me to my Maister
Tilney, to my good moder Wesenham, Henre Wyndessore, and ⟨..⟩
my suster his wif; and euere wele mote ye fare Norffolklyk.

Wreten at Longham the v day of Septembre. And þat my lord of
Wynchestre refuse nought to take administracion in ony case.

Your owen frende J. Bokkyng

The spelling and grammatical forms of this group of writers
show a number of variables of greater or less significance, of
which only a selection can be noticed here. References to
particular occurrences are limited to those of special interest.

Certain spellings which are characteristic of some East Anglian
writers—x- in *xal* 'shall', *qw*- for *wh*-—are all but unknown:
qw- never appears at all, *xal* only once in Bokkyng's early letter
G.140 / 169 (misread *zall* in the editions); otherwise *sh*-, rather
than *sch*-, is normal. Loss of a fricative before *-t* is shown directly
only in *ryth* 'right' in Bokkyng's early letter; otherwise *ryght*,
thought, etc. are regular, though loss of the fricative is shown
indirectly by unhistorical spellings such as *wryghtyng*, *oughtlaw*
by Barker, *wryghting* by Russe.[20] The letter ʒ is rare: it seems to
occur only once, initially in ʒow in no. 510 written by Russe for
Howes. The use of þ is one point on which the writers differ
substantially, especially at the beginnings of words. Russe never
uses þ- at all. Barker has in most of his letters only a sprinkling
of examples, in the form of y-, in words like þat, þerof, þerfore,

---

[20] On such regional spellings as they are used by some of the Pastons see N. Davis,
'The Language of the Pastons', *Proc. Brit. Acad.* xl (1955), 120–44, esp. pp. 124–5.

but in the late no. 925 there are nearly forty cases of *þe*. In striking contrast, Bokkyng at all times uses a real *þ*- not only in the short and abbreviated words like *þe*, *þer*, *þis*, *þat*, *þem*, *þus*, but also in longer words like *þing*, *þinke*, *þought*, *þrive*. This is not exclusive—he sometimes has *th*-, but in the short words as well as the others; he certainly did not attempt to distinguish voiced and voiceless consonants in this way.

There is variation also in the writing of *e* for normal Middle English short *i*. Russe often has *e* both in native words, *besy*, *dede* 'did', *leuyd* and *levyng*, *sethyn*, *wretyn*, and in words of French origin, such as *condecion*, *consedre* (and inflected forms), *commesyonerez*, *delygence*, *dysposecion*, *menut*, *openyon*, *Trenyte*. Similar forms, in addition to several of these, occur in the three letters written for Howys: *deleuery*, *delygent(ly*, *expedecyon*, *fulfellyng*, *preson*, *speryt*. Barker also uses such forms freely: *besynesse*, *ded*, *dreven*, *theder*, *wedow*, *wreten*, *contenu*, *preuy*. Bokkyng, on the other hand, has them very rarely—the Magdalen letter has *wreten* but the usual form is *writen*, and he has *prevy* in no. 568 for Fastolf. Howys in his holograph letter has *wretyn*, *wele* 'will', *preson*, *prevy*. A special case is the verb *wete*, presumably with a long vowel, which Russe has regularly (seven times in his own letters, also for Fastolf and twice for Howys). Barker happens to use the word seldom, but his form is again *wete*. But Bokkyng has two cases of *wete* against seven of *wite* / *wyte*, in letters for Fastolf as well as his own.

The spelling *ea* instead of *e* for the vowel in words like *please* is common in all these writers, unexpectedly at this date. Russe has *deceasyd*, *dyspleasure*, *ease*, *encreasyth*, *mean(ys*, *peas*, *please*, *seas* 'cease', *season* in his own letters, for Fastolf and for Howys *please*, though he has also *plese*, *mene*, *sesyng*. Barker has *please*, *pleasaunce*, *seale* for himself, *please*, *pleaser* for Fastolf and for Arblaster, *please* and *meane* for Howys. Bokkyng has *ensealed*, *meane*, *oneasid*, *please* for himself, *disseasid*, *meane*, *please* for Fastolf. Howys has *please*, but *mene* and *menys*.

Before *nd*, *a* and *o* may vary. Russe has *hand*es (once), *lond-* (6 ×), *stond-*, *vnderstonde*, *notwithstondyng* (10 × in all). Barker has *lond-* (8 ×, five of them in no. 925), *notwythstondyng* but *vnderstande*; for Fastolf he has *hand*es, for Howys *hand*es but *lond-*. Bokkyng has *hand-*, *noughtwithstanding*, but *fonde* 'found'. For Fastolf he has *stande*. Howys has *lond* but *nowth-wythstandyng*.

The form of 'any' in Russe (13 ×) and Bokkyng (9 ×) is always *ony*. Barker has *ony* himself, *any* for Fastolf (three times in one letter). Howys has *any* once.

The forms of 'much', 'such', and 'which' may vary. Russe has *mych*(e (8 ×), *suche* (3 ×), *whych*(e (23 ×) and a single *wiche*; for Howys he has *myche* but *wheche* (5 ×). Barker has *meche* (once), *suche*, *which*(e (5 ×), and *wheche* for himself; *moche* for Fastolf, Howys, and Arblaster, *suche* and *wheche* (13 ×) for Fastolf, *whiche* (5 ×) for Howys. Bokkyng has *moche*, *suche*, *which*(e regularly and often, both for himself and for Fastolf. Howys has *swyche* on the only appearance of the word.

In 'again', 'against', 'give', *g* may vary with *y*. Russe has *ageyn* (5 ×) and *ayens* (2 ×), *geue* (6 ×), *forgeue* and *foryeue* each once, *gaf* and *yaf*; for Howys *geue*. Barker has only *ayens* and *yaf* for himself; *ayenst*, *geve*, *yeve* for Fastolf, *ayenst* for Arblaster. Bokkyng has *ayen*, *ayenst*, *agayn*, *gif* (infin.) for himself and for Fastolf. (He also writes 'get' twice *ghete*, as Worcester also does.)

The endings of the plural and the genitive of nouns, where they are not simply *-s* as in *maters*, are variously written *-is / ys* and *-es*, with the alternative *-ez*. Russe uses all these forms at all periods of his writing, but *-is / -ys* more than the others; for example *termys*, *fermys*, *plasis* as well as *tymes* in no. 508 (1454), *coferys*, *shyppis*, *literys* as well as *tymez* in no. 725 (after 1466). His *-ez* forms are nevertheless a distinctive feature of his work. They are: *dayez* in nos. 551 (1456), 643 (1461), twice in no. 688 (1465), *tymez* in nos. 643, 725, twice in no. 688, *fermourez* three times in no. 551, *officez* twice in no. 666 (1462), *yowrez* twice in no. 666, *feez* in no. 551, *causez* in no. 643,

Seynt Oloffez in no. 675 (1462), *partyez* in no. 676 (1462), *aduersaryez* in no. 688. For Howys his forms are *personez, douterez, otherez, maisterez* (4 ×) in no. 510, *otherez, Jenneyez* in no. 511 (both 1454), *materez* in no. 516 (1455); for Fastolf *personez* and *frendez* in no. 514 (1455). Barker writes the ending -*es* almost regularly, with only an occasional -*ys*, until his late no. 925 in which -*ys* strongly predominates. There is a single example of -*ez* in *frendez* in the early G.79 / 104 (1450). Bokkyng often writes -*is*, as *prestis, maisteris, nedis*, but more often -*es*; a peculiarity of his is the frequent detaching of the -*is* of the possessive—*maister is* in no. 549, *God is* nos. 549, 552, G.315 / 366, and for Fastolf no. 570, *moder is* no. 552, and especially with names, as *Jenney is* no. 552, *Thomas is, Fulthorp is* no. 565, *Woodrove is* no. 569. Howys writes only -*ys* in *mannys, ellys, menys*, except for the unique *enemyndz* or perhaps rather *enemynez*.

The form of 'his' is sometimes *hise / hyse*, sometimes *hese*. Russe has mostly *hise / hyse*, but *hese* twice in no. 508, and in nos. 688 and 725, and five times in no. 894. He has *hese* for Fastolf twice in no. 514, for Howys in no. 510 and five times in no. 511. Barker's normal form is *his*, but he has *hese* twice for Fastolf, once each in G.79 / 104 and 142 / 173 (1450 and 1451). Bokkyng has only *his* and *hise* except for three cases of *hes* in G.140 / 169 (1451). Howys has only *his*.

The pronoun 'it' is sometimes *hit*. Russe has only *it*. Barker often uses *hit*: for example in no. 578 (1459) all five occurrences of the pronoun have that form, and in no. 667 (1462) there are five cases of *hit* beside one of *it*. But in the late no. 925 the only two occurrences of the word are both *it*. For Fastolf, Howys, and Arblaster Barker uses *hit* regularly—for example six times in G.79 / 104. Bokkyng has *it* almost everywhere, but there are two cases of *hit*, beside one *it*, in the early G.140 / 169, and two of *hit* beside six of *it* in G.275 / 322.

The pronouns 'their' and 'them' have both the old and the new forms. Russe has *ther(e* four times in no. 508 and twice in no. 688, but *here* still five times in no. 894; for Fastolf *there*, for

Howys *there*z each once. In contrast, *hem* is his usual form (some 16 times) against a single *them* in no. 676, where it functions as a specifying demonstrative in 'them of Ireland'. For Fastolf *hem* is again his form; for Howys it happens that no occasion for it occurs. Barker has few examples of either form: *ther* in no. 578, *theym* twice in each of nos. 667 and G.221 / 265. For Fastolf he has both *hem* and *theym* in G.79 / 104, *hem* and *them* in G.133 / 164, *hem* in G.142 / 173; for Howys *here* and *there* each once, *hem* once and *theym* three times. Bokkyng has *her* once in the early G.140 / 169, and *hem* three times only; *þere* / *ther* three times and *þem* / *them* six. For Fastolf he has *þere* / *þeire* / *there* five times, *þem* twice. Howys has *here* once.

Infinitives keep the -*n* ending irregularly. Russe has *takyn*, *stondyn* / -*en*, *syttyn*, *hurtyn*, in five different letters. Barker has *ben* six times, *don*, *gon*, and *seyn* each once. For Fastolf he has *ben*, *don* eight times, *seen*, and *labouren*; for Howys and for Arblaster each *don*. Bokkyng has -*n* only in *ben*, twice (before a word beginning with a vowel) in G.140 / 169.

Present and past tense plurals are similarly irregular. Russe does not use -*n* at all. Barker does not use it in his own letters, but has *ben* for Fastolf and Howys, *arn* for Arblaster. He also has *beeth* once for Fastolf in G.79 / 104, where the following *bothe* may perhaps have influenced it: 'as to my shippys, þei beeth bothe come in savetee, blyssed be God'. Bokkyng has a number of present plurals in -*n*: *sitten*, *faren* twice, *attenden*, *þinken* twice, and another *þinkyn* for Fastolf; and a few past plurals: *hadden*, *comen*, *speken*, *writen*, and *riden* and *writen* for Fastolf.

The present plural of 'be' is in Russe *be(e* four times, *ar(e* three; *be* once for Fastolf. Barker has *ben* for Fastolf (as well as *beeth* noticed above) and for Howys, *arn* for Arblaster. Bokkyng has *ar* twelve times, *er* once, *be* twice; *ar* three times for Fastolf.

The past participles of strong and anomalous verbs show much variation in the retention or loss of -*n*. Russe has with -*n be(e)n* (3 ×), *doon* (2 ×), *leyn*, *slayn*, *sworn*, *comyn*, *bounden*,

takyn (2 ×), *wretyn* (4 ×), *holdyn, spokyn, chosyn,* and without
it *bee, doo* (4 ×), *knowe, growe*. Barker has *ben* (5 ×), *don,
taken* (3 ×), *wreten* (2 ×), *dreven, knowen, holpen;* also *holde*
(2 ×), *know*. For Fastolf he has *ben, don* (4 ×), *boorn, forgeten,
geven, growen, holden, holpen* (2 ×), *wreten* (2 ×); also *be,
dreve, founde* (3 ×), *wrete, gete*. For Howys he has *ben* (3 ×),
leten; for Arblaster *ben, beholden,* and *gete, knowe*. Bokkyng
has most with *-n: ben* (4 ×), *doon* (6 ×), *se(e)n* (2 ×), *slayn*
(2 ×), *sworn, taken, writen* (7 ×) and *wreten, begonnen, biden,
drawen,* but *bounde, ley* (no. 548); for Fastolf *ben, founden,
knowen* (2 ×), *spoken* (2 ×), *writen* (5 ×), *vnderstanden,* also
bounde.

These varying usages may be summarized as follows. In his
frequent use of *þ* Bokkyng stands apart. He differs also in using
e for *i* rarely, whereas Russe, Barker, and Howys do so often.
The spelling *ea* is more or less equally favoured. Before *nd* Russe
and Barker prefer *o* except in *hand;* Bokkyng prefers *a,* but the
numbers are small. *Ony* is strongly preferred. *Suche* is general
except for a single *swyche* in Howys; *mych(e* is used by Russe,
moche (once *meche*) by Barker and Bokkyng; *whych(e* is Russe's
usual form, *wheche* for Howys; *which(e* is regular in Bokkyng
and frequent in Barker, but he also has *whech(e,* often for
Fastolf. *Ageyn / ayen* and *geue / yeue* are not clearly distinguished. In noun endings Russe often uses *-ez,* which otherwise
occurs only once in Barker; Bokkyng commonly writes *is* of the
possessive separately. As an alternative to *hise* Russe often has
hese, which is rare elsewhere. *Hit* is not used by Russe, very
frequent in Barker, rare in Bokkyng. In the third person plural
pronoun Russe has *ther(e* but *hem;* Barker has *h-* and *th-* forms
in both cases; Bokkyng mostly *þ- / th-* in both. Infinitives have
-n sometimes in Russe; sometimes also in Barker, all but one in
monosyllabic verbs; in Bokkyng only twice, in *ben*. Verb plurals
never have *-n* in Russe, rarely in Barker, but occasionally in
Bokkyng in past as well as present. In past participles Bokkyng
has *-n* more frequently than the others. In addition, Howys is
individual in writing *nowt(h, where* for 'were', and especially

-*t* as the ending of the third person singular in *hat, causet, maket*.

This group of writers, living in a household relatively remote from large centres and three days' ride from London, for the most part wrote an English less distinctively 'Norfolklike' than might have been expected as early as the middle of the fifteenth century. Some of the variable features of linguistic form they all treated in the same way, and it was not always the way taken by the incipient standard language. On the other hand, in many things individual choice had by no means been eliminated by their years of close association in the service of Sir John Fastolf. Their letters show something of the complexity of the process by which regional men of varied experience moved towards a common form of written English.

The Books of Philosophy Distributed at Merton College in 1372 and 1375[1]

NEIL KER

> For hym was levere have at his beddes heed
> Twenty bookes clad in blak or reed

The collections of books at Merton College grew steadily throughout the fourteenth century, as a result mainly of bequests from former fellows. To house them, the college set up first one and then another, larger 'libraria' in which the most valuable books could be chained and made careful arrangements for the safe keeping and use of the many books of theology and Aristotelian philosophy not included in the library, entrusting them for several years at a time to fellows of the college studying theology and arts. This bipartite method of keeping the books is basically that in use at the Sorbonne already in 1289.[2] At Merton in the second half of the next century the distribution was called an *electio* and the set of books each fellow received was his *sors*. All this is admirably set out by F. M. Powicke in his *Medieval Books of Merton College* (Oxford, 1931).[3] As material for the fourteenth-century part of his chronological survey Powicke had not only inscriptions in extant books to go on, but also four documents: a useful catalogue of the 'Libri philosophie' drawn up in the twenties probably, a useful catalogue of the books of theology (etc.) dating from about 1360, and two lists of books of philosophy 'in electione sociorum',

---

[1] I owe particular thanks to Dr Roger Highfield and Mr John Burgass; also to Dr Richard Hunt, who spent time on difficult titles and secundo folios, to my profit. [2] L. Delisle, *Le Cabinet des manuscrits*, ii (1874), p. 181. [3] See also the papers by P. S. Allen and H. W. Garrod in *The Library*, 4th series, iv (1924), 249–76 and viii (1928), 312–35.

one of 1372 and the other of 1375. He called them P, T, B, and C and printed them on pp. 47–67. These catalogues exist by good fortune only. Election lists in particular are ephemera, vitally important for a few years and then of no use. No doubt all Oxford colleges in which books were distributed had such lists, but they survive only at Merton, two from this century and two from the next.[4]

In making an election list there were five points to consider: as for the fellows, how many of them were taking part and in what order: as for the books, how many were to be distributed, their subject, and their value. Powicke considered that 'in general the fellows named in these lists were men of some years', often of many years', standing'.[5] Their order was evidently a set one, since the names of the seven fellows who took part in both the 1372 and the 1375 election are in the same order in both lists. The order is one of seniority, if the example of Oriel College earlier in the century is anything to go by: there, according to the statutes of 1329, each fellow was to be allowed one book in order of seniority, and if any books were left over, fellows might then choose them 'secundum ordinem personarum'.[6] The bursar's rolls at Merton provide some evidence on this point, although they are a defective series and unsatisfactory from our point of view because they do not provide lists of fellows, but only lists of those fellows who were responsible for commons on a weekly rota: in a term of seventeen or eighteen weeks we can expect only seventeen or eighteen names. The names in the lists of stewards are not in a set order, but elements of order can be detected, notably the run Dollyng, Lyndon, Caps, Stone, Gunwardby in Rec.3704 which comes again, less Dollyng, in Rec.3705 and is also in election list B.[7] All but one[8]

---

[4] Powicke's D and F, *c.* 1410 and 1451.   [5] *Medieval Books*, p. 15.
[6] *Statutes of the Colleges of Oxford* (ed. 1853), Oriel College, p. 15.
[7] Names follow the spellings in A. B. Emden, *Biographical Register of the University of Oxford to A.D. 1500*, 3 vols. (Oxford, 1957–9). Henceforth *BRUO*. The archives of Merton College are numbered in a single series beginning with Rec.1. The bursar's rolls, save a few strays, are Rec.3612–3965d in this series.   [8] Park. According to *BRUO* he was first bursar in 1373–4.

of the names in the two election lists occur also in the lists of stewards in the surviving rolls from the mid sixties to the mid seventies. Thomas Swyndon and Robert Rygge (B.1,2) were fellows in 1365 (Rec.3698). Stapilton and Staunton (B.3,4) first come to our knowledge in a defective list probably for 1368 (Rec.3701); More, Bryghtwell, Wotton, Potton, and Reynham (B.6,7,9–11) first in the list for Nov. 1368–Mar. 1369 (Rec.3703); Sampton, Coryngham, Wendover, Lyndon, Organ, Banbury, and Horsham (B.5,15,16,19, C.9,10,15) first in a defective list for Nov. 1369–Mar. 1370 (Rec.3702);[9] Hodersale, Fitzsymond, Dollyng, Caps, Stone and Gunwardby (B.13,17,18,20–2) first in the list for Mar. – Aug. 1371 (Rec.3704); Swyndon (if this is the receiver of B.8),[10] Halden,[11] Alkrynton, Risburgh, Balynden, and Pratt (B.8,14, C.11–14) first in the list for Nov. 1374–Mar. 1375 (Rec.3706); Pester (C.8) first in the list for Aug.–Nov. 1376 (Rec.3708).[12] In 1372 the books for distri-

[9] The regnal date in the heading of Rec.3702 is damaged and has had a reagent on it, but 'xliii Et sequente' seems almost certain. The roll is in a good hand rather like that of election list B.

[10] BRUO records only one Swyndon at this time, Thomas, but the name occurs twice in list B: Thomas Swyndon had sors 1 and Swyndon sors 8. The latter may have been the John Swyndon who, like Thomas, was a fellow of Exeter. Thomas transferred to Merton in 1365 and John (perhaps his younger brother) may have followed him a few years later. The matter is complicated by Thomas Swyndon's alias Styve. Styve is named in Rec.3705, Swyndon in Rec.3706, 3708, 3709: see below.

[11] There is a mention of Halden in Rec.3702.

[12] Seven bursar's rolls (and seven lists of stewards) remain out of twenty-five for the period from the November–March term of 1368–9 to the November–March term of 1376–7, the six mentioned in the text and Rec.3705 (Nov. 1371–Mar. 1372). The lists in Rec.3708, 3709 are for consecutive terms: only four names are common to both lists. The names (those not in the election lists B and C are shown by italics) are: (Rec.3703) *Caldwell*, *Green*, Rygge, *Cary*, *Bramley*, More, Brightwell, '*Bronnyng*' (Emden read Brounyng), Wotton, Potton, Reynham, *Tauk*, Stapilton, Staunton, *Hulman*, *Salisbury*, *Wyk*; (Rec.3702) *Salisbury*, Horsham, Coryngham, [...] *Uscher*, Wendover, *Bloxham*, [...] Sampton, Staunton, Lyndon, [...] Banbury, Organ; (Rec.3704) *Blankpayn*—he comes in Professor Bennett's *Chaucer at Oxford and at Cambridge*—Hodersale, Wotton, Dollyng, Lyndon, Caps, Stone, Gunwardby, Fitzsymond, Stapilton, Sampton, *Ramesbury*, *Caldwell*, Wendover, *Aylesham*, *Aston*, *Hulman*, Staunton, Rygge; (Rec.3705) Lyndon, Caps, Stone, Gun-

bution—all in Latin—numbered 137 and went to twenty-two fellows: numbers 1–3 on the list got eight books each, numbers 4–13 seven books each, and numbers 14–22 five books each, or, in two cases, four books each. In 1375 the books numbered 134 and went to fifteen fellows: number 1 got twelve books and the rest eight, nine, or ten.[13] The aim seems to have been to provide each fellow with as complete a collection of Texts of Aristotle, logical Texts, and Commentaries on Aristotle by Averroës as his position warranted and the resources of the college allowed, and to distribute Expositions and what I have called 'Extras' as equitably as possible, the better titles being higher rather than lower in the lists.[14] By a deliberate change in 1375 the two available copies of the Textus de Animalibus were promoted from being 'Extras' to a leading position in two *sortes* of list C.[15]

Only careful organization could achieve what we see in these lists. At Merton the subwarden was responsible for the philosophical election. Probably he had a priced and numbered list to work from, so that he could readily see what was available, how many Texts, how many Commentaries (Averroës and, for the Ethics, Eustratius and others, but the college had only one of these for distribution), how many Expositions (usually Aqui-

wardby, Stapilton, Wendover, *Aston, Aylesham,* Fitzsymond, *Caldwell,* Sampton, *Hulman, Maundour,* Staunton, Rygge, *Reyneyd, Styve;* (Rec.3706) Stone, Gunwardby, Fitzsymond, *Reyneyd,* More, Swyndon, Potton, Brightwell, Wotton, Reynham, *Hulman,* Risburgh, Alkrynton, Balynden, Pratt, Horsham, Halden; (Rec.3708) *Castell,* Horsham, Lyndon, Pester, Rygge, Swyndon, More, Doilyng, Potton, Coryngham, Wendover, *Ramesbury,* Organ, Banbury, Caps; (Rec.3709) Stapilton, Stone, More, Alkrynton, Risburgh, Balynden, Reynham, Wotton, *Offecote, James,* Brightwell, Alkrynton, *Castell,* Swyndon, Lyndon, Pratt, Staunton, Rygge.

[13] I have not taken B.14.6 and C.4.11 (Powicke, nos. 448, 498) into account, nor the books distributed to Stapilton as an afterthought in 1375, nor the evidence which suggests that C.1.11, C.1.12, C.7.10, and C.14.9, none of them in list B, are additions to list C.

[14] I have used a capital letter to begin the words Texts, Commentaries, Expositions, and 'Extras', when referring to books in election lists B and C.

[15] A third copy, now MS 270, was not available for the elections, as the donor had specified that it should be chained in the library.

nas), and how many other books on or related to natural philosophy and logic; and could see, too, how much each book was worth, in case a fellow should have the misfortune to lose a volume of his *sors*.[16] We might expect that he would take care also to see that each book was marked plainly with a title, say 'Textus philosophie' or 'Commentator philosophie', and a number. If such titles and numbers were used at Merton, the evidence for them has all gone: possibly they were written on now vanished bindings or end-leaves. They were used at Balliol College, however, where, for example, a copy of Eustratius on the Ethics, now MS 116, is marked 'primus commentator' at the head of the first leaf.[17] On the other hand, a scrap of evidence about prices remains. One of the books issued in 1372, B.17.3, was not returned at the right time, as was noted on the election roll, where there is also a valuation which must have been taken from a priced list.

Thanks mainly to the philosophy catalogue, we know the price of over forty of the books in these election lists, enough to show that the order within each of the four groups, Texts, Commentaries, Expositions, 'Extras', is a value order. If there were two in a *sors*, first Texts were worth more than second Texts, first Commentaries more than second Commentaries, and first 'Extras' more than second 'Extras', to judge from the prices attached to B.3.2 and B.3.3, B.4.2 and B.4.3, B.9.1 and B.9.2, B.11.2 and B.11.3, B.17.1 and B.17.2, B.21.4 and B.21.5, C.7.3 and C.7.4, C.7.5 and C.7.6, C.9.2 and C.9.3, C.10.1 and C.10.2, C.12.1 and C.12.2.[18] The only contrary evidence comes from C.15.2 and C.15.3. The commentaries in one-Commentary *sortes* are priced between 24s. and 15s. The least valuable Commentaries are seconds, B.10.5 and B.12.5.

The *sortes* themselves may have been arranged in a value

---

[16] Possibly the preparation of a list of this sort was intended in 1351–2 when sixpence-worth of parchment was bought 'pro rotulis librorum philosophie' (Rec.3686).

[17] For this and other marked books at Balliol see R. A. B. Mynors, *Catalogue of the manuscripts of Balliol College, Oxford* (Oxford, 1963), pp. xv, xvi.

[18] See the Concordances, below, pp. 383–93.

order. There is a little evidence about this, but nothing like enough. Some books in the first three *sortes* of list B were good books. B.2.1 (= C.2.1) was called 'bonus' when it was bought, B.1.1, B.1.4, and B.2.1 (= C.1.1, C.7.5, and C.2.1) have big prices attached to them, and we can see with our own eyes that B.1.6, B.1.8 (= C.11.1), and B.3.7 (= C.1.8) are handsome.[19] Thomas Swyndon's *sors*, B.1, may have been worth something like £6. The books called Quaternus or Questiones are at the far end in each list: they do not occur above B.15 or, except one, above C.8. The assumption that most of them were of no great value is supported by the under-a-shilling prices of B.19.4 and B.22.4 (= C.11.8). B.18.4, now MS 296, may be an exception, but it is certainly the least prepossessing of the surviving books.[20] Stone's *sors*, B.21, was worth about 21*s*. (or perhaps 31*s*.) and most of its value lay in the Commentary: every fellow could expect to have one costly book, Averroës, in his keeping.[21] The only other *sors* with a value which can be guessed at is Staunton's, B.4. It may have been worth a little over £3.

Probably some fellows had a say in the composition of their *sors*. Seven took part in both elections. One 1372 book came again to More in 1375 and one to Hodersale, two again to Wotton and two to Stone. This may be mere chance. But it can hardly be chance that one of the bursars in 1375, Geoffrey Potton, got again four of the seven books he had had in 1372.

One might expect that two nearly contemporary scribes writing lists of the same books in a different order would go about things in the same way; indeed that there would be a well-established formula for writing election lists by the 1370s. To judge from list C this was not so. The names of fellows are not set out as in B. Titles of books are in the accusative, not the nominative. Titles differ slightly from B's, sometimes for the better; in particular, the uninformative word 'quaternus' is

[19] MSS 274, 271, 273.
[20] B calls it 'quaternus', P,C, and D 'expositio', but in spite of the presence of Aquinas on the Posterior Analytics Powicke's title, 'Sentences and questions on logic', seems best.
[21] See the Concordance under B.21.3.

avoided. Abbreviations of words which come over and over again, like *naturalium*, *ethicorum*, *physicorum*, *commentum*, are not B's abbreviations.[22] There are odd variations in the abbreviations used, *comment'* for the first Commentary and *commentatorem* for the second Commentary in four successive *sortes* (10–13) and then *comment'* for the first Commentary and *commentum* for the second Commentary in four other successive *sortes* (10–13).[23] The scribe of C seems to have liked varying things.

What lies behind the titles? We know, of course, if the books survive, but that is seldom and only as a result of transfer from election to library in or before the fifteenth century: B.8.4, Commentum methaphisice, is MS 269; B.1.6, Exposicio super ce et M', is MS 274; B.3.7, Expo' methaphisice, is MS 273; B.11.6, Exposicio logicalium, is MS 289; B.1.8, Textus de animalibus, is MS 271; B.18.4, Quaternus or (list C) Expositorem sex principiorum, is MS 296; B.20.4, Tractatus lincolniensis cum aliis, is MS 280.[24] We know, more or less, if entries in lists B and C correspond to entries in the philosophy catalogue.[25] We can make some sort of estimate if we read the descriptions of surviving texts and commentaries in *Aristoteles Latinus*[26] and the philosophy sections of a full medieval catalogue like that of St. Augustine's, Canterbury, where nos. 1024–59, 1062–5 are texts of Aristotle, nos. 1066–75, 1078–9 commentaries on Aristotle by Averroës, Albertus Magnus, and Eustratius, nos. 1080–4 expositions, nos. 1085–1104 sententiae, questions, etc. on natural philosophy, nos. 1279–1308 texts of logic, and nos.

[22] B: n^{a}l' *and once* n^{a}lium, eth^{rum}, phi^{rum}, com^m (*reversed* c *for* com-). C: naturalium *or* n^{a}lium, ethi^{orum}, phi*si*corum, comment' *or* commentum (*both with reversed* c *for* com-).

[23] See *Merton Muniments*, ed. P. S. Allen and H. W. Garrod, Oxford Historical Society, lxxxvi (1928), Pl. 24.

[24] See below, Notes. All are in post-medieval bindings, but signs of chaining sometimes remain on the endleaves.

[25] See below, Concordance.

[26] *Aristoteles Latinus*, Codices descripsit G. Lacombe (*et al.*), supplementis indicibusque instruxit L. Minio-Paluello, 2 parts (Rome, 1939; Cambridge, 1955).

1309–36 questions, sententiae, summae, etc. on logic.[27] Evidently nearly all titles may and most titles do conceal part of the contents. MS 273 contains not only Aquinas on the Metaphysics, but also Aquinas on the Politics. A 'Textus naturalium' may or may not include the Metaphysics. A 'Textus methaphisice' is quite likely to include the Ethics and a 'Textus ethicorum' the Metaphysics: the precise title in the election lists will depend on which comes first. These lists are no guide, therefore, to the number of copies of the Metaphysics or the Ethics at Merton College. They are some guide to the number of copies of Averroës on the Physics, Metaphysics, and De celo, and of Eustratius (and others) on the Ethics, since two of these quite long commentaries, together with the texts commented on,[28] would not normally be fitted into one volume: 'Commentum methaphisice' is a complete description of the contents of MS 269.

The fifty-seven Texts distributed in 1372 have probably all disappeared. So have all but one of the thirty-six Commentaries and all but three of the seventeen Expositions. Enough English specimens of this kind of book survive, however, either as whole books or as binding fragments,[29] to give us a good idea of what they looked like and to suggest some generalizations about the Merton copies. One is that the great majority of these books were written probably after the middle of the thirteenth century. Another is that most of the Texts of natural philosophy and of the Metaphysics and Ethics are likely to have been fairly large books—over 300 mm high—written in textura of a good size, easily legible if one understood the abbreviations, and fairly widely spaced, and surrounded by wide margins in which extensive notes could be written. The secundo folio references, if identifiable, show us how much was written on the first leaf and provide a rough and ready means of estimating how closely

[27] M. R. James, *Ancient Libraries of Canterbury and Dover* (Cambridge, 1903), pp. 307–18, 349–55.
[28] See below, p. 356.
[29] Many English binding fragments are recorded in *Aristoteles Latinus*, nos. 1938–2012.

these Texts resembled extant copies.[30] Thus, fifteen Texts of the Physics, the leading piece in a Textus naturalium, can be ranged in a secundo folio order from the one with the most writing on the first leaf (B.1.1) to the one with the least writing (B.10.3). These two were exceptional copies, B.10.3 no doubt in long lines and perhaps something like BL Royal 12 G.ii, which has even less writing on the first leaf and in which the Physics takes up 113 leaves.[31] The rest, save one, all have secundo folios which occur between line 1 and line 48 of the text of Aristotle on p. 11 of the Leonine edition of Aquinas on the Physics. For most of them a two-column arrangement seems likely. Some may have looked like BL Royal 12 G.iii and Corpus Christi College, Oxford, 114, which also have secundo folios which fall between line 1 and line 48.[32] There are not many reproductions of books of this sort, but part of a page of an untypical English Textus naturalium is familiar from the *Specimina* of Ehrle and Liebaert: the lower margin is so wide in this manuscript that the whole of Aquinas' exposition is written in it in small current script, s.xiv.[33]

The Texts of logic are likely to have been written on a generous scale also, but since even a complete corpus of these texts is relatively short, the books tend to be smaller, the writing in one column, and the number of lines on the page not more

[30] Some allowance must be made for variations in the size of the initial beginning the first leaf.

[31] *Aristoteles Latinus* shows that this is an exceptionally large number of leaves, exceeded in existing English copies only by Corpus Christi College, Oxford, 111, an early fourteenth-century copy which belonged to William de Blythe, †1374 (*BRUO*, p. 207: he bequeathed law-books to Balliol College). The Royal manuscript measures 325 × 210 mm with 23 lines to the page in a written space of 137 × 80 mm. It is as though the *Oxford English Dictionary* had a Penguin-size text space.

[32] 12 G.iii: secundo folio *dendum est* (edn., p. 11 / 28). Physics on 76 leaves. Written space 165 × 92 mm. 2 columns of 34 lines. Corpus 114: secundo folio *omnia aut quale* (edn., p. 11 / 11). Physics on 72 leaves. Written space 145 × 100 mm. 2 cols. 29 lines. In both copies the space between one ruled line and the next is very close to 5 mm. See Pl. 4b.

[33] F. Ehrle and P. Liebaert, *Specimina codicum latinorum Vaticanorum* (ed. 1932), p. 140, from Vatican, Urbinates 206. *Aristoteles Latinus*, no. 1810.

than about thirty; that is to say an arrangement which is rather unusual for a copy of the Physics is here the normal arrangement. Probably the Merton Texts of logic were only as big as Balliol College 253 if they had very wide margins. That manuscript, Logica vetus + Logica nova, measures 290 × 185 mm and has 28 lines to the page in a written space of 142 × 82 mm. Cf. Pl. 4a.

The Commentaries will have varied more in appearance. They were expensive double-column books. As a rule, Aristotle's text is written in front of the commentary section by section, and is distinguished from the commentary by being in larger script, one line of text commonly taking up the space of two lines of commentary.[34] Some thirteenth-century copies arranged like this are not very big, because the commentary is in a small—too small—hand, not much bigger than the hand used for small thirteenth-century Bibles.[35] Later this was avoided and the copies containing the longer commentaries were perforce big books in one direction or another, that is to say either in leaf size, with a height of 350 mm or more,[36] or, like Merton 269,[37] in number of leaves. Sometimes only the size of hand differs, not the number of lines to the column: in such copies the space above each line of text is of course less than the space above each line of commentary.[38] Sometimes the whole manuscript is written in one size of script, and text and commentary are distinguished by headings 'Aristoteles' and 'Commentator',[39] or by underlining the text in red.[40]

[34] In *Aristoteles Latinus* Lacombe noted the two sizes of script in sixteen manuscripts from English medieval libraries, nos. 220, 234, 269–71, 312, 341, 347, 348 (Eustratius), 352, 365 (= Merton 269), 371, 374 (Eustratius), 384, 388, 393.

[35] BL Royal 12 D.xiv: text in 35 lines and commentary in 69; written space 168 × 103 mm; a caution in the Robury chest in 1321. New College, Oxford, 284: text in 39 lines and commentary in 78; written space 215 × 135 mm.

[36] Balliol College 114: text in 31 lines and commentary in 61; written space 252 × 170 mm. Balliol College 243: text in 26 lines and commentary in 51; written space 260 × 170 mm. Balliol College 244: text in 31 lines and commentary in 62 lines; written space 270 × 170 mm.   [37] See below, p. 371.

[38] Merton College 282: text and commentary in two columns of 50 lines; given by William Rede. Balliol College 94: text and commentary in two columns of 48–50 lines.   [39] Oriel College, Oxford, 7.   [40] Eton College 122.

The size of the script is important. In the existing books it is big enough, except in some of the earlier copies of the commentaries of Averroës, to be reasonably easy for scribes who had training, but no special expertise in textura. The Merton election lists and medieval catalogues like those of Christ Church, Canterbury, and St. Augustine's, Canterbury, in which donors are often named, give us some idea of the great number of manuscripts of philosophy in circulation in the fourteenth century. Many scribes must have been employed in writing them. The records do not tell us who these scribes were, nor when and where they wrote, and existing manuscripts are not much more informative. One precious exception is the '17us commentator' at Balliol College, Averroës on the De celo, priced at 10s.: Richard de 'Maincestria' (or perhaps 'Mamcestria': Mancetter, Warwickshire perhaps more probably than Manchester) wrote it in 1308 for Master William de Mundham.[41] Another is a 'Volumen de naturalibus' of about the same date, with a handsomely written *ex libris* of the Cathedral Priory of Rochester to which an addition has been made in current anglicana like that of glosses to the text: the addition says that Henry de Renham wrote the book 'et audiuit in scolis oxonie et emendauit et glosauit audiendo'.[42] Here is someone (a student ?) making a book for a master and a student making a book for his own use and then apparently passing it on to a cathedral library. Probably many books might have carried similar inscriptions.

Forty-nine of the books in election list B are identifiable in

[41] Balliol College 244. See above, n. 36. In 'Oxford College libraries before 1500', *The Universities in the Late Middle Ages*, ed. J. Ijsewijn and J. Paquet (Louvain, 1978), p. 300, I suggested that Richard of Manchester was a professional scribe. I now doubt this: his book does not look particularly professional. Probably I underrated there the importance of the student in the production of books of philosophy.

[42] BL Royal 12 G.ii. See above, p. 355. Renham is Rainham, Kent, a few miles east of Rochester. *BRUO* has seven people under the spelling Reynham, six of them fellows of Merton in the fourteenth century. A Henry de Reynham is recorded as a fellow of Merton in 1321 and only in that year. Royal 12 G.ii might be, but is not very likely to be, as late as 1321.

the philosophy catalogue compiled it seems in the twenties, and maintained for a decade or two after that, but probably only in a desultory way. Four are known to have been bought about 1360. One was a legacy from a fellow who died in 1347. The rest, about eighty books, are unaccounted for. Some may well have been entered in the philosophy catalogue, which becomes more or less illegible towards the end.[43] Some may have escaped the philosophy catalogue, though in college at the time it was compiled. Most came in the thirties, forties, fifties, and sixties, no doubt, by gift from fellows and—a few—by purchase. The theology catalogue names some twenty-five donors from the 1325–60 period: Henry Mamesfeld (†1328),[44] William Boys (†1329),[45] Henry de la Wyle (†1329), Roger Martival (†1330),[46] Robert Ripplingham (†1332), Stephen de Gravesend (†1338), Robert Babington (†1341), William Harington (†1344), William Inge (†1347), Gilbert Alberwik († by September 1347), John Staveley (†c.1358: cf. Rec.3970G); Stephen Boys, Thomas Buckingham, Richard Campsale, Roger Crosby, Richard Elyndon, Walter Horkstowe, William Humberston, Roger Lunde, John and William Reynham, Thomas Standon, Hugh Staunton, Nigel Wavere, and Richard Yately. It is not to be supposed that only William Boys, Crosby, Gravesend, Inge, and Lunde, of all these donors, gave books of philosophy to Merton;[47] nor that many followed the example of Henry de la Wyle who thought that his texts and commentaries on Aristotle would be better at Balliol. Nine years later Stephen de Gravesend left his books of philosophy[48] to the college where Bradwardine had lately been and

---

[43] The last but one entry seems to record the 'Ex legato' of Roger Lunde (Lunte) and the last of all perhaps that of Peter de Keynsham.

[44] The books with Mamesfeld's name against them are early additions to the theology catalogue. This suggests that they arrived c.1360, rather than in 1328.

[45] William Boys belongs here if he was the chancellor of Lichfield, † 1329. 1329 fits well with the position of this legacy in the philosophy catalogue.

[46] Lunde, not Martival, was the donor of nos. 138–40: Martival's name is not in the philosophy catalogue (see Powicke, p. 51, note).

[47] See Powicke, pp. 106, 99, 111, 115, and n. 46 above.

[48] BRUO, p. 806. The ten books in the philosophy catalogue 'ex legato magistri Stephani de Gravesend' are Powicke, nos. 147–56. They are not on the subject

Heytesbury still was a fellow. The election system was working then no doubt—the first casual reference to it is in 1338—and he will have been aware that his eleven books would make the *sortes* more ample and be a real help to students of natural philosophy. It is not fanciful to think that there is a connection between the *sors*, the row of books in a fellow's room, and the *opera* achieved by fellows of Merton from Bradwardine to Rede and perhaps Strode,[49] which made Merton internationally famous.

Election list B

The 1372 election list is on one side of a sheet of parchment measuring about 560 × 265 mm.[50] It is written in an expert small current anglicana, now faded, but for the most part easily legible by ultra-violet light. About 23 mm was reserved on the left of the sheet for the names of the fellows from no. 2, Rugge, to no. 22, Gunwarby. The written space is about 235 mm wide and extends to near the right edge of the sheet. The *sortes* take up just over two lines (no. 1), or between one and two full lines (nos. 2–17, 20, 21), or nearly one full line (nos. 18, 19, 22). Secundo folio references (the first word or two of the second leaf) are underlined. A space of 10 mm or more was left between each *sors* and some 55 mm remain blank after *sors* 22. A title, 'Eleccio librorum anno edwardi 3[i] 46 anno cristi 1372', was written at the foot of the dorse, so that it could be seen when the sheet was rolled up.[51]

of logic, as we should expect from Gravesend's will (Archives of St. Paul's Cathedral, Box 66, no. 27), in which he bequeathed to Merton 'omnes libros meas de arte dialectica', valued at £4. 6s. 5d.

[49] *BRUO* records first and last Merton fellowship dates for: Thomas Bradwardine 1323–35; Thomas Buckingham 1324–40; William Heytesbury 1330–48; Simon Bredon 1330–41; William Collingham 1331–41?; John Ashenden 1336–55; John Dumbleton 1338–48; John Swyneshed 1340–7; William Rede 1344–57; Ralph Strode 1359–60. The records are not full enough for all these dates to be exactly right. Thus, Strode, Chaucer's friend, may have been a fellow of Merton in 1361, a year for which there is no bursar's roll. Whether he ever qualified for a *sors* is doubtful.

[50] The seven texts printed by Powicke, P, T, B–F, and the Fitzjames indenture of 1483 (Powicke, p. 213) are kept together as Q.1.11. Photographs of B, C, and the last part of P taken under ultra-violet light are kept with them.

[51] This title may not be in the main hand.

The difficult parts are at the top on the left where Powicke was unable to read parts of *sortes* 1–5 and 7 and at the ends of full lines more or less throughout. Ultra-violet light is very helpful at the top on the left, but less so at line-ends, especially near and beyond a curving tear which has been mended, but not skilfully, so that the writing in *sortes* 5–10 beyond the tear is now a millimetre or two lower than it should be. The fourteen full lines 2, 3, 5, 7, 9, 11, 13, 15, 17, 19, 27, 33, 37, and 38 are the worst affected. In *sors* 1 the third Text and the second Exposition (or perhaps the first 'Extra') come in the faded part. After this the Commentaries are affected, probably nine in all. One can only suppose that they are to be found among the Commentaries in list C for which no equivalent has been found in list B.[52] Details of the extent of the damage are given in the Notes on *sortes* 1–9, 13, 16, 21, 22. A vertical stroke shows where a new line begins in the manuscript. Powicke's numbers are in parentheses.

Line 1
Eleccio et distribucio librorum philosophie Aule de Merton' facta die sancti Edmundi Regis Anno domini M° ccc^mo sept[uagesim]o secu[ndo]

Lines 2–4. B.1.1–8. (1–6, 6*, 6**)
In primis [. . .] est Magister Thomas Swyndon'
(1) textus naturalium secundo fo *non possibile est*
(2) Item textus ethicorum secundo fo *felicitate*
(3) Item textus ue lo secundo fo [. . .] |
(4) Item commentator phisicorum secundo fo *quanto magis*
(5) Item commentum de anima et 'textus' de plantis secundo fo *debemus*
(6) Item expo' super ce et M' et lib' [. . .]' secundo fo *par[tib]us* [*eius*]
(7) [Item . . .]
(8) [Item textus . . .] | de animalibus *et loqui*

Lines 5–6. B.2.1–8. (7–12, 14, 15)
Rugge
(1) textus naturalium secundo fo *vere esse*

[52] See below, p. 384

(2) Item textus ethicorum secundo fo *singula*

(3) Item textus no lo secundo fo *ficienter enim*

(4) Item commentum phisicorum secundo fo *vniuersaliori*

(5) [Item ...]|

(6) Item commentum ce et M' secundo fo *necesse est*

(7) Item expo' logica Algal' cum libris Auicenne secundo fo *sed quia hoc est*

(8) Item Almage [...] secundo fo *que hiis*

Lines 7–8. B.3.1–8. (16–23)
Stapult'

(1) textus naturalium secundo fo *si quidem*

(2) Item textus ethicorum *dinem inquirere*

(3) Item textus ve 1[o] secundo fo *species a*[...]

(4) Item commentum Eth[...] secundo fo *omnis doctrina*

(5) Item [...]|

(6) Item commentum methaphisice secundo fo *et veritatis*

(7) Item expo' methaphisice secundo fo *instinctu*

(8) Item Aalacen (*sic*) secundo fo *ex colore*

Lines 9–10. B.4.1–7. (24–30)
Stanton'

(1) textus naturalium *vere substancia*

(2) Item textus methaphisice secundo fo *socrates*

(3) Item textus methaphisice secundo fo *moue*[*tur ab*]

(4) Item commentum ce et M' secundo fo *autem recipit*

(5) Item commentum phisicorum [secundo fo...]|

(6) Item expo' super phisicorum thome Alquini secundo fo *vniuersaliori*

(7) Item planisperium secundo fo *transiens*

Lines 11–12. B.5.1–7 (31–34, 34*, 35, 36)
Santon'

(1) Ethicorum textus[...] (*this word cancelled*) secundo fo *ipsum et substancia*

(2) Item textus methaphisice secundo fo *et primos theolo*^tes

(3) Item textus naturalium secundo fo *tates* [*sunt*]

(4) Item commentum methaphisice secundo fo [...]

(5) [Item ...] |
(6) Item expo' methaphisice thome secundo fo *anima ex hoc*
(7) Item arsmetrica boicii secundo fo *de numero impari*

Lines 13–14. B.6.1–7. (37–39, 39*, 39**, 40, 41)
Mor'
(1) textus natural' secundo fo *et hoc inconueniens*
(2) Item textus methaphisice secundo fo *existimamus*
(3) Item textus de anima secundo fo *in subiectis*
(4) Item commentum methaphisice secundo fo [...]
(5) [Item...] |
(6) Item expo' ethicorum thome secundo fo (*these four words cancelled*) thome phisicorum *deinde cum dicit*
(7) Item geometria secundo fo *datum angulum*

Lines 15–16. B.7.1–7. (42–45, 45*, 46–7)
Bryttw[ell]
(1) textus naturalium secundo fo *namque de subiecta*
(2) Item textus lo ve secundo fo *sunt ab vno*
(3) Item textus m[etaphisice] secundo fo *magis speculatiu'*
(4) Item commentum methaphisice secundo fo *p*[...]
(5) Item [commentum de anima secundo fo] | *scire diffinicionem*
(6) Item expo' thome ethicorum secundo fo *equitand'*
(7) Item textus de animalibus`secundo fo' *sunt quedam*

Lines 17–18. B.8.1–7. (48–54)
Swyndon'
(1) Textus methaphisice secundo fo *totaliter*
(2) Item textus Metheororum secundo fo *nulli eorum*
(3) Item textus logical' secundo fo *vero et ab hiis*
(4) Item commentum methaphisice secundo fo *li et si gerosius*
(5) Item commentum de anima (?) secundo fo *vniuersaliter* (?) |
(6) Item expo' `methaphisice secundo fo' *corpora cum*
(7) Item questiones super phisicorum cum textu de anima secundo fo *totum perfectum*

Lines 19–20. B.9.1–7. (55–61)
Wotton'

(1) textus naturalium et t (et t *cancelled*) secundo fo *et tali*
(2) Item textus generacionis secundo [...] (*two or three letters cancelled*) fo *naturam fieri*
(3) Item textus logicalium secundo fo *specie predicantur*
(4) Item commentum de Anima secundo fo *que sit*
(5) Item commentum methaphisice secundo fo [...] |
(6) Item petrus de Aluernia super metheororum *de generacione*
(7) Item questiones secundo fo *vtrum consideracio*

Lines 21–22. B.10.1–7. (62–68)
Potton'

(1) textus logical' secundo fo *eo quod quale*
(2) Item textus methaphisice secundo fo *est illa que*
(3) Item textus phisicorum secundo fo *minime vt*
(4) Item commentum de anima secundo fo *endi[lechi]a*
(5) Item commentum methaphisice secundo fo *per secundum species* |
(6) Item expo' thome politicorum secundo fo *dii quorum*
(7) Item astronomia de conchis secundo fo *te tractaturum*

Lines 23–24. B.11.1–7. (69–75)
Reynham

(1) textus methaphisice secundo fo *quid et causam*
(2) Item textus de generacione secundo fo *motibus puta*
(3) Item textus ve lo secundo fo *quoniam* (?) *proprium* (?)
(4) Item commentum de Anima secundo fo *solli[citaretur]*
(5) Item commentum ce et M' | secundo fo *duarum quantitatum*
(6) Item expo' logicalium e (*sic*) secundo fo *est de primis*
(7) Item arsmetrica boicii secundo fo *vt grex*

Lines 25–26. B.12.1–7. (76–82)
Park

(1) textus ethicorum `secundo fo´ *principia bene*
(2) Item textus logical' no secundo fo *tacionum*
(3) Item textus logical' secundo fo *differentibus*

(4) Item commentum de celo secundo fo *in aliam magnitudinem*
(5) [Item commentum] ce et M' | secundo fo *perfectum*
(6) Item expo' thome Ethicorum *id est querunt*
(7) Item expo' priorum secundo fo *diuisio*

Lines 27–28. B.13.1–7. (83–89)
Hudersal'
(1) textus natural' secundo fo *vnum sunt*
(2) Item textus phisicorum secundo fo *iustis et*
(3) Item textus Metheororum secundo fo *re factas*
(4) Item commentum methaphisice secundo fo *cum* (?) *dixit*
(5) Item commentum [...]*iam* |
(6) Item expo' de anima secundo fo *que sit*
(7) Item thimeus platonis secundo fo [*in*]*cogniti moris*

Lines 29–30. B.14.1–5. (90–94)
Halden'
(1) textus logical' secundo fo *genus ab hiis*
(2) Item textus naturalium secundo fo *non solum*
(3) Item commentum phisicorum secundo fo *ligibile vniuersal-
iter*
(4) Item auic' super methaphisicam et sextum[...] secundo fo
consideracio (?) |
(5) Item expo' super primum Metheororum secundo fo *pars
diuiditur*

Lines 31–32. B.15.1–5. (95–99)
Coryngham
(1) textus meth[eororum] secundo fo *multi eciam*
(2) Item textus logical' secundo fo *in eo quod quid*
(3) Item commentum phisicorum secundo fo *quoniam illa*
(4) Item questiones super libros phisicorum *non continetur*
(5) Item questiones secundo fo | *ex^{cio}p^o*

Lines 33–34. B.16.1–5. (100–104)
Wyndouere
(1) textus logical' secundo fo *predicantur speciebus*
(2) Item textus phisicorum secundo fo *quemadmodum et quod*

(3) Item commentum methaphisice secundo fo *de principiis*

(4) Item questiones methaphisice secundo fo *in infinitum* [...]

(5) Item questiones (?) secundo fo | *capituli dicit*

Lines 35–36. B.17.1–5. (105–109)
Fitzsymond `non ad plenum´

(1) textus methaphisice secundo fo *ipsi et causas*

(2) Item textus natural' secundo fo *alie quantitates*

(3) Item commentum phisicorum secundo fo *in postremo* `deficit prec' xvi s''

(4) Item expo' et questiones secundo fo *habet su[fficienci]am* |

(5) Item quaternus de diuersis questionibus secundo fo *sed verum et falsum*

Line 37. B.18.1–5. (109–113)
Dollyng'

(1) textus logical' no secundo fo *contra* (?) *predictam*

(2) Item textus logical' ve secundo fo *quoddam est*

(3) Item commentum phisicorum secundo fo *et dixit*

(4) Item quaternus secundo fo *diuisione quod*

(5) Item quaternus secundo fo [...]

Line 38. B.19.1–5. (114–119)
Lyndon'

(1) Textus ce' et Mundi secundo fo *violencia*

(2) Item textus natural' secundo fo *quomodo plura*

(3) Item commentum de anima secundo fo *et vtrum*

(4) Item questiones secundo fo *ad que*

(5) Item quaternus secundo fo [...]

Lines 39–40. B.20.1–4. (120–123)
Caps

(1) textus ce' et M' (*these four words cancelled*) textus phisicorum secundo fo *stanciam*

(2) Item textus methaphisice secundo fo *eciam medium*

(3) Item commentum de anima secundo fo *diffiniciones rerum*

(4) Item tractatus lincolniensis cum aliis [...] | *pletum* (*cancelled*) *incomplexum*

Lines 41–42. B.21.1–5. (124–128)
Stone
(1) textus natural' secundo fo *quoniam multipliciter*
(2) Item textus predicamentorum et residua logica secundo fo
substanci*a autem*
(3) Item commentum ce et M' secundo fo *et dicimus*
(4) Item questiones methaphisice secundo fo *sua*[*m sine labore*]|
(5) Item mercurius de nupciis philiologie secundo fo *mos connubialis*

Line 43. B.22.1–4. (129–132)
Gunwarby
(1) textus de anima secundo fo *tibus nichil*
(2) Item textus natural' secundo fo *principium autem*
(3) Item commentum de anima secundo fo *bis et amplius*
(4) Item expo' ce et M' secundo fo *et hoc habet*

Line 44. B.14.6. (133)
H[alde]n'
Quaternus de ente et essencia thome secundo fo *secundum quod
dicit*

Lines 45–47.[53] *(134–136)*
Memorandum quod M Walterus Stanton' recepit ¦3ᵉˢ libros de
Medicina´ de libris simonis bredon' per manus custodis In die
Mercurii ante festum sancti petri | tres (*cancelled*) videlicet lilium
medicine secundo fo *de ista* Item librum Mesue cum amphorismis
aliis cum collector' aueroys 2° fo *fist* [...] | Item librum exposi-
ciones [...]s super amphorismos ypocratis secundo fo *oportet*

Notes on list B

References for the Physics (normally the first piece in a Textus
naturalium), Metheora, De celo, and De generatione are to page and
line of the Leonine edition of Aquinas, 1884 (Physics) and 1886, and,
in parentheses, to the conventional divisions of the Greek text derived
from the page, column, and line numbers in the Bekker edition of

[53] An addition in the hand of the scribe of list C.

1831; for the Ethics, Metaphysics, and De Anima to these divisions as given in the margins of modern editions of the Latin text; for the Isagoge of Porphyry (normally the first piece in a Logica vetus) to page and line of the edition by A. Busse, 1887. The bracketed sigla, A, C, E, G, L, Ln, Lv, M, Meth, N, P, Pol indicate respectively the De anima, De celo, Ethics, De generatione, Textus logicalium, Logica nova, Logica vetus, Metaphysics, Metheora, Textus naturalium, Physics, and Politics or Commentaries and Expositions on these texts. Bold type, for example **B.1.6**, shows an existing book.

Sors 1

Line 2, beginning. The present surface reading appears to be 'In primis est Magister Thomas Swyndon'' which makes sense. 'Thomas' seems to be an alteration from 'Thomam' and there is a space between 'primis' and 'est'. There are 8 mm between 'Swyndon'' and 'textus'.

Line 2, end. 35 mm not read, room for no more than the secundo folio of B.1.3.

Line 3, end. 60 mm not read after 'partibus'. I presume that the next word was *eius* and that a short item follows, B.1.7, and the words *Item textus* of B.1.8. Powicke did not allow for anything between his B.6 and B.7.

B.1.1 (N). For the probable donor, Boys, see p. 358. He gave other good books (Powicke, p. 106). This one is the highest priced book in the philosophy catalogue (P) and no doubt the finest Aristotelian text the college possessed. In 1452 a fellow had it in his election on condition that he gave it 'novam tunicam' (Powicke, p. 81). The secundo folio (edn., p. 22/6) suggests that the format was exceptionally large and the script not as big as it is in the large copies of the Libri naturales now Balliol College 232A, 232B.

B.1.2 (E). The secundo folio is edn., 95.a.20.

B.1.3 (Lv). The secundo folio not read.

B.1.6 (C). MS 274. s.xiii/xiv, xiv¹. England. Aquinas on the De celo and expositions of other Libri naturales by him, Peter of Auvergne, and Thomas Sutton. Secundo folio *partibus eius.*

fos. 317. 300 × 207 mm. Written space 215 × 140 mm. 2 cols. 45
lines. Informal textura and (fos. 89ᵛ–121) anglicana by a slightly
later hand. Initials are alternately blue and red with ornament
of the other colour, except on fos. 89ᵛ–121 where they are all
blue with red ornament. 'Liber scolarium de Merton' ex emp-
cione'. fo. 318ᵛ: the record of purchase for 13s. 4d., c.1360, is in
Rec.3970C, 'Item in expositore super libr' de celo et mundo cum
multis aliis', secundo folio *partibus eius*. Not part of a regular
sors in 1375, but one of several books handed over to Henry
Stapilton after the main distribution had been made.

B.1.7. Not read. From its position it may have been an
Exposition or an 'Extra'.

B.1.8. MS 271. s.xiii ex. Northern France. Textus de animalibus. Secundo folio *et loqui*. *Aristoteles Latinus*, no. 367.

fos. 150. 305 × 215 mm. Written space 205 × 140 mm. 2 cols. 44
lines. Textura. Each book begins with a handsome initial. A
chainmark, ..., at the foot of fo. 150ᵛ. Probably transferred to
the library before the time of election list D (1410).

Sors 2

Line 5, end. 45 mm not read after 'vniuersaliori', room for
one item, B.2.5 (Powicke, B.11).

B.2.1 (N). The 'Textus naturalium bonus', secundo folio *vere
esse*, bought for 16s, c.1360 (Rec.3970C). The valuation was
probably higher and this may have been the second best 'textus'
in college, the best after B.1.1.

B.2.4 (P). B.4.6 had the same secundo folio.

B.2.5. Not read.

B.2.7 (L). Not read by Powicke who allowed for two entries,
B.13 and 14, in the 110 mm after the 'Item commentum' of B.2.6.
Ultra-violet light shows that this space contained only the end
of B.2.6 and an unusually long entry, B.2.7.

Sors 3

Line 7, end. 45 mm not read after the secundo folio of B.3.4,
room for one item, B.3.5.

B.3.1 (N). The secundo folio is edn., p. 11/9 (185.a.27).

B.3.2 (E). The secundo folio is edn., 94.b.24.

B.3.3 (Lv). It is tempting to think that this is Trinity College, Oxford, 47, an early and important manuscript with secundo folio *Species autem dicitur*: the 1519 election list shows that the third word of the second leaf of B.3.3 was *dicitur* (Powicke, p. 251). B.3.3 was an unusual copy in that the whole of the first two chapters of the Isagoge of Porphyry was fitted on one leaf, a larger amount probably than in any of the seventeen copies listed in *Aristoteles Latinus*, apart from Gonville and Caius College, Cambridge, where *Species autem dicitur*, the opening words of chapter 3, comes at fo. 1^v / 29, as the College librarian kindly tells me. The fact that Trinity 47 was pledged (by someone whose first name was John) in an Oxford loan chest, the Vaughan and Hussey chest, with four supplements, in the 1390s and again in 1400, is no objection to its being a Merton College book (cf. below, B.8.4), but the evidence from the philosophy catalogue prevents us from making the identification. B.3.3 according to P was a 'Logica vetus' of no great value. In Trinity 47 the Logica vetus occupies only the first eighteen leaves in front of Boethius on the Topics, the Arithmetic and Music of Boethius, and Euclid's Geometry on 172 leaves. We can hardly suppose that the cataloguer would fail to mention all these substantial pieces: other gifts of Brice de Sharsted are listed in some detail.

B.3.4 (E). Perhaps the copy received by Merton College in 1366 in return for a loan of 20s. to Mr William Arderne (Rec.3700).

B.3.5. Not read.

B.3.7 (M). MS 273. s.xiii / xiv. England. Aquinas on the Metaphysics and Politics. Secundo folio *instinctu prudencia*.

> fos. 223. 330 × 230 mm. Written space 257 × 170 mm. 2 cols. 52 lines. Backward sloping textura. Bought for 13s. 4d., c.1360, 'Item in alio expositore super methaphisicam et politic'', secundo folio *instinctu prudencia* (Rec.3970C). '8us liber de sorte Abyndon'' (Henry Abingdon, fellow in 1390, warden 1421–37) and '5us de sorte Iohannis Look' (John Luke, fellow in 1390, first

bursar 1395–6), fo. vi^v. 'Exposicio sancti (?) thome de Alquino super xii libros methaphisice secundum stacionarios cum aliis politicorum prec' xl s', fo. iii^v, s.xiii / xiv. Not in election list D: cf. B.1.8.

B.3.8. Corpus Christi College, Oxford, 489, no. 86; 490, nos. 7, 8, 33, 115; Merton College 23.dd.11, pastedowns; Westminster Abbey 36, nos. 4, 5; Bodleian Library, 4° C.95 Art., pastedowns. s.xiv. England. Alhacen, Optica. Secundo folio (*ex colore illius*).

> fos. 17. Written space *c.*193 × 107 mm. 32 long lines. Textura. 'Liber domus scolarium de Merton' in Oxon' ex dono Magistri Ricardi Geddyng quondam socii' (Corpus 490, no. 115). Used as pastedowns by an Oxford binder, no doubt Dominique Pinart, *c.*1590: see N. R. Ker, *Pastedowns in Oxford Bindings*,[54] pp. xi, 101, 120–127. The two Bodleian leaves, not listed in *Pastedowns*, are inside the covers of T. Cartwright, *Second replie against Whitgiftes second answer*, London, 1575. They may have been used rather earlier than the others by some other Oxford binder than Pinart.[55]

Sors 4

Line 9, end. The 45 mm not read after 'Phisicorum' can hardly have held more than the rest of the B.4.5 entry.

B.4.1 (N). The secundo folio is edn., p. 11 / 23 (185.b.4).

B.4.2 (M). The secundo folio is edn., 983.b.17.

B.4.5 (P). The secundo folio not read.

B.4.6 (P). The secundo folio is edn., p. 6, col. 2 / 33.

Sors 5

Line 11, end. 50 mm not read after 'fo', room for the secundo folio of B.5.4 and one short item. Powicke did not allow for an item here (after his B.34), but there is room for one in the form *Item commentum* ..., where the title can take up less than 20 mm.

[54] Oxford Bibliographical Society, new series, v (1954).
[55] The ugly 'pincers' centrepiece (cf. *Pastedowns*, centrepieces i–vi) occurs with an Oxford ornament, no. 54 in *Pastedowns*, on Lanhydrock D.17.11, C. Obenhinius, *Promptuarium sacrosanctum*, Ursellis, 1576.

4a All Souls College, bb.5.10, part of pastedown at end reduced; see pp. ix–x
Reproduced by permission of the Warden and Fellows

4b Corpus Christi College, MS 114, part of fo. 96ᵛ, reduced; see p.x
Reproduced by permission of the President and Fellows

4c Merton College, MS 269, fo. 248, lower part of page; see p.x
Reproduced by permission of the Warden and Fellows

B.5.2 (M). The secundo folio is edn., 983.b.29, *et primos theologizantes.*

B.5.3 (N). The secundo folio is edn., p. 11 / 20 (185.b.1).

B.5.4 (M). The secundo folio not read.

B.5.5. Not read.

Sors 6

Line 13, end. 50 mm not read after 'fo', room for the secundo folio of B.6.4 and one item, B.6.5. Powicke did not allow for anything here between his B.39 (B.6.3) and B.40 (B.6.6).

B.6.1 (N). The secundo folio is edn., p. 16 / 11 (186.a.13).

B.6.2 (M). Bought for 5s., c.1360, 'Item textus methaphisice et ethicorum', secundo folio *existimamus* (Rec.3970C). The secundo folio is edn., 981.b.9.

B.6.4 (M). The secundo folio not read.

B.6.5. Not read.

Sors 7

Line 15, end. 48 mm not read after the first letter of the secundo folio of B.7.4, room for the rest of the secundo folio and the first six words of B.7.5 which can be reconstructed. Powicke did not allow for an item here (after his B.45).

B.7.1 (N). The secundo folio is edn., p. 11 / 15 (185.a.32).

B.7.2 (LV). The secundo folio is edn., p. 26 / 17.

B.7.3 (M). The secundo folio is edn., 982.a.29.

B.7.4 (M). The secundo folio not read.

Sors 8

Line 17, end. The 50 mm after 'gerosius' are indistinct.

B.8.1 (M). The secundo folio is edn., 982.b.7.

B.8.2 (Meth). The secundo folio is edn., p. 330 / 38 (339.b.27).

B.8.4 (M). MS 269. s.xiii². England. Averroës on Metaphysics. Secundo folio *li et si gerosius.* *Aristoteles Latinus*, no. 365.

fos. 286. 300 × 210 mm. Written space 180 × 115 mm. 2 cols. 21 lines of text and 41 of commentary, the text in a larger hand than the commentary. A good initial to each book. A caution of

Welpyngton (Richard Whelpyngton, fellow 1386–7, still in 1401–2), with two supplements (fo. 286ᵛ). Two erased cautions on fo. i. A chainmark, ... , shows on fos. 283–6, but not on the parchment binding leaves, fos. 287–90. Not in election list D: cf. B.1.8. Pl. 4c.

Sors 9

Line 19, end. The 40 mm after 'sit' containing B.9.5 are indistinct.

B.9.1 (N). The secundo folio is edn., p. 11 / 48 (185.b.25).

B.9.3 (L). The secundo folio is edn., p. 27 / 21 (?).

B.9.5 (M). The secundo folio not read.

Sors 10

B.10.1 (L). The secundo folio is edn., p. 28 / 12.

B.10.3 (P). The secundo folio is edn., p. 7 / 36 (185.a.16).

Sors 11

B.11.1 (M). The secundo folio is edn., 981.a.30.

B.11.2 (G). The secundo folio is edn., p. 271 / 3 (315.a.28).

B.11.3 (L). The secundo folio is edn., p. 27 / 15.

B.11.6 (L). MS 289. s.xiv med. England. An anonymous piece on the Categories, Kilwardby on the Prior Analytics, Grosseteste on the Posterior Analytics, and Giles of Rome on the Elenchi. Secundo folio *est de primis*.

fos. 186. 360 × 225 mm. Written space 285 × 170 mm. 2 cols. 56 lines. Widely spaced anglicana. Blue initials with red ornament. Chainmarks, ... and ∴ , on the flyleaf in front. Not in election list D: cf. B.1.8.

Sors 12

B.12.1 (E). The secundo folio is edn., 95.a.32.

B.12.3 (Lv). The secundo folio is edn., p. 28 / 9.

Sors 13

Line 27, end. The last 65 mm, containing the secundo folio of B.13.4 and the entry following it, B.13.5, are indistinct.

B.13.1 (N). The secundo folio is edn., p. 11 / 43 (185.b.20).

B.13.2 (P). Powicke read 'Ethicorum'. C.5.3 has a different secundo folio.

B.13.3 (Meth). The secundo folio is edn., p. 330 / 40 (339.b.29).

B.13.5 (M). The secundo folio not read.

B.13.7. The secundo folio is ed. Klibansky (1962), p. 11 / 2.

Sors 14

B.14.2 (N). The secundo folio is edn., p. 11 / 47 (185.b.23).

B.14.6. Added after B.22.4. Apparently an extra book given to Halden, the first of the fellows who had been given only five books in the election.

Sors 15

B.15.1 (Meth). The secundo folio is edn., p. 330 / 16 (339.b.8).

Sors 16

Line 33, end. The 30 mm containing the last words of the secundo folio of B.16.4 and the first four words of B.16.5 are indistinct.

B. 16. 2 (P). The secundo folio is edn., p.11/27 (185. b. 7).

Sors 17

B.17.2 (N). The secundo folio is edn., p. 11 / 20 (*alique quantitates*) (185.b.1). *alie*, not *alique* is the reading of the 'antiqua translatio' in Corpus Christi College, Oxford, 114.

B.17.3 (P). Fitzsymond failed to hand it in, hence the interlineation and the note in the margin: see above, p. 351.

Sors 18

Line 38, end. The secundo folio not read.

B.18.4. MS 296. s.xiii ex.–xiv in. England. 'Sentencie' on logic, Aquinas on the Posterior Analytics, and questions on the Topics, on matter and form, and on grammar. Secundo folio *diuisione quod genus.*

fos. 163. 287 × 200 mm. Written space 233 × 145 mm. 2 cols. 54 lines. Now fourteen quires. Informal textura and (fos. 131–63, arts. 7, 8) current anglicana. The first binding was a limp parchment cover, as appears from the description in P and the title ('quaternus') in B.[56] Not in election list F, so far as can be seen.

B.18.5. The secundo folio not read.

Sors 19

Line 39, end. The secundo folio not read.
B.19.1 (C). The secundo folio is edn., p. 13 / 7 (269.a.7).
B.19.2 (N). The secundo folio is edn., p. 11 / 36 (185.b.13).
B.19.5. The secundo folio not read.

Sors 20

B.20.4. MS 280. s. xiv in. England. Grosseteste on the Elenchi and Posterior Analytics, Kilwardby on the Prior Analytics, and questions on logic. Secundo folio *incomplexum*.

> fos. 140. 305 × 225 mm. Written space 260 × 180 mm. 2 cols. 52 lines. Incipient formal anglicana. Blue initials. 'Liber domus scolarium de Merton' in Oxon' ex assignacione Magistri Willelmi Ingge Archidiaconi Surr' quondam socii dicte domus ita quod a dicta domo non alienetur vel distrahatur quouis modo [...]' on the flyleaf; also there, 'De sorte Hereward' (John Hereward, fellow in 1381, still in 1390–1, first bursar 1387–8) and '5ᵘˢ de sorte Swyndon' (perhaps John Swyndon, fellow in 1390–1, still in 1400, rather than Thomas or (John ?) Swyndon who took part in the 1372 election). Not in election list F, so far as can be seen.

[56] The very common word 'quaternus' means as a rule a book bound in a limp parchment cover. The strings are usually exposed on the spine and the number of quires can easily be seen by counting the strings. Lincoln College, Oxford, Lat. 62 is a book of this sort which has escaped rebinding: it was formerly at Merton and may be recorded in the 1519 theology election as the 24th book given to Hoper, secundo folio *tropologice*—the secundo folio is *tropologicus*. Books with the word 'quaternus' on their parchment covers are Lincoln College Lat. 68 (rebound, with the cover inside: 'Iste quaternus constat Iohanni [...]', Canterbury Cathedral, Lit.D.12, the obit book compiled by Thomas Cawston, and Canterbury Cathedral, E.6, prior Goldstone's accounts for 1452, inscribed 'Quarternus W. Barnett'. Mr Graham Pollard thought that the quaterni containing the statutes of Oxford University were unbound (*Bodleian Library Record*, viii. 79), but it seems to me more likely that they were bound in limp covers. It would not be difficult to string an extra quire inside a binding of this sort.

Sors 21

B.21.1 (N). The secundo folio is edn., p. 11 / 1 (185.a.21).

Sors 22

B.22.1 (A). The secundo folio is edn., 403.a.21.

B.22.2 (N). The secundo folio is edn., p. 11 / 1 (185.a.20).

Lines 45–7. A convenient blank space used by the scribe of election list C for a memorandum about three medical books bequeathed to the college by Simon Bredon (†1372) which were handed over in some year to Walter Stanton. All three are listed in Bredon's will (Powicke, p. 84).

Election list C

In 1375 the blank dorse of list B was used for list C. The scribe began at the foot of the dorse. His writing is a less competent current anglicana than that of B, larger and looser. Thus, the nine words of C.9.1 take up 77 mm, against 48 mm in B. Difficulties in reading secundo folios near the right edge of the parchment are partly due to the script. In line 5 of the secundo folio of C.1.6 is not in the main hand and the same may be true of the word 'coment'' near the beginning of this line and the word 'coment'' towards the end of line 9. A blank margin on the left side of the sheet, about 65 mm wide, seems to have been used for some checking purpose: there is a triangle of dots, two and one, against nearly every *sors* and a lozenge was cut out of the parchment on a fold line opposite *sortes* 1, 3, 5, 7, 9–12, 14, 15, and perhaps *sors* 8.[57] The names of fellows are not in this margin, as in B, but within the written space which extends for about 200 mm to near the right edge of the parchment, except in *sors* 15 where the scribe realized he had much room to spare and began each new line with a new item. The first *sors* is in five lines and the rest in three or four lines. Secundo folio references are underlined, as in B. The space between each *sors* varies in width from about 10 to about 4 mm or less. The narrowest spaces are

[57] The hole against *sors* 8 is small and unconvincing. By good luck the holes have damaged list B at points where there can be no doubt about what the scribe wrote.

probably the result of filling up with afterthoughts. 220 mm remained at the foot of the sheet. In part of this space the scribe set out the names 'More', 'Wotton', 'Potton', and 'Hodersal', anticipating presumably that extra books would be distributed to the first four people named in the list, but he only entered one title in all this space (C.4.11). Below 'Hodersal' he wrote 'Stapulton' and a badly faded list of half a dozen books. Last of all he wrote 'Remanent (?) xiii volu''. On the other side of the sheet he entered the memorandum which now forms lines 45–7 of list B.

Damage consists of a small stain near the beginning of lines 1, 2, severe fading of lines 59–62 and fading of line ends, so that some parts of fifteen entries are illegible: C.1.2, 11; C.2.2, 6, 9; C.4.3, 7; C.5.3, 6, 9; C.7.9; C.9.7; C.10.6; C.12.3; C.15.2.

The first ten *sortes* of C are reproduced in *Merton Muniments*,[58] Pl. 24, and transcribed on the facing page.

Lines 1, 2.
Eleccio et distribucio librorum philosophie Aule de Merton' In Oxon' facta die concepcionis sancte Marie virginis Anno domini | Millesimo ccc° lxxv^to

Lines 3–7. C.1.1–12 (1–12)
In primis Rec' [per] Magistrum Iohannem More `Iohannes Wendouere habet totam sortem´
(1) textum naturalium secundo fo *non possibile est*
(2) Item textum Ethicorum cum aliis | secundo fo *ipsum* [...]*a*
(3) Item logicam totam secundo fo *predicantur speciebus*
(4) Item textum de anima secundo fo *in subiectis*
(5) Item comment' Methaphisice | [secundo fo] *paucioribus*
(6) Item coment' phisicorum secundo fo *monstratiue*
(7) Item comment' de anima secundo fo *vniuersale*
(8) Item thomam super libros Methaphisice secundo fo *instinctu* |
(9) Item perspectiuam alecen secundo fo *ex colore illius*
(10) Item geometriam ´euclidis,´ secundo fo *sciendum*
(11) Item epistolas senece de natural [...] |
(12) Item libros auicenne cart' de librario secundo fo *esse suum*

[58] Oxford Historical Society, lxxxvi (1928).

Lines 8–10. C.2.1–9 (13–21)
Stephanus Wotton
(1) textum naturalium secundo fo *vere esse*
(2) Item veterem logicam secundo fo *sunt ab v*[*no*]
(3) Item Ethicorum | secundo fo *singula*
(4) Item nouam lo secundo fo *ficienter*
(5) Item comment' de anima secundo fo *que sit*
(6) Item coment [...] de ce et mundo [secundo] fo [...] *a*
[...] |
(7) Item comment' celi et mundi secundo fo *necesse est*
(8) Item petrum de aluernia secundo fo *de generacione*
(9) Item almagest secundo fo [...]

Lines 11–13. C.3.1–9 (22–30)
Galfredus Potton'
(1) textum naturalium (*cancelled*) moralium secundo fo *Prin-cipia bene*
(2) Item textum methaphisice secundo fo *est illa que*
(3) Item textum logice secundo fo | *in eo quod quid*
(4) Item textum naturalium secundo fo *minime*
(5) Item eustacium secundo fo *omnis doctrina*
(6) Item coment' methaphisice secundo fo *per secundum* |
(7) Item comment' de anima secundo fo *que sit*
(8) Item thomam super methaphisicam secundo fo *corpora cum*
(9) Item philosophiam de conchis secundo folio *te tractaturum*

Lines 14–16. C.4.1–10 (31–40)
Hodursale
(1) textum naturalium secundo fo *et hoc inconueniens*
(2) Item textum methaphisice secundo fo *et primos the*[*tes*]
(3) Item textum naturalium secundo fo *non* [...] |
(4) Item methaphisice secundo fo *eciam medium*
(5) Item comment' de anima secundo fo *solicitaretur*
(6) Item comentatorem methaphisice secundo fo *de principiis*
(7) Item comment' phisicorum [secundo fo ...] |
(8) Item thomam super phisicorum secundo fo *vniuersaliori*

(9) Item planisperii secundo fo *transiens*

(10) Item lincoln' secundo fo *incomplex*^m

Lines 17–19. C.5.1–9 (41–49)

Dollyng'

(1) textum naturalium secundo fo *vero substancia solum*

(2) Item textum ethicorum secundo fo *felicitate et*

(3) Item ethicorum secundo fo *iusti* [..]|

(4) Item methaphisice secundo fo *magis speculatiua*

(5) Item comment' methaphisice cum aliis secundo fo *propter fortunam*

(6) Item comentatorem 2° fo (*these two words cancelled*) de anima 2° fo [...]|

(7) Item expositorem super librum phisicorum secundo fo *deinde cum dicit*

(8) Item questiones 2° fo *capituli dicit*

(9) Item textum metheororum celi (?) et (?) mundi (?) secundo folio [...]

Lines 20–22. C.6.1–8 (50–57)

Caps

(1) textum naturalium secundo fo *namque de subiecta dicuntur*

(2) Item textum methaphisice secundo fo *socrates ipse*

(3) Item textum logic' secundo fo *specie predicantur*

(4) Item ve logic' secundo folio *species autem*

(5) Item comment' phisicorum secundo folio *et dixit quoquomodo*

(6) Item comentatorem 2° fo (*these two words cancelled*) methaphisice 2° fo *veritatis*

(7) Item expositorem super methaphisicam secundo fo *anima ex hoc*

(8) Item Expositorem sex principiorum 2° fo *diuisione quod gen[us]*

Lines 23–26. C.7.1–10 (58–67)

Stone `Cum istis libris honeratur Willelmus Cates (?) per manus br[yttwe]ll'

(1) textum naturalium secundo fo *siquidem igitur*
(2) Item textum naturalium secundo fo *quoniam multipliciter*
(3) Item logic' secundo fo *subiecta autem*
(4) Item vetus logic' secundo fo *quoniam proprium*
(5) Item comment' phisicorum secundo fo *quanto magis*
(6) Item comentatorem 2° fo (*these two words cancelled*) de anima secundo fo *diffiniciones* |
(7) Item expositorem de anima secundo fo *possumus*
(8) Item geometriam euclidis secundo fo *dat' angulum*
(9) Item 'textum' methaphisice secundo fo [...] |
(10) Item iii libros geometrie secundo fo i^i *biis trianguli*

Lines 27–29. C.8.1–8 (68–75)
Pestur
(1) textum Methaphisice secundo fo *totaliter sutem*
(2) Item textum naturalium secundo fo *et tale*
(3) Item phisicorum secundo fo *summe partis* |
(4) Item logicalia secundo fo *vero et ab hiis*
(5) Item comment' phisicorum secundo fo *composicionis*
(6) Item comentatorem de plantis 2° fo *debemus*
(7) Item expositorem | logicalium secundo fo *est de primis*
(8) Item questiones phisicorum 2° fo *in hiis oculte*

Lines 30–32. C.9.1–8 (76–83)
Organ
(1) textum Methaphisice secundo fo *quid et causam*
(2) Item textum ethicorum secundo fo *dinem inquirere*
(3) Item textum naturalium secundo fo | *alie quantitatis*
(4) Item textum naturalium secundo fo *tates sunt*
(5) Item me (*cancelled*) comment' methaphisice secundo fo *ab ista causa*
(6) Item coment' de anima secundo fo | *endilechia*
(7) Item questiones secundo fo [...] *fi^m*
(8) Item methaphisicam auicenne 2° fo *consideracio*

Lines 33–35. C.10.1–8 (84–91)
Bannebury
(1) textum Metheororum secundo fo *multo eciam quibusdam*

(2) Item methaphisicam secundo fo *ipse et causas*
(3) Item' phisicorum secundo fo *parua | magis*
(4) Item logicalia secundo fo *tacionum genera*
(5) Item comment' phisicorum secundo fo *quoniam illa*
(6) Item commentum Methaphisice secundo fo [...] *dix*[t] |
(7) Item expositorem super polet' secundo fo *dii quorum*
(8) Item exposicionem super priorum secundo fo *diuisio et diffinicio*

Lines 36–38. C.11.1–8 (92–99)
Alkerton
(1) textum de animalibus secundo fo *et loqui*
(2) Item textum methaphisice secundo fo *existimamus*
(3) Item topicorum aristotelis '2° fo' *dialectice |*
(4) Item textum de vetere logica secundo fo *differentibus*
(5) Item comment' celi et mundi secundo fo *autem recipit*
(6) Item commentum methaphisice secundo fo | *idem est omni*
(7) Item expositorem super phisica (*cancelled*) libros ethicorum secundo fo *equitandum*
(8) Item expositorem super celi et mundi 2° fo *et hoc habet*

Lines 39–42. C.12.1–9 (100–108)
Riseborow
(1) textum de animalibus secundo fo *sunt quedam*
(2) te logi^cam (*sic*) 2° fo *eo quod quale*
(3) Item phisicorum secundo fo | *quemadmodum* [...]
(4) Item comment' metaphisice secundo fo '*li*' *et si gerosius*
(5) Item commentum de ce et mundo secundo fo *et dicimus |*
(6) Item thomam super ethicam secundo fo *id est querunt illa*
(7) Item questiones celi et mundi 2° fo *totum perfectum*
(8) textum de anima | secundo fo *anime vtrum sunt*
(9) Item commentatorem phisicorum 2° fo *in postremo*

Lines 43–46. C.13.1–9 (109–117)
Balyndon'
(1) textum phisicorum secundo fo *vnum sunt*
(2) textum naturalium secundo fo *violencia quidem*

(3) Item de generacione | secundo fo *naturam fieri*

(4) Item comment de a (*cancelled*) celi et mundi secundo fo *et vtrum*

(5) Item commentum de anima secundo fo *scire diffinicionem* |

(6) Item questiones secundo fo *suam sine labore*

(7) Item questiones antiquas 2° fo *vtrum consideracio*

(8) Item comment' methaphisice secundo fo *et eciam* |

(9) Item antiquas questiones secundo fo *rectos sed magis*

Lines 47–50. C.14.1–9 (118–126)

Prat

(1) textum celi et mundi et generac' secundo fo *motibus puta*

(2) Item textum logicalium secundo fo *genus ab hiis* |

(3) Item textum phisicorum secundo fo *stanciam vnam*

(4) Item comment' phisicorum secundo fo *hoc nomine*

(5) Item comment' celi et mundi secundo fo *duarum quan[titatum]* |

(6) Item questiones secundo fo *non continentur*

(7) Item arismetricam boicii 2° fo *de numero impari*

(8) Item questiones de gramatica secundo fo | *habet sufficienciam*

(9) Item antiquas et bonas questiones super (*sic*) secundo fo *more* (or *mire*) *sciencia*

Lines 51–54. C.15.1–8 (127–134)

Horsam

(1) textum de anima secundo fo *tibus nichil*

(2) Item metheororum secundo fo *nulli [eorum]* |

(3) Item methaphisice secundo fo *mouetur ab aere*

(4) Item comment' phisicorum secundo fo *ligibile*

(5) Item commentum celi et mundi secundo fo *perfectum* |

(6) Item questiones super metheororum secundo fo *ad quem*

(7) Item arismetricam boicii 2° fo *grex* |

(8) Item commentum abbreuiatum secundo fo *breues Me'*

Line 55. More

Line 56. Wotton

Line 57. Potton

Line 58. C.4.11 (*135*)
Hodersal' paruum quaternum de papiro secundo fo *generacionum* cum a [...]

Lines 59–62. C.16.1– (*136–141*)
Stapulton (59) [...] secundo fo *de* [...] Item quaternos xx de
    burlee [...]
    (60) [...] cum pluribus aliis secundo fo [...]
    (61) Item [...] mundi et alios multos secundo fo
    partibus eius [...]
    (62) Item [...]

Line 63. Remanent (?) xiii volumina

Notes on list C

Sors 1

At some point during the currency of the election list John
More's *sors* was taken over by John Wendover and a note to
this effect was added in the space below the heading. *BRUO*
shows that More was one of the bursars in every year from
1375 to 1387, except 1381. He was 3rd bursar in 1378 when
Wendover was 2nd bursar. In C.1.5 the secundo folio has been
added, perhaps *currente calamo* at the beginning of line 5, before
the scribe began writing C.1.9 at the beginning of line 6. C.1.11
and C.1.12 seem to be added entries, to judge from the way
they are placed, so it is not quite impossible that C.1.11, of
which the secundo folio has not been read, is the Seneca recorded
in the election list *c.*1410, now MS 250, fos. 156–245 (Powicke,
no. 351). This was a bequest from John Reynham who died by
November 1376. His books, or some of them, came to Merton
in 1377 (Rec.3973, an out-of-sequence bursar's roll). C.1.12 was
taken out of the library: I do not understand what 'cart'' means.

Sors 2

Traces of the secundo folio of C.2.6 (*Merton Muniments*, Pl.
24/9) favour identification with B.12.4.

Sors 4

The secundo folio of C.4.7 has not been read. Hodersale got an additional book (C.4.11) after the main list had been drawn up.

Sors 5

The secundo folio of C.5.9, perhaps an added item, has not been read.

Sors 7

Transferred like *sors 1* from one person to another, according to a faded note in the margin. The words 'Cum' and 'Cates' were read for me by Dr de la Mare and Dr Hunt. The words 'oneratur cum' followed by the title of a book occur six times in election list F (Powicke, pp. 79–82). A William Gates was fellow of Merton in 1381. Brightwell was 3rd bursar in 1377–8 and a fellow until 1382. C.7.9 (the secundo folio not read) and C.7.10 appear to be added items.

Sors 13

C.13.9 is perhaps the same as P 77, 'Questiones morales et naturales', secundo folio *rectum* (changed to *recto*) [...]', bequeathed by Stephen de Gravesend.

'Remanent (if that is right) xiii volumina' at the foot of the sheet may record the position before or after additional books were distributed. Six of them are noted above. Besides these there is the much damaged additional *sors* (*sors 16*) recorded in lines 59–62 under the name of Stapilton (Powicke read *Staunton*) who was 3rd bursar in 1376 (Rec.3708). It appears to have consisted of at least seven books.

Concordance of B with C, P, etc.

This list, divided under the headings Texts, Commentaries, Expositions, and 'Extras', shows where each B entry occurs in later election records, C, D (*c.*1410),[59] the electio of John Wodward (1418: Powicke,

[59] 185 items, of which seventy-six are now identifiable in B, C. The rest are presumably newcomers, except a few like D.8.12 which may have been recorded in now illegible parts of B, C—D.8.12 might be C.4.7.

p. 77), and F (1451),⁶⁰ and where it is to be found in Powicke's bold-type numeration. It contains, also, in a new line, the relevant entry in the philosophy catalogue, P (*c.*1325, with later additions).⁶¹ The sigla in parentheses are those used in my Notes, above. For list D the *sors* number is given, followed by Powicke's D number in brackets. Bold type shows an existing book.

As a result of damage nine Commentaries in B are not identifiable in C. They are: (title unknown) B.2.5, B.3.5, B.5.5, B.6.5, B.13.5; (Physics) B.4.5; (Metaphysics) B.5.4, B.6.4, B.7.4. The entries in C against which they can be matched are: (Physics) C.1.6, C.4.7, C.8.5, C.14.4; (Metaphysics) C.1.5, C.5.5, C.9.5; (De anima) C.5.6.

The secundo folios of thirty-one books in B, C occur in the 1519 election list (Powicke, pp. 250–1), which does not record titles:

B.1.1 Bal 5	B.10.3 Barlow 9
B.1.2 Pereson 10 (felicitate autem)	B.10.4 Tut 6
B.1.4 Serlys 5	B.10.5 Pereson 14
B.1.5 Tressam 18	B.14.4 Tut 17
B.3.3 Pereson 2 (species autem dicitur)	B.12.5 Serlys 4
B.4.2 Serlys 3	B.13.1 Serlys 7
B.4.4 Raynolds 7	B.14.3 Langley 3
B.4.6 Raynolds 12	B.15.4 Serlys 11
B.6.2 Serlys 1	B.17.2 Langley 4
B.6.6 Owyn 14	B.21.2 Langley 5
B.7.5 Raynolds 9	B.22.2 Langley 7
B.8.2 Tut 1	C.9.5 Barlow 10
B.9.1 Serlys 6	C.11.3 Tonsun 2
B.9.6 Tut 18	C.13.8 Tut 2
B.9.7 Tut 16	C.14.9 Owyn 25
B.10.2 Serlys 2	

TEXTS

B.1.1 (N). C.1.1. D.1.1 (1). F 158. Powicke 118.
P 64. 'Liber phisicorum cum aliis libris naturalibus de problematibus et metaphis'', secundo folio *et non possibile est*, bequeathed by William de Bosco (Boys), price 26s. 8d.

⁶⁰ Badly damaged. 228 items, of which forty-four are now identifiable in B, C.
⁶¹ P. 66, 72, 79, 83–5 may have been recorded in B, C. Their secundo folios have not been read. P 1–25 are reproduced in facsimile in *Merton Muniments*, Pl. 23.

B.1.2 (E). C.5.2. D.1.2 (2). F 98. Powicke 417 = 466.

B.1.3 (Lv). Possibly C.11.3. No Powicke number.

B.2.1 (N). C.2.1. Powicke 409 = 460.

B.2.2 (E). C.2.3. D.8.2 (77). F 119. Powicke 77.

P 13. 'Textus Ethicorum cum libro de causis in commento', secundo folio *singula talibus*, price 4s.

B.2.3 (Ln). C.2.4. D.15.7 (178). Powicke 393.

B.3.1 (N). C.7.1. D.11.1 (114). F 115. Powicke 410.

B.3.2 (E). C.9.2. D.12.2 (128). F 53. Powicke 49.

P 10. 'Textus libri Ethicorum', secundo folio *dinem inquirere*, given by John Martyn, price 4s.

B.3.3 (Lv). C.6.4. D.13.7 (145). F 46. Powicke 103.

P 56. 'Vetus logica', secundo folio *species autem*, bequeathed by Brice de Sharsted (†1327), price 2s.

B.4.1 (N). C.5.1. Powicke 457.

B.4.2 (M). C.6.2. D.12.3 (129). Powicke 108.

P 61. 'Textus methaphisice cum textu Ethicorum in nudis asseribus', secundo folio *socrates ipse*, bequeathed by Brice de Sharsted, price 6s.

B.4.3 (M). C.15.3. D.12.11 (137). Powicke 51.

P 6. 'Textus methaphisice libri phisicorum celi et mundi de anima et textus quorundam paruorum librorum naturalium antique translacionis', secundo folio *mouetur ab aere*, given by John de Pykering, price 3s.

B.5.1 (E). C.1.2. D.1.2 (2). F 141. Powicke 466A.

B.5.2 (M). C.4.2. D.10.2 (103). F 163. Powicke 403.

B.5.3 (N). C.9.4. Powicke 461.

B.6.1 (N). C.4.1. D.4.1 (26). Powicke 411.

B.6.2 (M). C.11.2. Powicke 404.

B.6.3 (A). C.1.4. D.14.3 (154) ?. F 118?. Powicke 69.

P 26. 'Textus libri de anima', secundo folio *in subiectis*, price [...].

B.7.1 (N). C.6.1. D.3.1 (17). Wodward 1. Powicke 458.

B.7.2 (Lv). C.2.2?. Powicke 394.

B.7.3 (M). C.5.4. D.8.11 (86). F 228. Powicke 74.

P 19. 'Textus Methaphisice Karneby', secundo folio *magis speculatiua*', price 3s.

B.8.1 (M). C.8.1. Wodward 3. Powicke 405.

B.8.2 (Meth). C.15.2. D.1.3 (3). Powicke 71.

P 3. 'Textus metheororum', secundo folio *nulli eorum*, price 2s. 6d.

B.8.3 (L). C.8.4. Powicke 395.

B.9.1 (N). C.8.2. D.9.2 (90). Powicke 60 = 611.

P 31. 'Textus libri phisicorum de anima Metheororum et de generacione et Ethicorum et celi et mundi', secundo folio *et tali igitur*, given
by William de Barneby, price 6s. 8d.

B.9.2 (G). C.1.3. Powicke 75.

P 12. 'Textus de generacione per se', secundo folio *naturam fieri* (not
neque fieri), price 1s. 6d.

B.9.3 (L). C.6.3. Powicke 396.

B.10.1 (L). C.12.2. Powicke 48.

P 5. 'Vetus logica cum noua in vno volumine', secundo folio *eo quod
quale*, given by John Martyn, price 4s.

B.10.2 (M). C.3.2. D.2.3 (10). F 10. Powicke 406.

B.10.3 (P). C.3.4. D.6.11 (61: De anima). F 196. Powicke 66 = 624.

P 11. 'Textus libri phisicorum et aliorum librorum naturalium',
secundo folio *minime ut tetragonismi*, price 1s.

B.11.1 (M). C.9.1. Powicke 153 = 407.

P 78. 'Textus methaphisice cum commento de causis et textu de
plantis in vno volumine cum proposicionibus procli'', secundo folio
quid et causam, bequeathed by Stephen de Gravesend (†1338).

B.11.2 (G). C.14.1. D.14.1 (152). Powicke 76.

P 23. 'Textus de generacione et aliorum paruorum librorum naturalium et celi et mundi', secundo folio *motibus puta*, price 3s.

B.11.3 (L). C.7.4. Powicke 61.

P 25. 'Vetus logica', secundo folio *quoniam proprium*, price [...]d.

B.12.1 (E). C.3.1. D.2.2 (9). Powicke 418.

B.12.2 (Ln). C.10.4. Powicke 397.

B.12.3 (Lv). C.11.4. D.11.13 (126). Powicke 398 = 455.

B.13.1 (N). C.13.1. D.15.1 (172). F 182. Powicke 125.

P 68. 'Textus phisicorum de noua translacione cum comentis phisicorum de substancia orbis de generacione de sensu et sensato de
memoria de sompno de longitudine et breuitate vite in vno volumine',
secundo folio *vnum sunt*, bequeathed by John de Sandwich.

B.13.2 (P). Powicke 419.

B.13.3 (Meth). Powicke 73.

P 18. 'Textus trium librorum Metheororum', secundo folio *re factas in hominibus in d* [...], price 1s. 6d.

B.14.1 (L). C.14.2. Powicke 398A.

B.14.2 (N). C.4.3. D.12.1 (127). Powicke 412.

B.15.1 (Meth). C.10.1. D.11.2 (115). F 94. Powicke 110 = 467.

P 63. 'Liber Metheororum de sompno de memoria de sensu de lineis de inundacione Nili de bona fortuna de longitudine et breuitate vite de vita et morte de pomo de proprietatibus elementorum', secundo folio *multo eciam*, price 5s. Added after the bequest of Brice de Sharsted (P 56–62) in another ink.

B.15.2 (L). C.3.3. Powicke 399.

B.16.1 (L). C.1.3. D.12.7 (133). F 110. Powicke 400.

B.16.2 (P). C.12.3. D.6.3 (53). Powicke 67.

P 36. 'Textus Phisicorum in sex quaternis `ligatus`', secundo folio *quemadmodum et quod est*, price illegible.

B.17.1 (M). C.10.2. D.6.2 (52) ?. F 78. Powicke 64.

P 9. 'Textus methaphisice solemnis', price 3s. 4d.

B.17.2 (N). C.9.3. D.15.3 (174). F 49. Powicke 65.

P 7, 'Textus libri Phisicorum et metheororum de antiqua translacione in vno volumine et alii libri naturales', secundo folio *Alie quantitates sunt*, price 2s.

B.18.1 (Ln). Powicke 401.

B.18.2 (Lv). Powicke 402.

B.19.1 (C). C.13.2. D.15.2 (173). Powicke 413.

B.19.2 (N). D.15.14 (185). Not in Powicke, whose 'P 2 = B 116, D 185' (p. 102) is the result of some confusion, since P 2 is a commentary = B.4.4.

B.20.1 (P). C.14.3. Powicke 416.

B.20.2 (M). C.4.4. D.9.3 (91). Powicke 408 = 456.

B.21.1 (N). C.7.2. D.5.2 (39). Powicke 414.

B.21.2 (L). C.7.3. D.7.7 (69). Powicke 63.

P 4. 'Vetus logica incipiens a libro predicamentorum cum noua logica', secundo folio *substancia autem est*, price 4s.

B.22.1 (A). C.15.1. D.13.1 (139). Powicke 68 = 463.

P 24. 'Textus libri de anima et aliorum paruorum naturalium', secundo folio *tibus nichil*, price 3s.

B.22.2 (N). D.11.11 (124). F 205. Powicke 415 = 614.

COMMENTARIES

B.1.4 (P). C.7.5. D.6.4 (54). Powicke 15.

P 35. 'Commentum Phisicorum ... in membrana vitulina', secundo folio *quanto magis*, bequeathed by William Burnell, price 24s.

B.1.5 (A). C.8.6. D.3.3 (19: 'Textum de Vegitalibus et plantis', secundo folio *debemus ymaginari*). F 117. Powicke 423.

B.2.4 (P). No continuous number in Powicke.

B.2.5. No continuous number in Powicke.

B.2.6 (C). C.2.7. D.12.4 (130). Powicke 481.

B.3.4 (E). C.3.5. Powicke 496.

B.3.5. No continuous number in Powicke.

B.3.6 (M). C.6.6. Powicke 420.

B.4.4 (C). C.11.5. D.7.4 (66). Powicke 80 = 482.

P 2. 'Commentum celi et mundi et commentum de sensu et sensato et de anima de generacione de causis longitudinis et breuitatis vite', secundo folio *autem r'*, price 15s.

B.4.5 (P). No continuous number in Powicke.

B.5.4 (M). No continuous number in Powicke.

B.5.5. Not in Powicke.

B.6.4 (M). Not in Powicke.

B.6.5. Not in Powicke.

B.7.4 (M). Possibly C.1.5 or C.5.5. No continuous number in Powicke.

B.7.5 ([A]). C.13.5. D.14.4 (155). F 139. Powicke 476.

B.8.4 (M). C.12.4. Powicke 391.

B.8.5 (A?). C.1.7?. D.6.10 (60)?. Powicke 473.

B.9.4 (A). C.2.5. Powicke 424.

B.9.5 (M). Powicke 420A.

B.10.4 (A). C.9.6. Powicke 425.

B.10.5 (M). C.3.6. F 11 (secundo folio *per secundam speciem*). Powicke 421.

B.11.4 (A). C.4.5. Powicke 474.

B.11.5 (C). C.14.5. D.12.9 (135). Powicke 442.

B.12.4 (C). C.2.6?. D.5.4 (41). F 161. Powicke 427 = 480?.

B.12.5 (C). C.15.5. D.7.11 (73). F 77. Powicke 107.

P 60? 'Commentum celi et mundi in nudis asseribus', secundo folio *presentiam et cet*', price 7s.

B.13.4 (M). C.10.6. Wodward 5. F 142. Powicke 14 = 470.

P 34. 'Commentum Methaphisice cum proposicionibus Procli commentatis', secundo folio *cum dixit*, bequeathed by William Burnell, price 16s.

B.13.5 (M). No continuous number in Powicke.

B.14.3 (P). C.15.4. D.8.5 (80). F 51. Powicke 428.

B.15.3 (P). C.10.5. D.4.4 (29: secundo folio *quando illa*). Powicke 429 = 646.

B.16.3 (M). C.4.6. Powicke 422.

B.17.3 (P). C.12.9. Powicke 430.

B.18.3 (P). C.6.5. Powicke 79.

P 1. 'Commentum libri Phisicorum cum paruis libris naturalibus', secundo folio *et dixit quoquomodo*, price 16s.

B.19.3 (A). C.13.4. F 9. Powicke 149.

P 74. 'Comentum C et M et super librum de anima in vno volumine', secundo folio *et vtrum habeat*, bequeathed by Stephen de Gravesend.

B.20.3 (A). C.7.6 (Expositio). D.11.9 (122). F 54. Powicke 106.

P 59. 'Commentum methaphisice et commentum libri de anima in nudis asseribus', secundo folio *diffiniciones rerum*, bequeathed by Brice de Sharsted, price 18s.

B.21.3 (C). C.12.5. D.11.10 (123). Powicke 82.

P 37. 'Commentum celi et mundi in membrana vitulina in nudis asseribus ... et continet commentum de causis et partem commenti de anima', secundo folio *et dicimus*, price [..] 6s.[62]

B.22.3 (A). Powicke 426.

EXPOSITIONS

B.1.6 (C). C.16. [ ]. Powicke 517.

B.2.7 (L). No continuous number in Powicke.

B.3.7 (M). C.1.8. Powicke 390.

B.4.6 (P). C.4.8. D.6.5 (55). F 12. Powicke 34 = 437.

P 33. 'Exposicio Thome de Alquino super libros Phisicorum de anima

---

[62] Powicke gives the price as 'xvis', but I cannot read what stood in front of 'vi'. An even larger price than 16s. might be possible for a manuscript *in membrana vitulina*: cf. the Commentary, B.1.4.

et aliis paruis libris naturalibus', secundo folio *vniuersaliori sensibili*, bequeathed by Thomas Bray, price 10s.

B.5.6 (M). C.6.7. Powicke 435.

B.6.6 (P). C.5.7. D.15.5 (176). F 99. Powicke 438.

B.7.6 (E). C.11.7. Powicke 439.

B.8.6 (M). C.3.8. D.5.5 (42). In F after 158. Powicke 33.

P 32. 'Exposicio Thome de Alquino super Methaphisicam', secundo folio *corpora cum superioribus*, given by Thomas Bray, price 6s. 8d.

B.9.6 (Meth). C.2.8. D.2.4 (11). Wodward 6. F 165. Powicke 83.

P 20. 'Exposicio libri Metheororum Aluerne', secundo folio *de generacione et corupcione*, price 3s.

B.10.6 (Pol). C.10.7. D.12.5 (131). Powicke 85.

P 38. 'Exposicio libri Pollethicorum', secundo folio *dii quorum vnus*, price 8s.

B.11.6 (L). C.8.7. Powicke 433 = 515.

B.12.6 (E). C.12.6. F 188. Powicke 440.

B.12.7 (L). C.10.8. Powicke 434.

B.13.6 (A). C.3.7 (Comment' de Anima). Powicke 436.

B.14.5 (Meth). Powicke 441.

B.17.4. C.14.8 (Questiones de gramatica). D.12.8 (134: Questiones gramaticales). Powicke 444.

B.22.4 (C). C.11.8. D.9.11 (99). F 65. Powicke 81 = 485.

P 16. 'Exposicio libri celi et mundi', secundo folio *et hoc habet racionem*, price 8d.

'EXTRAS'

B.1.7. Not in Powicke.

B.1.8 (Textus de animalibus). C.11.1. Powicke 392.

B.2.8 (Almagest). Powicke 86.

P 39. 'Liber continens Almagest' cum multis aliis in vno magno volumine', secundo folio *que hiis assimilantur*, price 8s.

B.3.8 (Alacen). C.1.9. D.4.6 (31). Wodward 10. F 146. Powicke 96.

P 49. 'Alacen', secundo folio *ex colore illius*, price 4s.

B.4.7 (Planisperium). C.4.9. Powicke 87.

P 40. 'Planisperium Tholomei cum Almagest'', secundo folio *transiens*, price 10s.

B.5.7 (Boethius, Arithmetica). C.14.7. Powicke 450.

B.6.7 (Geometria). C.7.8. D.5.6 (43). Powicke 97.

P 50. 'Geometria Euclidis. Algorismus demonstratus. Archimenides de curuis (*sic for* terrenis) superficiebus', secundo folio *datum angulum*, price 3s.

B.7.7 (Textus de animalibus). C.12.1. D.9.1 (89). Powicke 109.

P 62. 'Liber de animalibus noue translacionis in rubeo coopertorio', secundo folio *sunt quedam male*, bequeathed by Brice de Sharsted, price 20s.

B.8.7 (Questiones super phisicorum cum textu de anima). C.12.7. D.8.10 (85). Powicke 443.

B.9.7 (Questiones). C.13.7. F 122. Powicke 445.

B.10.7 (Astronomia W. de Conchis). C.3.9. Powicke 453.

B.11.7 (Boethius, Arithmetica). C.15.7. D.13.6 (144). Powicke 451.

B.13.7 (Thimeus Platonis). Powicke 449.

B.14.4 (Avicenna super Methaphisicam et sextum). C.9.8. Powicke 452.

B.14.6 (Quaternus de ente et essencia Thome). Powicke 448.

B.15.4 (Questiones super libros Phisicorum). C.14.6. D.13.9 (147: Questiones naturales). F 79 (Exposit' naturalis philosophie). Powicke 35.

P 8. 'Exposicio super libros naturales methaphisice et alia', secundo folio *non continetur*, bequeathed by Walter de Chilton, price 1s.

B.15.5 (Quaternus). Powicke 446.

B.16.4 (Questiones Methaphisice). C.9.7. D.13.8. F 167. Powicke 487 = 672.

B.16.5 (Questiones ?). C.5.8. D.10.8 (109: Questiones super libros phisicorum). Powicke 447 = 671.

B.17.5 (Quaternus de diuersis questionibus). D.14.11 (162: Librum logice) ? F 179. Powicke 128 = 431.

P 71. 'Sophistica disputata et varie questiones ligat' in nudis asceribus', secundo folio *set verum et falsum*, bequeathed by John de Sandwich.

B.18.4 (Quaternus). C.6.8. D.4.8 (33). Powicke 126.

P 69. 'Expositor super veterem logicam et librum posteriorum cum questionibus logicalibus et methaphisicalibus in xvii quaternis ligatus et sine asceribus', secundo folio *diuisione quod genus*, bequeathed by John de Sandwich.

B.18.5 (Quaternus). No continuous number in Powicke.

B.19.4 (Questiones). C.15.6. Powicke 84.

P 21. 'Questiones libri metheororum cum multis aliis', secundo folio *ad quem est processus*, price 6d.

B.19.5 (Quaternus). No continuous number in Powicke.

B.20.4 (Tractatus Lincolniensis cum aliis). C.4.10. D.7.8 (70: Lincoln' super libros Elenchorum). Powicke 207.

B.21.4 (Questiones Methaphisice). C.13.6. D.14.6 (157). Powicke 105.

P 58. 'Liber de questionibus super methaphisicam et de anima et super sexto phisicorum de celo et mundo cum aliis in nudis asseribus', secundo folio *suam sine labore*, bequeathed by Brice de Sharsted, price 1s.

B.21.5 (Martianus de nupciis philiologie). Powicke 89.

P 42. 'Sex pecie edicionis Marciani de vii artibus', secundo folio *mos connubialis*, price 6d.

Concordance of C with B and, failing B, later lists[63]

*C.1.1 (N)	B.1.1	*C.2.3 (E)	B.2.2
C.1.2 (E)	B.5.1	C.2.4 (Ln)	B.2.3
C.1.3 (L)	B.16.1	C.2.5 (A)	B.9.4
C.1.4 (A)	B.6.3	C.2.6 (C)	B.12.4?
C.1.5 (M)	Powicke 468	C.2.7 (C)	B.2.6
C.1.6 (P)	Powicke 477	*C.2.8	B.9.6
C.1.7 (A)	B.8.5	C.2.9	Powicke 491
C.1.8 (M)	B.3.7	C.3.1 (E)	B.12.1
*C.1.9	B.3.8	C.3.2 (M)	B.10.2
C.1.10	D.7.6 (68: secundo	C.3.3 (L)	B.15.2
	folio *Sciendum autem*). Powicke	*C.3.4 (N)	B.10.3
	492 = 688	*C.3.5 (E)	B.3.4
C.1.11	Powicke 495	C.3.6 (M)	B.10.5
C.1.12	D.7.5 (67: Logicam	C.3.7 (A)	B.13.6
	Algazel). Powicke 494	*C.3.8 (M)	B.8.6
*C.2.1 (N)	B.2.1	C.3.9	B.10.7
C.2.2 (Lv)	B.7.2?	C.4.1 (N)	B.6.1

[63] The valuation or cost of items marked with an asterisk is known: see the Concordance of B with C and pp. 351–2.

C.4.2 (M)   B.5.2
C.4.3 (N)   B.14.2
C.4.4 (M)   B.20.2
C.4.5 (A)   B.11.4
C.4.6 (M)   B.16.3
C.4.7 (P)   No continuous
   number in Powicke
*C.4.8 (P)   B.4.6
*C.4.9   B.4.7
C.4.10   B.20.4
C.4.11   Powicke 498
C.5.1 (N)   B.4.1
C.5.2 (E)   B.1.2
C.5.3 (E)   Not in Powicke[64]
*C.5.4 (M)   B.7.3
C.5.5 (M)   Powice 469
C.5.6 (A)   Powicke 475
C.5.7 (P)   B.6.6
C.5.8   B.16.5
C.5.9 (Meth)   No continuous
   number in Powicke
C.6.1 (N)   B.7.1
*C.6.2 (Meth)   B.4.2
C.6.3 (L)   B.9.3
*C.6.4 (Lv)   B.3.3
*C.6.5 (P)   B.18.3
C.6.6 (M)   B.13.6
C.6.7 (M)   B.5.6
C.6.8 (L)   B.18.4
C.7.1 (N)   B.3.1
C.7.2 (N)   B.21.1
*C.7.3 (L)   B.21.2
C.7.4 (Lv)   B.11.3
*C.7.5 (P)   B.1.4
*C.7.6 (A)   B.20.3
C.7.7 (A)   D.14.5 (156).
   Powicke 484 = 658
*C.7.8   B.6.7
C.7.9 (M)   Powicke 459
C.7.10   Powicke 493
C.8.1 (M)   B.8.1

*C.8.2 (N)   B.9.1
C.8.3 (P)   Powicke 464
C.8.4 (L)   B.8.3
C.8.5 (P)   Powicke 478
C.8.6 (A)   B.1.5
C.8.7 (L)   B.11.6
C.8.8   D.14.10 (161). F 21.
   Powicke 486
C.9.1 (M)   B.11.1
*C.9.2 (E)   B.3.2
*C.9.3 (N)   B.17.2
C.9.4 (N)   B.5.3
C.9.5 (M)   D.9.4 (92). F 209.
   Powicke 483
C.9.6 (A)   B.10.4
C.9.7   B.16.4
C.9.8   B.14.4
*C.10.1 (Meth)   B.15.1
*C.10.2 (M)   B.17.1
C.10.3 (P)   Powicke 465
C.10.4 (L)   B.12.2
C.10.5 (P)   B.15.3
* C.10.6 (M)   B.13.4
C.10.7 (Pol)   B.10.6
C.10.8 (P)   B.12.7
C.11.1   B.1.8
*C.11.2 (M)   B.6.2
C.11.3 (L)   D.6.7 (57: secundo
   folio *dialectice cum*). Powicke 454
C.11.4 (Lv)   B.12.3
*C.11.5 (C)   B.4.4
C.11.6 (M)   D.2.7 (14: secundo
   folio *id est cum venio*). F 120.
   Powicke 471
C.11.7 (E)   B.7.6
*C.11.8 (C)   B.22.4
*C.12.1   B.7.7
*C.12.2 (L)   B.10.1
C.12.3 (P)   B.16.2
C.12.4 (M)   B.8.4
*C.12.5 (C)   B.21.3

[64] See note on B.13.2.

C.12.6 (E)	B.12.6	C.14.3 (P)	B.20.1
C.12.7	B.8.7	C.14.4 (P)	Powicke 479
C.12.8 (A)	D.10.1 (Textum	C.14.5 (C)	B.11.5
nat.phil.). F 138. Powicke 462		*C.14.6	B.15.4
*C.12.9 (P)	B.17.3	C.14.7	B.5.7
C.13.1 (P)	B.13.1	C.14.8	B.17.4
C.13.2 (N)	B.19.1 ?	C.14.9	Powicke 489
*C.13.3 (G)	B.9.2	*C.15.1 (A)	B.22.1
C.13.4 (C)	B.19.3	*C.15.2 (Meth)	B.8.2
C.13.5 (A)	B.7.5	*C.15.3 (M)	B.4.3
*C.13.6	B.21.4	C.15.4 (P)	B.14.3
C.13.7	B.9.7	*C.15.5 (C)	B.12.5
C.13.8 (M)	D.10.10 (111)?	*C.15.6	B.19.4
Powicke 472		C.15.7	B.11.7
C.13.9	Powicke 488[65]	C.15.8	Powicke 497
*C.14.1 (C)	B.11.2	C.16. [ ]	Powicke 490
C.14.2 (L)	B.14.1	*C.16. [ ] (C)	B.1.6

[65] See Note on C.13.9.

A List of the Published Writings of
J. A. W. Bennett

COMPILED BY P. L. HEYWORTH

Editor, *Medium Ævum*, 1956–81
General Editor, Clarendon Medieval and Tudor Series, 1958–75.

1930

'New Zealand and the Pacific.' *Open Windows* (Christchurch and Wellington, New Zealand Student Christian Movement).[1]

1931

'A Future for Our Language Departments.' On the teaching of literature in New Zealand universities. *Kiwi*, xxvi. 45–7.
'Gerard Manley Hopkins: Poet of Surprise.' *Kiwi*, xxvi. 55–7.
Editorials and notes in *Open Windows*.

1932

'The Necessity of Criticism.' In defence of literary criticism. *The Phoenix* (Auckland, the Literary Club at Auckland University College), vol. 1 no. 1, March, pp. 21–4.
'After Which.' A riposte to a reply (vol. 1 no. 2, pp. 36–40) to 'The Necessity of Criticism.' *The Phoenix*, vol. 1 no. 2, July, pp. 40–1.
Review of P. W. Robertson's *Life and Beauty: A Spiritual Autobiography*. *The Phoenix*, vol. 1 no. 2, July, pp. 44–7.

1933

'Habent sua fata libelli: A note on the literature of the College.' *The Golden Jubilee Book of the Auckland University College 1883–1933*, pp. 49–52.
Review of *New Zealand Best Poems*, 1932. *The Phoenix*, vol. 2 no. 1, March, pp. 50–1.
Review of Pearl Buck's *Sons*. *The Phoenix*, vol. 2 no. 2, July, p. 63.

[1] From memory. No copy of the magazine can be traced.

1936

'Concerning Wade ...' A note on *Canterbury Tales* E. 1424. *MLR* xxxi. 202–3.

Review of Henry W. Wells's translation of *The Vision of Piers Plowman*. *MÆ* v. 132–6.

Review of Ethel Seaton's *Literary Relations of England and Scandinavia in the Seventeenth Century*. *Saga-Book of the Viking Society for Northern Research*, vol. xi part iii. 295–7.

Letter: 'Bernard's Catalogue.' Note on Humfrey Wanley's draft of the Preface to Bernard's Catalogue, 1698. *TLS*, 31 October.

1937

'Dryden and All Souls'. Dryden's candidature for the Wardenship of All Souls. *MLN* lii. 115–16.

'The Beginnings of Norse Studies in England.' *Saga-Book of the Viking Society for Northern Research*, vol. xii part i. 35–42.

Review of Robin Flower's *Laurence Nowell and the Discovery of England in Tudor Times*. *MÆ* vi. 219–21.

Review of Gudmund Schütte's *Das Südjütische Dänentum. Zwölf Wahrheiten. Saga-Book of the Viking Society for Northern Research*, vol. xii part i. 44.

1938

'Broadcasting in the British Dominions.' Variations in the speech of radio announcers in Australia, Canada, and New Zealand. *Proceedings of the Third International Congress of Phonetic Sciences, Ghent 1938*. 160–5.

'A Note on the Bodleian.' Humfrey Wanley's proposals for improving the Bodleian Library. *Oxford Magazine*, 16 June.

Reviews of T. P. Dunning's *Piers Plowman: An Interpretation of the A-Text. MÆ* vii. 232–6; *Oxford Magazine*, 17 February.

Review of Haakon Shetelig and Hjalmar Falk's *Scandinavian Archaeology*, translated by E. V. Gordon. *MÆ* vii. 161–3.

'Shadow of a War.' On England's preparations for war. *Tomorrow: a New Zealand independent fortnightly paper*, 25 May.

'Aftermath.' Further remarks on war preparations. *Tomorrow*, 9 November.

1939

'A Middle English Inscription.' At Horley, Oxon. *Notes and Queries*, 176. 387–8.

'Oxford in 1699.' Letters of William Adams, 1673–1714. *Oxoniensia*, iv. 147–52.

Review of Mildred Elizabeth Marcett's *Uhtred de Boldon, Friar William Jordan, and Piers Plowman*. MÆ viii. 169–71.

1940

'Free Speech in Quay Street.' On pro-war sentiment in New Zealand. *Tomorrow*, 21 February.

1941

'English as you teach it in America.' Reflections on English studies at universities in the United States. *College English*, ii. 675–81.

1942

'Old English *hrohian*.' A note on an emendation by Junius. MÆ xi. 90.

Review of H. L. Mencken's *A New Dictionary of Quotations on Historical Principles from Ancient and Modern Sources. The New Republic*, 1 June.

Review of Margaret Schlauch's *The Gift of Tongues. The New Republic*, 13 July.

1943

'The Date of the A-Text of *Piers Plowman*.' PMLA lviii. 566–72.

'The Date of the B-Text of *Piers Plowman*.' MÆ xii. 55–64.

'English as it is spoken in New Zealand.' *American Speech*, xviii. 81–95. Reprinted in *English Transported: Essays on Australasian English*, ed. W. S. Ramson (Australian National University Press, Canberra, 1970), pp. 69–83.

1944

'Oxford Revisited.' *The American Scholar*, xiii. 367–9.

1945

'New Zealand Literature and Art.' *Encyclopedia Americana*, xx. 262–5.

'Writing in New Zealand.' *The American Scholar*, xiv. 200–8.

'Traherne and Brasenose.' An unnoticed reference to Traherne in the Brasenose Book of Benefactors. *Notes and Queries*, 188. 84.

'Lombards' Letters ('Piers Plowman', B. V, 251).' *MLR* xl. 309–10.

Review of Gladys I. Wade's *Thomas Traherne. New York Times Book Review*, 28 January.

1946

'The Early Fame of Gavin Douglas's *Eneados*.' *MLN* lxi. 83–8.

Review of Nevill Coghill's *The Pardon of Piers Plowman. TLS*, 6 July.

Review of Ian Maxwell's *French Farce and John Heywood. TLS*, 3 August.

1947

Foreword (biographical note) to John Mulgan's *Report on Experience*. London: Oxford University Press, pp. v–xi.

Review of E. K. Chambers's *English Literature at the Close of the Middle Ages. RES* xxiii. 271–3.

Review of J. W. Adamson's *The Illiterate Anglo-Saxon and other Essays on Education, Medieval and Modern. Oxford Magazine*, 19 June.

Review of Nevill Coghill's *The Pardon of Piers Plowman. Oxford Magazine*, 23 October.

Review of A. M. D. Hughes's *The Nascent Mind of Shelley. Oxford Magazine*, 20 November.

1948

A List of the Published Writings of Charles Talbut Onions. Oxford: At the Clarendon Press. With a biographical note. pp. 18.

'Hickes's "Thesaurus": A Study in Oxford Book-Production.' *English Studies 1948: Being Volume One of the New Series of Essays and Studies Collected for the English Association by F. P. Wilson*, pp. 28–45.

'A New Collation of a *Piers Plowman* Manuscript (HM 137).' *MÆ* xvii. 21–31.

1949

'The Decay of Romantic Love.' *The Listener*, 24 March.

Review of Eugène Vinaver's edition of *The Works of Sir Thomas Malory. RES* xxv. 161–7.

Review of Wilhelm Levison's *England and the Continent in the Eighth Century. MÆ* xviii. 33–5.

Review of Haldeen Braddy's *Chaucer and the French Poet Graunson. MÆ* xviii. 35–7.

Review of Eleanor Shipley Duckett's *Anglo-Saxon Saints and Scholars. MÆ* xviii. 37–8.

Review of Kenneth Allott's edition of *The Poems of William Habington. Oxford Magazine*, 3 November.

Review of Rosemary Freeman's *English Emblem Books. Oxford Magazine*, 17 November.

1950

'Caxton and Gower.' A note on a borrowing from Gower in Caxton's translation of Ovid, Metamorphoses, xi. 583 f. *MLR* xlv. 215–16.

'William Langland's World of Visions.' *The Listener*, 2 March.

Review of H. S. Bennett's *Chaucer and the Fifteenth Century. MLR* xlv. 78–9.

Review of Nevill Coghill's *The Poet Chaucer. Landfall: A New Zealand Quarterly*, vol. 4 no. 3, September, pp. 246–50.

1951

'The Beginnings of Runic Studies in England.' *Saga-Book of the Viking Society for Northern Research*, vol. xiii part iv. 269–83.

Review of John Harvey's *The Gothic World, 1100–1600. TES*, 9 February.

1952

Review of E. Talbot Donaldson's *Piers Plowman: The C-text and its Poet. MÆ* xxi. 51–3.

Review of Marchette Chute's *Geoffrey Chaucer of England. TLS*, 4 January.

Review of M. C. Bradbrook's *Shakespeare and Elizabethan Poetry. TLS*, 1 February.

Review of A. H. Smith's *Piers Plowman and the Pursuit of Poetry. TLS*, 8 February.

Review of Rossell Hope Robbins's edition of *Secular Lyrics of the XIVth and XVth Centuries* and D. W. Robertson and Bernard F. Huppé's *Piers Plowman and Scriptural Tradition. TLS*, 25 July.

Review of David Talbot Rice's *English Art 871–1100. TES*, 1 August.

Review of H. S. Bennett's *English Books and their Readers, 1475–1557. Oxford Magazine*, 30 October.
Review of *London Medieval Studies* vol. II part i. *TLS*, 5 December.
Review of J. A. Asher's *Amis et Amiles. An Exploratory Survey. Landfall: A New Zealand Quarterly*, vol. 6 no. 4, December, pp. 333–4.

1953

'Chaucer, Dante, and Boccaccio.' A note on Chaucer's use of Boccaccio at *Knight's Tale* 635–6 and *Troilus* III. 1092. *MÆ* xxii. 114–15.
'The Grey Collection.' An account of the medieval manuscripts and early printed books in the library of Sir George Grey. *New Zealand Libraries: Bulletin of the New Zealand Library Association*, vol. 16 no. 4, May, pp. 82–6.
Review of Eleanor Shipley Duckett's *Alcuin, Friend of Charlemagne. MÆ* xxii. 48–9.
Review of Paul Christophersen's *The Ballad of Sir Aldingar: Its Origins and Analogues. TLS*, 12 June.

1954

Chaucer, *The Knight's Tale*. Edited, with notes and glossary, by J.A.W.B. London: Harrap's English Classics. pp. 205. Revised edition 1958.
Note (p.v.) and bibliographical note (pp. xcv–cii) to the third impression of W. W. Skeat's edition of *The Vision of William concerning Piers the Plowman*, Oxford, 1886.
'A Medieval Manuscript in New Zealand.' A manuscript of Gregory's *Moralia. Bodleian Library Record*, vol. v no. 1, April, pp. 25–7.
'A Note on Donne's *Crosse.*' *RES*, NS v. 168–9.
Review of Albert H. Marckwardt's edition of *Laurence Nowell's Vocabularium Saxonicum. RES*, NS v. 398–9.
Review of Robert W. Ackermann's *An Index of the Arthurian Names in Middle English. MLR* xlix. 221–2.
Review of G. H. Cook's *The English Mediaeval Parish Church. TES*, 2 July.
Review of Christopher Woodforde's *English Stained and Painted Glass. TES*, 6 August.
Review of Margaret Rickert's *Painting in Britain: The Middle Ages. TES*, 1 October.

Review of Antony Alpers's *Katherine Mansfield. Landfall: A New Zealand Quarterly*, vol. 8 no. 4, December, pp. 301–4.

1955

Devotional Pieces in Verse and Prose from MS Arundel 285 and MS Harleian 6919. Edited by J. A. W. B. Scottish Text Society, 3rd Series, no. 23. Edinburgh and London: William Blackwood for the Society. pp. xxxviii, 349.

The Poems of Richard Corbett. Edited by J.A.W.B. and H. R. Trevor-Roper. Oxford: At the Clarendon Press. pp. lxv, 177.

Review of Morton W. Bloomfield's *The Seven Deadly Sins. MLR* l. 65–6.

Review of Thomas A. Knott and David C. Fowler's edition of *Piers the Plowman: A critical edition of the A-Version. MLR* l. 193–4.

1956

Review of Claes Schaar's *Some types of narrative in Chaucer's poetry. MÆ* xxv. 57–9.

Review of Sir William A. Craigie's *Sýnisbók Íslenzkra Rímna. Specimens of the Icelandic Metrical Romances. MÆ* xxv. 59–60.

Review of Henry A. Person's edition of *Cambridge Middle English Lyrics. RES*, NS vii. 68–9.

Review of Josephine Waters Bennett's *The Rediscovery of Sir John Mandeville. Oxford Magazine*, 23 February.

Reviews of David M. Taylor's *The Oldest Manuscripts in New Zealand. Landfall: A New Zealand Quarterly*, vol. 10 no. 2, June, pp. 149–51; *TLS*, 2 November.

Letter: on a reference in Gibbon to Captain Cook's voyages to the Antipodes. *Landfall: A New Zealand Quarterly*, vol. 10 no. 1, March, p. 84.

1957

The Parlement of Foules: An Interpretation. Oxford: At the Clarendon Press. pp. 217.

'Dunbar's *Birth of Antichrist*, 31–2.' *MÆ* xxvi. 196.

Revision of the sections on Geoffrey Chaucer (pp. 130–45), and The Fifteenth Century (pp. 146–51) in *The Cambridge Bibliography of English Literature*, vol. V, *Supplement*.

'Vivat C.T.O.' Leading article on C. T. Onions. *TLS*, 29 March.

Review of Maria Wickert's *Studien zu John Gower*. *RES*, NS viii.
54–6.
Review of Dudley David Griffith's *Bibliography of Chaucer 1908–
1953*. *RES*, NS viii. 180–1.
Review of Hardin Craig's *English Religious Drama of the Middle
Ages. Oxford Magazine*, 2 May.
Letter: 'Medieval English Poetry.' A note on *Sir Gawain and the
Green Knight* lines 802, 865. *TLS*, 8 November.
Obituary notice of Richard Selig. American poet, pupil of J.A.W.B.
The Times, 22 October.

1958

'Lefunge O Swefne. O Nore.' A note on some parallels. *RES*, NS ix.
280–1.
General Index to Medium Ævum Volumes I to XXV. 1932–1957.
Compiled by J.A.W.B. *et al*. Published for the Society for the Study
of Mediaeval Languages and Literature. Oxford: Basil Blackwell.
pp. 35.
Review of Richard Cleasby and Gudbrand Vigfusson's *An Ice-
landic–English Dictionary*, second edition, with a supplement by
Sir William Craigie. *MÆ* xxvii. 220.
Review of J. S. Purvis's *The York Cycle of Mystery Plays: A Complete
Version. Oxford Magazine*, 30 January.

1959

Review of *Studies in Heroic Legend and in Current Speech by Kemp
Malone*, edited by Stefán Einarsson and Norman E. Eliason. *MÆ*
xxviii. 229.
Review of E. H. McCormick's *New Zealand Literature: A Survey*.
New Statesman, 15 August.
Letter: 'Rewards and Fairies.' On Richard Corbett's 'Farewell,
Rewards & Faeries.' *TLS*, 20 November.

1960

'Sum Rex, Sum Princeps, etc. (*Piers Plowman* B, Prologue 132–8)'.
Notes and Queries, 205. 364.
'Landfall in Unknown Seas.' On New Zealand culture and literature.
The Listener, 21 January.

'Sketch-Plan for a College.' *Landfall: A New Zealand Quarterly*, vol. 14 no. 3, September, 274–80.

1961

'Research: the Tyrant.' *The Listener*, 26 January.

Review of Charles Muscatine's *Chaucer and the French Tradition: A Study in Style and Meaning. RES*, NS xii. 70.

Review of C. E. Wright's *English Vernacular Hands from the Twelfth to the Fifteenth Centuries. Archives*, v. 112.

1962

'Why Men Cry "Seynt Barbara".' *RES*, NS xiii. 283.

'Wanley's *Life of Wolsey*.' *Bodleian Library Record*, vol. vii no. 1, June, pp. 50–2. Earlier summarized in a note to Richard S. Sylvester's edition of George Cavendish's *The Life and Death of Cardinal Wolsey*, Early English Text Society, OS 243 (1959), p. 288.

'Climates of Opinions.' On figurative uses of 'climate' in English. *English and Medieval Studies Presented to J. R. R. Tolkien on the Occasion of his Seventieth Birthday*, edited by Norman Davis and C. L. Wrenn. London: George Allen and Unwin, pp. 280–305.

'Remembrance of Things Past.' A note on the sources of the title. *Notes and Queries*, 207. 151–2.

Review of *Eirik the Red and Other Icelandic Sagas* selected and translated by Gwyn Jones. *MÆ* xxxi. 80.

Review of *Studies Presented to Sir Hilary Jenkinson*, edited by J. Conway Davies. *MÆ* xxxi. 223–4.

Review of *Medieval England*, edited by A. L. Poole. *MÆ* xxxi. 224–6.

Review of Lars-Ivar Ringbom's *Paradisus Terrestris: myt, bild och verklighet. MÆ* xxxi. 226–7.

Review of Titus Burckhardt's *Siena the City of the Virgin*, translated by Margaret McDonough Brown. *MÆ* xxxi. 228–9.

Review of Norman Cohn's *The World-View of a Thirteenth-Century Parisian Intellectual: Jean de Meun and the Roman de la Rose. Durham University Journal*, NS xxiii. 143.

1963

Essays on Malory. A collection with contributions by Walter Oakeshott, C. S. Lewis, Eugène Vinaver, and others. Edited by J.A.W.B. Oxford: At the Clarendon Press. pp. vii, 147.

Review of George Kane's edition of *Piers Plowman: The A-Version. Will's Visions of Piers Plowman and Do-well. RES*, NS xiv. 68–71.

Review of David F. C. Coldwell's edition of *Virgil's Æneid translated into Scottish Verse by Gavin Douglas, Bishop of Dunkeld*, vols. ii–iv. *RES*, NS xiv. 73–4.

Review of A. B. Emden's *A Biographical Register of the University of Oxford to A.D. 1500*, vols. ii, iii. *MÆ* xxxii. 167–8.

Review of Marc Bloch's *Feudal Society*, translated by L. A. Manyon. *MÆ* xxxii. 168.

Review of Laura Hibberd Loomis's *Adventures in the Middle Ages: A Memorial Collection of Essays and Studies. MÆ* xxxii. 168–9.

Review of William Croft Dickinson's *Scotland from the Earliest Times to 1603. MÆ* xxxii. 169.

Review of Philip E. Jones's edition of *Calendar of Plea and Memoranda Rolls preserved among the archives of the Corporation of the City of London, A.D. 1458–1482. MÆ* xxxii. 169–70.

Review of *The Romance of the Rose* translated by Harry W. Robins, edited with an Introduction by Charles W. Dunn. *Notes and Queries*, 208. 473.

Review of E. H. McCormick's *The Fascinating Folly: Dr Hocken and his Fellow Collectors. The Library*, Fifth Series, xviii. 247–8.

Letter: 'Milton's "Cato".' An unnoticed Horatian allusion in Milton's sonnet 'Laurence, of Vertuous Father vertuous Son'. *TLS*, 5 April.

1964

Review of Gilbert H. Doble's *The Saints of Cornwall. Part One: Saints of the Land's End District. Part Two: Saints of the Lizard District. MÆ* xxxiii. 85.

Review of *Didactic Literature of the Middle Ages* (*L'Esprit Créateur*, vol. ii no. 3). *MÆ* xxxiii. 85.

Review of Heather Peek's and Catherine Hall's *The Archives of the University of Cambridge*, and A. C. Chibnall's *Richard de Badew and the University of Cambridge 1315–1340. MÆ* xxxiii. 86–7.

Review of C. S. Lewis's *The Discarded Image. TLS*, 16 July.

Obituary notice of P. S. Ardern, 1881–1964. New Zealand medievalist and scholar. *Comment: A New Zealand Quarterly Review*, vol. 6 no. 1, October–November, pp. 11–12.

1965

The Humane Medievalist: An Inaugural Lecture. Delivered by J.A.W.B. at Cambridge, 20 November 1964. Cambridge: University Press. pp. 32.

'Grete Clerk.' *Light on C. S. Lewis*, edited by Jocelyn Gibb. London: Geoffrey Bles, pp. 44–50. Reproduces some passages in *The Humane Medievalist.*

Review of John H. Fisher's *John Gower*, and Terence Tiller's translation of *Confessio Amantis. TLS*, 18 November.

Review of *Oxford New Zealand Encyclopaedia*, and *Encyclopaedia of Modern Knowledge. TLS*, 9 December.

Review of J. A. Burrow's *A Reading of Sir Gawain and the Green Knight. TLS*, 23 December.

Letter: 'Maitland by Mail'. An emendation to, and a note on, two letters of F. W. Maitland. *TLS*, 8 April.

1966

Early Middle English Verse and Prose. Edited by J.A.W.B. and G. V. Smithers, with a glossary by Norman Davis. J.A.W.B. was responsible for the following texts, introductions, and commentaries: I, VIII s–y, X–XIII, XVI, XIX. Oxford: At the Clarendon Press. pp. lxi, 620. Second edition 1968.

'Caxton's Ovid.' On the two halves of the Pepysian MS of Caxton's copy of Ovid's *Metamorphoses. TLS*, 24 November.

'Gower's "Honeste Love".' *Patterns of Love and Courtesy: Essays in Memory of C. S. Lewis* edited by John Lawlor. London: Edward Arnold, pp. 107–21.

'Donne, "Elegy", XVI, 31.' *Notes and Queries*, 211. 254.

Review of R. S. Loomis's *A Mirror of Chaucer's World. TLS*, 10 March.

Review of R. C. Alston's *A Bibliography of the English Language from the Invention of Printing to the Year 1800. Vol. I: English Grammars written in English and English Grammars written in Latin by native speakers. The Library*, Fifth Series, xxi. 334–5.

Review of *The Dark Ages: the making of European Civilization*, edited by David Talbot Rice, and Françoise Henry's *Irish Art in the Early Christian Period (to 800 A.D.). MÆ* xxxv. 177–8.

Review of E. J. Palmer's *The Rise of English Studies*, and W. W.

Robson's *English as a University Subject*. *Southern Review* (University of Adelaide), vol. ii no. 2, pp. 178–81.

Review of *Letters of C. S. Lewis* edited by W. H. Lewis. *Magdalene College Magazine and Record*, New Series no. 10, pp. 14–16.

1967

Review of *Malory's Originality: a critical study of Le Morte Darthur* edited by R. M. Lumiansky. *RES*, NS xviii. 190–1.

Review of David F. C. Coldwell's edition of *Virgil's Aeneid translated into Scottish Verse by Gavin Douglas, Bishop of Dunkeld*, vol. i. *RES*, NS xviii. 310–13.

Review of Beverly Boyd's *The Middle English Miracles of the Virgin*. *MÆ* xxxvi. 93–5.

Review of Rosemond Tuve's *Allegorical Imagery: Some Mediaeval Books and their Posterity*. *English Language Notes*, v. 52–7.

Review of B. G. Koonce's *Chaucer and the Tradition of Fame: Symbolism in The House of Fame*. *TLS*, 4 May.

Review of V. A. Kolve's *The Play Called Corpus Christi*. *TLS*, 4 May.

Letter: 'Caxton Saved'. *TLS*, 19 January.

1968

Chaucer's Book of Fame: An Exposition of 'The House of Fame'. Oxford: At the Clarendon Press. pp. xiv, 191.

Selections from John Gower. Edited, with introduction, notes, and glossary, by J.A.W.B. Clarendon Medieval and Tudor Series. Oxford: At the Clarendon Press. pp. xxii, 189.

'Corbett, Richard (1582–1635)', vol. 6, p. 488, and 'Langland, William', vol. 13, pp. 693–5, in *Encyclopaedia Britannica*.

Review of G. O. Sayles's edition of *Select Cases in the Court of King's Bench, vol. vi, Edward III: 1341–1377*. *MÆ* xxxvii. 363–4.

Review of Alain Renoir's *The Poetry of John Lydgate*. *Studia Neophilologica*, xl. 242–3.

Review of William R. Crawford's *Bibliography of Chaucer, 1954–63*. *TLS*, 22 February.

Review of Kenneth Varty's *Reynard the Fox: A Study of the Fox in Medieval English Art*. *TLS*, 22 February.

Review of V. Pritchard's *English Medieval Graffiti*. *TLS*, 22 February.

Review of R. T. Lenaghan's edition of *Caxton's Æsop*. *TLS*, 23 May.

Review of *Sir Gawain and the Green Knight* edited by J. R. R. Tolkien and E. V. Gordon. Second edition revised by Norman Davis. *TLS*, 25 July.

'Return of Zuleika (Manibus M.B. et S.C.R.).' *Oxford Magazine*, 9 February.

1969

'Chaucer's Contemporary.' *Piers Plowman: Critical Approaches* edited by S. S. Hussey. London: Methuen, pp. 310–24.

Review of R. C. Alston's *A Bibliography of the English Language from the Invention of Printing to the Year 1800. Vol. VIII: Treatises on Shorthand. The Library*, Fifth Series, xxiii. 259–60.

Review of R. C. Alston's *A Bibliography of the English Language from the Invention of Printing to the Year 1800. Vol. V: The English Dictionary. The Library*, Fifth Series, xxiii. 358.

Review of G. M. Story's edition of *Lancelot Andrewes: Sermons. Notes and Queries*, 214. 112–14.

Review of *A Mind Awake, An Anthology of C. S. Lewis*, edited by Clyde S. Kilby. *New Blackfriars*, l. 223–4.

1970

Review of the second edition of Eugène Vinaver's *The Works of Sir Thomas Malory. RES*, NS xxi. 192–3.

Review of A. G. Rigg's *A Glastonbury Miscellany of the Fifteenth Century: A Descriptive Index of Trinity College, Cambridge, MS.0.9.38. The Library*, Fifth Series, xxv. 162–3.

Review of V. Pritchard's *English Medieval Graffiti*. M/E xxxix. 77–8.

1971

Review of Astrik L. Gabriel's *Garlandia: Studies in the History of the Mediaeval University*. M/E xl. 90–1.

Review of John V. Fleming's *The Roman de la Rose: A Study in Allegory and Iconography. Notes and Queries*, 216. 187–8.

Review of Robert S. Kinsman's and Theodore Young's *John Skelton: Canon and Census. The Library*, Fifth Series, xxvi. 271–2.

Review of *The Oxford Book of Medieval English Verse* edited by Celia and Kenneth Sisam, and Peter Dronke's *Poetic Individuality in the Middle Ages. TLS*, 23 April.

Review of A. C. Spearing's *The Gawain-Poet: A Critical Study*, and P. J. C. Field's *Romance and Chronicle: A Study of Malory's Prose Style. The Spectator*, 22 May.

1972

Langland, Piers Plowman: The Prologue and Passus I–VII of the B-text as found in Bodleian MS. Laud Misc. 581. Edited, with notes and a glossary, by J.A.W.B. Clarendon Medieval and Tudor Series. Oxford: At the Clarendon Press. pp. xiv, 259.

Supplementary Notes on Sir Gawain and the Green Knight, 1. Cambridge, privately printed. pp. 28, i.

Introductory note to the Paradine Press facsimile of William Caxton's edition of the Canterbury Tales, 1484. Reprinted from the Pepys copy at Magdalene College, Cambridge.

Review of *The Medieval Literature of Western Europe: A Review of Research, mainly 1930–60* edited by John H. Fisher. *MÆ* xli. 240–1.

Review of Chauncey Wood's *Chaucer and the Country of the Stars: Poetic Uses of Astrological Imagery. University of Toronto Quarterly*, xli. 174–5.

Review of Alice Chandler's *A Dream of Order: The Medieval Ideal in Nineteenth-Century English Literature. RES*, NS xxiii. 376–8.

Obituary notice of W. A. Sewell. Professor of English at Auckland, 1934–46. *The Times*, 9 May.

1973

Supplementary Notes on Sir Gawain and the Green Knight, 2. Cambridge, privately printed. pp. 22.

Review of Sir Edmund Craster's *The History of All Souls College Library* edited by E. F. Jacob. *MÆ* xlii. 297.

Obituary notice of T. P. Dunning. Vincentian and medieval scholar. *The Times*, 8 May.

Obituary notice of Charles Brasch, 1909–73. New Zealand poet and editor. *The Times*, 24 May.

'Charles Brasch, 1909–73: Tributes and Memories from his Friends.' *Islands: A New Zealand Quarterly of Arts and Letters*, vol. 2 no. 3, Spring, pp. 236–40.

1974

Chaucer at Oxford and at Cambridge. The Alexander Lectures delivered at University College, University of Toronto, in December 1970. Toronto: University of Toronto Press. pp. 131.

Supplementary Notes on Sir Gawain and the Green Knight, 3. Cambridge, privately printed. pp. 25, i.

'Henryson's *Testament*: a flawed masterpiece.' *Scottish Literary Journal*, i. 5–16.

Section on John Gower in *The New Cambridge Bibliography of English Literature*, vol. I, 600–1660, columns 553–6.

Ordo Missae. Order of the Mass. A translation into traditional liturgical English of the New Order of the Mass, with a selection of Prefaces, by J.A.W.B. Association for Latin Liturgy. pp. 123.

'Little Gidding. A Poem of Pentecost.' On the Magdalene College, Cambridge, drafts of T. S. Eliot's *Four Quartets. Ampleforth Journal*, vol. lxxix part i, Spring, pp. 60–73.

Review of G. D. Squibb's *Founder's Kin: Privilege and Pedigree. MÆ* xliii. 320–1.

Review of Meg Twycross's *The Medieval Anadyomene: A Study in Chaucer's Mythography. TLS*, 15 March.

Review of Sheila Delany's *Chaucer's House of Fame: The Poetics of Skeptical Fideism. Notes and Queries*, 219. 191–2.

1975

'A King's Quire'. On the *King's Quair* of James I. *Poetica: An International Journal of Linguistic-Literary Studies* (Tokyo), no. 3, pp. 1–16.

'The Blessed Mutter of the Mass: Maimed Rites?' *Cambridge Review*, 21 November.

Review of Marion Stewart and Helena M. Shire's edition of *King Orphius; Sir Colling; The Brother's Lament; Litel Musgray: Poems from Scottish manuscripts of c.1586 and c.1630 lately discovered. MÆ* xliv. 92–3.

Review of *A New Historical Geography of England* edited by H. C. Darby. *MÆ* xliv. 105.

Review of *Geoffrey Chaucer* edited by Derek Brewer. *TLS*, 14 February.

1976

Supplementary Notes on Sir Gawain and the Green Knight, 4. Cambridge, privately printed. pp. 21.

The Knight's Tale: A Commentary, 4 parts. Cambridge, privately printed. pp. 117, i.

'Langland (William).' *Dictionnaire de Spiritualité Ascétique et Mystique Doctrine et Histoire*, tome ix, columns 219–21.

'Gibbon and the Universities.' *Cambridge Review*, 22 October.

Preface to Kathleen L. Scott's *The Caxton Master and his Patrons*, Cambridge Bibliographical Society Monographs no. 8, pp. ix–xv.

Endnote to the Paradine Press facsimile of Robert Crowley's edition of the Vision of Pierce Plowman, 1550. Reprinted from the Pepys copy at Magdalene College, Cambridge.

Endnote to the Paradine Press facsimile of William Caxton's The Historye of Reynart the Foxe, 1489. Reprinted from the Pepys copy at Magdalene College, Cambridge.

Review of Alice S. Miskimin's *The Renaissance Chaucer*. *Renaissance Quarterly*, xxix. 266–7.

1977

'Chaucer, Dante, and Boccaccio'. *Accademia Nazionale dei Lincei. Quaderno N.234. Problemi Attuali di Scienza e di Cultura*. Rome: Accademia Nazionale dei Lincei. pp. 22.

Review of George Kane's and E. Talbot Donaldson's edition of *Piers Plowman: The B Version. Will's Visions of Piers Plowman, Dowell, Do-better and Do-best. RES*, NS xxviii. 323–6.

Review of Gisbert Kranz's *C. S. Lewis: Studien zu Leben und Werk*. *MLR* lxxii. 673–4.

1978

'Carlyle and the Medieval Past.' *Reading Medieval Studies*, iv.3–17.

Review of *Islands*, vol. 6 no. 3: Frank Sargeson at 75. *TLS*, 4 August.

1979

'Nosce te ipsum: Some Medieval Interpretations.' *J. R. R. Tolkien, Scholar and Storyteller: Essays in Memoriam*, edited by Mary Salu and Robert T. Farrell. Ithaca and London: Cornell University Press, pp. 138–58.

Review of Judith H. Anderson's *The Growth of a Personal Voice: Piers Plowman and The Faerie Queene. Renaissance Quarterly*, xxxii. 642–3.

Review of *David Jones: Letters to William Hayward*, edited by Colin Wilcockson. *Cambridge Review*, 29 June.

1980

'Some Second Thoughts on *The Parlement of Foules.' Chaucerian Problems and Perspectives: Essays Presented to Paul E. Beichner C.S.C.*, edited by Edward Vasta and Zacharias P. Thundy. Notre Dame and London: University of Notre Dame Press, pp. 132–46.

Prefatory memoir to T. P. Dunning's *Piers Plowman: An Interpretation of the A-Text*, second edition revised by T. P. Dolan. Oxford: At the Clarendon Press, pp. v–viii.

'Faulkner and A. E. Housman.' Echoes of Housman in Faulkner's *Absalom, Absalom! Notes and Queries*, 225. 234.

'One hundred and twenty years of *The Eagle.' The Eagle*, St John's College, Cambridge, Magazine, lxviii. 3–8.

Review of *On the Properties of Things. John Trevisa's translation of 'Bartholomaeus Anglicus De Proprietatibus Rerum'*, edited by M. C. Seymour and Gabriel M. Liegey *et al*, and *Bartholomaeus Anglicus On the Properties of Soul and Body: De Proprietatibus Rerum Libri III and IV*, edited by R. James Long. *MÆ* xlix. 151–2.

Essays on Gibbon. Cambridge, privately printed, pp. [ix], 85.

Forthcoming

The Poetry of the Passion. A study of the Passion in English poetry from the earliest times. Oxford University Press.

'Scottish Pre-Reformation Devotion: Some Notes on MS Arundel 285', in Festschrift for Professor Angus McIntosh.

'Those Scots copies of Chaucer', in *Review of English Studies.*

'Langland's Samaritan', in *Poetica* (Tokyo).

'The Antipodean Connexion', in *The Eagle*, St John's College, Cambridge, Magazine.

Reviews of R. S. Kinsman's *John Skelton, Early Tudor Laureate* and his *John Skelton: an Annotated Bibliography*, F. P. Pickering's *Essays on Medieval German Literature and Iconography*, and Elisabeth G. Kimball's *A Cambridgeshire Gaol Delivery Roll 1332–1334*, in *Medium Ævum*, xlix.

Articles on C. T. Onions and C. S. Lewis in *Dictionary of National Biography.*

Memoir of C. T. Onions in *Proceedings of the British Academy.*

'Recollections of David Nichol Smith.'

In Progress

The Oxford History of English Literature vol. II, part i.

A commentary on *Piers Plowman*, the B-text.

Index

---◆---

References are to pages of the text. Footnotes are indexed only where texts and primary authorities are cited.

Fastolf, Sir John—(*cont.*)
  Correspondents—(*cont.*)
    330, 331-2, 333, 335, 336, 337,
    338, 339; Paston, John II, 336;
    Paston, Margaret, 333, 335,
    338; Paston, William II, 337;
    Rothwell, Master, 338; Wayte,
    William, 339
  Others: Cutler, Robert, 333; Elys,
    Bartholomew, 333; Fastolf,
    Thomas, 331, 333;
    Felmyngham, Friar Clement,
    333; Heydon, John, 334; 'Long
    Bernard', 333; Osbern, John,
    334; Pecock, William, 336;
    Pykeryng, William, 334;
    Wainfleet, William, 339;
    Wentworth, Sir Philip, 333, 337;
    Woodville, Anthony, Lord
    Scales, 334; Yelverton, William,
    332, 333, 335, 337
  Manuscripts, see Manuscripts
    noticed, *below*
Fastolf, Thomas, *see* Fastolf, Sir
  John
Felmyngham, Friar Clement, *see*
  Fastolf, Sir John
Fisher, J. H., *John Gower: Moral
  Philosopher and Friend of
  Chaucer*, 162, 171
Fitzwilliam, Lord, 10
Fitzwilliam Museum, 185, 186
Flavius Mithridates, his translation
  of the *Bahir*, 249-53 (printed);
  236-7, 240, 242
Flower, Robin, 18
Fourteenth Century Verse and Prose,
  10
Frost, Robert, 46n
Fulgentius, 93

Gairdner, J., *The Paston Letters,*
  331-44 *passim*
Gawain and the Green Knight, Sir,
  154; 'Supplementary Notes on', 12
Gesta Romanorum, 169
Gibbon, Edward, 12

Gibson, Edmund, 3
Gilbert, A. H., 169, 170, 171
Giles of Rome, on the Elenchi, 372
Giovanni da Serravalle, 32n
Glossa Ordinaria, 22, 28, 279n
Glover, Robert, *see* Fastolf, Sir John
Godfrey of Viterbo, 169
Goethe, 207-8, 209
Golden Letany, The, 191
Gollancz Prize (British Academy), 10
Gonville and Caius College,
  Cambridge, 369
Gordon, E. V., 2
Gospel of Nicodemus, 288
Gosse, Edmund, 139
Gower, John, 10; *Confessio Amantis*
  Book VII, 159-83 *passim; Mirour
  de l'Omme,* 161, 162, 163, 174,
  179, 181; *Vox Clamantis,* 161,
  162, 163, 174, 178n, 180; *In Praise
  of Peace,* 163; *Cronica Tripertita,*
  163, 164; 'O Deus Immense', 163
Gray, Douglas, article by, 185-205;
  288
Great Yarmouth (= Jermuth), 332,
  334, 338
Greene, R. L., *The Early English
  Carols,* 193
Gregory the Great, Homily on Luke,
  22, 23, 24, 30n; *Moralia,* 174n,
  225n
Grosseteste, Robert, on the Posterior
  Analytics, 372, 374
Guillaume de Lorris, 69, 93, 136,
  162, 174n
Guillaume le Clerk, and the *arbor
  caritatis,* 217-18, 219 (*Bestiaire*)

Halifax, Lord, 3
Hamilton, George L., 171
Hananīkh, the, 180
Hardie, Colin, 4, 5
Harrowing of Hell, see Mystery
  plays
Hart, Robert, *see* Fastolf, Sir John
Harvard University, 11
Haxey, Thomas, 180